The School of Rome

The publisher gratefully acknowledges the generous
support of the Classical Literature Endowment Fund
of the University of California Press Foundation.

The School of Rome

Latin Studies and the Origins of Liberal Education

———

W. Martin Bloomer

UNIVERSITY OF CALIFORNIA PRESS

Berkeley   Los Angeles   London

University of California Press, one of the most distinguished university presses in the United States, enriches lives around the world by advancing scholarship in the humanities, social sciences, and natural sciences. Its activities are supported by the UC Press Foundation and by philanthropic contributions from individuals and institutions. For more information, visit www.ucpress.edu.

University of California Press
Berkeley and Los Angeles, California

University of California Press, Ltd.
London, England

Library of Congress Cataloging-in-Publication Data

Bloomer, W. Martin.
 The school of Rome : Latin studies and the origins of liberal education / W. Martin Bloomer.
    p. cm.
 Includes bibliographical references and index.
 ISBN 978-0-520-25576-0 (cloth, alk. paper)
   1. Education—Rome—History.   2. Education, Humanistic—History.
 3. Latin language—Study and teaching—History.   I. Title.
 LA81.B45   2011
 370.937—dc22   2010031698

Manufactured in the United States of America

19 18 17 16 15 14 13 12 11
10 9 8 7 6 5 4 3 2 1

This book is printed on Cascades Enviro 100, a 100% post consumer waste, recycled, de-inked fiber. FSC recycled certified and processed chlorine free. It is acid free, Ecologo certified, and manufactured by BioGas energy.

CONTENTS

ACKNOWLEDGMENTS

This project began well over a decade ago, and I owe thanks to many for material, moral, and intellectual support. My colleagues at Stanford University—especially Anthony Raubitschek and Susan Treggiari—fostered the project's small beginnings. The deans' offices at Stanford and the University of Notre Dame, and the Institute for Study of the Liberal Arts at Notre Dame, generously supported my research. Two institutions gave me time to work, the Spencer Foundation (which audaciously funded a project far removed in time from their customary research focus) and the American Council of Learned Societies. Much help came from students: Paul Chenier, Margaret Imber, Brendon Reay, and Luke Roman at Stanford; Robert L'Arrivée, Thomas Clemmons, Emily Gandolfi, James Kriesel, Hailey LaVoy, Nathan Ristuccia, and Harold Siegel at Notre Dame. Silvia Dupont, Chris McLaren, Corradino di Sante, and Joseph Stanfiel read early drafts. That this work finally drew to a close I owe to the advice and encouragement of Keith Bradley, Thomas Habinek, Ralph Hexter, Brian Krostenko, Blake Leyerle, and Daniel Sheerin.

Introduction

Three Vignettes

In the summer of 44 B.C., an aristocratic youth studying in Athens wrote his father's agent assuring him, a bit too eagerly, that all was going well with his Greek philosophy teacher. The man no longer seemed so severe and now even dropped by unannounced for dinner. Could the agent send the young man a trained slave, preferably a Greek, to transcribe notes? Three months earlier the youth had been visited by a friend of his father on the way out from Rome to serve as a short-lived governor of Asia. Trebonius wrote back to the father to report that the son was living modestly and devoting himself to his studies. The father clearly was not so sure: he had managed to get his son to dismiss one professor of rhetoric, a bad sort according to a later historian, and was tightening the purse strings.[1]

Three centuries later in a city of the northern Roman Empire, where Greek was still known, but where trousers and beer were more common than togas and wine, a first reading exercise imagines a boy writing an account of his daily routine. He calls for his clothes, breakfasts, and still in the cool of dawn walks to school with a slave retinue—pedagogue, book-bag porter, perhaps others. He returns home for lunch and greets his parents and the extended *familia*. He writes too of breaking away from his studies to go to the forum or the baths with his pals.[2]

A century and a half later, across the Mediterranean in North Africa, a teenager fresh from school realizes his mother's dreams by setting up as a teacher of rhetoric. School had been traumatic, or at least emotional. He was beaten but still failed to learn Greek. Yet Virgil moved him: he wept for Dido as Aeneas sailed away, leaving her to die by her own hand.[3]

The three students are Cicero's son Marcus, an anonymous youth in Marseilles, and the young Augustine. Each in a different setting pursued a liberal education, the training befitting a freeborn Roman. Liberal education bound them to the great texts and men of the past, marked them as participants in the culture of free men, and anticipated their adult rights and roles. The connection of past, present, and future men of learning helped constitute a sense of identity. The identity of culture is not a historical reality but a fiction, an imaginative act that takes the student beyond his place, present abilities, and even background. If the differences among the students strikes the historical observer, the students themselves were united by a fierce pride in their literacy and knowledge. Students in the late empire believed their educational culture bound them to the long-perished republic and its literary masterpieces. The young Cicero, however, would have found the Latin of the students from Africa and Gaul barbaric, their poor Greek disgraceful. Roman students for at least the first five centuries A.D. read the *Aeneid* of Virgil and tried to write speeches like Cicero's, yet their education was a fluid, dynamic practice rather than a uniform experience dictated by a conservative tradition among an elite. Schools, curriculum, pedagogy, the status of teachers, and the demographics of teachers and students changed in response to the evolving needs of literate classes, to the impulse of new literatures, new religions, and new governors, and to the rediscovery of old texts.

To take the very long view, Roman education is situated just past the midpoint in the history of formal, literate education. The earliest evidence for training in literacy skills comes from Sumer and the subsequent users of its cuneiform script and script-teaching systems, the Babylonians. Throughout the ancient Near East and in Egypt, boys have left records of their arduous preparation to enter a scribal class for service in an extended court bureaucracy. The curriculum of lexical lists was also, as has been recently emphasized, an introduction into a culturally specific organization of knowledge. Petra Gesche's critical study of Babylonian education reminds the reader that the Western ideas of the development of the individual and an individual ethical outlook are not found in the ancient Near East.[4]

For Romans of the classical period, education was a Greek import, and they somewhat mistily contrasted an education founded on literary texts and conducted by Greek speakers beginning in the third century B.C. with an older, native primitivist and paternal training in the manly arts.[5] That many of the first teachers in the middle and late republic were Greek-speaking slaves and freedmen aggravated the muddled contrast in this view.[6] Educators in the Greek world had innovated by adapting training originally designed for a scribal class to a citizen class. Roman education had ventured its own new adaptation, which an emphasis on continuity with the older and grander intellectual culture of Greece has obscured. The connections with Italic cultures from the eighth century on and, in particular, with Etruscan culture were little understood, either by the Romans who wrote of their own institutions or by later students of culture, predisposed to discover decisive cultural transfers from one great civilization to the next. In particular, "school" may have seemed a familiar and unproblematic term that linked great civilizations, including those of the European historians of classical or medieval education. But a classical *paideia* was a shifting construct, and the school of Athens (or better, the many schools of the Hellenistic cities from North Africa to the Black Sea) was not the school of Rome.[7]

In their haste to move from the classical Greeks to the Renaissance and the Enlightenment, histories of liberal education have tended to belittle the Romans. The Romans sometimes are treated as placeholders, intermediaries who provided a synthesis of learning, the seven liberal arts, so that it might be preserved by the Middle Ages, until the Renaissance restored the original, Greek complexity and fullness of literature, philosophy, music, and so forth. In fact, the Romans educated on a vast scale, instituted bilingual education, and developed rhetorical training significantly, with a variety of teachers, students, materials, and methods that reflected the diversity of the empire itself.[8]

From the third century B.C., prominent Roman families had attached to their family circle various Greek experts, philosophers, cooks, doctors, and poets, and among these specialists trainers in grammar and rhetoric also found receptive patrons. A system of school practices modeled on the Greek resulted, not from the enactment of laws or citywide policy, but from the keen interest of the elite in the skills and substance of a Hellenistic education. The adaptation of education to Roman ends was part of the city's fascination with Greek culture, which was encountered anew in the military conquests of the third and second centuries B.C.

To detect, describe, and explain the changing educational culture of the Roman world would require a work of many volumes, several lifetimes, and a community of scholars.[9] As a contribution to the study of Roman education, this book asks what the ancients thought education would do to and for children, and what in practice it offered students.[10] Roman theorists of education certainly provided rationales along with description of practices, but claims about an institution, stemming from the elite of that institution, while good evidence for the mentalité of its agents, offer an insufficient account of methods and purposes. The theory and practice of education are like an old married couple whose differences, plastered over for polite society, break through unasked and unpredictably, and so vehemently that one wonders what their relationship to each other could possibly be. Roman education was not simply the ideal script of progress from unruly illiteracy to mastery of self and speech that the theorists present. Concrete skills of reading, writing, speaking, and thinking were won by boys and girls with what all agreed was hard work.

That work included arithmetic and geometry. Dancing was taught, although the elder Scipio and others disapproved. Music, science, and more advanced mathematics could be learned from expert teachers but had been removed from the typical curriculum. Physical education was also a casualty as the Hellenistic cycle of civic education in school, gymnasium, and palaistra was replaced by the Roman schools of literacy. From Hellenistic education the Romans adopted above all the expert preparation in reading, writing, and speaking. Quintilian described the ideal Roman education—what he wished a student in the greatest school of Rome (his own) would accomplish. He wanted the grammar-school teacher to teach grammar only and leave the rhetorical exercises to the rhetorician. The strict division of Roman schooling into three separate institutions—elementary literacy and numeracy at the school of the *litterator* or *ludi magister,* reading of the poets and historical and oratorical prose along with some composition exercises at the school of the *grammaticus,* and then training in speech and debate (declamation) at the rhetorician's—is inaccurate. We can imagine, following Quintilian's guide, that the Roman boy or girl came to grammar school at age seven, eight, or nine already knowing the alphabet. Reading, writing, and arithmetic were learned here. The child would learn to write and then read Greek; Latin followed. After basic literacy (including memorization and recitation) the child learned grammar, mythology, and literary criticism all together while reading a poetic text and listening to the teacher's exposition. The grammar-school teacher would deliver a brief opening lecture. The child might recite an assigned passage. The teacher would proceed to comment on the spelling, diction, and rhetorical figures of the passage (the scholiasts, particularly Servius on the *Aeneid* and Priscian in his *Partitiones,* give an idea of the qualities of this instruction). A set of exercises from the aphorism to fable and description, up through a series of increasingly complex narrative building blocks, led to the finished speech. At the final stage, known as declamation, the advanced student learned a system of composition and delivery of mock deliberative and legal speeches.[11]

The avowed ideal of this education was the orator, who embodied the expressive speech capacities that the Roman elite needed as lawyers, politicians, diplomats, governors, and generals and the receptive capacities needed by the friends, counselors, and audience of these. Only the rare boy would become a Cicero or Julius Caesar or even enter the *cursus honorum,* the itinerary of high public office. Rhetorical education had other, less grand aims. Students of rhetoric learned to understand and criticize speeches and texts. They were also schooled in the categories and techniques for argument and exposition, advocacy and attack, and conflict resolution and the bringing of grievance. Thus Roman education trained jurors as well as senators, women as well as men.

The first half of this book moves from the introduction of Hellenistic schooling and the rise of the schools (chapter 1, with special treatment of the physical place of the school; chapter 2, stories the Romans told of their first schools; chapter 3, the Romans' discovery of crisis in a change of schooling) to the theory and ideology of education as expressed by two great educators at the turn of the first and second centuries A.D. (Plutarch and Quintilian, in chapters 4 and 5 respectively). Their prescriptive works, a treatise from the circle of Plutarch entitled *De liberis educandis* (On the Education of Children) and the monumental work of Quintilian, the *Institutio oratoria* (The Orator's Education), offer the most cohesive statements of the ideology of education in the first century A.D. (Both texts are also of tremendous importance in the history of education, including the Renaissance revival of classical education.) These works also theorize, though not always explicitly or consistently, the idea of a child and the child's development of academic skills and intellectual capacities.[12] Whereas in the past these authors have been mined for details concerning the use of letter blocks or the techniques of teaching reading, for example, and have been justly celebrated for policy, such as their common opposition to corporal punishment, in fact these roughly contemporary texts deserve a reading that generously takes them at their word: education is a treasure, and the two works powerfully exhort the reader to its pursuit. With such protreptic the heart of the educationalist justifying his institution is revealed. By looking at Romans looking back at the history, purpose, and process of their schooling, these opening chapters consider the ideas and assumptions implicit in Roman educational narratives.

The relationship of these ideas to learners is taken up in the second half of the book, which seeks to understand how the educational exercise shaped its users. School exercises may be designed to transmit ideals of education, but they also communicate attitudes and demand skills that the teachers or theorists have not fully planned or even imagined.[13] Chapters 6 (grammar and the fable), 7 (the educational precept and persona), and 8 (declamation and rhetorical habitus) treat the goal of education: the rhetorical culture that marked the Roman man as a free citizen whose words and learning merited respect. The adolescent had toiled at school to earn this recognition. His exercises had shown him many victims and the need for advocacy. The dumb animals of fable were to be given voice. The generals and statesmen of old were to be addressed again in speeches of counsel. The canonical texts were to be reread, recopied, and reperformed. Indeed, the reading of literature supplied the student with excerpts and arguments, metaphors and images, for his own writing and speaking. Among the roles that the rhetorical curriculum presented to be played, interpreted, or rewritten, I have been particularly concerned to trace the cues given the adolescent to learn, or revise his understanding of, social categories. At times the student received outright directives, as when the outline plot of a declamation required him to write of the conflicting roles of an accused man as son and soldier. At times there were more subtle conditionings of attitudes and responses, as when the young declaimer had to frame emotional responses from the characters of a conflict, such as what a freedwoman, what a stepson, would appropriately feel and do when family, social, or civic order started to unravel. That a student "needed" a slave to carry her books and mind her on the street was itself a daily practice of the divisions of labor, in turn reinforced and relearned in school exercises. In the final stage of rhetorical schooling, the young man's declamatory speeches patched the fictional breaks in the familial, moral, and sociopolitical fabric of the Roman city. His skill in speech enabled him to emerge as the master of the personae of his fiction and the winner of applause, who could amuse and move his audience. Or perhaps he failed utterly or bored his peers or wrote a silly sententia. As throughout his education, his faults would be castigated.

In the ludic place of Roman education, not only were the exercises fictionalized conflicts, but as so often at school they could be repeated again and again. Turn taking and restarting, with correction, makes the player of a game better at that game. The student becomes a better student, but he and she have been told that this is a serious enterprise, a preparation for and a version of adult roles. The school exercises aim to create an elite literary subjectivity by means of a graduated curriculum that moves from the simple exercises of recasting fables or supplying an aphorism with a speaker and context so as to make the sparest of plots into a full-blown speech in character to the mock-trial speech of defense or accusation. Those habits of thought and expression fostered by the school can be deemed a subjectivity at the point that the student comes to view himself as a speaker and writer. Ancient schooling had the student read, write, recite, fragment, gloss, recombine, expand, and evaluate narratives of several kinds from an early age. The student was required to do more than read (perhaps unlike many a modern college student, who reads once or partially, and for whom the professor's lecture and secondary reading provide replay and synthesis). He or she might have had the text modeled by teacher or by a slave pedagogue, or their own performances might have the whole or parts praised or corrected. This correction ranged from corporal punishment to the correction of the pronunciation of a word, the delivery of a phrase, or the punctuation of a dictated text. The text might be delivered as dictation or as a text to be copied (from papyrus to wax or wax to wax), or as a finished product—a papyrus roll of Virgil's *Aeneid*, for example. The content of a lesson and the various formal skills required to read, write, vary, and interpret would be encountered again. Indeed, the same content and form, a fable for instance, could serve as a first writing exercise, and later as a reading exercise, become still later a prompt for a composition, then even a discussion exercise in which the student might be asked to critique the stylistics of the fable, and finally a piece to be inserted as an argument in a larger composition.

This play with narratives that pose plots of competing ethical impulses and consequences may well have had greater effect on subjectivity than the sententious moral or point of the tale.[14] From a humble exercise such as the bilingual glossaries in which children practiced translation as they practiced writing commands to their slaves, the student reads and writes a narrative that portrays him at the center of a social world designed to serve him and to respond to him. The world is imagined as a series of encounters or conflicts, where the student's own virtuosity may allow a successful, pacific outcome or at least closure. In fable, the fox may eat the sheep, but the student learns a moralizing lesson. The hero and speaker of the sayings tale, the *chreia* that has a famous speaker make a withering reply to some challenger, manages to evade violence or verbal attack by his wit. The disastrous consequences threatened by the facts of the declamation will be avoided only if the boy can construct some clever but plausible escape. A man speaking and writing fluently, without interruption or the interference of another's expertise, is the ideal mode of adult behavior imagined by much of this curriculum.

With such a definition of rhetorical subjectivity, we need not imagine that education is a simple process of cultural hegemony that relentlessly replicates established attitudes and practices. We can, however, trace through the writing and speaking exercises and in the ancient pronouncements about education a process that, with difficulty and considerable effort, led a few to remarkable intellectual abilities. The difficulty of the process certainly winnowed the set of the learned governors of a society, which no doubt was doubly useful, as it served established interests and instilled in its new practitioners a sense of their distinctiveness. In that sense of distinction we witness the Roman rhetorical system at its most efficacious. The successful student believes in the lessons of schooling. He need not believe that his teachers are right and all his toil well spent; but if he imagines that he has become like the censorious Cato, whose precepts he has memorized, and Cicero, whose speeches he has studied, and that now like the old Romans he too possesses a masterful culture, then he has emerged against the threats of chastisement, correction, and rebuke as one who can speak for others. His right to speak for others is of course no right but a learned disposition that depends on and recreates a segregation of classes and genders, that understands that the violence of his world— murder (by the wolf in the fable, by Marc Antony in the historical declamation), civil unrest, robbery, adultery, infidelity—can be mediated by the educated speaker. In describing the school of Rome, then, I have tried to keep the student before the reader's eyes, as he works his way through a curriculum, as he grows into an accomplished stylist, and as he learns to justify the very distinction his schooling has produced.

The Roman curriculum retrained the child in how to tell a story, in part by fostering a stance of objectivity—as if there were only one well-ruled way to speak, which requires systematic control of the persona of the speaker. As the student learns figured speech, he learns to reduce individuals and individual cases to formulae, to stereotypes, and to arguments (discussed in detail in chapter 7). He writes repeatedly in Greek "work hard [*philoponei*: love pain/toil] lest you be beaten."[15] Intellectual labor becomes an alternative world to his previous family life and also a daily practice in resolving the imagined conflicts of categories and in framing and understanding his own evolving social role. The move from fable to the morality tales of the *chreia* to the role playing and categorical thinking of declamation constitutes a radical training of the imagination, and this effective schooling is far more imaginative than the traditional accounts, which stress the dryness and complexity of rhetoric, have allowed. We may well reinterpret the enduring legacy of Roman education not as the seven liberal arts or a lapidary prose style or the virile texts of the canon, but as a trained habit of mind that insists that texts and tests, through a competitive display of reading, writing, and reciting, form the child into a worthy Roman.

1

In Search of the Roman School

The centuries-long efforts and activities of students, teachers, parents, and patrons in Roman schools will be explored in this book as an important and innovative component in the making of Roman culture, with significant consequences for the methods and agents of education in the West. Histories of education tend to celebrate founders and revolutionaries. In such dramatic narratives, the Greeks have fared better than the Romans. No matter that the the notions of "Greeks" and "Romans" are rather vague, and, in our period, overlap; that the Greeks too were transmitters (and modifiers) of techniques and institutions of the training of children in literacy and numeracy; and that the broad strokes of this understanding reflect an Enlightenment prejudice that reduces to nearly unself-conscious mediators any, especially the Roman and the medieval, who stand between the Greek founders and the European spiritual and cultural revivers and heirs of early modernity. Modernity, however, should not take all the blame. The Romans themselves furnished the outlines for a history of education that misappraised their own roles. This chapter traces the origins of the underestimation of the Roman contribution to schooling and depicts the early centuries of schooling at Rome as a complex and thriving period.

The narratives and anecdotes of early schooling display the strong colors of an institution's and a society's mythmaking. Roman schoolmen reflected on the origins of their cherished institution, and, more generally, writers from the late republic and early empire investigated their past with complex presuppositions about the transfer of culture from Greece. Typically, they imagined a native hardiness and simplicity, long since lost or even spoiled by luxury and civil discord. This chapter recalls what Roman cultural etiology and archaeology forgot—the existence of schools before the influx of Hellenistic teachers after Rome's successful wars of the third and second centuries. Scholarly investigation has revealed that Roman archaic culture was bound to a broader Italic cultural community. The native history of the school, rich in symbolic contrasts and dramatic beginnings, deserves serious attention both for its influence and for its insight into the thinking of Roman educators. As mobile, flexible, and impermanent places and as an institution of and for children, Roman schools have left only a small imprint in the historical record. What *is* clear, nonetheless, is that the model of sudden cultural transfer is flawed and partial; that the Romans' reluctance to adopt gymnastic education during the third century can be explained; and that the educational milieu that the Hellenistic experts encountered and exploited needs to be differently, and better, understood.

Suetonius, most famous as a historian of the emperors, also included grammarians and rhetoricians in his study of famous men. In his biographies of the grammarians he noted that the old Romans had neither studied nor esteemed grammar and that its first teachers were those half-Greeks Ennius and Livius Andronicus. Suetonius had little to say of them and began his account of the origins of schooling with the first theoretical grammarian whose presence at Rome he could verify, the learned Crates of Mallos. The better-documented teaching of the internationally famous Crates appealed to Suetonius far more than did that of the republicans Ennius and Livius, of whom he knew much less, perhaps only a few anecdotes, which he could have drawn from Cicero and the early Latin poets' versions of Greek tragedies and of Homer's *Odyssey,* more unusual Hellenistic texts like the *Epicharmus,* and the works on Roman subjects, such as the *Annales.* The achievements of poets from Virgil through Lucan, Martial, and Statius had eclipsed those of the early poets. Crates' embassy to Rome in 168 formed instead a concrete and more dramatic point of origin—the bringer of culture arrived fully laden.

Writing ca. A.D. 100 in the *Quaestiones romanae* (Roman Questions) (59), a work of decidedly antiquarian flavor, the Greek scholar Plutarch similarly imagined a point of origin that inaugurated the history of Roman schooling as a cultural transfer of Hellenistic education to Rome. Plutarch identified Spurius Carvilius as the first teacher to have a school of letters in the city of Rome. He was probably wrong, but no more so than the Romans themselves. He chose the freedman of the consul of 235 B.C., Spurius Carvilius Maximus, because Spurius Carvilius was the first to charge for his services.

These two accounts of the origins of the Roman school serve as intimations of the understanding of the category "school" in the year A.D. 100 rather than as an archaeology of education in the city. School was what Suetonius and Plutarch had been to and what a scholar such as Crates represented—the Hellenistic grammatical and literary curriculum taught by a man for pay. It is instructive that neither Plutarch nor Suetonius wrote of a building or a place.[1]

Young Romans learned to read and write, do arithmetic, and deliver advice and speeches. They may have attended a place of instruction outside the house for at least some of their lessons.[2] In understanding the beginnings of their cultural history, Romans of the late republic, who not only served as the chief sources for Roman scholars in the imperial period but still hold a privileged place among modern historians, focused on a period of innovative cultural practices. They traced the theater, literature, schooling, and scholarship back to the arrival of Greeks captured in the Punic Wars or visiting in the aftermath of these wars or, especially, the Third Macedonian War.[3] Their adventitious archaeology of culture had some truth: like Toynbee in the nineteenth century, contemporary classicists follow Livy and Sallust in recognizing the important legacy of the Punic Wars for the Romans. Contemporary scholars, however, do not stigmatize renewed Greek cultural influence as the introduction of luxury; rather, like Andrew Wallace-Hadrill, modern scholarship asks about the effect of imports upon Roman social and political life.[4]

Is schooling, then, another luxury introduced to Rome by the Greeks as late as the mid-third century B.C.? If so, for what end? Was it merely to create and nourish Roman taste or cosmopolitan feeling? We might ask also, Did schooling contribute to the aristocracy's sense of self (and if it were a matter of social distinction, who were the uncultivated)? Were the Romans adopting schooling awed by Greek culture? Did it, like the theater, have native or Italic antecedents all but forgotten by the Romans of the middle and late republic? These schematic questions, all of which assume that Greek culture was a belated and accidental visitor to the city that would be great, hardly do justice to the complexities of Roman social life or the traditions of Italic literacy and cultural systems. But in asking these questions, we imitate the ancients themselves, most especially Suetonius, who tells us that Livius Andronicus and Ennius, the first practitioners of Latin literature, were also the first to keep school at Rome. He knew that one Plotius was the first to have a school of rhetoric (and we have seen that, in Plutarch, Spurius Carvilius was the first to have a grammar school).[5] No doubt, Suetonius, writing a sort of biographical encyclopedia ca. A.D. 100, recorded the best information he had. His sources were all documentary and primarily literary. He knew Livius and Ennius were Rome's first poets, and somehow had an additional item of information: they had taught in both Greek and Latin in their own homes and outside their homes. The second notice of place (*foris*) may imply a public place or may simply mean that they taught at other people's houses. At any rate we have an early notice of two categories of place devoted to teaching. For Suetonius, "school" seems to mean not so much a particular space dedicated to instruction as a master, a distinct curriculum (in grammar, rhetoric, or philosophy, i.e., on the Greek model), and a number of students.

Roman writers of the late republic and the early empire remembered the origins of their schools in clear and forceful stories. The lack of apposite written sources before the third century and changes in the Latin language and in the institutions of the city go some way toward explaining why Romans did not recall their early schooling, but stories of schooling have particular ideological characteristics. They speak of the training of youth in a society's or a class's values, and this symbolic weight can easily lead to idealizations and associations that have more to do with the present and with a wished-for identity, and less with the past as a historical reality. The Roman stories reflect lines of imagination of simple, fundamental contrasts: of old, Roman fathers had educated their sons at home. Greek-style education, with a literary curriculum, paid teachers, and a school outside the home for social peers of different families, came to Rome in the recent past, the third and second centuries B.C. Here too were to be found the origins of Latin literature. The Romans' interest in their own institutions apparently arises in the same period. The poet and teacher Ennius wrote a work entitled *Origines*. The statesman Cato, who looms large in accounts of early Roman schooling, consistently contrasted Roman customs and institutions with the recently arrived and corrupting Greek.

Later Romans and Greeks followed the lead of these sources in three ways: they assumed this period to be one of origins; they understood the origin of schooling to be a transfer of the superior Greek culture to their (rude and hardy) ancestors; and they ascribed the impulse to adopt a new cultural practice to a named individual. This thinking, at once etiological, cultural, and biographical, has a powerful, ideological appeal. It identifies the Romans as valid (if only recent) participants in the Hellenistic *paideia*—that literary culture that identifies civilization and empire and the civilized inheritors of a great tradition—and grants then something in addition, a nativist, ancestral virtue that makes the Romans superior to those who have only schooled customs and schooled virtue.

No long-enduring building or locale, or great sentimentality about the institutions of childhood, guided Plutarch in his notice of the first school at Rome. Rather, he saw education as a cultural translation. The techniques, texts, and teachers of schooling came, he thought, from Greek cities in the aftermath of the wars of the third century. A history of Roman schooling could begin only when a curriculum, if not a place, modeled on Greek practice had made its way to Rome. Further, as noted above, a biographical tendency informs the accounts of early schooling: developments are attributed to a named individual. Before that, the Romans concocted stories of paternal instruction in the manly arts of farming and soldiering, a theme that owes much to proud propaganda from the elder Cato about how he handled the training of his son (without need of the entourage of Greek experts who attended other wealthy Romans). But before we come to the stories of Cato and his generation, we need to look beyond the limits of Plutarch's knowledge.

The Roman school is a difficult place to visualize.[6] With one noteworthy exception, archaeologists have found no Roman classroom, in part because the school did not necessarily depend on dedicated space.[7] Many places would do, and a particular grammar school was not a long-lived institution. Searching for the places of Roman schooling requires a reappraisal of the physical requirements of a school. In contrast to the modern furniture-stuffed, well-lit, blackboard-at-one-end-behind-the-teacher's-desk plan for the schoolroom, the ancient grammar school did not prize so highly the line of sight. Instead, students came individually to the teacher to read lessons and receive instruction. In addition, the students' own slaves, the pedagogues, helped provide discipline. Similarly, acoustics were not important when students were all murmuring their own lessons, and the single student ordered to perform spoke within two or three feet of the seated master, thus—at least for a young student—at the ear level of the older man.[8]

The school had no desks and need not have had any bookcases. Students, or their pedagogues, brought lamps, papyrus rolls in a book bucket, wax tablets, pens and styli (whose flattened end served as an eraser for writing on wax), and also perhaps ink in a handy case (see the funerary relief from Neumagen), even abaci. The teacher sat in a large chair at the front. He provided benches or perhaps, in the deluxe setting, the round-backed chairs we see on a funerary relief, sometimes wax tablets, far more commonly the instruments of punishment: the *ferula* or *virga* (the cane but not the whip—the *flagellum*—that the Romans reserved for slaves as the more severe and humiliating device).[9] Children did not have school uniforms, although we are told that Plato's scholars wore a uniform.[10] Of course, the free boys and girls who went to school wore their own version of a class uniform: the *toga praetextata* for boys, a tunic for girls, and for both the *bulla* (amulet) about their necks that signaled their free status. In the rhetorical schools older boys might well have advanced to wearing the *toga virilis* for declaiming in Latin and the Greek *pallium* for declaiming in Greek. The school could be a well-equipped place, with maps and busts of famous authors.[11] It certainly was often crowded or close, at least to our eyes, for children bent over their reading and writing, with wax tablet or papyrus roll balanced on their knees. They read by rolling the scroll out with the left hand and taking in with the right, even steadying the roll with their chin.[12] A slave pedagogue (tutor and mentor as well as daily companion) and perhaps a slave porter (the *capsarius*) attended each student.

The physical requirements for a grammar school were minimal: school, like any small ancient business, could be held on the street, under or above a portico, near an important public building such as a temple, or at a rented shop. A wall painting from Pompeii, now lost, showed school near a portico and decidedly amid the bustle of the city. School could be held "in private," at the teacher's home or the house of the patron. The famous schoolman Verrius Flaccus taught Augustus's grandchildren in the atrium of a villa on the Palatine (Suet. *Gramm.* 17). Augustine on coming to Rome in A.D. 383 held school at home ("at first" he writes; perhaps he transferred to some other facility; cf. *Conf.* 1.5.12). Augustine, of course, was teach-

ing rhetoric; the home is apparently that of his host. He would move, presumably
to grander facilities, when in the succeeding year he went to Milan to teach rhetoric at the imperial court. But this was the acme of the teaching/performing profession of the rhetorician.[13]

More elaborate structures have occasionally been interpreted as educational venues. Ray Laurence has explained the second, seemingly superfluous, theater in Pompeii by reference to similar structures in Corinth, Argos, Athens, and Epidauros,
which apparently were used for the performances of rhetorical or literary works.[14]
Aurelius Victor (*Caes.* 14.2–3) wrote that the Athenaeum at Rome, built by Hadrian,
was first a school of the liberal arts. This assembly hall was later used by declaimers,
but we do not know where it was. A library was attached.[15]

Part of the difficulty in evaluating the ancient evidence for the location, design,
and functions of schools stems from the plasticity of the term *school,* whose semantic
range extends from a modest room or the corner of a street for teaching basic literacy and numeracy to a performance place for elite youth and professionals to declaim. My list of the places of Roman schools is by no means exhaustive, even for
Rome, and every city had its schools. One fragment of an Egyptian papyrus letter,
apparently from a wife to her husband, who has learned Egyptian letters, affords a
glimpse into a modest school, or the hope for a school, which classical, literary
sources would scarcely admit. The wife congratulates the addressee for now having a job prospect: he will be able to teach boys at the house of the enema doctor.[16]

Subliterary evidence, the correspondence of the modestly literate, the graffiti on
city walls, does not so much round out the evidence from literary authors as tan-
talize with the suggestion of a larger, less sophisticated world of literacy and schooling. The best preserved of ancient Roman cities, Pompeii, has an unrivaled breadth
of graffiti that implies, like the Egyptian school at the enema doctor's house, schools
and schooling that a Cicero or Quintilian would ignore. Graffiti indicate schooling
took place at several locations in Pompeii and at Rome. The places of instruction
are unremarkable shop stalls.[17] Two exceptions to these modest locales merit attention, since they seem to have dedicated space and indicate an education that is
decidedly not modest. The emperor's palace had a slave-training complex known
as the *paidagogia,* and the villas of the wealthy had as part of their design semicir-
cular recesses, or exedrae. The latter, like private libraries, are places of culture, perhaps of poetry reading or rhetorical training. Varro portrays the gymnasium and
the new-style villas as exemplars of the new urbanization—part of his habitual complaint that the Romans have abandoned their ancestral agricultural ways (*Rust.* 2
pr.)[18] More positively, Varro is commenting on a new lifestyle, an association of the
Roman elite with Hellenistic *paideia,* or with physical places that evoke the great
paideia of the Hellenistic cities. The civic gymnasium, the private and imperial libraries, the frescoes of poets on villa walls, and the presence of small but discrete
places within the grand Roman house for reading, recitation, or education demon-

strate an increasingly visible connection of the Roman elite with places of culture. The villa of course also made room for slaves, who included the expert scribes, accountants, readers, and teachers. Slaves were trained within the emperor's complex for bureaucratic positions, which no doubt centralized for the growing imperial administration what was already common practice both within elite households and in private enterprises, such as the training of slaves in literate skills by Atticus.[19]

Activity and agents, rather than a designed, dedicated, or abiding place, defined the Roman grammar school. The Roman *ludus* did not translate a Greek place or institution, as it also kept a Latin name and did not borrow the Greek *scholē*.[20] Stanley Bonner argued that the application of the term *ludus* to a gladiatorial school and Augustus's use of the expression *lusus Troiae* for his revival of an archaic rite of military training of young boys suggested that *ludus* had originally meant "a group of boys in training for war." *Ludus* would thus be the play form of war, and the term was extended to the group training of boys, whether mental or physical.[21] The grammar school, the *ludus litterarius* or *ludus magistri,* was where one found a teacher training children in early literacy (and perhaps numeracy) skills for a fee. Thus when young Marcus Cicero, the son of the orator, received tutoring at home, he was not attending a *ludus*.[22]

The search for a single architectural correlate to a social or cultural institution is perhaps misguided. The Roman senate did not always meet in the curia. Trials were not attached to a specific building. The Roman house was itself "multi-use," flexible, and permeable space.[23] The Mediterranean climate also allowed a flexibility of location: the street schools would be dreadful, even impossible, in Rome in March.[24] One would love to track some struggling schoolmaster, searching for a dry venue in the Italian winter, decidedly unlike the well-off Quintilian, perhaps a freedman with a niggardly patron, who sold his learning to centurions' sons, and those even lower on the social ladder.[25] He did not need papyrus or many books. Writing materials could be of humble, recycled material, pottery shards and bits of wood, or the eminently practical and reusable wax table. Fees were not always paid; the place was noisy; the rod much used; and perhaps he moved his school as the weather and his pocketbook allowed. Flexibility of place, equipment, and personnel, and ease of entry into the profession favored the impecunious schoolmaster.

Unlike the grammar school, the school of rhetoric required an audience, even if the assembled body numbered only students, their slave companions, and a teacher. No matter the size, the group of orators in training made for a different sort of school. First, all were aware that they were engaged in higher studies. They had left behind, if they had not quite been graduated from, grammar school. In fact, curricular change may not have been as important to the scholars' sense that they had taken up a new and superior enterprise as the change to an all-male student body and to new, more sustained, and complex modes of performance and evaluation. Quintilian informs us that in his day grammar-school teachers had taken over much of the rhetorical curriculum (adding *controversia* and *prosopopoia* to their traditional duties, the *progymnasmata*, or exercises in composition and delivery).[26] Indeed, one of the great legacies of Quintilian's work is its educational outlook of an integrated curriculum. Many of his fellow teachers did not share his attitude: they did not deign to teach the earlier parts of the curriculum. Instead, they gave instruction in declamation. Rome probably had so many well-prepared students and so many experts that this kind of specialization succeeded: declamatory schools could become institutes unto themselves. The declaimer Latro, celebrated in the pages of his fellow Spaniard Seneca the Elder, gave no instruction. Rather, students came to his school to hear his model speeches and divisions of the case.[27] Quintilian did not like the lecture format, passive learning, or the style of speaking so created. He certainly practiced declamatory training, but as the final stage of education. He suggests a carefully controlled environment: boys speak in the order set by the master, which moves from the best to the weakest speakers; he suggests revising the order from time to time.[28]

We do not know if other schools followed these principles, but both Quintilian's school and the schools that relied on extemporaneous speaking or declamation alone (of which he disapproved) reflect the same needs for organization of space. Boys sat in front of their master, who in turn sat on a large chair known as the *cathedra*. Such a disposition suits the needs of both performance and group teaching. The declamations that stem from Quintilian's school bear some marks of teaching practice. The master presented the facts of the case, then divided the case into two or three tactical approaches, and delivered a sample speech. From the collection of the elder Seneca it is clear that boys competed in a set order. The whole class seems to have declaimed on the same theme, each boy walking to the front of the room to deliver his declamation.[29]

The performance of a rhetorical exercise in school mimics the relations in Roman adult life of advocate and jury, magistrate and assembly, and adviser and great patron. As the boy spoke in the persona of lawyer or adviser, the immediate place of the school might have to be imagined away, the listeners transported to other times and places through the fantasy of the plot, and through specific rhetorical figures such as apostrophe and description. The boys might speak as if they were at the centumviral courts in Rome or among the intimate advisers to the reigning Caesar. As in grammar school, they could, in fact, have been in widely different venues. For special performances, the boys might perform in the same space that Pliny or Martial or the leading professional declaimers rented for a recitation or competition.[30] Seneca reports that the declamatory teacher Cestius had the gall to perform his own reply to Cicero's speech in defense of Milo. It sounds as if Seneca had been there to witness the presumption, and one can conclude more generally from his collection that the rhetoricians wanted visitors. They courted fame—and no doubt new students—in a competitive display. Perhaps Cestius had a special place for this special occasion. Seneca does not remark on it, and in all probability he simply dropped in on one of the leading schools of his day, probably at a colonnade *cum exedra*. The rhetorical school seems to have been treated as a public place where even the mighty might drop by: the declaimer Latro made a most unfortunate gaffe when Augustus, Maecenas, and Agrippa were in the audience. A generation earlier, Cicero and other illustrious men attended the declamations at the school of Gnipho (a freedman who had first taught in Julius Caesar's household).[31]

At home Cicero practiced his own declaiming, perhaps only in Greek and only with his leading set, without the public.[32] During the close of the republic, as declamation spread as an educational and cultural form, elite Romans also performed or attended performances in their own homes. Private villas reveal spaces dedicated to literary practice and performance. The exedrae are small enough that they might be suitable only for the practice of a speech before a few friends or family and expert slaves. They also have a symbolic element: they evoke larger, public cultural spaces (and events), as does a small domestic library. As a recess in a rectangular room that in turn opens on the colonnade and looks out beyond to the garden, an exedra was not a closed space. In all particulars, like the school, this is a set—the recapitulation on a smaller scale of a larger, more serious space—in which a play version of real events is rehearsed. The school did not develop a separate architecture for good reason: it needed only to anticipate a place of real oratory, the noisy law court or the open-air assembly.

An awareness of the fluid meaning of "school" clears away the prejudice that education must take place in a standard architectural site. The search for the schools of early Rome or for schooling in early Rome must proceed on different criteria. Contact with Italic, Etruscan, and Greek city-states and merchants probably exposed Rome to various literacies. The success of the city as a commercial, religious, and political center probably required literacy among some of its citizens. This does not mean that there were schools or, if there were, that instruction was given in Latin. For this reason we must begin not with the strong, polar thinking of the late republic that set an early nativist Rome against an imported and transforming Greek culture, but with the city of Rome in its cultural contacts with Greek, Etruscan, and Italic neighbors.[33] While Suetonius has shortsightedly provided a history only of the school form familiar to him, he may well have been right in believing that the literature-based schooling of the Greeks was not present at Rome before the early third century. The Romans appropriated Greek culture in a selective fashion. Scipio described and deplored a dancing school for young Roman lads and lasses.[34] Cato would go farther and criticize Scipio as a philhellene.[35] Amid the polemic, it is important to remember that schooling was not a sudden, overwhelming introduction of an unknown culture and technology.

The literary record would have us look to the third century B.C. and the richly flourishing Greek culture of the cities of southern Italy as the point of origin for

Roman literature and Roman schooling. Possibly, we can push the originary moment back at least a century, but we must shift the place of contact from Magna Graecia to Etruria. From the evidence of the history of Latin writing, this is not surprising. The Roman alphabet had been borrowed from (or at the very least was certainly influenced by) the Etruscans. Aldo Prosdocimi has stressed that the alphabet came with schooling.[36] The literary record contains one (problematic) clue of Etruscan influence in the schooling of Romans: Livy writes (9.36.3) that it is reported that Roman nobles sent their sons to the Etruscan city of Caere to learn Etruscan. He is telling the story of a Roman explorer and finds it more likely that the Roman had learned Etruscan from friends. Livy treats the ability as something exceptional (*aliquid praecipuum*) and adds that a slave learned in Etruscan accompanied the explorer. Livy may be discounting the evidence—and adding details that made the learning of a foreign language by a Roman more reasonable (to his generation): special connections or an expert slave. One may speculate that more generally some Roman youth were learning the copious and expert religious lore that the *libri etrusci* contained.[37] The need to learn Etruscan or to communicate through writing involved wider circles than noble youth who wished to travel or prepare perhaps for service in official religion. Rome had increased contact with the cities of Etruria in the fourth century as changes in Etruscan society were replacing the traditional mercantile aristocracy with a group who for centuries would provide Rome's favored contacts in various settings—a landed aristocracy. At the same time Etruscan cities show an increasingly sophisticated use of Greek art forms. It is unreasonable to assume that Etruscans made use of Greek mythology solely for graphic purposes.[38] Otto Brendel drew the connections between Etruscan-Roman contact in the fourth century and the possible contact with Greek literature. He cited the words Aulus Gellius (17.21.45) attributed to Porcius Licinus: "In the Second Punic War the winged Muse descended among the rough and bellicose people of Romulus"; and noted that winged Muses are an Etruscan not a Greek motif. Greek cultural forms could have taken several avenues to Rome, but the Etruscans are implicated. We are lucky to have Livy's notice of the possible early contact of elite Roman youth with Etruscan culture.[39] It is a hint of the significant changes in the social, agricultural, economic, religious, and political relations of these neighbors in the fourth century. Without these indications of the Roman debt to Etruscan literary and artistic culture, we would have only the later material evidence to deduce the connections of the two elites, such as the Romanizing funerary monuments in Etruscan cities, which testify to the strong, almost obliterating influence that Roman cultural forms would have on their conquered neighbors.

The achievement of Roman culture in the middle and late republic and the cultural memory that privileged an unmediated contact with the Greeks have obscured earlier Roman cultural forms. Scholars have recently begun again to argue for a Roman literary culture of long duration—against what the Romans themselves remembered—by emphasizing such aristocratic institutions as the symposium and the sodality (religious fraternity) where song played a vital role.[40] But aside from these partial glimpses of early Roman culture, the institutions and educational practices that contributed to the formation of a governing or a literate class remain opaque. Still we may remind ourselves that we have only touched upon the fourth century, and wonder what the seventh, sixth, and fifth centuries have hidden: periods of song, treaty, and law; of contact with Etruscans, Greeks, and Italic peoples; and of literacy. At a minimum, Rome had schools throughout these periods, and school equipment like alphabet-inscribed writing tablets, and ink jars. Perhaps we must share Livy's uncertainty that in the fourth century there had been a move to educate noble youth in what was probably conceived of as an older, higher (and perhaps religiously more authoritative) technology of literacy, and that boys were being sent not simply outside the house but out of the city.

A sketch of the Etruscan material evidence proves suggestive. Most germane to the student of education are not the ritual texts but the abecedaria, alphabets incised on durable materials. The earliest of these do seem to be grave goods, namely, markers of status that, though perhaps in use in daily life, are often preserved in a funerary context as deluxe, precious versions of objects essential to the identity of the deceased. In an Etruscan milieu these may be Greek or eastern Mediterranean objects, imported as luxury goods, the earliest of which date from the seventh century and include inscribed letters that are not used in the subsequent epigraphic materials (beta, delta, samek, omicron).[41] One such is an ivory tablet from the second quarter of the seventh century from Marsigliana in the Museo Archèologico in Florence, on one long side of which run, from right to left, twenty-five letters. The object represents a wax tablet, but it is something of a deluxe miniature, perhaps not meant for real practice.[42] A similar ivory miniature wax tablet, though not inscribed, was found in 1935 on a hilltop of Puglia outside Arezzo. This tablet dates from the second half of the first century B.C. and is part of a girl's grave goods, which also include toys and small daily objects. Certainly, five hundred years separate the objects, but the two do demonstrate the importance of commemorating literacy and schooling for a dead child.[43] From the beginning of the sixth century come examples of an Etruscan alphabet with only the letters used in inscriptions. There are further reforms of the alphabet, but from this point on, the inscribed abecedaria correspond to the language being used in contemporary Etruria.[44]

In addition to abecedaria, incised syllabaries show the familiar, if tedious, process of learning to read. With some of these we may have artifacts of the Etruscan school (although whether this was at home or outside, tutoring a few or schooling a group, we do not know). In their adoption of Greek literary and artistic culture, and in the prominence of writing in their funerary iconography (ranging from the incised abecedaria and syllabaries to the reclining sculptures of the dead who hold inscribed texts in their hands), the Etruscans show a keen and enduring interest in literacy. The evidence indicates that far from developing from modest utilitarian beginnings, literacy was part of an elite's religion and commemoration. Etruscan religious technology was certainly part of Rome's tradition. Much later, in the fourth century, it may be that elite Romans sought out Etruscan learning. In between, in all likelihood, schooling in Latin had its own Roman institution.

To insist on an exclusively Etruscan milieu for the introduction of schooling would require ignoring direct contact with both Greek city-states and the Italic literary culture seen in hymns and law codes. Among the evidence for Italic literacy training, a Venetic votive plaque, in bronze representing a wax tablet (dating to the fifth–fourth centuries B.C.), is especially important. Again, as with the funerary objects, we do not have the "real" artifact of a school but a symbolic version that attests to the important status of literacy, as well as to the fact of school training. In the sanctuary of Reitia at Este, a Latin writing exercise was found among Venetic exercises on a lamina.[45] No doubt this exercise attests to the process of "Romanization," but it also reveals one practical way the language was learned and spread before the standardization (of sorts) that Greek-style schooling would help achieve.[46] The early Italic history of the uses of literacy, and the uses of different languages and scripts on the peninsula, lie beyond our topic. Aside from general indications of the level of literacy and of a ritual, diplomatic, and legal culture, the first-century B.C. historian Livy has some stories that presume there were schools in the fifth and fourth centuries. Like his contemporary Dionysius of Halicarnassus, Livy tells the story of Verginia and has her going to school in the forum in the year 449 (Livy 3.44.6; Dion. Hal. 11.28); Livy also mentions schools at Falerii and Tusculum (5.27 and 6.25). It is conceivable that all are anachronisms, but they are additional chinks in the well-armored story that schooling began in the third century.

Whether or not the Romans first experienced advanced literacy training in an Etruscan school or in some system of apprentice learning, or simply learned the alphabet with the aid of Etruscan abecedaria, they were not awaiting the arrival of Greek teachers. The material evidence undercuts the stories from Roman literature that schooling had suddenly irrupted into a cultureless third-century city of Italy. The materials and the disposition for education were centuries old by the time Livius Andronicus wrote the first Latin translation of a Greek school text (the *Odyssey*, sometime in the third century B.C.). We should conclude that in the third century there came to the most powerful Italic city, one with various elite activities (religious, legal, political, and diplomatic) dependent on literacy, an international technology of schooling in the mobile form of human experts. The dazzling qualities of the expert performers—the trained memory abilities that seem miraculous, the achievements of philosophical argumentation, the pyrotechnics of virtuoso oratorical delivery—riveted the Romans. Even more importantly, these experts (and the less dazzling, more commonplace teachers of grammar and rhetoric) fundamentally changed Roman institutions. As the Romans secured and came to govern a far-flung empire, and as the elite competed for positions of leadership and came to forge a new Roman culture of governors, memories of an earlier educational culture, one informed by contacts with the Etruscan, Greek, and Italic worlds, were displaced by stories that celebrate a new founding—the era when Roman patrons befriended and employed Hellenistic scholars. The qualities of the Romans' memory of the capture and transformation of the educational culture of the Greeks concern us next.

2

First Stories of School

Several stories constitute the chief evidence for how, in the third and second centuries B.C., literary education became part of the city elite's communication of status, merit, and achievement. The century following the arrival of the first teachers of historical record, Spurius Carvilius, Ennius, and Naevius, did see a refounding of education at Rome. Although at the expense of an accurate memory of the earlier history of Roman education (some of the reasons for which I have touched on above and will consider further below), Hellenistic experts and expertise changed Roman education profoundly.[1] The experts brought with them an advanced technology of instruction. One immediate accommodation was the production of school materials in Latin. If the transformation of education entailed simply a question of a change in language or if the transformation were but part of the formation of aristocratic culture as the city's empire grew dramatically, the processes and agents of change would be of interest in their own right. Consistently, however, the sources describe a public display of private education.

Both the biographies of famous republican Romans written in the early empire and the comedies of Plautus and Terence, which were contemporary with the transformation, depict families communicating the education of their children as a showpiece, a view into the house for those not usually allowed access. The excellent care of high-status children makes a number of important claims about a family. Certainly, the family has the resources—slaves, books, money—to lavish on children who decidedly do not have to work. The family that educates distinctively well sets itself apart from other elite families and declares its concern for the future. There is then a dynastic, diachronic, as well as a rivalrous, synchronic, tendency. The family that defers present goods onto the future return is concerned—so seems the drift of the ideology—with its own future certainly but also with that of the group for whom it is preparing another good generation of leaders. In addition, in keeping with Roman ideas about leadership and the governing class, we shall see education depicted as an exemplary practice. The families of a Cato or a Scipio are creating a system of distinction, but ostensibly the distinction is based on judgment and training not wealth and social position. Consequently, that distinction can be emulated by the not-so-wealthy and not-so-prestigious. Education is, then, like other social practices (such as the building of houses), a display of rivalry and a practice of emulation. Thus, too, it seems to have contributed to an exemplary culture that competed in displays of elite status on the unstated assumption or ancillary animating principle that emulation of such display, in a lesser key, bound the larger society together.

The bulk of the evidence for education at this time comes from biographies of famous men (yet another refracting lens in Roman exemplary culture), but the earliest reflection on education occurs in two scenes from Roman comedy, where education serves as a barometer for the moral health of society at large. Both the stage characters of early comedy—an errant youth, a cantankerous father, and a coddling uncle—and the diligent parents with outstanding children in the pages, two and a half centuries later, of the idealizing biographers depict the institution of schooling at an important phase of development. Roman comedy is of special importance for two reasons. Light is shed on the practice of education and attitudes toward education at an early stage; and, perhaps, even more importantly, since Roman comedy continued to be performed and also to be read in Roman schools, these scenes had a long influence. Roman comedy represents part of the public comment on education that the republican families of Cato and Cornelia sought to influence.

The tripartite structure of this chapter (which treats the character of Roman memory of early education, the family display of sons and educators, and comic reflection on the value of an education) arises from the particular challenge of disparate evidence but also attempts to reflect the variety of attitudes to education in the transformative period of the third to second century. The sections are also united as analyses of the Roman crafting of the experience of education—not in the sense of the design of a curriculum but as a presentation of the compelling purpose of a specific training. That the later sources have their own interests does not disqualify them from the historian's analysis. Indeed, as educational history, what may seem anachronism or bias by strict modern standards is an effect of educational thinking—that recurrent mode that explains and reexplains why a past generation was educated in a certain way and why the present or future student should be educated in the same way. Whether the past is the author's childhood or what he takes to be his ancestors' ways, the contrast of then and now abounds in symbolic potential.

THE CHARACTER OF THE ROMAN MEMORY OF EDUCATION

That symbolic potential has proved too irresistible for some twentieth-century in-terpreters. On the impulse of ancient sources, especially the figure and rhetoric of the elder Cato, it has proved tempting to imagine the adaptation of education at Rome as a polarized struggle between a nativist camp of enthusiasts for an old-fashioned Roman education and a Hellenophilic salon of the new arrivals and their devotees. Cato, who would be celebrated a century later by Cicero (and others) as the type of the hardy, independent, sagacious Roman, has, however, much in common with other members of the Roman elite who were making a display of an education that manifestly depended on Greek models and expertise. In fact, Cato did not so much deny this dependence as demonstrate that it should be subject to the judgment and direct supervision of the Roman master. The first century of this new Hellenistic but bilingual education shows not the struggle of Rome with Greek culture but a competition at Rome in how to use that culture.

The story of the uses of that culture depends on two distinct sets of interested parties, those upper-class Romans who made a display of their educational culture in the late third and second centuries B.C. and the chief reporters of these events, Suetonius and Plutarch, both writing in biographical modes at the beginning of the second century A.D. Neither of these sets focused on studying the history of edu-cation or even of schooling as a cultural institution. The aristocrats presented their children as exemplary, and education seems to have been a (new) vital part of this commemoration of family and advertisement of the family's ongoing, even dynas-tic importance for Rome as a whole. The biographers depicted subjects in a manner that presupposed the culture of the Romans as a transfer of Greek *paideia*, reinforced by native Roman virtues. Plutarch notices the education of a famous man because the rhetorical encomium included education, along with family background and birth, as a standard, illustrative element of the early life of the great man.[2] Suetonius comes closest to studying the institution of education in itself because his collected biographies of illustrious men included sections on grammarians and rhetoricians.

Roman narratives of the origin of Roman education describe educational activ-ities as public actions of the patrons and include the names of the most notable po-litical actors of the times: the great general Aemilius Paulus, for example, and his son, the even greater general, the younger Scipio; also the censor Cato; and, in a moment of great importance that splinters the exclusively male focus, Cornelia, the mother of the political reformers the Gracchi brothers. These first stories attest to public displays of education. In their most basic form, they are notices in a separate narrative: the elder Cato, for instance, notes in a speech that he attended to the edu-cation of his own son. At times they constitute more dramatic parades of culture: the author recreates for his reader the Greek entourage that accompanied the sons of the elite, or the grand, triumphal procession of Paulus's victory over the Greeks at Pydna, among whose captives was Polybius, known to posterity for his history but who first made his career at Rome educating and advising the younger Scipio.

The Romans' memories of the early history of the school cluster around the names of exemplary individuals. In part, the commemoration of third- and second-century teachers in Suetonius and Plutarch reflects a Greek cultural habit of thought that privileges the first founder.[3] In this kind of thinking, gradual change, contacts of groups, and distinctive new ideas or institutions hardly play a role. Rather, cultural change occurs in lightning leaps that are the work of great individuals. A cultural good, known and important in the present, is attributed to a distant founder. As a primal scene of education, the Greeks had the mythological exemplum of Achilles taught by the centaur Chiron, a scene where mortal and immortal, man and beast, youth and experience, killer and civilizer, meet. In addition, education was tied through founding stories to the city-state: the sixth-century Sicilian lawgiver Charondas was believed to have included among his laws free education for citizen sons.[4] The Romans did not possess a culture scene comparable to the centaur and the hero or even the archetypal lawgiver, which loads schooling with such strong cultural and civic significance. The legendary Roman king Numa received religious lore from Egeria (and later was imagined as a student of Pythagoras), but the story, while significant as a statement of the Romans' unique status as religiously favored, shows no interest in the process of education. For Romulus and Remus a she-wolf sufficed.[5] Alain Hus has noted that the Romans, uniquely among the Indo-Europeans and unlike the Etruscans, had lost the idea of instruction from a supernatural being. The she-wolf is a substitute mother only, neither a wondrous hybrid nor the substitute father that Chiron plays to Achilles. She is a mute beast providing physical nourishment to infants. The articulate beast-man Chiron provides intellectual and cultural nourishment to the exemplary ephebe. Greek teacher and student represent the transitional category and process of education. By contrast the Romans imagine the history of schooling in historical fashion. A biographical mode locates the first founders as the Greek experts who arrived at Rome beginning in the third century B.C. and subsequently made such a strong impression upon their captors and hosts. The Romans were thereby historical, real heirs and practitioners of the great *paideia* of the Hellenistic and the classical Greek past.

The Romans, however, did not commemorate education on a scale commensurate with the enduring, physical legacy of the Greek world. The Hellenistic cities designed and maintained large civic buildings to accommodate the classes of ephebes who boxed and declaimed, danced and wrestled, and played the lyre. In addition to the inscriptions from various cities that record the yearly contests of the ephebes, we have stories of school embedded in descriptions of the famous institutions of Plato, Isocrates, and Aristotle. In other stories of education, the institution is not the schoolroom but the symposium or the circle of Sappho, which one can follow the poet in calling the abode of the Muses or term a *thiasos,* a religious sorority. The variety of institutions and practices of the education of Spartan boys likewise far exceeds the bounds of the "school."[6] The Greeks often said that Homer was an education in himself, or that pederasty was the most beautiful education.[7] Greece remembered a variety of educational practices where the Romans would re-member, against a semifictitious ancestral simplicity, the imported literary and rhetorical training exemplified by patrons, their freedmen, and sons.

Roman memory differed both from Greek civic commemoration and from the Greek cultural belief in mythological first founders. At Rome individual teachers were recalled, but in connection to leading, historical Romans.[8] A Roman name— a great one such as Scipio or Cato—hangs as a sort of counterweight to the freed-men clients who were the teachers. In part, this double naming reflects the nam-ing practices of the Roman freedman—the slave on his manumission takes his name from his former master. Even in the case of the famous Crates, stories connect the visiting ambassador to the distinguished Romans of the day. Such stories reflect the Roman cultural tendency to temper the debt to Greek culture. Education at Rome is thus imagined as essentially a hybrid creature, bilingual and bicultural, but with the Roman as patron. This focus in stories of education also puts the private and the familial on view for the larger Roman public. The rise of schooling is thereby linked to the competition among the elite for the display of their singular status and participates in the development of the media of display (including drama and or-atory—which in turn supply texts for the educational curriculum). In addition, these stories depict the governing class of Rome captivated by new ways of understand-ing their enlarging world and themselves.

The Roman elite celebrated and communicated their connection to the Hel-lenistic experts. Without discounting the genuine intellectual interests of the fam-ily of Aemilus Paulus, for instance, the display made of these interests is striking. A corona of Greek philosophers followed the father or the four boys through the streets of Rome. The daily scene mimicked in miniature the triumphal parade of Paulus, who as victor at Pydna had brought Greece under Roman sway (and had kept from the booty of the Third Macedonian War only the great library of King Perseus, another enduring and visible trophy of triumph).[9] Rome would see in the decades surrounding the funeral games of Paulus other Greek arrivals, whose sym-bolic significance was at times resisted by Cato. In 168 Crates of Mallos, literary scholar and philosopher, had an enforced extended stay at Rome after breaking his leg during a visit as ambassador for King Attalus II.[10] In 155 Carneades the skep-tic directly drew Cato's ire when he lectured on both sides of moral questions. The scholarly performance was part of a diplomatic mission: three leading philosophers, each a representative of the one of the three major Hellenistic systems—the Aca-demic Carneades, the Peripatetic Critolaus, and the Stoic Diogenes—had come to Rome on behalf of the city of Athens.[11] Scholars made good ambassadors in the

Hellenistic world, where Greek culture was a blazon of legitimacy and where the philosopher-scholar was seen as a master of argument—the successor to Isocrates and Aristotle, each of whom in his own way attempted to mediate the strong Platonic opposition between philosopher and orator. Carneades' lectures have been taken as moral relativism since he argued both sides of the issue. Far more likely, they demonstrated the need for systematic philosophy by revealing the inconsistencies in basing moral decisions on received norms. Crates' lectures were well attended, although Suetonius exaggerates Crates' singularity and his influence: he was one of many Greek experts coming to Rome.[12]

Nonetheless, to witness Crates or Carneades in action was a terrific thrill. These were not philosophers of the walled-off academy debating recondite points of epistemology. They were practiced experts in speaking and would have spoken with argument, style, and speed (apparently from later complaints about the Greek style affecting Latin oratory) unknown to the Romans. Clearly, the Roman audiences knew Greek, and here they met the best trained speakers of Greek, men who had risen to the top in a tremendously competitive, Mediterranean-wide system. Suetonius's account makes it seem that the Greeks captured the Romans in one fell swoop, whereas the Romans had been primed, as it were, by the eighty years since Livius Andronicus had put on the first play translated from Greek and had set up school. The political subtleties of the situation surrounding the embassy of the various philosophers may well elude us, yet we see the Roman elite in a scramble of enthusiasm for the new expertise.

With the Macedonian Wars over, Rome had received a new influx of luxury goods (including vast numbers of slaves) from the East but perhaps more importantly had seen that the East could be a permanent source of wealth and prestige. Attitudes to the stuff and technologies (religious, educational, agricultural, military) encountered in these wars and their aftermath were no doubt changing.[13] For the training of a ruling elite, whose composition, opportunities, and duties were evolving in the growing empire, education in language, literature, rhetoric, and, to some degree, philosophy promised access to and control of important Hellenistic technologies. Most immediately, education on the Hellenistic model formed speakers. In the history of the reception of this Greek culture, the elder Cato demands special attention, since he portrayed himself as a contrarian resistant to the role of Hellenism and to the new education.

SONS AND EDUCATORS

Whereas only a small fraction of Cato's speeches and writings has survived, two literary portraits have ensured his canonical place as a symbol of Roman values and decidedly Roman education. Cicero made him the central character of his dialogue *De senectute* (On Old Age). In addition, for readers of the Roman empire, Plutarch's biography ensured that Cato would be remembered as a champion of Roman republican virtues. From these literary works and the notices of his own works addressed to his sons emerges a picture of self-reliance. Plutarch reports that Cato wrote in his own hand and in big letters a history of Rome—for his son to read (*Cat. Mai.* 20.7). He takes education into his own hands, directly supervising his son, unlike others, who delegate the care of the son.

However, Cato was not the champion of all things Roman against the philhellene Scipio, as a strain in scholarship once believed.[14] Family connections in fact suggest contact and good relations: Cato's son Licinianus married Scipio's daughter.[15] Cato, whose same, elder son had been a legate at Pydna, supported a triumph for Paulus against Sulpicius Galba's opposition. Cato's own relation to Hellenism has been thoroughly reinterpreted. Most germane to the present question, Cato was not opposed to Greek education. He was something of an educational entrepreneur and innovator (as I argue in chapter 7). He had a Greek freedman—Chilon—who kept a school.[16] Both the client and son represent Cato's family, and we see Cato manipulating these extensions of himself. Cato's great extant work on agriculture shows considerable concern with the proper management by the father of his delegates. The estate reflects the virtue and the control of the master, even or especially when absent.

Perhaps the school of Chilon was a rival in some small way to the intellectual circles in which Scipio Aemilianus matured. Thanks to the Greek historian Polybius, who presents himself as a sort of second or third father to the precocious Scipio, and to Plutarch in his biography of Paulus, we are better informed regarding the distinguished education of Scipio.[17] But we know, in addition to the notice of Chilon's school, that Cato had brought Ennius to Rome. The relationship with the poet-schoolmaster did not last. Ennius found patronage elsewhere: he gained the rights of a Roman citizen in 184 and came under the patronage of M. Fulvius Nobilior.[18]

The attraction of Greek culture at this time has been redescribed in terms of the cultural capital it provided to the changing Roman aristocracy.[19] The formation and evolution of Latin literature thus, like the rise of schools, accompany changes in the ruling elite, and specifically in their opportunities for fighting abroad, for putting on games, and no doubt also for building houses, for dressing, for adorning their *familiae* with expert slaves, cooks, doctors, poets, and teachers. In distinguishing himself, Cato had well publicized that he did not have very many slaves, that his wealth and status came from a traditional farm and the traditional practice of defending his clients in the courts. Cato was in fact far more like Scipio than his self-portrait allows.[20] It is true that Cato rather dramatically chose not to send his son to the school of his freedman. Instead, like Paulus, Cato attends to his own son's education. Two passages from Plutarch purport to show the schooling he and Paulus gave (these are also the impulse to the allegorical interpretation that some scholars have applied to two characters in the Roman play *Adelphoe* (Brothers), which I discuss below). The affinities of the stories will emerge, including a markedly dynastic quality, by comparison with a third famous upbringing of two Romans just junior to Scipio Aemilianus, his wife's brother's children Gaius and Tiberius Gracchus.[21]

> When his son came to the age of intelligence, Cato took the boy under his own care and taught him to read and write even though he had an expert slave, Chilon by name, a schoolteacher then teaching many students. As Cato himself says, he did not think it right that his son should be verbally abused or pulled by the ear if he stumbled in his studies nor that the boy should be indebted to the slave for such a thing as education, but Cato himself was his son's elementary teacher, his expositor of law, and his physical trainer, not limited to the javelin, fighting in armor, and riding but also including boxing, enduring heat and cold, and swimming the Tiber manfully in its full rush and swirl. He says he wrote out in his own hand in large letters his history [of Rome] so that the boy would have at home a source for his acquaintance with the ancient patriotic deeds. [Plutarch continues with notices that Cato always spoke chastely before the boy and never bathed with him.][22] (Plut. *Cat. Mai.* 20.3–5)

In his life of Aemilius Paulus (6.8) Plutarch describes Paulus educating the boys in the traditional way he had been educated and also having them educated by a passel of Greek experts (scholars, equestrians, artists). As Alan Astin points out, Plutarch does not set the two educations at odds.[23]

No more than thirty years separate the two upbringings described above from that of the Gracchi brothers: at Paulus's death Scipio was twenty-three or twenty-four; Cato's son Licinianus, who had first seen military action in Liguria in 173—in all likelihood still in his teens—was perhaps thirty; in eight years' time Cornelia, the younger daughter of Scipio Africanus and Paulus's sister, would take over the education of her three children following the death of her husband (153 B.C.). The young Tiberius Gracchus would be a friend to another Cato, the grandson of Cato and Paulus.[24] In addition to the difficulty of determining political allegiances in the mixed lines of familial allegiance, the evidence points to carefully orchestrated youths. The education of elite children has become worthy of record. The training of the heirs of great families is exceptional—it demands the resources of a noble family or the direct tutelage of Cato, who is patron to many and magistrate of the republic—but this exceptionality is advertised for Romans to read and see.

The Gracchi children were nearly as much princes as the children of Augustus's family would become. The mother of the Gracchi refused marriage with Ptolemy VIII (so Plutarch reports, *Ti. Gracch.* 1.7); and, at least according to Roman anecdote, when a visiting Campanian lady showed off her jewels, Cornelia "delayed her in conversation until the boys returned from school and said, 'These are my jewels.'" The story is an educational *chreia,* a sayings tale that promotes the value of children (and education).[25] The education of the prince is a literary genre unto itself (beginning with Xenophon's *Cyropaideia*), but Cornelia acts like other old-time Romans to champion Roman values against imported luxuries (cf. Manlius Curius

Dentatus, the conqueror of the Samnites and Sabines in 290, who spurned the Sabines' gold, preferring his dinner out of a wooden bowl—so opines Valerius Maximus at 4.3.5a, who sets Cornelia at the opening of his next chapter). Native son, like native food, is better than foreign gold and jewels. Children figure in the discussion of luxury because they are objects of display. Like Paulus and Cato, Cornelia directed the audience's attention to the direct contact of parent and child. Valerius Maximus began chapter 4.4 by asserting: "Children are the greatest ornament of a matron" (*Maxima ornamenta esse matronis liberos*); but, as the story makes clear, it is schooled children who are the family's finest object of display.

The feelings of Cornelia and the elder Cato for their children are not at issue here. However devoted they felt to their children, the decision to communicate the direct supervision of a parent reveals much about contemporary perceptions of education. Given the extended *familia* with its client, freedman, or servile experts, unmediated parental instruction was unnecessary, even surprising. This paternal instruction, however much it presents an image of an integrated, strong family (with Cornelia a stand-in for her father, the great Scipio, as much as for her husband), did not recuperate a lost, ancestral practice. It was informed by Greek school texts and methods. In addition, the solitary parent draws attention to his or her self-sufficiency. Her husband and father may be gone, but Cornelia exhibits the dynastic connection living on in her children. Cato may lack the extravagant resources of a huge family, but he makes a strong show of this lack. Aemilius Paulus also participated in the education of his boys, although he did not act alone; according to Plutarch's account, he joined in the family training, which included resident philosophers and men of letters such as Polybius. Cato, ever brilliant at undercutting the opulent display, made his own curricular supplies and taught his son to write. Almost two centuries later, the first emperor Augustus would make a point of doing the same with his grandsons—such care of the young reflects a good share of dynastic propaganda, but it is not mere showmanship: one must emphasize the symbolic importance of having the heir write (and speak) like the father for a civilization that judged genius in family terms and for which speech and handwriting were emblems of authenticity and legitimacy.[26] It may be that Cato was trying to beat Paulus at his own game—showing the city not Greek doctors and philosophers and statesmen-in-exile fussing about the boys but the father himself taking direct charge. All these elite families show a dynastic instinct with their children; they have that keen, political sense that display of the young advertises the house's prosperity, its order, even its rightness. And for the religious community that was second-century Rome, fecundity and the thriving of children show divine approval. In its ornaments of well-ordered youths the house is provident and providential.[27] And the education of these young people is an essential part of the status and legitimacy of the elite family.

The elite practices described by our sources share a common appreciation of the public utility of education. All the families apparently used similar methods and texts. Indeed, Paulus and Cato produced their own school texts. In Cato's case at least, this seems to have been an exemplary text, one meant to be used by Roman students generally. The differentiation of education is thus marked not as Greek versus Roman but as rival materials authored or endorsed by great, rival families. The elite Roman father does not abdicate the right of supervision of his sons. Rather, he makes a show of direct, judicious, individual supervision (and does not make a show of the education of his daughters in the same way, although Cornelia reveals that daughters were educated and that an educated mother was an asset). The reception of elite displays of education can be surmised by the success of the families, the success of education, and by the inclusion of education as an important constituent of the great Roman man by the biographers. But the contemporary reception of education can be seen far better in scenes from the comic stage.

COMIC REFLECTIONS

The first extant extensive reflection on schooling and the first instance at Rome of the literary use of school as a theme comes in a comedy of Plautus, the *Mostellaria* (Haunted House), written between the time of his first datable play, 204 B.C., and the production date of his last play (traditionally mistaken as the date of the death of the poet), 184 B.C. The young lover Philolaches (Laughter-Lover) appears on stage for the first time for a mock scholastic discourse on how educating a boy is like building a house.[28] The opening words set the tone of academic parody in a sustained rhetorical querying, a *dubitatio,* about what simile to develop. Philolaches reports that long cogitation has led him to consider many *argumenta* (and note the professorial color of *diu disputavi,* line 87). A hyper-academic, self-correcting, speech-qualifying skepticism (line 86: "and in my heart, if I have a heart") makes clear this is a spoof, as does the comic gap between the traditional sententious style (complete with the doublets, at times alliterative, and synonymous dicola found in archaic prayers; e.g., line 89: *similem esse arbitrarer simulacrumque habere*) and the love-smitten state of the speaker. In this elaborated, exaggerated conceit, we have a glimpse into Roman ideas of and Roman play with schooling at a time that the elder Cato (234–149 B.C.) could well have been in the audience.[29]

Part of the soliloquy reflects Hellenistic practice (and the Greek original for Plautus's version): in lamenting his changed state, Philolaches says he once was outstanding in the exercises of the gymnasium (lines 150–53). Indeed, all the other youth used to come to him for advice. The Romans did not adopt the gymnasium, especially not the physical exercises, preferring instead the more military training of the Campus Martius.[30] Plautus had two Greek models for the play. Arguably, he might only be providing a Roman idiom for Greek practice. Roman moralizing, expressed by such key terms as *industria* and *parsimonia,* might be such an addition. Against this interpretation, it must be noted that the humor of the scene does not depend on the contrast of Roman and Greek elements. Education is not marked as Greek or as corrupting; rather, Philolaches has fallen from a correct youth, full of educational training, to an appetitive adolescence. The speaker does not attack or even undermine any particular curriculum. Certainly, the lover's self-sophistry, the rhetorical division of his status, the description of the search for material known as *inventio*, the elaboration of a simile and its use as an argument, are all meant to raise a laugh at the expense of Greek-style schooling. The speaker declares that his fall began when he left his family to rely upon his own *ingenium*, but the contrast is not the facile one between traditional family and new-fangled literary identity and subjectivity.

The simile supposes that a family can be judged by its house upkeep as by its child rearing.[31] The family values are distinctly Roman: the bad father shows the spectrum of Roman social faults: *nequam homo, indiligens / cum pigra familia, immundus, instrenuus* ("a useless fellow, idle, with a house of sloths, ill-kept and moribund himself"); before leaving his family, the young man was *industrior* than anybody else (150) and *victitabam volup, / parsimonia et duritia discipulinae alieis eram* (153: "I lived perfectly satisfactorily, my self-restraint was an education for others"). This is the very language that we will see associated with Cato.[32] Indeed, the farfetched simile, while no doubt made academic by its exaggeration and thorough enumeration, may recall Cato: he counseled that a field can be judged like a man: *scito idem agrum quod hominem; quamvis quaestuosus sit, si sumptuosus erit, relinqui non multum* ("Think of it this way: a field is just like a man: he may be as profitable as you like, but if he has expensive tastes, not much will be left").[33] Cato also writes in considerable detail of buildings, their expense, upkeep, and utility. Perhaps Plautus here turns the tables on him, reversing tenor and vehicle and developing Cato's moralizing equation of building and man. Cato writes that in early adolescence a *pater familias* should be keen to sow, think long and hard before building. Only when he has reached the maturity of thirty-six, should he begin to build. Philolaches' adolescent self-building seems to have more comic point with this Roman text and contrast in mind.[34]

To use an idiom as academic as Philolaches: the language of hardy, continent youth constitutes a social protocol of the Roman son that defined the son in terms of work and nonexpense. That is, he wastes not. Fathers, however, spend all on him (125: *nec sumptus ibi sumptui ducunt esse*, "Fathers don't count that expense as expense") and do all the paying and sweating (127–28: *sumptu suo et labore / nituntur*, "They strive with their own expense and labor"). In contrast, the son's labor is reflexive, self-contained, not expansive, marked by *parsimonia et duritia* (154), virtues not of expenditure but self-control and containment. An antithetical economics underlies the idealized, pre-comedy contract of father and son.[35] In the new situation that comedy presents, the father's attachments have not changed; he does not become suddenly severe. Rather the boy is no longer a schoolboy. A play of New Comedy depends on the violation of the earlier socially and familially contracted relationships: the son must fail to live up to the ideal protocol and assume another stereotype for comedy to take place. In comic economics, patrimony must verge on being squandered, whether immediately on drink and prostitutes or potentially by the purchase of a slave girl or marriage to one. In the passage from the *Mostellaria,* school represents the pre-comic order. So we should be wary of crediting the well-moraled past where good fathers taught basic literacy and the law, either by themselves or out of their pocket (126: *docent litteras, iura, leges / sumptu suo et labore*). This sounds like a Roman education, whereas the gymnastic arts of line 153 with discus, javelins, running, weapons, and horse seem to blend Greek gymnasium and Roman Campus Martius. The earlier passage imagines the *tirocinium,* the single year of service spent under arms by a young Roman, and not the ephebeia of the Greek cities; for not only is the idiom Roman (131: *unum ... stipendium*) but so is the practice of sending a relative along (129–30: *ad legionem ... aliquem cognatum suum*). The details of the military training and the prominence of law in the curriculum correspond to Roman practice. The playgoer thus does not simply laugh at an overeducated Greek character. The young man's language of self-description, while parodic, declares him a real Roman: he once was *frugi* and *probus* (133).[36]

In short, schooling does not convey a contrast of old Roman practice and newly introduced Greek rhetorical or gymnastic education. There is a hint of the difference between Roman practice and the Greek world of Plautus's sources, but the fantasy setting of comedy exploits without resolving the contrasts. Schooling is presented as consonant with Roman traditions, indeed productive of serious moral virtues. I stress this point because it has been customary to contrast Roman old-time education with the new-fangled Hellenistic curriculum. This contrast is posited upon the authority chiefly of the elder Cato. Finally, the contrast has been read into another scene from Roman comedy (from Terence's *Adelphoe,* discussed below). The passage from the *Mostellaria,* the earliest Latin source describing education, attests to an audience who can joke with schooling. It is one of the institutions, such as law, religion, marriage, and a father's moralizing, whose language and concepts comedy delights in exploring. Education can be a conceit with which to raise a laugh and which bears reflections on moral subjectivity, relations within the family, and the public estimation of the family. From the start of the Roman literary record, education acted as a social barometer; and whether or not the idea of comparing child rearing to maintaining a home was the Greek playwright Menander's or Plautus's twitting of Cato, the Roman writer has given it a Roman context and made it a social metaphor.[37]

In Plautus's play the son-in-love laments his fall from a well-schooled past. Schooling was not the source of corruption, but inherent in the comic conceit of the schoolman turned rake was the contrast of the boy's strict adherence to the rules of school, family, and father with the new attractions of la dolce vita. Approximately three decades later, the playwright Terence presented an equally brilliant scene whose humor depends again on flouting education. A tough-minded, country-dwelling father upbraids his urban brother for the indulgent rearing of the son he has had him raise. The duo have been interpreted as thin allegories for the elder Cato and the philhellenic Scipio Aemilianus. In fact, this interpretation has more interest as an instance of reception history—how critics following the lead of Cicero have interpreted the cultural history of the first half of the second century B.C. as a contest between *Romanitas* or *rusticitas,* figured in Cato, and *urbanitas,* the Greek-leaning sophisticated culture of Scipio and his alleged circle—than as an account of the actual relations and programs of Cato and Scipio.[38] The identification wrongly retrojects a contrast from Cicero's dialogues that used Cato and Scipio as characters, and, it must be said, recoups claims made by Cato himself about his character and his enemies.

For the history of education at Rome, Terence's play signifies more than an erroneous, allegorical identification. The playwright has modulated the characters found in his Greek original, the suave sophisticate (*senex lepidus*) and the misanthrope, and so softened the philosophical contrast in his model's play, which had set the Epicurean father against the curmudgeonly, antisocial father. The Roman audience sees instead a more Roman contrast of the *pater durus* and the kindly uncle.[39] This accommodation of Greek culture has its own importance in the history of Roman culture. In addition, the play, *Adelphoe,* stands at the end of the first period of Roman schooling on the Greek model.

Terence was the first Roman author whose work would endure in the school curriculum. His conscious emulation of the style of Menander, an author of great importance for the Hellenistic school curriculum, recommended him to schoolmen (in particular, his characters might not be better behaved than Plautus's, but they, and their monologues, could be lifted from a play as a more consistent ethopoeia, and his ethical reflections abounded in sententiae). The older Latin poets were gradually abandoned. Their Latinity soon proved old-fashioned, not simply because the language was changing but because the literary genres and literary language were flourishing. The first practitioner of Latin literature, Livius Andronicus, had his *Odyssey,* written in an archaic meter, replaced, perhaps in his lifetime, by a hexameter model, which in turn, like Ennius's historical work, the *Origines,* would be displaced by the introduction of the Augustan poets into the schools by the freedman of Augustus, Quintus Caecilius Epirota. Horace finds fault with the Romans' taste for the old authors but remembers well learning Livius' poems in the school of the menacing Orbilius.[40] Terence endured for reason of his style, a Latin of a new aesthetic (the schoolmen's stated reason does not acknowledge the racy plots and fine scenes of the dramatist).[41] The stylistic achievement, so unlike Plautus, of a smooth and urbane Latin, which was more fit for the suave father Micio, perhaps contributed to the rumor that Terence was aided in his writing by noble Romans. The line of suspicion pointed to Scipio.

The prologue of the play is the ultimate source for these reports (15–16: *homines nobiles* / ... *una scribere*). If poet could be confused with patron, why not a character from the play? There are additional complicating factors: the play was produced for the funeral games of Lucius Aemilius Paulus, the general who was victorious over the Macedonians at Pydna in 168 B.C. and the biological father of Scipio (who had been adopted by the son of the elder Scipio). Perhaps then the play was well chosen for its reflection on double paternity. In addition, the urbane father's name, Micio, is Greek for "tiny" (in Latin, *paullus*).[42] If then Micio were the historical Paulus or his son Scipio, and Demea a stage Cato, we would have in their opposing ideas of child rearing evidence for an uneasy transition between the new Greek education and an allegedly old-fashioned Roman upbringing.

Yet Demea makes an unconvincing Cato, even if one imagines that a Roman audience remained deaf to the representation of the differences of the brothers as differences in philosophy. Micio dated their difference from the time of adolescence, when each took to his own course of study, and of life. The Greek prototype of Demea may have represented the simple life more clearly as the position of a Cynic or a Stoic.[43] Would a Roman audience have interpreted this account of difference and the actors' subsequent speeches as a contrast in educational modes recognizable as Cato's and Scipio's? The two fathers do not embody an opposition of the Greek and the Roman but give voice to the rival understandings of a Roman son—the creature of his father without legal rights, and the scion of a free family with all the dignity and status of the governing class.

These public notices of education agree that the boy must be educated (Cornelia who took over her sons' education must have been superbly educated—comedy and the stories passed down to Plutarch did not advertise the reality of girls' education). The theme of *puer educandus est* (the boy must be educated), which we will see so thoroughly developed by the late first-century A.D. teacher and theorist Quintilian, should be added to the elder Cato's set of imperatives. Perhaps we should take the simile of Philolaches seriously. For the Romans, education is like building a house. The schooling of the boy, not simply what he learns but how and at whose hands, played a part in family representation. As an elite, public practice, this schooling no doubt attracted imitation. Not everyone could afford the expert entourage that accompanied Aemilius Paulus and his sons. More could afford Chilon's school. Perhaps even more could use the schoolbooks authored by Cato. In this way, Cato's family would be the most widely used model. Chapter 7 will explore the traces of one of Cato's school texts and his paternal persona in the Roman curriculum. Roman schooling, like the rise of Latin literature, the proliferation of festivals, and the introduction and domestication of intellectual experts, is one ingredient in the increased culture and display of culture at Rome in the third and second centuries B.C. Roman families felt that children like houses were worthy of regard. In particular, the son has skills worthy of experts, and his performance shows his family's character and distinction.[44]

Education is of course only part of the story of changes in the Roman family and society: the boy, as symbol of the family and its ambitions, changed at this period both because of the new techniques of education and because of the opportunities that Roman expansionism of these decades provided.[45] The ongoing need for trained officers and administrators was recognized by the Romans who placed their sons as legates under a leading general, as orators in training, perhaps too as legal experts, which is what Cato's son Licinianus would become. Part of the placement occurred through adoption and marriage, and part, no doubt in the Romans' minds a less important part, depended on shared teachers or shared literati, as we see poets coming to be of interest to Roman patrons. A proper appreciation of the schooling of children at this time would have to range education against other public appearances of children: we would need to track children accompanying a father to court, children in the funerary parades, as well as children going to and from school and perhaps performing in school contests. We have instead the occasional boasts and complaints, of the exemplarity of a particular family, of the wrong course in schooling boys taken by others, of Cornelia exhibiting her gems, of the elder Scipio complaining that some children are taught to dance.

Our focus has been on the reports of the education of the distinguished Romans young Aemilianus and young Cato Licinianus. We do not know who the freedman Chilon's scholars were, or what Ennius's school looked like. More positively, from the early period of the evidence, Rome shows a variety of schooling, with home-schooling of the aristocrats and one rung below that, apparently, the school of the freedman tied to a considerable patron (Chilon's school). From the comic poets Terence and Plautus we see that school was treated as a kind of personal, familial, or social barometer, a way to talk of youth that was freighted with social and moral resonances. Education has become an important part of a culture of exemplarity, a token of a family's *disciplina*. Thus it contributed to the system of praise and blame in complex fashion: in the sight of free children going to school, perhaps on occasion performing; in the anecdotes and scenes reported to fellow Romans; and in the gradual development of an ethical language about good and bad child-rearing. Despite the positive pictures of the education of the noble youths treated above, the Roman record abounds in complaints about new curricula, teachers, and students. The censorious record now concerns us, both for its details about the practice of education and as a cultural reflection on the rise and spread of education.

3

The School of Impudence

Between the century of the first teachers (roughly 240–140 B.C.) and the efflorescence of literary activity in the first centuries B.C. and A.D., a small hint of the variety of Roman schooling is provided in a notice about a single school. The innovative methods of a rhetorician had so offended the censors of 92 B.C. that they issued an edict of disapproval. The identity of the teacher, the nature of his offense, and the motives of his critics are, in fact, not easy to discern, but the sense of crisis is palpable. The censors' disapproval left a strong mark on the Romans of the late republic and early empire, in great part because major literary figures—Cicero, Suetonius, and Quintilian—commemorated the event as a perilous moment in the history of education.

The intended target, Plotius Gallus, may not have inaugurated the practice of training advanced students in making speeches in Latin (without the use of Greek study materials or Greek practice speeches), but this practice, or perhaps his students' success, drew official ire. The censuring of Gallus's school itself constitutes important evidence for the rise of the institution of schooling and its check by official and traditional institutions. Yet Gallus's Latin-only curriculum anticipates later Roman practice. Despite the censure, such techniques would prove successful and lasting.

In keeping with their biographical understanding of the rise of education, the Romans stigmatized individuals rather than reporting debates of educational method. The strong criticism of the school of Plotius Gallus has masked the conditions of education at the turn of the second and first centuries B.C. In his dialogue *De oratore* (On the Orator), Cicero has cast one of the censors, Crassus, both as the spokesman for opposition to upstart innovation and as a champion of the compendious expertise and civic responsibility that reflect Cicero's first-century ideal. The complaint repeats a polemical commonplace: innovation, attributed to an individual, often a social inferior, threatens ancestral ways. This nativist history of education ineluctably associates educational practice with social change and social discipline. When a practice typical of Hellenistic education—the training of the voice for oratorical performance and practice in mock legal speeches on contemporary themes—becomes invested with issues of the corruption of youth and the health of society, the historian will have good reason to proceed with caution. In addition, Cicero's characterization of these issues seems disingenuous: in fact, he had found the methods of the school enticing. The portrayal of the issues in the *De oratore* may well be an act of revisionism.

Criticizing academics is a sport of long tradition. The foolish professor or self-absorbed student is an endless source of fun. Amid a string of ancient jokes at the expense of the clueless student, the *scholasticus,* the following is typical: "A student was going to sell his house and so sent around one of its stones as a sample" (*Philogelos* 41: *Skholastikos oikian pōlōn lithon ap' autēs eis deigma periepheren*).[1] The humor depends on the contrast between the school and the community at large, especially the contrast between the specialized language of the one and the generally received and readily intelligible expression of the other. Here the word for "sample" or "demonstration," *deigma,* has an academic ring: the student has sent around a sample proof or literary foretaste rather than an architectural drawing or advertisement.[2]

Socrates himself provided the model for the seriocomic schoolman who transgresses (or is it transcends?) the divide between the scholastic and the public (as also the mercantile and the civic) spheres of the city. Unlike the *scholasticus,* who was the butt of jokes, he at least had a sense of irony and the self-conscious knack of using a term current in both a specialized and a general sense (a cobbler and a statesman have *aretē,* or so they may think). Socrates' portraits in Aristophanes, Plato, and Xenophon, for all their differences, enshrined the educator of the young as a problematic character.[3] The question of whether the teacher is a prattler or a sage, an innovative corrupter of the community's youth or its most important source of values and skills, did not die with Socrates.

Plotius Gallus was no Socrates, but in his case too the conflict that arose ostensibly over issues of educational method masked larger social or even political issues. Gallus has not received sufficient attention in educational history because the ancients disparaged him as a vulgar pleader and because the theorists, especially Cicero and his great admirer Quintilian, advocated a Greek-intensive, long, theoretically informed, and graduated training of the orator.[4] In fact, Cicero dominates the ensuing discussion of Gallus. In reconstructing his early education, Cicero has Gallus play the role of the road fortunately not taken. On the subject of his own formation, the great author and speaker merits a certain skepticism. The customary anachronism of Cicero's dramatic dialogues, where speakers of antiquity are summoned for the sake of their authority and not for their genuine sentiments, is compounded by the tendency of the educational treatise to idealize curricula of the past. The rhetorical manuals earlier than Cicero's *De oratore* or Quintilian's hefty treatise—the *Rhetorica ad Herennium* and Cicero's own youthful (and later regretted) *De inventione* (On Invention), a lightly polished version of lecture notes from a rhetorical school—offer a less polemical and idealizing insight into the educational milieu at the beginning of the first century B.C. These earlier texts, and, one suspects, the schools from which they sprang, like that of Plotius Gallus, held out the promise of oratorical excellence through the medium of Latin.

In 161 B.C. a *senatus consultum* gave the praetor the legal authority to expel rhetoricians and philosophers from Rome. A different *senatus consultum,* in either 173 or 154, was directed at two individuals, Epicurean philosophers who were thereby banished. Individual philosophers and poets did suffer from legal opposition; in addition to the anonymous Epicureans already mentioned, it is possible that the edict against philosophers and rhetoricians had specific targets. The praetor's authority to expel academics was a legal power, which the year's praetor could apply at his discretion, not the generalized policy of a modern, bureaucratic state.[5] In his study of astrology at Rome, Frederick Cramer referred to the various official edicts against the astrologers as "emergency measures."[6] Certainly, no evidence suggests that Tiberius Gracchus's tutor or the other Greek experts attached to the great houses were forced from the city.

Indeed, the intellectual history of Rome from 170 to 140 can be described in terms of the Greek luminaries who came to Rome at this period: Crates of Mallos, Diogenes the Babylonian, Carneades of Cyrene, Critolaus of Phaselis, and Panaetius of Lindus.[7] The arrival of the philosophers makes a dramatic story, but the educational historian must look at the more humdrum tutors and teachers, and those who were not well received. To the list of oppressed literati we might add the poet Naevius, imprisoned by the rivals of his patron, apparently for his plays' political wit.[8] As always in the republic, the foreign man of letters was a client who needed a citizen patron to prosper. Whereas Terence and Polybius succeeded in this regard, Roman literature abounds with the envy that the competition for patronage generates; and despite a strong literary tinge to the author's complaint that he or his work is slighted, writers faced threats more material and damaging than unkind criticism or malicious gossip. The foreign intellectual client made a convenient, substitute target for the patron. Naevius and later the poet Archias seem targets of opportunity.[9] Romans' ambiguous feelings about Greek intellectual culture, and indeed about the influence of the teacher, would likewise continue.[10] The nativist posturing that contrasted innate Roman morality with learned Greek philosophy was not limited to Cato. Cicero indulges in it when it suits his purpose: thus in the *De oratore* he makes the philhellenic Crassus, the censor who passed the decree of 92, a curmudgeonly critic of the influence of Greek culture.[11]

The *senatus consulta* of 161 and 173/154 intimate the senate's reaction to cultural experts without communicating any details of the state of education or the growth of philosophical instruction at Rome in the 160s. Indeed, these actions of the senate are better compared to other exclusion orders than to the notices, treated above, of Roman nóbles' contact with Hellenistic cultural experts. The senate had intervened in the introduction of foreign technologies (astrology, cult practice, education) most famously in the restriction of the Bacchic cult in 186. The targets of exclusion make a fascinating who's who of enemies of the Roman order throughout its history: Bacchus's new priests, priests of Isis, Jews, and astrologers.[12] Cato advised his estate manager (and all the readers of his agricultural manual) not to consult astrologers. Two centuries later, when the second emperor, Tiberius, excluded astrologers, Rome was not rid in any systematic way of this group of experts. No doubt the politics of his day, in which a horoscope could be part of the propaganda wielded by an aspirant to the throne, brought about the emperor's order.[13] While the restriction of the Bacchic cult and the disorder that accompanied it were severe, these measures had a strong proportion of the symbolic and, for our period especially, should probably be associated with other strongly symbolic legislation, such as the difficult-to-enforce sumptuary legislation that limited the amount of jewelry a woman could wear.[14] The assertion of control over freeborn, elite women and children is an index of change, perhaps both of the public style of the (nonadult male) *familia* and of the set of citizens who are in fact displaying their wealth and status. Education, like dress, may offend not because it makes some bold change but because more and different people are sporting it.

Whereas the senate did not have the apparatus of coercion that in the twentieth century has successfully directed what a citizen is to wear or who his teachers are to be, the Roman *senatus consultum* did invest the praetor with the power to banish. This distinguishes it from the censors' decree of 92, which had no such administrative bite. The senate seems to have shared Cato's aversion to Epicureans. Two Epicureans were banished. Similarly, Cato had objected to the lectures of an individual philosopher (the skeptic Carneades). Certainly, the *senatus consulta* and Cato's admonitions betray an anxiety about the influence of some of the teachers who were coming to Rome in increasing numbers.[15] Paulus's, Cato's, and Cornelia's advertisement of direct supervision of their children's studies seems to recommend the avoidance of education through slaves, freedmen, and schools. But the actions of great families did not constitute policy statements advocating homeschooling; rather, they seem motivated by the fact that family status depended upon a number of exclusive, expensive, and visible distinctions, which included a segregated education.[16] For those lower down the social ladder, such as the students of the school of Chilon, the children of the Scipios or the Gracchi might represent an ideal. The more modest might have to comfort themselves with the thought that they too pursued a Greek-style education. Whereas Cicero would come to articulate a counterplan to Gallus's methods, attainable for the wider public who could read his dialogues, second-century opposition to techniques and practitioners of education seems episodic, even symbolic, not systematic or theoretical. Further, the evidence suggests a vibrant and diverse educational culture—in recognizably Greek disciplines.

Amid the spotty chronology of official responses to teachers and declarations of social discipline, the edict of the censors Crassus and Domitius Ahenobarbus properly returns us to the history of the school. Here Suetonius's notice of the censure of those conducting and attending Latin schools and Cicero's recreation of the issues agree that an innovation had been introduced into the curriculum. In 92 B.C. the censor Domitius Ahenobarbus joined his colleague, with whom he seems to have been in near-constant disagreement, to issue an edict castigating one particular school. They did not, as is often stated, close the school.[17] Suetonius, in describing the difficult fortunes of the teachers of rhetoric at Rome, cites the censors' edict:

> We have been informed that there are persons who have established a novel sort of instruction and that the youth gather at their school; that these people have styled themselves "Latin rhetoricians," and that young persons idle away whole days there. Our ancestors established what manner of things they wished their children to learn and what manner of schools they wished them to attend. These new practices, which do not accord with ordinary custom and the way of our ancestors, are vexatious and wayward-seeming. Therefore we have determined to make our judgment plain both to those who preside over these schools and to those who have become accustomed to attending them: we do not approve.[18]

The censors did not approve, and neither did the subsequent, written Roman tradition. Practice was a different matter. The distinguished authority of the critics has perhaps distorted a proper appreciation of both the innovation and the success of the school, or its approach. Cicero has Crassus, set as a character in the dialogue devoted to the training of the perfect orator, explain his opposition. Tacitus, in his account of the new style and the new proper orator, recalls Cicero's Crassus and the dialogue's words: this establishment was "a school of impudence." Suetonius includes one more important detail: in a letter he had read but which has not survived, Cicero said that he had wanted to attend this school, but that he had been dissuaded by friends.[19]

A thicket of scholarly opinion has grown up around the school and its critics. Plotius Gallus and his school have been understood to represent demagogic forces, with the censors in turn understood as conservative *optimates*. A second political analysis has seen the event as an attempt by the senatorial class to restrict access to the practice of oratory. Bonner argued that the objection of the censors was moral not political,[20] but the moral, aesthetic, social, and political certainly supplement each other in explanations of why human beings cleave to one group. Erich Gruen has recently pruned the assumptions of these approaches, by demonstrating in detail that the alleged demagogic agents involved, the teacher and Marius, had no such connection (in fact, in the 90s Marius was making connections with Crassus); further, Crassus's political allegiances cannot be classified as "optimate." Indeed, the mutual hostility of Ahenobarbus and Crassus raises the important question, What coincidence of interest could move the censors to brand publicly one particular teacher a moral threat? The thorough study of Roman political interests and familial allegiances splinters the old divide of Roman cultural history into pro-Hellenic and pro-nativist camps or, as in this case, the demagogic and the senatorial.[21]

The threat perceived in Gallus's school and curriculum deserves additional study. The essential question remains, Why did a training for oratory through the medium of Latin exercises draw the condemnation of these two customarily fractious censors? To this must be added, Why did Cicero's advisers counsel him not to attend, and why did the issue of this particular school remain important in histories of the rise of Roman oratory and Roman schooling? In brief, the school of Gallus represented an innovation in curriculum, one that was effective and that, importantly, despite the censors' and Cicero's and Tacitus's invective, did not go away. In fact, the currency of setting speeches in Latin with Roman contexts is paralleled in the *Rhetorica ad Herennium* and would prove a hallmark of Roman declamation. To disentangle the strains of memory and polemic we must consider Cicero's reconstruction of Crassus's opposition and of his own early education.

When Cicero had finished his grammatical studies, that is, after he and his brother had come to Rome for school, where he had as classmates the young Atticus and his cousins and would prove a great success, he thought of attending a new school.[22] Older friends, including L. Crassus, dissuaded him from attending the rhetorical school of Plotius Gallus. Instead, he served as a sort of apprentice to a famous Roman jurist.[23] The precise chronology of Cicero's early schooling is not clear: for instance, in the *Brutus* (207) Cicero tells that he studied under Stilo, the famous Roman grammarian and antiquarian. This may mean simply that he attended the old man (as a dependent friend, a client); certainly, Stilo set no course of study. We do not know at what age Cicero first called on Stilo or how long the relationship continued.

The *Brutus* typifies the difficulty of interpreting Cicero on the early history of Cicero, and hence the difficulty of assessing his reliability as a source for the history of schooling at the beginning of the last century B.C. The dialogue sketches the history of Roman oratory but as a narrative series of great men in which Cicero seeks to enshrine himself.[24] One way to advertise status was to mention friends (Romans did the same in their wills and forensic speeches). When, for instance, Cicero comes to defend the Greek poet Archias, he mentions as friends of the defendant, it would seem, all the leading men of Rome he can (*Arch.* 6—at 20 Cicero recalls Marius's strong devotion to Plotius). Cicero does not mention famous names indiscriminately, nor should we believe that in a speech delivered to a Roman jury he could fabricate contemporary relationships. His list of mentors reveals patterns both of social relations—centering on Crassus and politically conservative—and of his own abiding intellectual interests: the old Roman poets, Roman law, and Greek intellectual culture. Cicero would become a true expert in Roman law, and no doubt his interest was nurtured by the early encounter (from 90 B.C.) with the famous jurist, the octogenarian father-in-law of Crassus, Q. Mucius Scaevola.[25] As with Stilo one is tempted to conclude that had there been significant lessons given and learned or significant patronage from the older mentor, Cicero would have details to relate. Perhaps, as Elizabeth Rawson has suggested, Cicero met his lifelong friend the scholarly T. Pomponius Atticus at Scaevola's.[26] Scaevola died during the Social Wars, when Cicero served under Pompeius Strabo, father of the famous Pompey. To the everlasting confusion of students, Cicero then attached himself as a "student" to Scaevola's cousin, the like-named *pontifex maximus* Q. Mucius Scaevola (see *Amic.* 1 and Rawson 1983, 16–17), a friend of Crassus. The list of scholarly influences could be continued (Cicero's introduction to Greek philosophers occurs at this time), although biographers naturally emphasize his three prosecutions as the formative events of his early career. In this same period he took lessons in oratory from the Greek Molo (with whom he would later study at Rhodes), perhaps after his first treatment of the science of speaking, the *De inventione*.[27] As an ambitious orator and intellectual, Cicero sought out those with expertise and power. The connections he cites reflect the flexibility of his training and the volatility of Roman politics. No single institution, no single alliance, served to prepare him or perhaps to satisfy him, but the more general conclusion for Roman education is that for the Roman elite opportunities and experts abounded.

By this point Cicero's education has advanced far beyond the rhetorical curriculum treated by the present book, and in significant ways far beyond the curriculum Cato Licinianus or, in its focus on developing an integrated but distinctive Roman oratory, even Scipio Aemilianus had pursued some six or seven decades earlier. Cicero now left Rome (79 B.C.), by his own account for his health, although historians have often suspected political caution hurried him from the city—Plutarch alleged that following the prosecution of Roscius Cicero feared Sulla.[28] Cicero explains his departure exclusively in medico-rhetorical terms. His physicians and friends counseled that should he persevere in his forceful delivery of law-court speeches he would ruin his health. Cicero was capable of dissimulation especially in regard to his own motives, but he was of a rhetorical temperament: he saw the voice as a specimen of the body's condition and as an index of character; he trained himself with physical exercise and a regimen of diet and massage understood to be beneficial to one's abilities as a speaker.[29] In addition, he did work very hard; he is known to have been frail; and his style of speaking did change from the sustainedly overwrought manner of his early speeches. He would in turn send his own son to

Greece for study at the same stage of life.[30] The medical reasons are credible, perhaps especially so given the stress and peril of remaining in Rome.

In trying to determine why Plotius Gallus became for Cicero a failed candidate,
one might speculate that Gallus's school and expertise did not have the status or
the curriculum as Cicero prepared to enter public life. The orator was always in
search of good teachers, but the best teachers were the free men who taught in their
native Greek cities.[31] By implication, the freedmen at Rome were second-class teachers; and while there is patent social snobbery in this preference, in truth Rome at
this time paled as a center of Hellenistic learning. Not until the great patronage of
Augustus and the further spread of empire and peace would Rome become a rival
to Athens, Rhodes, or Alexandria. Plotius Gallus probably did not have the expertise
of a great rhetorician. He may have been a freedman, which perhaps with the ple-
beian form of his name, Plotius, rather than Plautius aroused social snobbery and
so contributed to his disqualifications.[32]

Plotius's style of speaking sounds like it was of the unremitting and unvaried quality, with its attendant physiological effects, that so worried Cicero's friends.[33] Cicero may have been far closer to this teacher or his style than he would later have
his readers know. Gallus would then have been part of the problem, not the cure.
Cicero's recollection in the *De oratore,* which forgets his attraction to the school,
smacks of revisionism. The evidence for the curricular practice in this school depends preeminently on Cicero, and upon a particular kind of Ciceronian voice
within a literary dialogue.

The practice of Plotius's students has been deduced from what Cicero has Crassus say in the dialogue *De oratore.* Interlocutors press the old man on how the young
should form themselves into the perfect orator. The literary pattern where a dialogue depends on the last oral recollection of an old-timer is meant to convey an
air of authority and authenticity. Crassus serves as a symbolic linchpin, between
young and old, Cicero and the early orators, and Greek-infused culture and an alleged, prior Roman nativism. The dialogue's recommendations, however, neatly con-
cur with Cicero's theory and practice. As in the more historically oriented *Brutus,*
Cicero here represents proper oratory as the perfect fusion of Greek and Roman.[34]
By this he means more than that Greek rhetorical theory gradually wormed its improving way into Latin practice. The study of Greek language and literature affords
the orator the *copia* that he needs to meet all contingencies of any given speech situation. In the *De oratore* Crassus also outlines a practice of imitative performance
and translation that we know to have been Cicero's own: the orator must declaim
in Greek and translate this performance into Latin.[35] Cicero has Crassus provide
the rationale for such double translation or double performance: first, reading a
speech in Greek and repeating it trains the memory, then one's Latin style is developed by translating and reperforming it in Latin. Translation from Greek to Latin
works better than reading, then reciting, and finally recasting in one's own words

a Latin speech of Gracchus or a poem of Ennius (his earlier practice—or so Crassus of the dialogue confides) because at times Gracchus and Cato have used the proper words and one is forced in the effort at variation to employ a less apt Latin expression.[36] Working from the Greek has the further advantage, Crassus says, that one enriches Latin vocabulary. Again, Crassus's guidelines directly reflect Cicero's practice, one that he theorizes when speaking of the difficulty of writing his philosophical dialogues in Latin.[37] The *De oratore* purposefully intervenes in or even deforms the history of speaking at Rome.[38] Cicero's dialogue presents a genealogy, complete with archetypes and antitypes, that with a revisionist simplicity discovers a history that seems on critical inspection to reflect Cicero's biography, or the autobiography he chooses to present.

Beyond his genuine admiration for Greek culture and the high artistry of Greek oratory, Cicero has recognized the special challenge posed and reward gained by bilingual performance. Translation puts pressure on the target language. Certainly, one comes to understand the original language better (here, we are talking of advanced understanding: neither Cicero nor Crassus learned Greek as students learn Greek even now with the help of a bilingual crib). Literary Latin, as many of the vernaculars in the Renaissance, was enriched by the work of translators. Cicero's reading of Latin literature was also informed by the sensibility of a reader experienced with translation and of an author adept at translation.[39] The early Latin poets were not simply producing translations but versions of Greek originals.[40] An educated Latin reader like Cicero was such a double reader—he read Ennius with Homer and Euripides in his memory. In addition, Cicero was a translator in his own right (of Aratus and Plato, especially). The declamation of a Greek original with immediate Latin translation, practiced in the company of a select few, is something between an educational practice and professional maintenance. Other evidence points to the fact that Cicero maintained his art privately and publicly. Thanks to Suetonius (*Gramm.* 7.3) we know that Cicero went to the school of Gnipho even during his praetorship (in 66 B.C.), where there was declamation on market days (every ninth day). The historical Cicero demonstrates a range of interest in schools of speech that is not consonant with the censorious pronouncements put into the mouth of Crassus in the *De oratore*.

Cicero's own practice presents a model without parallel in Greek literary culture, and one at odds with Plotius's transferal of Greek educational practice to Rome. The declamation in one language followed by translation into another does have parallels in the subsequent history of Latin pedagogy, as for instance in Roger Ascham's recommendation that the Renaissance English gentleman practice double translation, turning his Latin into English and then retranslating the English into Latin.[41] Ascham pushes the fluidity of expression one step further. Turning one's native language back to the original surely trains the memory as well as the command of diction, idiom, and syntax. Ascham's method shows two great affinities with Cicero's and Quintilian's approaches. First, as a composition exercise, it is extremely liberating. There is no need for invention or analysis. The topic is given and no interpretation asked, which features together allow the learner to focus all effort on the verbal surface. This focused stylistic exercise in variation owes much to the Hellenistic curriculum, which set a number of exercises on the same theme or the same text. The theme of a familiar fable could be given, and the student asked to produce his own version. A paraphrase of a developed passage or the expansion and ornamentation of a plain passage could be set. Verse could be turned to prose and vice versa.

All of these exercises develop stylization—where the student concerns himself with the *how* and not the *what* or *why* of discourse. A crucial innovation was that at Rome stylization was associated with translation. The Hellenistic student always worked from Greek to Greek (although Homeric and Thucydidean Greek were a far cry from his or her daily speech). Cicero's recommended practice sprang from the Hellenistic grammatical-rhetorical exercises in stylization and at the same time reflected the concern of a bilingual culture. The linguistic complexity is even greater since the curriculum included Greek of various periods, dialects, and genres; Roman students were also learning to speak Hellenistic Greek; and they were fashioning a literary language of their own. Of course, the individual student did not determine the rules for his performance, but composition did occur in this complex of linguistic codes and registers. A fundamental principle of this schoolwork (and of the literary practice for which it prepares) is the conviction that an authoritative original merits multiple versions. The performance and re-performance that move from the set version to one's own are also actions of play that treat language as a primary medium and object. Language is to be varied for its own sake. Authoritative Latin versions (Cato or Gracchus or Ennius) are less useful, on Cicero's judgment, because they hamper the student's freedom.

A slightly utopian, fantastic quality colors the recommended pedagogy. Cicero's instructions smack of an idealized classroom where time and talent are so ample that inconsequential things, a long dead speech or poem, can be taken up, cast this way or that, discussed, poked, and played with. The remove of time, of language, of seriousness or at least of closeness to daily life and pressing affairs, encourage the play with form. We have entered the school of virtuosi. Plotius Gallus offends against this entire literary sensibility. His exercises are in Latin and are practical (related to Roman contexts), distinctly not literary. Cicero and his peers have the time and resources for such play and for the deferred return on investment that such intensive training promises. The idealized leisure stands purposefully distant from the workaday, successful training of speakers practiced by Plotius Gallus.

Cicero's portrayal of Crassus's practice shows strong affinities with his other, leading account of the development of oratory and the orator at Rome. The *Brutus* details the development of Latin oratorical style, a movement Cicero crafts as a linear progression from the nativist Latin of Cato through an increasingly perfect acquaintance with Greek culture to culminate with the death of Hortensius. The endpoint is significant because Hortensius was the orator second to Cicero, and more dramatically the orator who dies with the republic. The *Brutus* and the character L. Licinius Crassus in the *De oratore* share the conception that Latin oratory advances in proportion to its knowledge of Greek culture. The *Brutus* also shares the technique of characterization of the *De oratore* whereby Roman aristocrats make distinctive, individual contributions that seem to anticipate Cicero's own synthetic virtuosity. Some scholars have argued for the historical accuracy of Cicero's Crassus, chiefly on the grounds that Cicero would not have dared deform the attitudes of a famous speaker whom the older members of his audience might have heard.[42] Yet one of Cicero's great talents was that species of rapprochement that makes great men look similar despite their personal, philosophical, or ideological differences. This is a republican tact or knack that can make a great communicator useful, a facility not simply to draw together opposed leaders but to articulate a common ground. The same quality shaped Cicero's historical imagination, so that despite the anachronism Roman historical characters serve as exemplary spokesmen for Greek ideas. These characters succeed within the text and as memorable confabulations because they do not simply ventriloquize Greek ideas but rather craft artfully drawn syntheses of Roman exemplarity and Greek science. Crassus may have practiced some such oratorical exercises, but the evidence points much more strongly to the fact that Cicero practiced this way in private. The mature Ciceronian understanding of the development and importance of Latin oratory left no room for a schoolteacher who was the client of demagogues.

Within the *De oratore*, against the high-minded and aristocratic exemplary cultivation of the oratorical self, Plotius Gallus plays a vulgar foil. Although not named in the dialogue, his style of teaching seems the target of Crassus's disapproval (thus the dialogue gives Cicero's version of Crassus's opposition known from the edict). In the *De oratore* Crassus is asked his views on the proper kind of exercises. The question and the responses come in formulas that suggest his authoritative, even magisterial role: *nunc de ipsa exercitatione quid sentias quaerimus,* immediately answered with his sententia, *Equidem probo ista* . . . (148–49: "Now we ask your judgment of the exercise . . . ; I approve that . . . ").[43] He approves the contemporary practice of setting a theme based on an actual law-court speech but immediately voices his disapproval of the end to which these exercises are at times employed: some use them for voice training and rejoice in the speed and power of delivery. Further, those addicted to this sort of speaking overvalue extemporaneous speaking; they do not properly appreciate the role of writing in good oratory. From here Crassus is off, talking about the role of writing in improving speaking. The censured speed and volume of delivery suggest that the anonymous "some" are orators similar to Plotius Gallus. Gallus was teaching *declamatio,* which at this point meant voice training (and not the use of *suasoriae* and *controversiae*).[44]

Crassus does not object to the modeling of speeches on Roman cases, nor even to instruction or performance occurring in Latin. This important point is often lost in recapitulations of the issues. He does object to the particular style of delivery that is swift and loud without reliance on written preparation. References from other sources imply that Plotius is the target here. Quintilian, immediately after mentioning that the Greeks began practicing on themes drawn from the law courts and the legislative councils in the time of Demetrius of Phalerum, asserts that the Latin teachers active at the end of Crassus's life were the first to set exercises modeled on contemporary speeches and that Gallus was the best known of these. Quintilian here (2.4.42) cites Cicero as his authority. Still, Quintilian's conclusion is no doubt right. Other sources associated Gallus or his students with loud delivery. A fragment of Varro's *Saturae Menippeae* (Menippean Satires) (p. 157 Riese) mixes social and stylistic criticism of Gallus in his characterization of someone who "had brayed like an ox-driver in the school of Plotius the rhetorician": *bubulcitarat* suggests the same mix of vulgarity and sheer decibel level that so offended Crassus. In another fragment Varro puns on the name of the schoolmaster so as to deride "this *gallus* (cock) who stirs up a tribe of brawlers" (p. 186 Riese). The cock produces mad dogs, not free men. Cicero strongly censures these *rabidi;* they are the "brawling advocate from the Forum" and "the declaimer from the schoolroom," contrasted with the truly cultured orator. (Cic. *De or.* 1.202: "We are not seeking through our dialogue some nameless pleader or a shouter or a mad-dog speaker [*rabulam*]"; *Orat.* 47: "We are not seeking some declaimer from school or mad-dog speaker [*rabulam*] from the Forum"; at *Brutus* 226 Cicero characterizes P. Antistius as *rabula sane probabilis;* Quintilian [12.9.12] reuses the doublet, substituting *latrator* for Cicero's *clamator* or *declamator*.) The mad-dog speaker is one foil to the good orator, an opposition similar to that of the actor and orator.[45]

Varro has here provided a valuable piece of evidence, which corroborates the picture derived almost exclusively from Cicero, and his *De oratore* in particular. In the dialogue Crassus's younger interlocutor, the famous orator Antonius, described the third, worst sort of student as one who does not orate but shouts, exceeding the boundaries of good taste and his own physical abilities: "To shout beyond the limits of what is appropriate and of his own powers characterizes the man who, as you, Catulus, once said of a certain bawler, gathers as large as possible a crowd of witnesses to his own folly with the service of his own herald."[46] Here Cicero may well be interweaving a famous *sententia* of Catulus with Crassus's known opposition to the school of Plotius. Again, Cicero may have tilted the balance of evidence so that we see Plotius Gallus as the convenient target of a broader opposition to demagogic and low-class speakers (he is also distancing himself from his own youthful style, that loud and unremitting delivery that threatened his health and drove him to Molo).[47] Greek orators were notorious for the speed of their delivery.[48] Asianist Latin orators were also criticized for their speed (and for their floridity—a vice supposedly to be checked by reliance on written preparation).[49] Plotius is receiving bad press with considerable prejudice. A minority report comes from a great authority: Quintilian (11.3.143) cites his work on gesture as an authority for the obsolete custom of wearing the toga long, down to the feet.

Cicero was seeking an originary moment for various phenomena in Roman public speech: the role of paid rhetoricians, Latin exercises modeled on actual Roman cases, the strong reliance on extemporaneous speaking, perhaps even Asianist style, and voice training independent of a larger curriculum—all of which he disapproved at the end of his career, and some of which he had clearly pursued in his youth. Late in life, Cicero sought to distance himself from his earlier stylistic excesses. He had overstrained his delivery and had to check this fault, indeed had to be retrained. The richer style of the Asianists he seeks to excuse as the style fit for a young man, a rich abundance to be pruned by age, judgment, and the pen. Cicero's view of the rise of Roman oratory and his selection of a generic form, the dialogue, contribute in the *De oratore* to a preference for dramatic dates about which to collect the names of old orators and range them in debates strongly colored by Cicero's own interests and career. Further, the course of oratory at Rome moves in tandem with the development of oratorical powers in the individual. Here Cicero seems guilty of that writerly fallacy of destiny wherein the present writer sees history, his own life, and the process of writing leading irresistibly to the moment of composition and likewise to the composer. Plotius Gallus deserves to be disentangled from a narrative that would cast him as the foil for Crassus' and Cicero's and Varro's ire or as a misstep in the history of Roman schooling.

Plotius Gallus was neither a strictly academic rhetorician nor a humdrum teacher of shortcuts. He did write a book on delivery, which shows his interest in the practice of Roman oratory. There are two indications that he was a ghost writer for important speakers: M. Caelius, defending himself against the plaintiff Atratinus on a charge of *vis,* alleged that his opponent's speech had been written by Plotius (Suet. *Gramm.* 26). One can imagine that this was a joke, a sneer to denigrate the style of Atratinus's attack, but Fronto, that inveterate lover of old books, reports that he had seen a manuscript of a speech of Gracchus written in Plotius's own hand (*Ad M. Caes.* 1.7.4). If Gracchus and Atratinus were patrons, Plotius was something more like a voice expert to the stars than master of upstart demagogues. We know that Tiberius Gracchus had a pipe player who would play to recall the orator's pitch to a moderate level during his speeches.[50] We should not forget the range of experts needed by the Roman citizen ambitious to become a successful orator-cum-politician: the slaves who would know the names of all the citizenry, the masseuse, the voice expert, the physician who guided the physical regimen of the speaker, the former schoolmaster or pedagogue who continued in his ward's later life to be a speech counselor. Cicero does not call attention to this spectrum of hired and owned help. His letters, like his dialogues, make it seem that a community of high-minded and high-status Romans discuss things with him in the privacy of his home or one of his villas. Yet the truth is that he was an avid seeker of experts: he would travel to find the best teachers; he would ask Atticus for trained specialists; he would foster and even flatter expert freedmen; and of course he depended greatly on his freedman Tiro, note taker extraordinaire.[51] Plotius probably figured in the lower half of the spectrum of experts, which led from cook and masseuse up to the freeborn teacher or the Greek philosopher who might be part of the greatest family households. Plotius was not the sort of expert later sought by Cicero. Crassus disapproved of him in 92; Caelius finds him a convenient target in 56 B.C. Here again it may have been Cicero and Crassus who disapproved, for they had joined together to defend Caelius in the case of *vis* (itself a backlash from Caelius's failed prosecution of Atratinus's father, Bestia).

Perhaps we should not pursue Cicero's and Crassus's determined enmity any further. It would be more rewarding to consider what course of education a young man like Caelius, born ten years after the censors' edict of 92, pursued. But no record recalls his education, at least until he has contact with luminaries. At the end of his studies he became an apprentice to Cicero, as Cicero had been in turn to the two great lawyers the jurist and the pontifex Scaevola, although the English term "apprentice" does not do justice to the personal, practical, and fluid relationship between the great man and the young men who would attend him. By the time he was admitted to the circle of friends attending the jurist Scaevola's daily routine, Cicero had in all likelihood been to the finest teachers in Rome. At this stage, having completed what we might call the formal work of rhetoric, he seems to have been casting about and so considered Plotius's school before being dissuaded, in all likelihood by Crassus. In the volatile years of the late republic the volatile time of young manhood for the politically ambitious can be characterized as a search for opportunities: opportunities to defend or, failing that, to prosecute some leading man; and opportunities to secure patrons. The two processes were inextricably intertwined. We are here well beyond the period of schooling. In 90/89 Cicero would serve as military legate for Pompey's father. Caelius in turn would abandon Cicero's patronage to try the more meteoric prospect of Catiline. The prosecution of Caelius would send him back to Cicero. Cicero's volte-face with the choice of a schoolmaster is not so dramatic, but in retrospect he forgets how close he had come.

The importance of the choice of a teacher can be gleaned also from that famous story of Roman family education, that of Cornelia and her children. Plutarch has included a small detail: Diophanes of Mytilene was tutor to Tiberius Gracchus (Plut. *Ti. Gracch.* 8.4). Why did Plutarch here—or Suetonius more generally—think it significant to include the names of the Greek teachers of illustrious Romans? Like Cicero, they were interested parties: they too believed that Greek culture had transformed Rome and remained an essential, constitutive part of the formation of Roman youth. In addition, by commemorating a teacher, Plutarch gives his reader a piece of the moral as well as intellectual genealogy of his subject. Finally, a Roman reader sees in such notices not simply a statement of personal debt but a display of family resources and connections. The teachers of a Gracchus or of a Cicero were impressive personalities.

The school of Plotius Gallus could undermine all of these perceptions and signs of relationship. Plotius held school late in the education of a youth, perhaps a stage where school was unprecedented.[52] He also took a fee for preparing speakers who, to judge from Cicero's options, otherwise would have attended a practicing orator as client friends to a patron, where payment was inconceivable. Plotius's school promised the same excellence in the performance of Latin speeches, an excellence that was to be won, according to Crassus and Cicero, by diligent, personal study with Greek experts in the privacy of a great home and then by consultation as a junior friend of some established, practicing upper-class Roman. Plotius Gallus's school circumvented both sets and types of relationship.

Finally, the choice of type of education resulted in significant stylistic differences. The students of Plotius Gallus did not sound the same as someone of Cicero's train-ing. This does not mean that Plotius's disciples were all low-class demagogues. Cer-tainly Cicero felt the pull of this new school. It was exciting, and to judge from the indications of Plotius's continued activities and from the prominence of his patrons and denigrators, the new kind of impudence was successful. The reliance on actual cases and a strong emphasis on practical training in voice and bodily delivery seem to have distinguished the speakers of this school. Despite the denigration of the loud-ness of this school of speakers, the school marks the first exclusively Latin, advanced curriculum, a step as important in its way as Ennius providing a Roman topic and Latin style for epic (the very stuff of grammatical schooling) or Cato providing Latin aphorisms and history in Latin.

Plotius's school may have disappeared with him. The practice of having students focus on Latin speeches at the end of their curriculum persisted. Whereas Quin-tilian, like Cicero, insisted on the importance of Greek, the evidence of declama-tion shows a majority interest in Latin. The complaint leveled against Plotius's voice coaching and speech training will be repeated against the declamatory training in *suasoria* and *controversia* that developed in the second half of Cicero's lifetime. Quin-tilian will complain that extemporaneous speech was too highly prized and that the pen and theoretical training were proportionally despised. Complaints about the style of delivery continued, yet the style faulted by Seneca the Elder or Quintilian would change: there may be no direct inheritance from Plotius except that those disposed to lavish time and money on education would continue to snub those who took shortcuts.[53]

The censors' edict against the school and Cicero's nonattendance do not in fact constitute a crisis in schooling. They do indicate a lively, contentious community of schools, teachers, and patrons. We do not really know what tempted Cicero to or dissuaded him from attending, but he did attend a school about this time, and this too embarrassed him later in life. In the 90s Cicero went to somebody's lectures on rhetoric, which were given in Latin. He composed, and later regretted, a short handbook on rhetorical invention, the discovery of what to say, whose similarities with the anonymous *Rhetorica ad Herennium* indicate a common origin.[54] The anonymous Latin rhetorician who gave the lectures was no Plotius Gallus: he was interested in Greek theory, but like Plotius he was providing a shortcut to the traditional curriculum of study and practice in Greek. In the end Cicero would broadly and insistently advertise his connection to Crassus and the Scaevolas; later he would travel to Greece for better teachers; and in his practice he would declaim in Greek as well as Latin. Yet although he would turn against the strictly Latin and practical curriculum of the *De inventione* or of Plotius Gallus's book on delivery, and eventually produce a range of Latin theoretical works on rhetoric and oratory himself, in the 90s he had all but tried two schools at Rome that offered a curriculum in Latin.

The model of education within the aristocratic home for the sons of the family was not sufficient, as it had not been for the students of Cato's freedman Chilon. The written records tend to relate the censure of aristocrats toward the schools and so promulgate a nostalgic story of old schooling being replaced by the upstart institution. The schools of declamation at the very end of the republic and on into the empire, however, had better precedent and better continuity than a Cicero, Suetonius, or Seneca allows. Romans were not good educational historians in part because they told a story of native lore replaced by Greek expertise, thus belittling the traditions of Italic literacy. In addition, the contrast of Greek expertise and Roman ignorance could be read into the structure of schooling where the teacher was often a Greek freedmen in charge of freeborn Roman children. Each generation could read in this social reality a typology of the coming of education and culture. Paradoxically, the effort to supplant the Greek altogether, to forge an entirely Latin curriculum, would be met by the opposition of the elite, for whom Hellenistic culture had become a distinguishing badge and a cherished pursuit.

4

The Manual and the Child

The exemplary education of the young Roman, glimpsed so far in anecdotes told by or about exemplary fathers and a mother (Cato, Aemilius Paulus, Cornelia), receives systematic treatment in two manuals of education of the late first century A.D., the *Institutio oratoria* (The Orator's Education) of Quintilian and the *De liberis educandis* (On the Education of Children) written by a student or follower of Plutarch. Like the evidence for education in the republic, the works of the imperial age dispense praise and blame to exhort the reader toward an ideal education, and away from disapproved methods and teachers. In the *De oratore* Cicero had delineated the training and knowledge of the ideal orator but had explicitly neglected the early period of education. The educational manifesto of Pseudo-Plutarch and the rich treatise of Quintilian abundantly fill this gap. The Plutarchan text in particular provides an unrivaled insight into the ancient teacher justifying his ways.[1] Chapter 5 below, devoted to Quintilian, considers his influential theorization of the boy as a learning subject. The boy's dispositions, his growth, and his proper bookish formation interest Quintilian, and for the history of children, education, and psychology, such interest is novel and important.

Despite their manifest differences of scope and detail—the follower of Plutarch writes an essay urging fathers to delegate but supervise their sons' literary education, while Quintilian offers a nearly encyclopedic guide to the training of the speaker/writer—both texts communicate an imperial educational ideology. As prescriptive manuals of nurture, they contribute to a hierarchy of knowledge and labor in the complex and differentiated world of the early empire. Quintilian is manifestly imperial in the basic presupposition that imagines a standardized education as crucial to producing a citizen class worthy of the Roman past and of governing the Roman Empire. While the *De liberis educandis* may well have had a Roman audience in mind, it is not Romanocentric; yet it too imagines that a single class of citizen intellectual laborers will gain its principles of living and governing from a common education rooted in the classics. Neither work contains any intimation that education will do anything but foster the imperial system, and like Cato's writings to his son, both seek to form the ideal heir, for family and state.

Both texts also celebrate the ancient traditions of rhetoric and philosophy. Yet they do not simply synthesize Hellenistic manuals of rhetoric. Certainly, the authors are widely read and ready to display their authoritative sources. Their perspective departs from these intellectual predecessors through a sustained reflection on the toil that children carry out as students. The child of the Roman Empire has "his" special duty (which is consistently presented as his, though girls are clearly to be engaged in education): his learning will make him the sort of citizen to sustain family and empire. The abundance of teachers and schools, the success of Roman education (itself in part a result of the stability of empire and the great achievements of Augustan literature), the weighty tradition of Greek writings on grammar and rhetoric, and the contrast of restricted elite schooling with more widespread literacy form the backdrop to the theorization of how and why the child learns.

THE MODE OF THE MANUAL

The *De liberis educandis* and Quintilian's *Institutio oratoria,* for all their novel emphasis on the life of the child, belong to the genre of the technical manual. But beginning with Xenophon's treatise on the education of Cyrus, the Persian King, the handbook of nurture and culture thinks *with* the child as much as it thinks *about* the child. The strong link between the good government of the child and of the state is an enduring legacy of the educational, literary genre. Quintilian writes perceptively and originally of the process of inducing the child to learn. He recognizes the differing capacities of individual children (chiefly conceived as differing in promptness to learn) and focuses on differences in what one might be tempted to call maturity of intellect but which he seems to understand as different stylistic dispositions—more advanced students have different styles of expression. Neither Quintilian nor the author of the *De liberis educandis* has an interest in the interior process of transformation. The mental, emotional, and imaginative life of the child did not spark Quintilian and Pseudo-Plutarch as it would Augustine and Rousseau. But like the *Confessions* and *Émile,* the earlier pedagogic treatises divide the life of the child into educational stages and functions as they seek to make orderly and transparent the shaping of the boy into a man.[2]

A comparison with the later manuals, whose authors knew their classical models well, reveals broad commonalities in the prescriptive mode of writing about the young. The manuals explain and justify their approved pedagogy on three levels.

Practices are described; explanations of the purposes of the recommended actions are given; and the book's own harmonization (of practices, explanations, traditions, objections, innovations) becomes a compelling mode of expression and comprehension. The orderly presentation of the manual corresponds to its great optimism—the confidence that the child can be formed into a speaking subject. As a systematic synthesis the manual promises completeness and actuality. All necessary knowledge of the topic can be learned from this source or with this text as a guide. The manual seeks to calm turbulent impulses—the thought that youth will not be trained, that a different sort of schooling is called for, that traditions are being neglected, or that book-learned youth will not repair society.

Both in its theorizing and in the form of presentation, the manual of education was one of several genres exploiting the well-articulated expertise of the Hellenistic world. Like the manual of architecture, it also aimed to make more uniform the various practices of an empire. This tendency toward consistency may be a reflex of settled empire. The manual of education, architecture, or medicine is political not just in implicit assumptions about the roles and relationships of the various agents but also in its fundamental conviction that there is one proper way to educate (or to build for or to doctor) all students. Educational chauvinism is more strongly political, since the intended product is not doctor or architect but citizen. Quintilian and Pseudo-Plutarch believed that liberal education produced an ideal type of man whose attitudes and practices reflected, or even constituted, his status as a member of the governing elite. The educational texts are of a different order from the agricultural manuals or the home-economic or hunting writing of Xenophon, for example, for they take up the question of how to shape not field or slave or dog or wife but the future generation.[3]

The Romans' interest in reading and writing synthetic books of knowledge is perhaps so familiar, so much a part of what we take to be a legacy of the classical world, that its uniqueness is missed, or, at least, not given due prominence as a phase in Roman intellectual life. Cato wrote a manual of agriculture; he would be followed by Varro and Columella; and we have reviewed the early Roman works on oratory.[4] Strabo's geography, Vitruvius's architecture, Quintilian's rhetoric, Celsus's compendium of medicine, agriculture, law, military science, and rhetoric, and Varro's or later Columella's agriculture created a formidable Latin encyclopedia in the span of a century and a half. Varro also wrote on the nine liberal arts.[5] By A.D. 100 the consular and governor of Britain, Sextus Julius Frontinus, had written his art of war (*Strategemata*).[6] More esoteric works could be added to these primers of Roman culture, but such texts as the *Attic Nights* of Aulus Gellius are avowedly more literary, more entertaining, than these practical books. Certainly, the works of useful knowledge written during the early Roman Empire represent an offshoot of ancient *technai*, perhaps a more literary offshoot that derives some impulse from the philosophical and rhetorical dialogues of Cicero, who had made available to a Latin reading public both the matter of important Greek areas of knowledge and a body of literary works that now set the model for cultural discourse in Latin. The Latin didactic works communicated spheres of knowledge important for the father of the household in his familial and social role—the care of himself at home and at war, and of his family, buildings and properties, and sons. The chosen mode of precepts and illustrations in Pseudo-Plutarch especially and in Quintilian may have had a particular advantage over the dialogues of Cicero in that this method of exposition was itself familiar from a schooling in rhetoric. It also could be more easily excerpted into reusable tags.

To understand why Romans of the early empire turned to a new mode of didacticism, we need to lay aside the sharp distinction between original inquiry and résumé that informs so much of our literary and scholarly judgment. Cultural résumé clearly had a great appeal, and the making of books recognized as valuable necessarily involved the reading and excerpting of many books and the recapitulation of the positions and findings of the past. It is not the case that the Romans had a blinkered attitude to information, as if they thought all that was worthy had been said and that the present generation had only to adorn the discoveries of the past or vie with the great stylistic formulation of those discoveries. Such an unsympathetic understanding of Latin literature would grant the belated author only two choices: either he must simplify the form of expression and so make the classical more accessible or he must torture the form of expression in a drive for distinction that does not allow new material but impels mannered style. Both the functionalist communicative and the formal aestheticist models miss the animating principle of this genre and even era of literature. The authors of the late republic and early empire did produce aids (e.g., the minimalist account of rhetorical figures in the rhetorician Gorgias's *De schematibus*) and did produce some obscurities (e.g., some of the lines of the declaimers in Seneca's collection, the sorts of work satirized by Juvenal and Petronius for their pretense and bombast). But the work of the encyclopedist Celsus or of the universal historian Velleius Paterculus or the monumental *Natural History* of the elder Pliny aims to communicate knowledge that needs rearrangement for the present generation to use easily. Pliny and Velleius are not useful in an identical way, either as physical books or as bodies of knowledge. They did purport to communicate with a dignity appropriate for their subject, author, and audience the fruits of great study. This is ultimately a bookish habit or gesture. It does not imply that the old books are unavailable, but seems to imply that there are very many books and that the reader needs a guide. The affinities with the pedagogic writers are instructive.

Behind the essay attributed to Plutarch or Quintilian's great book runs the same sense of daunting knowledge now brought to useful reduction. Like Dionysius of Halicarnassus's universal history, Pseudo-Plutarch's essay and Quintilian's treatise are written as guides to a vast system of knowledge. As indices to a rich tradition of education, they parallel the encyclopedic impulse that cataloged and reduced the peoples, cultures, and events of the past to a ready textual form made newly accessible for a Roman imperial audience.[7]

The shaping of material to this useful end and the appreciative reader's sense of the structure and utility of the works depended on an attitude to composition shared by author and audience. In the postclassical generations after the great accomplishments of late republican and Augustan literature, writing was a rhetorical practice, one of *inventio* (discovery), *dispositio* (arrangement), and stylization (*elocutio*).[8] A practice of reading, excerpting, and rewriting shaped the mentalité of the literate. In rhetorical theory, *inventio* was the term for the speaker's collection of materials fit for a speech under preparation. *Dispositio* can refer to the general structuring of a speech or, more mechanistically, to the placing of the found objects that had to be restylized to fit the current composition (for they were not simply embedded). The technical manual particularly benefits from this traditional mode of composition: it is itself a compilation of past manuals and practices, and it reproduces the excerpt, sententia, or theory of past masters in such a way and in such a structure that the reader can now take them for himself. The manual need not advance bold new theories; its chief virtue comes in its reformulation of the rules and regimens for the intensive training of youth.

For later readers, the educational manual might come to be a weapon in their arsenal of culture. The term *manual*, in Greek *encheiridion*, itself means a handbook, a book of a size to be carried in a hand.[9] The strict etymological sense of the word might not suit the large work of Quintilian, except that the manual was a book that grew up on the periphery of the ancient school: it is a handbook meant to help the student, a ready aid in his studies, in the case of Epictetus's famous work the *Encheiridion*, a shortcut to the complex world of Stoicism. In its other, leading meaning *encheiridion* signifies a hand weapon, a dagger, and the manual could be a means of defense, an intellectual weapon at hand. Its practical quality derives from its size and its relation to school studies. In Quintilian and Pseudo-Plutarch especially, the book's assertion of its practicality contributes to the larger apologetic for liberal education. The target of such claims may well include other books (the authors have no time for a treatise on grammar, for example), and, in Quintilian's case, a more philosophical education. Fathers may rely upon the papyrus rolls of Pseudo-Plutarch or Quintilian and not upon any flesh-and-blood expert. The manual emerges not so much as the how-to of antiquity but as a maintenance checklist for the busy father. This genre reassures parents that sons educated in the recommended manner will not be led astray by the freedmen, often Greek, who numbered so significantly among the teachers at Rome. The educational manual is not yet the weapon of the humanists; rather, it intervenes between father and expert by disclosing methods and goals.

THE CONCEPTION OF *PAIDEIA*

To judge from the popularity of both Quintilian and Pseudo-Plutarch, readers have found considerable pleasure in being regaled with the advantages of a liberal education. Reading about education by the educated may represent an attraction like the mysterious allure of fishing stories for anglers. Perhaps nostalgia and voyeurism coincide in these peculiar literary forms. As a call to classical education, the *De liberis educandis* was a cherished text of the Renaissance and a favorite of the translators.[10] The great educator Guarino translated it into Latin in 1411 (thus before the rediscovery of Quintilian). The Aldine edition (1509) of Plutarch's *Moralia* preserved its (second) position in the MSS. Since Henri Étienne's Paris edition of 1572, the *De liberis educandis* has stood at the head of Plutarch's works. It appealed to the humanists as a manifesto of the new education, in part because it set in a vivid drama opponents to a classical education working against the all-important transformation of the child into a man, the cultured and reasoned height of civilization.[11] The humanists cherished a text that promised the great good worked by a classical education, and paraded as opponents to this good work flatterers, the corrupt, the servile, and the illegitimate—useful stand-ins for the Scholastics, reactionaries, indifferent nobles, and practical or even vernacular mercantile class who were perhaps not properly smitten by the advantages of reading Greek and writing Ciceronian Latin.

In fact, while it most likely stems from Plutarch's school or circle and is not the finished work of the master, this text offers remarkable insight into attitudes to education, even the ideology of education, Greek and Roman, in A.D. 100.[12] In other works Plutarch gives some attention to the what and how of education: he wrote on how to interpret the poets and how to listen to lectures—the stuff of elementary and advanced education. Even in these works he is ethically prescriptive, and negative. He writes of how to moralize apparently indecent passages or tells us not to interrupt the speaker. Whereas Aquinas's *De magistro,* following Augustine, would scrutinize the relation of student and teacher and define learning as the unblocked disposition of the subordinate to the supraordinate, the Plutarchan work assumes learning will take place, provided we attend to the good morals and language of the teachers. We need not hail the *De liberis educandis,* after the fashion of the Renaissance humanists, with self-seeking exaggeration as the insight into true culture long lost (and now to be restored by us). Rather, we should ask what Plutarch believed education and his text would do.

Whereas Quintilian organized a wealth of detail and experience in a compelling, synthetic presentation, the *De liberis educandis* is more hortatory than descriptive; yet its economic rhetorical form underscores a potent, ideological message. The author develops his argument on two, analogical fronts: father as sire is the true educator, and *logos* as master is the true emancipator. The exclusions worked by this strongly gendered thinking are significant. The treatise promises that freedom of birth and freedom of speech will coincide if the reader (imagined as a father) remembers to keep at bay the forces hostile to master *logos* and father: the influence, and particularly the speech, of wives, concubines, nurses, slaves, freedmen, flatterers, and the vile.

The Latin title conventionally assigned to the Plutarchan tract arose from the description of topic in the first sentence: *Ti tis an ekhoi eipein peri tēs tōn eleutherōn paidōn agōgēs kai tini khrōmenoi spoudaioi tous tropous an apobaien, phere skepsōmetha* (rather literally: "What someone might say about the rearing of free children and relying on what [rearing] these boys might turn out serious in their manners, come let us consider"). The sentence sounds more conversational than a title such as *On the Education of Children* might suggest. The conventional title also misleads on three accounts. The author did not mean to limit education to formal schooling, and by "child" he means a boy and a free boy at that.[13] A title truer to the stated aim is *Child to Citizen Transformation* or *The Technology of Child Production,* where the child is to be understood only as male and freeborn.[14] The text covers child production from procreation through the age of puberty. The author, like many others in antiquity, did not see childhood as a symbol of a beneficent nature or as a stage to which one should want to return. But where modern historians of childhood might fault the text's neglect of the psychology of the child, especially of the child's evolving point of view or mental capacities, we should recognize the particular vantage point of the treatise, which answers the questions essential to its culture: Who should teach the child, should the child be beaten, and is the recommended education only for the rich?[15]

The author aims to intervene in the process of child rearing, with the restorative, ideological end of putting father back in place and in charge. In the complex, differentiated, and slave-owning society of the Roman Empire (and Italy in particular), the idea that a father of the elite class would educate his own son is almost nonsensical. It might have been possible for some eccentric to direct the education of his son. Horace relates that his father, who was a freedman, served as his pedagogue—this exceptional practice testifies to the humility and devotion to learning of the poet and his family (as well as to their straitened circumstances).[16] But both Roman and Greek society had experts and institutions for all of education. An upper-class slaveholder would no more educate his son than he would change a diaper, plow a field, or set the table.[17] It was not simply that these were menial tasks. The performance of such tasks by delegated agents, while partly functional and efficient, also advertised the status of the owner, the man who does not have to work, at least not in the conventional sense of manual labor. Having one's sons educated by others shows, in Veblen's terms, conspicuous consumption and leisure.[18] The impulse seems triple: the son as an extension of the father does not have to work; the father's work of training the next generation is displaced onto his subordinates; and that work seems very much like leisure. The role or category of son is being redefined with that of work itself. Mental labor belongs to the owners, menial and domestic tasks to others. And the mental work in which the young heir is being trained itself rehearses the need for subordinates and the lavishing of resources upon this distinctly different member of the household.

The *De liberis educandis* conceives of the education of the young as a paternal project vital to family values, not as a transcendental or philosophical process within or for the self.[19] The text offers prescriptions and prohibitions more concerned with creating ideal relationships among men—father, teacher, and young student—than with any particulars of curriculum or method.[20] Education is thereby theorized neither exclusively as a process of nature nor as one of culture but rather as one of male bodies—allegedly, the paramount site of natural excellence and cultural (linguistic) training. The treatise imagines that *paideia* will establish *andreia*, manliness; indeed, its processes and relations are in a sense manliness.[21] The author hopes to direct the growing boy with nature and culture, the family and the teacher conspiring in an ideal harmony. The longed-for, ideal relationships that education depends on and will effect are set against a menacing background of inappropriate bodies, especially the female and the servile. The treatise also describes the positive work, the series of routine actions, that establish proper relations. These routines are patterns of human association and also habits or styles of reading, writing, and reciting. To ensure that the heir will turn out like the father, the treatise calls for the creation of a textual community, bordering on a fantasy of male relations, where bodies correspond to kinds of speech and both mirror the free status of the owner.

A defense of education necessarily requires an explanation of why a set of children is pursuing a particular set of activities. Often, such apologies do not acknowledge that any other thing or person is needed: teacher and student proceed in a heady vacuum. Indeed, talk of curriculum, canons, or methods tends to displace or even suppress the material and human labor that fuel the approved education. The not-so-free constraints of time, labor, and money that enable youth to be free for education are easily lost in prescriptions about what the child should do. A particularly complex challenge faced the follower of Plutarch as he wrote to explain, defend, and rationalize the schooling of boys. Other sets of children and of the educated and other pursuits of children lurk somewhat menacingly on the margins of his treatise.

Two aspects of ancient schooling were especially problematic: the educators were often of lower status than the students, and children other than free, elite children were educated, at times to professional standards. The *De liberis educandis* must define its approved education so as to differentiate it from the highly skilled literacy and numeracy of the slave experts. Further, since the severe training of children in these skills seems to treat the student as a slave, requiring him, even beating him, to perform, the author will argue for a different conception of the work of learning (and vigorously oppose corporal punishment). It is difficult to associate virility with education when the boy to be educated is difficult to distinguish from the punished slave, when elite girls and women are well educated, and when slaves and freedmen are among the best educators.

In order to differentiate an approved, elite education from the high expertise of a group of socially inferior practitioners, the educational ideologue may denigrate the activity of such practitioners as professionalism, trade knowledge, or pedantry. In a similar vein the author of the De liberis educandis exploits an existing Greek division between menial and mental labor so as to redefine the nature of the work, ponos, of the liberally educated boy as a free compulsion. The child does work, but with a willing spirit that distinguishes his work from the forced work of the slave. The author seeks to create a disposition in father and son, a habitus (to use Bourdieu's renewal of Aristotle's term hexis), which is both a set of attitudes and a daily practice.[22] In an important ideological development, the text imagines that this habitus actually sequesters the servile and the feminine. By redefining education as mental, not menial, labor and as a free compulsion that protects the family from attack (the inexpungible stain of reproach, as Plutarch terms it at 1B), the De liberis educandis constitutes a new chapter in educational thought.

The author writes most directly, however, to fathers. The De liberis educandis, along with Plutarch's various writings on education, Quintilian's great treatise, the encyclopedia of Celsus, and a wealth of ethical writing, might suggest that fathers in the first century A.D. needed advice on how to doctor their households or farm their estates or raise their sons. The pretense that a book is needed serves authors well, and the appearance of one self-declared "useful" book may encourage imitators. At the start of Roman prose literature, as we have seen, the elder Cato had set a strong precedent: the Roman father need only consult his text to put house and son, estate and servants (no matter how expert), in proper order, that is, well subordinated to the father's wishes. Literature is not here simply appropriating specialized discourses in the course of its growth as a cultural institution. More specifically, such literature purports to provide the master with disciplinary expertise. Reading and the reader trump experience. Perhaps for the literary culture of the early empire, Augustus's own policies and image making had contributed to a sense of the importance and possibilities of a hortatory, moralizing, paternal mode of presentation. Certainly, the De liberis educandis privileges the role of fathers, who have decidedly not, as in Plato's Laws, lost their place to experts and a state apparatus.[23]

In practice, education does not replicate paternal order (either the established institutions that tend to maintain social and cultural norms or more abstractly the attitudes and dispositions that aid the existing hierarchy of power) with rigorous sytematicity. Whereas the teaching and reading of the Aeneid in the schools provided each generation with a strong dose of the ideal father/son relationship,[24] ancient literature did not always represent the father in charge: comedy especially dramatizes the failure of his control, and in an extended family a father's control could not match the idealized order of Cato's writings. The gap between the strong figure of the idealized father and the actual dynamics of power in the family had been shaping Roman literature from the first Roman comedies of the third century B.C. In addition, Augustan political ideology, which depicted the emperor as father and made so much of family values, may have contributed to a concern over paternal order, perhaps especially because the realities of family life did not correspond to the political ideals. Had education and ideology been as effective as the treatise writers or legislators would have had it, the emperor's daughter Julia would not have been the colorful character she was. What is novel and interesting in the *De liberis educandis* is not so much the stance that education will reinforce the rule of fathers but the prescriptions for how to ensure proper growth in the son.

GROWING SONS

The *De liberis educandis* does not celebrate this period of training. The scholar of ancient education must give up the hope that he is going to find enthusings over the glorious season of childhood, those fine days of awakening at school. Emerson could rouse his reader's nostalgia with "Cannot memory still descry the old school-house and its porch, somewhat hacked by jack-knives, where you spun tops and snapped marbles . . . ?"[25] Plutarch's follower has no such feeling for the place of education, nor does he communicate any sweet longing for school games and school chums. It is not simply that school was some bleak exile, the sort of soul-parching, interminably rainy setting familiar from any number of nineteenth-century Bildungsromans. The author is not interested in the individual subjectivity of the young, nor does he see childhood as a formative period or a site of nostalgia for a lost and better identity.

First, the child's education will culminate with philosophy, which is a mode of disciplining one's life, not a professional career or technical field.[26] In modern terms, the child is to be trained toward an ethical disposition, the habit and outlook of an ideal adult man. Second, the child strikes the author as vulnerable. Nurse, mother, slave, pedagogue, teacher, base men, and rhetorical training itself threaten the child in line after line of attack upon his maturing male style.[27] The author sees the problem of education not as its potential failure to create the right relationship between teacher and student or to socialize the individual among peers or community or even to frame a moral or intellectual psyche. All of this he supposes may happen, but education can fail most fundamentally through a neglect of oversight that leads inevitably to the malformation of the child.

The child is imagined as a soft body, liable to an injury in its growth that will deform it for all time. At 3E infants' bodies must be massaged so that their limbs will grow straight; at 3F children are like soft wax ready for the seal.[28] The nurse must be Greek—a simile explains the aim: to avoid bodily deformity (3E). The child is imagined as a young plant in need of stakes (4C). At 5F the admonitory proverb again cautions that the child's companions must be the right sort ("If you dwell with a lame man, you will learn to limp"). The metaphor of 1B (those not well-born—he means of mixed birth—have an indelible reproach (*anexaleipta*) and are liable for all their lives to vituperation and insult) suggests that the soft bodies of such children are permanently, visibly marred. Bodily purity parallels verbal purity (e.g., 7B: "As the body ought to be not merely healthy but also sturdy, so also speech should be not merely free from fault but vigorous too"). Corporal punishment has a similarly indelible, physical effect: the children "grow sluggish and bristle at undergoing labor" (8F).

The propensity to be educated, to become the right sort of man, is a given (a consequence of free birth, it would seem). It is in keeping with Plutarch's thinking to summon a metaphor from the body and from medicine to make the point. Like health, educability is the default or natural condition. A famous Greek tag maintains that letters are the physician of the soul. We do not know what the comic poet who used this had in mind, but, like so much New Comedy, it was excerpted as a commonplace.[29] A romantic interpretation of the thinking behind the aphorism might conclude that literature communicates a positive force that shapes our selves and instills imagination and insight. An ancient interpretation, however, might think of literature as more consolatory, advisory, and sapiential; letters provide object lessons in dealing with adversity. More positively, the reading man relies on his texts and decidedly not on experience for the lessons of life. *Pathōn de te nēpios egnō*, "Only the fool learns from experience," runs another Greek tag (Hes. *Op.* 218). In line with this commonplace thinking, the ancient academic feels that literary schooling and study make the growth of the soul healthy. They prevent deformity and sickness and dispose men toward a mental self-sufficiency, although decidedly not the psychic salvation or personal emancipation imagined by modern theorists.

The educated man possesses from his reading a stock of material along with a capacity to read, write, and speak without the assistance of another, yet this mental self-sufficiency depends on external, material realities. His state of mind is marked by a freedom of speech, which is in fact a social and material condition as well as a disposition to understand and talk of the world in certain textual patterns. The author's science of text therapy has little of the magical about it. Specific texts are not charms or remedies. Rather, the freeborn are disposed to develop freedom of speech through the *paideia* that is the reading and writing of texts. One need do little to prepare for this text medicine since *eugeneia,* the legacy of good birth and upbringing, has bestowed this right to culture upon the freeborn.[30] Such a eugenics is in fact coextensive with the ideological cluster of rationalizations justifying the advantages of free birth and the thinking about the body that devolved from these mystifications (and hence neither an ancient version of the pseudoscience of the twentieth century nor the science fiction of the twenty-first century, each of which imagines the genetic improvement of the species). The relation of education to eugenics is an active, fostering one. Much must be done by and to the free boy to maintain and accentuate the distinctions from the base-born. Disease has to be avoided, actively and by design. And so education, and more broadly we might say the ongoing ethical conduct of life, are envisioned as a kind of preventative dietetics and calisthenics meant to preserve and strengthen eugenics. The *De liberis educandis* offers fathers a health program for growing sons.

In example, theme, and argument, Plutarch comes back again and again to concerns of purity. Above all, the body and speech of the son must be kept from tainted bodies and speech. Through the use of shared diction and direct metaphor, the care of the body is associated with care of the soul. The author engages in an intellectual zeugma that is more developed and significant than simply an embellishment of the commonplace *mens sana in corpore sano*. Body and soul are not sundered. The author realizes that injury to the body taints the soul, and here a social ideology of the hierarchy of the free and the slave informs his categories. The preservation of health depends on the subordination of the bodily to the mental, but the internal self-composure, wherein the individual orders his own wants and capacities, does not suffice to produce the desired state. Since his untainted body naturally and appropriately produces unsullied speech, the educated man rightly orders those about him. His eugenics is proved by his eulogics—his excellent, orderly, and ordering speech. With this mutually affirming cycle, the author can assure all fathers that their offspring is legitimate, that the child bodies of their sons are growing straight into speaking subjects without contagion from subordinates within the house or from the school.

The treatise began with the conception of the boy. Here the author develops his argument against bastards by using what will be typical forms of argument for this work, the especially schoolmasterly forms of citation from the poets, *chreia*, gnome, and historical exempla (*paradeigmata*). So after asserting his point that fathers should not have children with the lowborn, he supports this with one nasty consequence—the child of such a union is subject to verbal insult all his life—but then the author turns to his poetic and academic proofs (1B):

> Wise was the poet who declares:
>> The home's foundation being wrongly laid
>> The offspring needs must be unfortunate.

> A goodly treasure, then, is honourable birth, and such a man may speak his mind freely, a thing which should be held of the highest account by those who wish to have issue lawfully begotten. In the nature of things, the spirit of those whose blood is base or

counterfeit is constantly being brought down and humbled, and quite rightly does the
poet declare:
> A man, though bold, is made a slave whene'er
> He learns his mother's or his father's disgrace.[31]

The author has cited two passages of Euripides, *Hercules Furens* 1261 and *Hippoly-
tus* 424, and after these will bring on the historical exempla of Themistocles and of
King Archidamas. The passage performs in miniature the argument of the treatise:
the educational mode of reading, excerpting, and applying texts will guarantee the
legitimacy of the son. The texts of the classical authors offer the guide for the imperial citizen, as, more generally, imperial education sought to found identity on
the "prestigious past," although the author of the *De liberis educandis* seems to fear
that the present generation may show itself a bastard race.[32]

Anxieties riddle the directions for growing sons—not the child's worry that he
may not grow, but the father's worries that this growth may not be his own or may
not be "proper." One basic premise of the educational manual is that growth can
be analyzed into stages and categories. Rousseau would indict society for the improper administration of a child's early years: books are of no use to the young
child; let him play. Theories of experiential learning, of learning by toys and with
peers not with the solitary book, even the much disputed cognitive stages, all are
deeply indebted to Rousseau's *Émile,* although he is all but forgotten in professional
literature, replaced by his empiricist heir Piaget. The *De liberis educandis* also in-
dicts improper administration of the child, although the text is never a culprit. Instead the child advances from stage to stage without much advance in intellect (apparently for the historical Plutarch only the intellectual capabilities of the mature
student are of interest; perhaps this gap in Plutarch's writing and thinking encouraged our author). Up each rung of a ladder of perils, from mother's milk to
slave playmates and nurse, to pedagogues, and, at last, out of the house to school,
the child must avoid threats to his bodily well-being, and to his language. The cat-
alog of potential culprits makes interesting reading—nurse, mother, slaves, pedagogues, immoral teachers, those fathers swayed by the flattery of underlings or simply indifferent to the process of education. As a sure defense, the father has the
author's directives.

A reader might reasonably expect the treatise to discuss the nature of the freeborn male. What makes man (and not woman or slave) fit for education and for his
governing role? And since there are highly literate and numerate women and slaves
and freedmen, why should culture, education, be viewed as the defining essence of
the free man? Plutarch's contemporary Epictetus stands out as a slave-philosopher
who recommended philosophical education for women. But in a mode more typical of ideologies of knowledge, the defense of education maintains a universalist
stance—education is for the child, for every man. The rather indirect justification

of the superiority of the educated freeborn male comes in a series of comments, anecdotes, and rhetorical figures that serve to describe divisions of labor.

The author is masterful in his techniques of rationalization. Where a philosopher would want definitions and where a consistent educational theory pressures one to think that intellectual talent might be the one necessary ingredient of growing the educated person, the author describes typical activities. Through metaphor and anecdote he entwines the spheres of agriculture and education so as to champion natural growth. The child grows away from woman and slave as much as he does toward any positive attributes of virility. At the same time his body is celebrated as something distinctly different (if vulnerable). Nature, *phusis,* is thereby represented not as the common condition of human beings, but as a special birthright.[33] Tied to this division of *phusis* is the division of labor, *ponos,* whereby the free son alone can learn to speak properly.[34] Nicole Loraux has described the social semantics of *ponos* as a valorized effort that, starting in the classical period, distinguished master from slave, male from female, citizen from noncitizen.[35] The educational theorizing of toil can best be appreciated from the extant fragments of Musonius Rufus's treatment of the theses "Is *ponos* an evil?" (fr. 1) and "That toil matters little" (fr. 7). By the latter, Musonius means that great toil means nothing for the man intent on becoming a philosopher (compare Sen. *Ep.* 31.4). The present treatise delivers a little encomium on *ponos* (2C). Proper speech becomes the proper labor for the proper body: eugenics and eulogics coincide through the application of *ponos.* Sections 2C-F expound the importance of *ponos* for repairing the defects of nature and illustrate the point with a series of similes that begins with an almost Lucretian set of hard objects changed by the constant action of nature or man and moves on to agriculture, arboriculture, physical education, equiculture, and the domestication of animals. Education implicitly, then, is a kindred hard, male labor at the top of this series of those processes that bend nature to man's use.[36] In reality, children of school age, perhaps especially boys, most closely resembled slaves. In the name that summoned him, in the labor he was commanded to perform, and in the physical compulsion that harried, threatened, and beat him to perform, the boy was not only treated like a slave but was subject to slave or freedmen pedagogues and teachers. Despite the high valuation and social restriction of education, in learning to wield stylus and tablet, brush and papyrus, the boy was performing manual tasks. He was undergoing a physical regimen, walking to and from school at set times, sitting and standing, reciting, answering, learning gesture, learning when to speak and when to keep silent. The author presents this educational process as a *ponos* not simply analogous to but superior and rival to the servile. The ancient schoolboy internalized these metaphorical fields and relations by such repeated actions as the laborious copying out, time after time, of lines set by the master: *philoponei mē dareis* ("Love *ponos* lest you be beaten").[37] Eulogics are not neutral linguistic skills (e.g., the memorization of historical exempla, the ability to use metaphor, practice in extemporaneous speaking) but the trained disposition to produce and to regard a certain register of speech as a medium of hierarchy. The vision of education as emancipatory, a tendency stemming from the origins of the curriculum and reading list in democratic Athens and from Platonism's grand claims for the powers of philosophy, is severely curtailed by the doctrines of eugenics and eulogics.

"PLUTARCH" 'S EUGENICS

Kalos oun parrēsias thēsauros eugeneia.
Free birth is the honorable treasure chest of free speech.

This aphorism, coming at the outset of the *De liberis educandis* (1.10), assures those fathers desirous of worthy sons that their contribution is all-important.[38] Legitimacy will abide as a social, cultural, and intellectual capital that cannot be alienated.[39] The author does not delineate how one achieves free or independent thinking, nor, like some Stoic or transcendentalist or ascetic, does he advocate that man become self-sufficient so that he may be an independent agent, able like Thoreau from his spare sanctuary of surroundings and self to cry against injustice. Rather, the author has a more mundane and material point of view: the freeborn will not have the inequality of status or resources that requires the subordinate to keep silent. Free birth is a freedom from physical and material constraint, and importantly from doing the bidding of another. Aristotle had expressed this memorably: *eleutherou gar to mē pros allon zēn* (*Rh.* 1367a33: "The free man need not live at another's beck and call"). The *De liberis educandis* applies this thought literally: the freeborn child will not feel the lash and will be able to speak out.

In writing to reassure an elite that it is independent, despite all the slaves and women directing the young heirs, the author delivers a tripartite message that blends social apologetics with educational protreptic. First, education is all-important to train and distinguish the freeborn. Indeed, educability is their natural characteristic. Second, genius is not sufficient for education. Third, free birth is all but a necessity. The author does not argue this in an explicit, sustained fashion. Rather, his values and preferences emerge and are underscored by his preferred rhetorical modes of demonstration. So at 5D a priamel offers the things judged good by men as the unworthy foils for his preferred value, education. The first of the series is *eugeneia,* good birth. Despite the thoroughgoing conventionality of outlook (e.g., the denigration of wealth compared to education), the author will later admit that wealth is necessary (8E), and despite the presence of *eugeneia* as a foil in the priamel, the author's focus returns repeatedly to the status of the bodies of the agents of education. In this passage, however, he asserts at the end of his priamel that the two most important aspects of *phusis* are intellect and reason (5E).[40]

The reader of this text may begin to feel that he swims in a soup of unrealized propositions to be arranged into syllogisms or better rhetorical enthymemes as the topics and arguments demand: The man with *nous* and *logos* is the educated man; only the man with *nous* and *logos* is worthy of education; to have *nous* and *logos* one must have *eugeneia* and wealth. The author attempts to maintain a consistently high-minded protreptic to education, yet bodies and status keep interrupting "argument." Other ancient accounts of education certainly could leave unexpressed the prerequisites of resources and status needed for an education. So Cicero was repeating customary knowledge when he said there were three elements necessary to become an orator: *ars, exercitatio, ingenium,* "learned technique, practice and experience, and talent" (a traditional division; see Cic. *De or.* 113 ff., and cf. the opening of the *Pro Archia*). The author of the *De liberis educandis* recognizes that these are as necessary for moral excellence (*aretē*) as for skilled professions (*technai* and *epistēmai,* 2A).[41] Plato did not interrupt his dialogues on how or what to learn, or how to achieve philosophical *noēsis* with the codicil "This is only for me and you, Glaucon, Euthyphro," although it was no doubt self-evident that one had to be Greek and citizen of a polis. For Plutarch it was not so evident, partly because his contemporary the slave Epictetus was a great philosopher, and Epictetus's teacher had written an essay recommending that women study philosophy.[42] In the imperial Roman world, the ranks of slaves and ex-slaves were the true treasury of literate teachers and experts.

Plutarch's contemporary the great Roman teacher Quintilian had similarly restricted who could be the educated. His repetition of the elder Cato's definition of the orator as the *vir bonus dicendi peritus* (a good man skilled in speaking) asserts that expertise in language will not suffice for his educational ideal. *Bonus* (good) is as much a social as a moral term.[43] The first sociopolitical use of the term *bonus* comes in the earliest extant prose treatise, the elder Cato's *De agri cultura*. While there is nothing surprising in the conflation of moral and political terms (or the mystification of social divisions as moral differences), this first usage has a surprisingly strong literary afterlife. In the preface to his work, Cato wrote that, of old, when men wanted to praise another, they called him a good farmer (*bonus colonus*). Cicero describes his idealized readership as the *boni omnes.* Quintilian follows both Cato and Cicero in insisting that only the good can be the educated. For the author of the *De liberis educandis,* the ideological impasse that culture, a form of nurture, is all-important and that only the free man can be a philosopher requires a redefinition of the nature of (the free) man. It would seem that education cannot make every man free or good (socially worthy).

Whereas Quintilian relied on definition so as to restrict the set of the educated, in the *De liberis educandis* the tension between education's emancipatory, universal tendency and a restricted claim for its true practitioners surfaces in a number of metaphors, aphorisms, and anecdotes. The author must redefine *phusis,* the concept of the natural, so as to accommodate this contradiction between education as a natural right and education as a restricted social practice.[44] The text's exclusive interest in the freeborn boy and his father suggests that only one growth and one *phusis* are worthy of record. Indeed, growth seems to define male difference and superiority. The free boy grows away from woman and slave as the text details how fathers may reproduce the free. There is much association and little argument in this prejudice, but such association—the equation of natural growth with the developing ability of the boy in intensively trained literate skills (most often represented as skills of speech)—is crucial for the success of this educational rationalization.

The text begins with child production (*agōgē* and *genesis* at 1, *paidopoiia* at 1B). The author insists on a natural division: those born of a free father and an unfree mother (he uses the expression "chance women," which he glosses as "prostitutes and courtesans") are tainted. He makes this point again and again, with all the tools of his rhetoric (e.g., quotation of poetry, the sententia already noted of the treasure of free speaking found in good birth, and metaphor). It is natural, he says, that those who are counterfeit sully their thoughts. The surreptitious insertion of base metal is not a metaphor he continues, although he refers to the unexpungible stain of illegitimate birth (he means always a free father and an unfree or libertine mother).[45]

While impurity draws from him various metaphors of contagion (the son feels shame when he realizes the *kaka* [evil deeds, but also the crap in his lineage] of his parents), purity is presented in a sustained and recurring metaphor of agriculture.[46] Pure sower produces pure offshoot. The agricultural metaphor elides the mother's role.[47] The author will develop the simile: father is to son as farmer is to plant, but the agricultural metaphor first comes in his discussion of the role of nature, technique, and practice (2B). After the sweeping generalization that *aretē* like any art or science requires three things, he "proves" this with his statement that each of the three is necessary but not sufficient. The synthetic comparison of plant and child production then constitutes the second argument. Farming depends on good soil, an expert farmer, and potent seed (*spermata spoudaia*, 2.8), and child production likewise on nature, the teacher, and verbal injunctions.[48] *Phusis,* the teacher, and *logos* seem collectively to have displaced the base simile of sowing father and mother earth. The author then continues to discuss how the defects of nature can be remedied by instruction—he is back in his proper subject, having attempted a redefinition of nature. Both Plato's concerns about whether moral excellence can be taught and the social reality of the role of the mother are ignored when *aretē* is but a matter of teacherly, paternal farming of the boy.

In fact, the author continues here to develop the idea of *ponos*, of the proper work that improves or repairs nature.[49] This brings him easily again to agriculture at 2E (and compare 4C, where the good teacher is like the good farmer who stakes his tender plants). No doubt the economy of metaphors, the restricted, systematic quality of his symbolic field, contributes to the rhetorical unity of his piece. At the same time these early sections treat the early life of the child, as is clear from 2C when he takes up breast-feeding. But the care of the very young has become a sustained embellishment of the commonplace of the need for talent, training, and practice. His vignettes of the theme *labor omnia vincit* show sturdy growth as the sure result of the farmer's or the horseman's toil. So in his conceit of land requiring man's labor, trees will prove fruitful if they receive the right *paidagōgia*.[50] His crowning example is the story of the Spartan lawgiver Lycurgus, that all-but-mythic figure of paternal order. Lycurgus gave a different *agōgē*, upbringing and training (the key term of the Greek title of the *De liberis educandis*), to two puppies from the same litter. One he made wild (a scavenger for food), one obedient. These he exhibited as a visual parable for the Spartans, who did not get the point; the law writer then gave the proper interpretation. The author concludes with this powerful image, but what has been illustrated? The importance of toil and training and the relative non-importance of *phusis*, a category that has lumped together parentage, birth, and talent? Unlike Rousseau, Plutarchan nature is not a state of savagery. The dog is made fierce and self-reliant, made into a good Lacedaemonian, like the Spartan boys who had to steal their supper.[51] Beyond stipulating the status of the mother, the author has little interest in birth; growth is his main concern.

Growth will emerge as the arena of men (the farmer who stakes the tender plants has displaced the good soil as generative force). Indeed, as the narrative traces the development of the boy, the reader witnesses him growing away from his mother. Ancient fathers are often imagined as cultivating, seeding, plowing, their wives. Theocritus, in singing the praises of Helen's marriage, asserts that she will leave behind her childhood play for the work and deeds of a wife: she has hitherto been a field without grain, a garden without trees, a horse without a rider.[52] The father who follows the *De liberis educandis* seems to have transferred this cultivating activity from wife to son. Indeed, this account of the process of maturation suppresses the role of agents other than the father. An education of men and for men sounds more like social fiction than social history. Yet the mother does have a role to play in the text's directives. She is distinguished from improper women, and her duties are recovered from the slave wet nurse. The father-reader is warned away from intercourse with chance women: "First I advise fathers intent on producing respectable children not to cohabit with chance women" (1B: *prōton tois toinun epithumousin endoxōn teknōn genesthai patrasin upotheimēn an egōge mē tais tukhousais gunaixi sunoikein*), as later he is told, if a wet nurse must be employed, do not use "chance" women (3D: *tas ge titthas kai trophous ou tas tukhousas*).

The advocacy of marital fidelity is centered on the ensuing child: the legitimate son will have no stain, no shame, no verbal abuse. If courtesans are women of chance (*tukhē*), and the father is a figure of technology (*tekhnē*), how does the author represent this proper mother? She interests him as a feeder; the mother's role is essentially milk provider. This has two consequences: she replaces a slave in this function, and she thereby performs her natural role, as indicated by her bodily difference. Again, nature is invoked to argue for a social practice. 3C declares that nature instructs us (*dēloi de kai ē phusis*) that mothers should nurse their young. Nature has written evidence on women's bodies: they have milk, and two breasts in case there are twins.[53]

This argument from the female body illumines the author's gendered, class-sensitive typology of bodies. In advising the father on the production of a male body without blemish, the author sets the father the task of reading the bodies around him. At the same time, growth caused by the father is distinguished from the feeding of the mother, if one will attend to diction (*trophē* at 3C versus the *agōgē* that is his subject). Improper women are marked by chance (so again nurses are not to be selected from this random set, 3D) and by pay (*misthos,* 3C). Maternal love is superior to the purchased affection of the nurse, but the illustration has also distinguished feminine love from a father's training. It is perfectly reasonable that mothers who nurse will love their children more, for even animals separated from their "fellow feeders" feel some pang: "For fellow feeding is as it were the tuning key of friendly feeling. For even beasts appear to long for those of their trough mates who are dragged from them" (*ē suntrophia gar ōsper epitonion esti tēs eunoias kai gar ta thēria tōn suntrephomenōn apospōmena tauta pothounta phainetai.* 3D). This commonplace, dignified as it is because of its literary pedigree—it is drawn from Xenophon's treatise on education (*Cyr.* 2.1.28)—responds to the puppies raised by Lycurgus. The untrained, homebound cur eats from a dish; the other, disdaining the food set out for him and showing his master's training, chases a rabbit. Father trains the child to leave home and chase his dinner. Mother has an indefinite longing for her trough-mate.

In themselves, these notices are instances of male talk about women and women's place. In his manual of education, with its thematically restricted, often metaphorical thinking about nature, such reflections on naturalness and the body's functions and roles communicated a quasi-systematic view of the social order as a natural order. The impression of systematicity arises from a general ideological tendency to represent divisions of labor as natural and from the rhetorical mode of presentation and of hermeneusis that presents a unified reading of slave, woman, child, and father. The author relies heavily on metaphor, *chreia,* exemplum, and commonplace to argue his case. In male metaphors, the child is imagined as a crop, the fruit of powerful seed, watered, with soil well broken and plowed by the farmer father. Or he is the well-brought-up, aggressive hound, on show for a larger body of male spectators. In female symbols, he is the babe at the breast compared to less useful animals, not the master's dear hound, his servant in that essentially nonessential, leisured, and high-status activity, hunting, but the more productive and hence menial cattle and sheep (though *theria* includes wild animals as well). Such traditionalist thinking presents the bond of status, friendship, and well-directed appetite as the higher calling. These reflections further distinguish the boy's body and his proper training; indeed, the two come to be understood as naturally associated.

The lack of notice or theoretical analysis given to early periods of childhood and to the processes of acquiring language and subjectivity are, then, not simply an omission in the development of the science of human psychology. Nor should we believe, as have some historians of medieval and early modern Europe, that lack of theoretical discussion of childhood and adolescence implies that there was no concept of childhood.[54] Just as the agents of child rearing are all but passed over in silence, the educational treatise stigmatizes the early stages as preliminary or puerile. The fact that others had control, influence, and time for the child is denigrated through theorization as early and insignificant stages of development, worthy of comment only insofar as the author feels he must advise the master in the proper administration of subordinates. Writing in this disciplinary mode recreates an idealized hierarchy of the house where no individual or class or woman is granted large or ongoing authority, and the father's control is exhibited in the virtues of delegation, choice, and taste. And the father can monitor the fine production of his child, the author assures, by checking the boy's language.[55]

"PLUTARCH"'S EULOGICS

Correctness of language becomes here more than an aesthetic principle or social protocol. In the abstract, a traditional educational treatise provides the rules for correct reading, writing, and speaking, samples of that correct style, and an account of how to achieve that stylistic excellence. The *De liberis educandis* is especially concerned with the verification of speech. Of course, in its own Greek and in its use of classical sources, the essay demonstrates the approved style, but the verification of speech is a prominent theme that allies the narrator and the reader, the persona of Plutarch or the master teacher and the good father. The treatise is in part an index by which the father can be assured that his son is learning properly. This technique of reassurance depends on several factors. Positively, by speaking well, the boy gives living proof that he is his father's son. The teacher's role is almost elided here, as if education were simply developing or making manifest that natural relation of father and son. Negatively, the treatise relies on scare tactics. As part of its protreptic to education (and its special protreptic to fathers, to send their sons to Greek literary schooling), the text consistently parades the perils of bad teaching and bad teachers.

In this negative, apotreptic mode, the treatise allies faults of speech with slaves and women. The author had worried that a father's union with chance women would produce the stain that cannot be removed. The directions for the selection of a wet nurse repeat this characterization of women. The author allows the use of this sort of slave only if the mother's body is weak or pregnant (3D). He here describes a second best, but the recommendations of the ersatz mother reveal his criteria of feminine worth. She must produce milk and Greek.[56] In striving to create a definite subjectivity in the boy and the father, the treatise deploys received categories of gender and class so as to specify how the male is not servile and not feminine. At his most positive, the author promises to produce speaking bodies that are healthier, more powerful, and more confident than the uneducated. The circularity of the argument is clear: the free body is the vessel of free speech; free speech marks the worthy body and person.

The association of proper speech with a healthy body is the author's, who gives the justification again not by argument but by illustrative comparison with the body. Just as physical deformity is to be avoided, so is deformity of speech (3E). The author's worry about the visible physical contamination of the body by speech is evident in his directives for the selection of proper age mates for the freeborn boy. A sociolinguistic distinction maintains their difference from the child: they are *ta paidia* (5F), the legitimate children *hoi trophimoi* (in Latin, *pueri* as distinguished from *liberi*). Speech and character are seen as one, as in the rhetorical commonplace: *talis hominibus fuit oratio qualis vita* ("Men's speech is a mirror of their character," Sen. *Ep.* 114.1; although one is tempted to translate: "The tongue makes the man"). The author insists on this linguistic characteristic. He does not say the slave boys must be moral, loyal, or kind; he offers a rather general qualification: these slaves must be earnest in their manners. This vague moralization he then concretely defines: "Most importantly they are to be earnest in their character, speaking good Greek in clear fashion, lest, colored with barbarism or vulgarity, they import some of their baseness" (*prōtista men spoudaia tous tropous, eti mentoi hellēnika kai peritrana lalein, hina mē sunanakhrōnnumenoi barbarois kai to ēthos mokhthērois apopherōntai ti tēs ekeinōn phaulotētos*).[57] Their speech is to be Greek and very distinct; otherwise they will contribute a degree of servility to the boy. He will become barbarian, base (*moxthēros*), and cheap (*phaulos*)—all of which characterize the slave.

The use of quasi-medical diction strengthens the corporal quality of the author's argument: contagion or contamination is inherent in the verb *sunanakhrōnnumi*. Again, the author mixes positive and negative arguments: his positive health program comes to sound like those diets that detail all the things that one cannot eat. Fear for the body seems always close-by. A proverb provides the seal on his corporal contagious thinking: "If you dwell with a lame man, you will learn to limp" (*an khōlōi paroikēsēis, huposkazein mathēsēi*).[58] The maimed man verges on the female. The Greek word for "lame" is *khōlos*. Perhaps the Greek reader heard another censorious gnome as a latent echo. A Hellenistic epigram has as much time for wives as the author does: "Every woman is bile (*kholos*): she has two good moments / One on the marriage bed, one at the deathbed" (*Anth. Pal.* 11.381). "To dwell with the lame" is a deformed echo of marrying bile, *sunoiken* responds to *paroiken*, *khōlos* to *kholos*. The good father will, unlike the bad woman, stick to his own house, in this respect. The wish to keep the son distinct and free from any visible mark of inferior status is theorized as a physical protection. The bodies about him, even though slaves, must be unslavish, and the only way to achieve this exemption from servility is to have the slaves speak like free men.

The contradiction lurking in the social protocol that the ideal householder's slaves sound like free men (and perhaps thus deserve to be free men) does not elicit a direct response. Rather, the author develops a far from seamless thinking that attempts to stratify implicated layers—linguistic, corporal, and social. The slave body approaches the free inasmuch as it partakes of clean Greek. The free body teeters on the brink of servility every time its tongue makes a mistake (or its body is subjected to physical punishment). Free and slave seem to have as a common ground the tongue, as if this were the one true constituent of what it is to be human. The organ customarily understood as common to men has remarkably been displaced; the author addresses the control of the tongue directly at 10F.

In addition to being a rationalization, indeed mystification, of a difference grounded in social practice, the belief that language reflects and creates character is a reflex of rhetorical thinking. The treatise aims to create personae fit for the young man, and as in any prosopopoeia or ethopoeia (a passage that introduces a character as if he were present to address the audience), speech must fit character. Indeed, speech becomes a corporal attribute: like gesture or dress, it is an adornment to the body of the freeborn. Again the author thinks rhetorically: speech is a physical characteristic not because of any materialist theory of sound production but because of the physical process of language acquisition at school and because speech marks the body as free. One consequence of the training in linguistic skills, aside from the disciplining of the boy's own body through handwriting, reading, reciting, writing, and voice exercises, and beating, was the final division of speakers into those who had received schooling and now as free citizens had unmarkable bodies and those whose bodies continued to be subject to physical chastisement (just as their names continued to be boys, ta paidia, whatever their age).

Indirectly, the treatise strives to dampen the (patriarchal) anxiety about what happens inside the house, where women and slaves come and go and where the father cannot see everything. The author had warned the father not to "dwell together" (sunoikein, "to marry") with a prostitute or concubine; it is significant that the author does not want the stain of such a union to be in the house (oikos).[59] Likewise his proverb about the lame man warns that if you dwell with a cripple you will learn to limp (the verb "dwell," paroikeo, is a compound from the same stem as sunoikein). Similarly, pedagogues must not be prisoners of war, barbarians, or palimboloi (4A—this word means something like "throwbacks"; LSJ says, citing Menander 445, that palimbolos is a synonym for palimpratos, "sold again," that is, a good-for-nothing slave who passes from hand to hand—the lack of fidelity, the ease of passage, even the backwardness of the palim- prefix, have sexual connotations unremarked by the lexicographers). The positive message is not given, but it is clear: use homegrown slaves (in Latin, vernae). "Plutarch" laments the division of slave labor in some households. There are masters who use their diligent and worthy slaves (4B: *spoudaiōn*) as farm stewards, ship captains, factory managers, and bankers and save the most servile (he says drunkards, gluttons, and the untrained) for the management of their sons. Socrates in Xenophon's *Memorabilia* 1.5 had asked rhetorically what father would entrust his children to a man who was *akratēs,* not in control of himself. In "Plutarch"'s thinking, however, the unphilosophical man is not the source of worry. He has been replaced with the socially inferior, the vile slave or men who resemble slaves. In outline the text has been following the life of the child, and now with the selection of pedagogues, the sons are ready to leave the house. So the topic turns to the selection of teachers (4C).

The treatment of these more advanced agents of education differs significantly, primarily because these men were not slaves. Here the author does use moral language to describe the proper teachers, and, for the first time, he is concerned not with fathers' worries about education but about the role of fathers in the education of their sons. We now enter the world of professional teachers, whose number included Plutarch and perhaps the author of the *De liberis educandis.* The author worries that fathers, on the verge of this most important of decisions, will fall prey to cheapness or to flattery and the requests of friends. He had just introduced yet another agricultural metaphor: children like tender plants need stakes to support them. The expected items in this analogy, given that the analogy is illustrating the need for blameless teachers, are teacher is to student as stake is to young shoot. The author swerves from this to have the teachers as the farmers, and the stakes their words. So children need the precepts and instruction of teachers to grow straight. The slippage, which helps to downplay the influence of the teachers themselves, reintroduces the linguistic into the formative, creative process of education. The father's farmer role is taken over by the teacher's words. "Plutarch" is in fact weaning the son from the father, but he does so delicately and indirectly. The poor (nonapproved) father is like a weak growth, swerving to flattery and suggestion. Similes liken these fathers to someone who prefers his shoe to his foot (4E) or who entrusts himself to a bad skipper or an incompetent doctor (4D). These are all mistakes of choice and delegation, and importantly they are imagined by metaphorical association as imperiling the body or body part of the father.

The child does not risk destruction, however; he risks being turned into a slave. The author employs anecdote, a *chreia,* to make his point: Aristippus once told a cheapskate father that he would charge a thousand drachmas to teach his son. The father said he could buy a slave for that, and Aristippus's somewhat predictable punch line was "Then you will have two slaves, your son and your purchase" (5A). The boy become a slave is a recurrent bogeyman in the text's tactics to have dad ante up for education. At 5A the reader is warned of the result of poor education: youth is addicted to slavish pleasures (*tas ataktous kai andrapodōdeis hēdonas*). The author holds out two courses of life to his students: either become a practical father or study with Plutarch; the third sort of life after the practical and the con-templative is dissolute and a slave to pleasures (8A).

The author invests all those who interfere with education with the status of slaves. His habitual slander develops into a generalized rhetorical social census where everyone has his place and his speech. Any departure from this scheme is a form of slavery. Thus he denigrates flatterers, who would convince a father to send his son to a cheap teacher. They upset his tidy arrangement where only the morally and socially good speak well. So he terms their free birth accidental: "free-born by freak of fortune, but slaves by choice" (13C: *tēi tukhēi men eleutheroi, tēi proairesei de douloi,* Babbitt's translation). The oxymorons are strong, especially since the son of chance is a bastard.[60] The author is making a rhetorical gnome out of the com-monplace opposition of chance against choice, slavery and misfortune against free-dom and happiness. He twists a Stoic sentiment for his own polemical point.[61]

During a son's adolescence, a new corrupter may threaten fathers. This target is quite similar to the flatterer; the text describes them as *ponēroi*—in slightly old-fash-ioned English one might call them the vile or base, which collapses the economic and the moral fields exactly as does the Greek.[62] Again the author fears contagion, and to ward off this threat he summons a most schoolmasterly weapon, a list of aphorisms with exegesis. These form almost an incantation of moralizing practi-cality, especially the one that directly takes up the theme (and vocabulary) of the vile, 12F: "'Do not put food into a chamber-pot'; this means that it is not fitting to put urbane speech into a vile soul. For speech is the food of thought, and vileness in men makes it unclean" (Babbitt's translation, slightly adapted). The good father is further directed to steer a middle road: do not be harsh but mix honey with the wormwood (13D).

This advice-mongering may seem soupy scare tactics that mix proverb, school forms, and tags from the poets, Xenophon, and Plato. Repeatedly, this familiar fare presents education as a species of delegated labor wherein the father protects that important symbol, the body, and hence the status of his son. Fathers who fail to heed the various directives not to put something where it does not belong risk mar-ring that body or even enslaving their own. In the course of his admonitions, the author can deliver a tired bit of misogyny: the maxim "'Keep to your own place' is wise, since those who take to wife women far above themselves unwittingly become not the husbands of their wives, but the slaves of their wives' dowries." This expla-nation, however, reinforces the place of the free father: heeding the text, he will not be subject to slave, flatterer, rich wife, in sum the figures of appetite, of reason mis-led, of bodies that perhaps counterfeit the male. The enemy of education is conve-niently social and moral; he or she is reducible to memorable types, rhetorically arranged. Aphorism, *chreia,* metaphor, and notions of rhetorical decorum (the fit-ting, especially) create an orderly social and intellectual continuum.

The strongest evidence of the complex relation of rhetorical argument to concerns with the body comes in the treatise's most dramatic protection of the boy: the earnest disapproval of corporal punishment. The author's position, shared by Plutarch's contemporary Quintilian, has been celebrated as a fundamental statement of humanism.[63] In fact, it is but one part of his effort to prevent the deformation of the boy into a slave. The author disapproves primarily because the boy will look and feel like a slave. And the boy will be confused about his own identity. Blows and torture (*plēgais mēd' aikismois*) are not to be used—the Greek words suit slave punishment and slave interrogation. The author then offers a rhetorical argument, one that depends on the notion of the fitting (*to prepon*): *Kakeino phēmi, dein tous paidas epi ta kala tōn epitēdeumatōn agein parainesesi kai logois, mē ma dia plēgais mēd' aikismois. dokei gar pou tauta tois doulois mallon ē tois eleutherois prepein; aponarkōsi gar kai phrittousi pros tous ponous* (8F: "And I believe that children should be encouraged to noble pursuits not, by god, by blows and torture but by praise and words, for somehow it seems [right] that the former suit slaves more than the freeborn"). Much lurks beneath the *pou* (somehow), but we get no explanation. Instead, a rhetorical division again helps to ally the free and words, on the one hand, and slaves and the maimed body, on the other. The author writes that praise and reproof are more helpful for the freeborn (better than torture, *aikias*, he says). He describes the effect of corporal punishment upon the lads in medical terms: "They grow sluggish and bristle at the prospect of work" (*aponarkōsi gar kai phrittousi pros tous ponous*). Words preserve the health, the *phusis*, of the free; for the unfree body blows are the meet style.

On the verge of the topic of adolescence, the author has one more worry about the young man's body. For the sexually precocious, early marriage is the answer (13F). More discomfiting for the author is homosexual activity. He is most unsure if he should talk of it (11D: *polus d' oknos ekhei me*; cf. 11E: *eulaboumai tautēs eisēgētēs genesthai kai sumboulos*); and in this general section, where he has urged the father again and again to keep his son from low speech and low men, where he has urged passions be checked and warned of the perils of overindulgence and excessive severity from the father, he has a most revealing answer to the query that troubles him so. He resorts to textual authority. "Socrates, Plato, Xenophon, Aeschines, Cebes, and that whole chorus" (11E) say yes, so the author will hardly say no.[64] The status of the authors and perhaps of the male bodies of the lovers suggests for the author that homosexual practices may not enslave or degrade. The subject makes him uneasy. He quickly passes to a brief treatment of the vices of adolescents before taking refuge in the scholarly tour de force, the exegesis of proverbs (attributed to Pythagoras), which nicely combines his idea of conventional morality with schoolmasterly authority.

The author's turn to anecdote allows him to emphasize again the authorizing precedents of Greek writers and philosophers in a memorable form that often involves bodily purity or integrity. The sage in action in these sayings tales is active

and exemplary as a speaking subject. Amid these education heroes, introduced as
the seal on the comparatively brief treatment of what the adolescent will study,
Socrates enjoys pride of place. At 8F the author had inveighed against corporal punishment; he follows this instance of educational excess with an account of fathers
who make excessive demands on their sons. The soul requires the alternation of toil
and rest as the body is made healthy by satiety following upon appetite (9C:
katholou de sōizetai sōma men endeiai kai plērōsei, psukhē d' anesei kai ponōi). The
author does not tarry much over the studies in which the souls should toil (other
than the perfunctory notice to train the memory first, the author does not discuss
how or what to teach). Rather, he is hurrying toward the apex of the boys' education,
philosophy. In the course of his all too general recommendations on what to do—
do not overtax the boy, do train his memory, do not let him curse—he at last gives
examples of educated virtues.

Socrates and Plato are summoned, among others, as positive exemplars of
speech. They testify not to mental virtues and the avoidance of errors but to virtues
of speech. In particular, the philosophers return physical harm with verbal riposte.
The author rather grandly announces he is laying down what the young must say
and do (10B); in fact, he has put here, in place of any definite curriculum, negative
injunctions about how to speak. He does not pursue his advice that the memory
must be trained. Instead we read that children should not swear and should be circumspect in their speech (10A: tactful and polite). Virtues of speech are now presented as analogous or even identical to bodily virtues. He lists four virtues, with
each abstract virtue followed by a bodily virtue. The proper deeds and words of the
young consist in this: live an unpretentious life, restrain your tongue, get in charge
of your anger, control your hands. The Greek idioms all are tinged with a physical-
ity: the unpretentious life is the uninflated life, that of one who does not puff himself up. What I have translated "get in charge of anger" means to get the upper hand
of, that is, to best physically.[65]

Compared to the volumes written on the passions, the nature of human error,
and the weakness of will, these notices are trivialities, and so Plutarch holds the reputation of a humdrum repeater of Platonic generalities. But the author is in fact a
rhetorical thinker, one for whom the method and divisions of rhetoric are far more
important, even though he follows the centuries-old tradition of disparaging rhetoric and urging his young readers on to philosophy.[66] It may seem that he has given
short shrift to the rhetorical curriculum by invoking the philosophers. In fact, he
has subverted the Platonic conception of philosophy to suit his rhetorical program.
He seems to have in mind the four virtues of Plato's *Republic:* justice, prudence,
courage, and moderation (which occupy respectively the whole soul, reason, *thu-
mos,* and desire). To illustrate his fourfold virtues the author cites that staple of
rhetorical argument, historical examples. Collectively, these demonstrate the sort
of restraint toward which the boy is being trained. The illustrations of restraint re-

inforce this corporal conception of linguistic virtue. Socrates, when kicked by an impudent young man, declined to reciprocate in kind. Justice was done when everyone called the fellow "Kicker" from then on. So a verbal riposte responds to physical injury. The author catalogs proper responses to physical and verbal injury (the next example has Socrates receiving Aristophanes' stage abuse in good humor). Two examples follow (10D) of Archytas and Plato each not beating an impudent slave. Injury to the master results in verbal chastisement for the offender. The examples for holding one's tongue are of verbal attacks upon tyrants (Ptolemy Philadelphus, Alexander, Antigonus). The tyrant is not a philosopher, and so the truth-telling free-speaking actor comes to a bad end. So despite the customary, easy distinction of the speech of slave and freeborn (at 11C the aphorism that truth speaking is for children; lying for slaves, *douloprepes*), adult speech seems to have other considerations.[67] Questions of power and status are not so easily evaded.

In the earlier sections of his work and of the boy's life, the author was concerned that physical impurity and deformity be kept from the house. The son's body thus attracted worries about the activities of the mother and slaves within the house. A schema of different bodies with different roles contributes to the representation of a contrast between *paideia* and deformity. *Paideia*, education, is a formative process that must be shown to be opposite to the deformity of slavery. The Greek lexicon easily admits such confusion: *paideia* must be made distinct from *paidia*—the household slaves who were the boy's playmates, and also the slaves who were involved in education. In addition, *paidia* can refer simply to children, although usually preschool-age children.[68] The crucial difference between these two groups in the ideological description of the treatise is articulated in a theory of *ponos*, what is work for the slave is unfit for the master, just as the mental work of the master does not suit the slave; it is food in a shit pot. The educational treatise has rationalized socially differentiated practices of punishment, education, and labor through a rhetorical scheme of different bodies and their appropriate characteristics. The greatest challenge to this rhetorical division comes from education itself, and the expert slave. The author manages to resist treating the mind as an overarching category, one not susceptible to divisions of status, by tying certain speech, and thus thinking, to certain bodies. Further, he theorizes a distinction in the activities of these two classes of bodies. Again he relies on a common substratum of diction with an important division. Both slave and free engage in labor (*ponos*), but the slave's labor is menial and manual; the free's is higher and mental. This heavy-handed distinction attempts to represent the division of labor between owned and owner as orderly, bodily, and natural. As mind governs body and as metaphor governs thought or argument by making a hierarchy out of similitude, the free is always the dominant, organizing item. An association of the governors with the mind and the governed with the body is a frequent feature of a ruling class's parables, speeches, religion, and literature. The author strengthens the commonplace by means of the strong symbol of the (free) child. The boy grows away from manual labor and becomes a figure of intellectual labor.

Studying hard, expressed in the oxymoronic love toil, is the alternative to being treated as a slave. The author, like other teachers, worked hard himself to instill in his pupil the sense that their common activity was a mental labor, the superior correspondent to productive work. The moralizing injunction to work hard tells even the lazy scholar that he is at work. To the daydreaming boy, the alternative may seem to be play, but the ideological other half is work that actually is of some more immediate or more material use. Whether or not the boy learns his lesson well, continues on to study philosophy or to become a successful pleader in the courts, he will have learned to view certain literate activities as distinct spheres, if not quite the life of the mind, at least the work of the freeborn. *Paideia,* liberal education, will come to be rationalized as what is worthy of a free man, but as a process of social distinction and identity, ancient education was what distinguished one group of youth from another. This would become a visible and audible distinction, but it had to be learned. The transmission of such a right would be vigorously restricted, and this restriction vigorously rationalized, theorized, and championed.

5

The Child an Open Book

The *De liberis educandis* communicates a confident educationalism. Through well-managed mental labor the child amasses a reserve of linguistic and cultural capital that demonstrates his legitimacy. Successful learning furnishes the requisite proof that his body has been kept from contagion and that his speech and ongoing self-culture will remain worthy of a free man. Quintilian shows remarkable similarities in his discussion of the proper education of the male heir, perhaps understandably since Plutarch and Quintilian taught at Rome at the same time. Quintilian was so popular that students pirated some of his work.[1] In fact, the *De liberis educandis* and the *Institutio oratoria* provide unique insight into elite schooling at Rome at the turn of the first to second century A.D. In addition, the two treatises have an unrivaled importance for the legacy of educational thinking.[2] New movements in pedagogy, in philology, and in art and literary criticism have charted their beginnings from these works.[3] Whether as protreptics to an encyclopedic culture, or as digests of rhetoric, these texts have held their appeal, perhaps most fundamentally because (without gainsaying the special clarity of Quintilian's language and range of his information) they make the attractive claim that the present text can direct the fashioning of a new man. All seems possible, even the reader's return to proper culture (no matter what the divide of years or languages), if one will but follow the schoolboy's course.

Quintilian is much richer than the author of the *De liberis educandis* in details of instruction. Chapters 6, 7, and 8 below consider the chief, separate stages of the recommended training in grammar and rhetoric. Now we must start again where all histories of Roman education have begun, with the grandest theoretical account of schooling in the Western tradition. It is difficult not to be swept away, for Quintilian writes with an elegance and precision that, though not attaining the grand heights of Cicero's dialogues, are supported by a balanced judgment that judiciously weighs and sifts books, theories, and experts. Occasionally, like some motes of fine ore amid this heavy mining work, there gleam the jewels from the experience of a dedicated teacher. We are all students and teachers, and these asides draw us in as certainly as any novelistic experience of identifying with a character.

In the *Institutio oratoria* Quintilian has synthesized one of the most important technological systems invented by the ancients: rhetoric. He treats it not with the exotic vocabulary of a theorist but with the practical aims of a teacher of children. My modest enthusing is nothing compared to the salvos of celebration launched when Poggio "discovered" Quintilian's text in 1416.[4] The lost key to humanism, heralded as the code for reading, speaking, and writing, the full text of the *Institutio oratoria* received all the hyperbole the humanists could muster in their melodramatic sense of the ancient text's importance and their own importance for society.[5] Visit the cloister below the library of the Medicis, and amid the groups hushed and waiting patiently in a line stretching out from Michelangelo's stairs, you will hear the same story being told, with proper rhetorical climax, to Italian schoolchildren. Poggio is the agent of culture, of Latin, symbol of discovery and communication, collector and celebrant for the Medicis and the new age. Probably the text of Quintilian was not so important. Poggio trumpeted his sudden discovery of a text already known. But if we must deflate the claims of the efficacy of this text or the high symbolism of this moment, undoubtedly Quintilian became a major weapon in the reorganization of the university's curriculum and of the self-fashioning of the humanists.[6] Perhaps we need to take a harder look at Quintilian's appeal.

In writing an ideal script for the education of a boy, Quintilian has transmitted a synthesis and classical statement of Roman education.[7] The several dedications announce the work as a guide for the education of Quintilian's son and for the son of his dedicatee. It is also a showpiece on the education of the grandsons of the emperor Domitian's sister, whose supervision brought Quintilian out of retirement and interrupted the writing of his great work. This new charge and the death of his own sons may have moved the author to a broader conception of his audience and his purposes in writing. Yet like Cato's or Cicero's before him, Quintilian's inscription to his sons presents the author as an authoritative *pater familias* and would have been recognized as introducing an exemplary, not a private or familial, text.[8]

Quintilian shares with Plutarch the confidence that his text points the way to an education that is more than technical. He writes for the freeborn, whom his sons and the princes represent in ideal form. The very writing exhibits his own excellence—stylistic, pedagogic, and moral—and promises to produce the same results with the Roman boy. In the milieu of Plutarch's school, *paideia* was recognized as the essential difference between the free and the slave. Although not at odds in points of detail (Quintilian too opposes corporal punishment for its deformative effect), Quintilian does not see the agents of education as the pernicious threat that, as we have seen, the author of the *De liberis educandis* made them out to be; nor does Quintilian depend upon any thematics of the free body to unify his work and impel his father-readers toward expensive out-of-home schooling. For Quintilian, education did not need such sustained apologetics. He does not summon the threat of malformation to strike home every recommendation. One is tempted to conclude that this model text from the capital city of the ancient world did not stoop to consider the margins—the education of slaves or lower-class freeborn, of provincials—or contemplate the prospect of middling teachers. Quintilian has the scholar's arrogance: the present subject is best, perhaps only, presented in my book. Education is wholly contained here; it is not preliminary to philosophy or later life; it alone is responsible for the most important transformation, that of boy into man, in fact, the ideal man, the orator. The author of the *De liberis educandis* admitted there were three kinds of life (for the freeborn): the practical, the contemplative, and the pleasure-seeking (8A). Quintilian's focus does not admit any variety: all should want to go to school to learn to be an orator. Of course, not every upper-class Roman, even among the most prominent families of the capital, was going to be an orator. Yet the ideal never wavers, at least in Quintilian's pages. The straightforwardness of his assumption and the impression that we have in his text a distillation of his years of teaching have contributed to an understanding that the *Institutio oratoria* is the best evidence historians have for Roman educational practice in the first and second centuries A.D. In fact, Quintilian represents a new moment or new focus in the history of education.

THE CHILD AS A LEARNING AGENT

Quintilian gives far more attention than his predecessors to the child as a learning agent.[9] The presence, dispositions, and curricular progress of the child distinguish Quintilian's work. He describes the training of the child in meticulous detail, all the while deeming the process of education essentially an encounter with texts. It is inaccurate to reduce Quintilian's conception of education to those points of familiarity and similarity to later educations or even our own education. Certainly, in Quintilian's program the child develops increasingly sophisticated interpretive and expressive abilities, but Quintilian seems to understand what one might term the child's growing capacities or even the evolution of his subjectivity as a kind of textualization. The child's development becomes assimilated to the texts he reads, recites, annotates, and composes. Classroom procedures are described not from any abstract motive of complete reporting of the institution or as an aid to the uninformed teacher or parent. They merit reporting to the reader insofar as they directly contribute to an exercise, a specific act of reading, writing, or reciting, or more narrowly in the cases where they might impede the continuous growth of the child's abilities.

In addition to placing a new emphasis on the child's progress in and through texts, Quintilian makes new claims for education. He vigorously redescribes the topic of education with a bold synthetic approach that assimilates Roman theory (especially Cicero) and Roman practice (his own schoolroom and especially the relatively recent and intense training in analysis and performance known as declamation) to the authoritative accounts of Greek theory. This eclectic synthesis lies somewhere between a virtuoso salvage act and a recombinative or even cannibalistic apologetics. As his education will make the boy whole, his book seeks synthesis and the elimination of controversy or contradiction. Quintilian's great success is, then, that he presents grammatical and rhetorical curriculum as a moral routine, not the morally indifferent sequencing of skill-building tasks but the deliberate acquisition of the necessary expressive and interpretive faculties that underlie the well-ordered, capable self.[10]

The integration of routine, moralization, and textualization represents Quintilian's greatest achievement. Education comes to be understood as something different from and better than Plutarch's (and others') superior labor, which was to be pursued and savored as a superior category, as an essentializing distinction of the free. Child training in advanced linguistic skills has become the ethically constitutive process of being fully human. Plutarch is one witness to the traditional thinking that insisted that education makes the young good and useful. Quintilian differs significantly by not postponing (or deferring) to philosophy the creation of an ethical disposition. As a champion of the power of the processes of schooling, Quintilian insists, against both a satirical, polemical tradition and actual experience, that this process is essentially moral.

Quintilian rightly grasps that textualization seeks to instill definite attitudes. Of course, descriptions of process make many assumptions about order, logic, effective and ineffective impulses to change, and the very nature of change. An idea of what and who a child is lies at the heart of any purportedly objective description of education. Quintilian has specific ideas that underlie his descriptions of process, especially about how the child learns. He worries about the efficiency of education, considers the effect of different practices upon the student, and justifies his curriculum on this basis. Throughout his discussion of the curriculum, Quintilian will keep the child before the reader's eye. He will not let us forget that the interest of the child, not some Greek theory, directs his every move. The child's goal remains fixed, varying neither with locale nor with ability: it is a steady, verifiable progress toward the perfected subjectivity of a mature, moral speaker.

Concern for the welfare of children marks the text both in its content and in its stated gestures of origin and intent. Quintilian represents children as the impulse to write his work. The claim that children's needs and his students' insistence have impelled him to publish comprises another (more complex) way in which the child constitutes an important category, and not simply an object of report, in Quintilian's text. Those modern theories about the process of learning, which ultimately derive the idea of the solitary learner or the solitary user and maker of language from Cartesian ideas of the self, will not serve here. For Quintilian learning necessarily takes place within the context of a social community, in fact the same community of children, youths, and friends that he claims impelled him to publish in the first place. Certainly, Quintilian has adapted the presentation of a technical topic, rhetoric, under the stimulus of a moralizing pedagogics, and perhaps most specifically the influence of the Stoic thinking that only the sage can be a great orator. At the beginning of book 10 he reused Cato's definition of the orator as a *vir bonus dicendi peritus,* a good man skilled in speaking, and in his preface (9) he had laid down that the orator was to be a *vir bonus.* The insistence that the orator be a good man has a social foundation.[11] That *vir bonus* is doubly social—a member drawn from the elite, the Roman *boni omnes,* and an individual hailed as good by his public. While Quintilian never pauses to consider systematically the nature of the child, his text presents a unified thinking about and with the child. Quintilian describes an educational process in which children are agents, certainly susceptible to bad influences, but agents with capacities and dispositions distinct from adults though playing at and aiming at adult society.[12]

I take up below Quintilian's conceptions of the child: the dedicatory comments that present the child as the impulse to write, the processes of *eruditio* and *castigatio* that redirect the child's curbed passion toward manly use, and the competitive (yet social) process of learning itself. I conclude with his redefinition of rhetoric, certainly an act of intellectual poaching but also an index of his fundamental position that education is not child production but the construction of orators. In these reflections Quintilian far exceeds the predominantly negative anxiety about the malformation of the child that so possessed Pseudo-Plutarch's text. Indeed, we have to wait for Rousseau or perhaps even Freud and his students for an equally important, systematic reflection upon the ideology and the practice of child training.

PUER SCRIBENDUS EST:
THE CHILD AS IMPULSE TO COMPOSITION

Quintilian invites his reader into the long process of reading his book and of educating a child with a letter to his bookseller followed by a preface. This double initiation, with plenty of authorial explanation, might be required simply by the length and detail of the treatment, which then rolls on for an epic twelve books. Quintilian, however, used the double beginning to present the impulse to write as the same as the impulse to educate. With his preface, Quintilian draws us into the passion of education. He also presents a characterization of the student and the teacher, and their relationship, that will be of fundamental importance for his work. The letter that precedes the preface advertises readers' desire for his book and his own reluctance to part with it. The letter opens, after a customary salutation, with a rebuke: "You have hounded me with daily demands"—*Efflagitasti cotidiano convicio.* Quintilian repeats this colorful verb toward the close of the brief letter; now it is Quintilian's books that are so insistently desired (*efflagitantur*).[13]

At the outset, however, Quintilian maintains that he is the circumspect, careful, and reluctant author. He has delayed publication and cites Horace in his defense. The latter's *Ars poetica,* that careful, well-wrought classic, serves as more than a tag (Quintilian quotes from the work, which is read as the manual of Roman poetic aesthetics). The thematics of authorial worry regarding the premature departure of his text are also Horatian. Horace had treated his book of poetry as a young slave overeager to see himself bought at Rome's stalls. Quintilian, like the poet, tries to check the ardency of his work; he says the books are not old enough yet (*nondum . . . satis maturuisse*) and should be given a cooling-off period before sallying forth into the public world (*refrigerato inventionis amore* is his striking phrase—with a Ciceronian flavor).[14] This apology depends on the contrast between the author's care and the haste and imperfection demanded by the world—the author's act of publishing is not just tardy but grudging: *iam emittere incipere.* The first-person pronouncements are those of laborious, time-consuming effort: *impendi* and *repetitos . . . perpenderem;* and at the end, like his tentative beginning, *Inciperem,* the author is no direct agent but the well-wisher looking on from the shore as his beloved sails away (*permittamus vela ventis et oram solventibus bene precemur*). Finally, he puts his trust in his bookseller. Between author and reader comes this delegate, yet another mediator between author and the work in its final form, and between work and audience. All this rhetoric of reluctance, of work pried from the night light of the study, may seem conventional, but Quintilian develops both the imagery and certain ideas of the publication so as to shape the reading of his work and his readers' ideas of *studia,* the passion for education, for literary study, for youth itself.

The author is consistently reluctant, as he will be reluctant to hurry along the child's education, but most immediately, the proem continues to depict an author all but overwhelmed by the process of composition (*diu sum equidem reluctatus*—compare Quintilian's contemporary, the poet Statius, who began the dedicatory letter of his lyric collection, the *Silvae,* with similar hesitation, *diu multumque dubitavi . . .*). A press of books in both languages impedes him. Still, in what is a *topos* for the postclassical author, he attempts nothing new, only a selection of the old. Verbs that suggest slow movement, burden, and imposition, indirect expressions such as the litotes *non ignorabam,* and the sense of a multitudinous and authoritative tradition that daunts the present writer (*difficilis esset electio*) spring from the carefully constructed statements of diffidence in Horace (and the other Augustan poets). The state Quintilian describes, this developed *recusatio,* leads him to ask his audience's pardon. He calls it a *deprecatio,* the figure he discusses at 9.1.32—Cicero may again have inspired Quintilian, for in talking about the daunting Greek experts who have written on rhetoric, Cicero limits his own topic and asks his brother's indulgence (*veniam, De or.* 1.22–23). Further, Cicero says that he will not treat the puerile exercises—thus leaving an opening for Quintilian. In this variation on the Augustan poets' indirection about their literary ambitions and methods, the reluctant author is won over by the demands of his friends. So writing may evade a Horatian impasse (after Horace it would seem to take a Horace to write at all) by being cast as an act of patronage, a *beneficium* toward *amici*.[15]

The preface, which follows immediately upon this letter, especially exploits the contrast of Quintilian's readerly, time-consuming diligence and his students' oral, impetuous desire. Quintilian had said that he had cooled his own passion and then, like a reader, more carefully returned to favorite passages. In his letter to his book-seller he had moved from the loud and constant demands of the bookseller to the demands of his potential readers (*efflagitasti* is answered at the end with the mod-est *si tantopere efflagitantur quam tu adfirmas*). Now, in his preface, his students clamor, *quidam familiariter postularent* (and cf. *exigebatur* at 3). Marcellus Vitorius, Quintilian's first dedicatee, both loves Quintilian and has an excessive passion for the literary life (*cum amicissimum nobis tum eximio litterarum amore flagrantem*); perhaps the reader is to understand that the youth, unlike the author, has not had a cooling-off period for his passion: youth is inclined to be aflame (*flagrare*), our author to play it cool (*refrigerare*).[16] The mixing of personal and intellectual pas-sion recurs in Marcellus Vitorius himself: Quintilian has written these books to be useful for Marcellus in the education of his son Geta (*erudiendo tuo Getae*). Pas-sion and erudition are connected in the educational process. Quintilian conceived of elementary education as the channeling of this youthful passion—processes that he calls *castigatio* and *eruditio*.

The three dedications allow Quintilian to link a deflected, extreme passion to the process of education and of his own writing. In the first dedication, Quintilian imagines that his book will serve in place of himself as an aid in Marcellus's teach-ing of his son. The book replaces teacher. And perhaps we can sense a parallel to Pseudo-Plutarch's anxieties about delegated paternity and patriarchy, examined in the previous chapter: Quintilian's book makes the father into the complete teacher. But in his rededications Quintilian reconsiders both the connection of passion to education and the role of his book as a replacement for personal instruction and even as a substitute or recompense for personal relations. At the beginning of the fourth book Quintilian again salutes Marcellus, announces that a major section is done, a fourth of the journey made, and declares his new topic (actual judicial cases and their component parts). At 4.proem.4 he defends the rededication first by invok-ing the poets' practices (and we are to think of Homer above all others) of invoking the Muse a second time. In fact, circumstances had changed, and Quintilian did have the example of Cicero and no doubt others in rededicating a new portion or version of a major work.[17]

The emperor Domitian himself asked Quintilian to educate the grandsons of his sister. For all his subsequent nasty reputation, Domitian was a major literary force, and his mention adds luster to Quintilian's project.[18] The honor of his appointment was great. Declamatory education and performances gathered the city's elite for rivalrous performances and evaluations. Seneca and others had taken pride in being Nero's educators.[19] Quintilian succinctly evaluates the effect of the honor: with his added responsibility, he no longer writes for domestic use but for princely training.[20] The princes now eclipse his sons and young Geta. This proem augments the dedicatory fiction in which the author writes as if for the use of his own small circle, that is, for *familia* and *amici*.

The proem to the sixth book again starts with Marcellus and moves out to the new impulses affecting Quintilian's writing: the students who harried him to write (as the first preface put it) reappear in more generic form. He classes them simply as well-born youth (*iuvenes bonos*). Next comes the subject of the second proem, here economically noted as his new *officium*. His son is mentioned: Quintilian wrote with the thought that should he die, his son would have in the book a proxy for his father (*praeceptore tamen patre uteretur*). A sustained, rhetorical, and moving lament recounts the shock of the loss of his wife and younger son and, later at the age of nine, his elder son, brilliant and compassionate, and brave through the course of a protracted illness.[21] Bereft, Quintilian can only turn to his studies (6.pr.14: *Sed vivimus et aliqua vivendi ratio quaerenda est, credendumque doctissimis hominibus, qui unicum adversorum solacium litteras putaverunt*, "We live on and some principle of life must be resolved upon, and the most learned authorities must be followed who judged that literature was the sole solace in adversity"). Where youth's passion and his love for his son and friends had prevailed upon him to write, letters themselves are now the only solace for his state of longing (in Latin terms *amor* has changed to *desiderium*). In his final words Quintilian imagines that the book that was to be his replacement for his son now goes to surrogates of that son: *Nos miseri sicut facultates patrimonii nostri, ita hoc opus aliis preparabamus, aliis relinquemus* (6.pr.16: "Just as in my misery with the wealth of my estate so I was preparing this work for some and will leave it to others").[22]

In the first proem he had written that some students, misguided in their love of him, had used slave scribes to take down his lectures and that these unauthorized copies had been put into circulation under his name.[23] Part of his reasons for writing had been to supplant these supposititious writings. At the end of the third proem his legitimate work is being passed on to substitute heirs. Certainly, an elegiac strain has replaced that familiar epistolary topic that entreats the author to part with his much-needed work. In the present case, a complex interplay among the errant passion of the less than scrupulous students, young Geta's great passion for literature, and Quintilian's reasoned and cooled passion has produced a work that is his only solace for his loss of family. Quintilian's evocations of passion are all the more interesting in that they help evoke and direct readers' attitudes toward his book, paternal attitudes toward the child to be educated, and finally scholarly and technical attitudes toward literary, rhetorical study itself. As the teacher, writer, and book are substitute fathers, the book and studies come to be a proxy for the child. The slippage between the categories of child and book is not simply a phenomenon of the proems or the accidental consequence of his actual loss. It constitutes a continuing strain in his thinking about education. The child comes to be associated with the book, and studies themselves come to be understood as a maturing child.

At the outset of the grand work, we read that Quintilian had acted as a restraint upon youth (and his bookseller) in their agitation for his book. He has turned a studious and mature deaf ear to the demands of youth, just as he has shaped that youth from its early rude state. This deliberated curbing of youth's passion is essential to Quintilian's project and life—such is the force of his autobiographical notices in the prefaces. At 1.pr.3 Quintilian presents himself as the author at ease or even the public man now *privatus* again, now returned to *otium,* like Cicero at ease in a villa outside the city: "After I had won a respite from the scientific and zealous training of youth, which had consumed me for two decades" (*Post impetratam studiis meis quietem, quae per uiginti annos erudiendis iuvenibus inpenderam*). Quintilian has won his discharge, yet the occasion of writing makes clear that he is not yet free from correcting youth, nor from *studia,* scholarly researches and interested care.[24] He is of course also presenting his readers with his authority. In his artful indirection we learn ever so modestly of his preeminent experience.

The proem masterfully weaves an epistolary reluctance with the *topoi* of the Roman friend called to aid, the businesslike or even political Roman called to literary matters, and the Roman author, especially a poet, called to a grand topic with rich, even overwhelming traditions and precedents. For all the protest about well-earned *otium* being interrupted, we, like his friends, are to know that he has never paused from the education of youth—the conceit expressed in a phrase (*erudiendis iuvenibus*) that is grammatically a statement of purpose.[25] This phrase, "youth" with the gerundive—"children to be educated"—draws Quintilian back. Indeed, in the next two books Quintilian will use the word "boy" or "youth" with a gerundive to remind his reader of his purpose and to mark out significant stages in the progress of his project, this *institutio oratoria,* construction of an orator, which must start with an *institutio puerilis* and move step-by-step to maturity. Protesting that resignation of the task is impossible, the author presents a persona defined by a relationship to youth and to studies. All of Quintilian's care has been and will be, for the twelve weighty books that the slight preface introduces and for the eighteen years or so of a student's life, devoted to the process of *erudire,* the purpose of helping young men mature, most literally, of removing what is rude in them.

Cicero especially loved to use the word *erudire* as a synonym for "teach, educate, fashion the young."[26] An ancient definition of the root reveals its semantic range: *omnis fere materia non deformata, rudis appellatur* ("Rude denotes all material that has not been shaped," Cincius ap. Festus, p. 265 Müller). Rude is opposed to the well-shaped (the ancient definition does not exploit the second sense of *deformatum*, that which has had its natural shape, *forma*, mishandled, although Quintilian seems to exploit both meanings). The rude awaits man's shaping hand (so the word is used of the unformed medium that the artist takes up). The child is then like unworked marble, whereas the educated child can be commemorated as *eruditus*. A first-century B.C. funerary inscription commemorates a fourteen-year-old girl as schooled and learned (*erodita*) in all the arts.[27] In Quintilian, *rudis* is a favorite term in discussions of the educational process. Indeed, *eruditio* is conceived as existing along a continuum, at one end of which stands the unworked boy, while at the other stand the erudite poets and scholars whose diction and inquiries further purify *Latinitas*. Foremost among the latter are some famous poets and the incomparable (and many-booked) Varro (1.8.11).

Quintilian is interested, however, in the diction of the learned, not their doctrine. Quintilian seeks a supply of words from the erudite. These words are a sort of blanket to cosset the child, for erudition means in Quintilian an environment and process rather than an abstract mental state or codifiable set of principles. Speech itself or the single word can be *eruditus*. A striking indication of this linguistic bias is that Quintilian says *consuetudo*, actual practice in language, has much erudition. He is cleaving to one side of an ancient debate about how to determine the proper form of a word, but it is important to note that *eruditio* is here used of a discovered trove of words. Mother and father, and slave pedagogues too, must have *eruditio*. Every bit of language the boy encounters should be *eruditus*. The Latin lexicon concerns Quintilian: so he discusses the form of a word and the avoidance of solecism. In this linguistic environment the boy will enter the road to *eruditio*. There are other courses—pleasures he calls *ineruditae* (1.18.10)—and he notes that faults of language are hard to remove.

Amid this nurturing speech environment Quintilian imagines the boy developing in carefully structured and scrutinized ways. To continue with his diction, we may ask: How is the boy to be pruned of his rudeness or molded to maturity? Perhaps too we should ask what metaphor to use, for Quintilian does not rely much on metaphors of pruning or cutting or sculpting. By way of contrast, Martianus Capella imagines a Dame Grammar who takes from her box a sharp instrument to rasp the tongue and cut out improper words—this violent and intrusive iconography is a feature of the late antique and medieval traditions, not of Quintilian, and is perhaps a reflection of the common use of parchment, a writing surface more durable and capable of erasure and rewriting than the medium of Quintilian's day, papyrus.[28] Quintilian imagines that the boy who comes to his care passes easily from home to school. This ideal boy arrives free from linguistic blemish—so far he has met no inerudite word.

Again and again in his description of the progress of the boy, Quintilian joins a gerundive to the word "boy": the boy is to be trained (1.1.12 and in the final sentence of the book, 1.12.19), nourished, educated, advised; his inborn intellect is something to be sharpened.[29] At the beginning of book 2 the boy has become a *discipulus* or a boy to be passed on to the rhetorician or a mature child or an adult child on his way to being an *iuvenis*. The repeated age terms mark the progress of education and the reader's progress through Quintilian's work, which begins: *Igitur nato filio* ("Therefore once a son is born . . . "); book 2 charts the boy's development with new terminology: the *pueri* are now *discipuli* (2.1.1) or the *puer* who is to be sent to the rhetorician (2.1.3) or *puer maturus* (2.1.7) or *adulti . . . pueri* (2.3.1). Book 2 clearly represents a new stage, but the first stage demands more of our attention; for it is here that we can isolate the first of Quintilian's most distinctive ideas about education: the boy is worthy of training and of theoretical comment. This we must immediately qualify: whereas Quintilian realizes different children have different degrees of talent and different aptitudes, he does not give directions corresponding to those varying abilities. At 1.3.6, where he does allow that children progress at different rates, the teacher is told simply to push only those who are ready. Quintilian's theoretical account is satisfied with the boy, *puer,* as a simple category, whose growth may vary in speed but not in kind or direction.

The category *puer* comprises at once a stage of life, a stage of education, and a section of the book and the curriculum. While the first two books chart the progress from birth to puberty, Quintilian hardly employs biological terms.[30] Rather, the reader is presented with the space of the *puer.* The proem announced that Quintilian would trace the boy's studies *ab infantia* (pr. 1.6), and the book signals the movement with notices of the maturing boy. The boy is replaced by the "robust boy" in book 2, whose curriculum and ability now differ, since the boy has left behind the poetry he encountered with the *grammaticus* and now engages the more manly and truer subject of history (2.4.2: *apud rhetorem initium sit historica, tanto robustior quanto verior*).

Of course, these sections of Quintilian treat the subjects of grammatical instruction. If we were to provide him with summary paragraph headings, the topics would be spelling, music, geometry, and all the subjects that the grammarian and others would teach before the boy went on to the rhetorician. Certainly, Quintilian's work has been described this way, but what is remarkable is that Quintilian has chosen to include the preliminary training at all and punctuates it with introductory notices that mention the boy. Indeed, Quintilian has a certain diffidence about his technical subject—he reports that he is not teaching grammar but advising those who will (1.4.7: *non enim doceo, sed admoneo docturos*). He keeps the boy and not the technical subdiscipline before his reader's eye. After the initiatory *Igitur nato filio* come other notices of the child that also serve to introduce a new topic or stage: *A sermone graeco puerum incipere malo* (1.1.12: "My preference is that the boy begin with Greek"); *Sed nobis iam paulatim adcrescere puer* (1.2: "But the boy in our school already begins to grow"); a stronger echo and change of stage is announced with *Tradito sibi puero docendi peritus* (1.3: "Once the boy has been entrusted to him, the expert teacher . . ."). Quintilian joins this *puer* with the gerundive, as we have noted, or with a jussive subjunctive, *Quare discat puer . . .* (1.4.12: "Wherefore have the boy learn . . ."; cf. 1.4.22 and 1.5.11: *Scire autem debet puer,* "Moreover the boy ought to know . . ."). After a technical passage Quintilian reminds the reader of the topic at hand by setting the boy before his reader (again early in the sentence as a kind of programmatic recall): *superest lectio: in qua puer ut sciat* ("There is finally reading, in which that the boy know . . ."). Here Quintilian curbs the monotony of the technical material by setting down one guiding principle: amid all the instructions and exercises on how to read, the chief thing is that the boy is to understand (1.8.2: *intellegat*). At times Quintilian even omits *puer* in these sorts of notices. He uses a subjectless third-person verb when declaring a new stage: *Cum vero iam ductus sequi coeperit . . .* (1.1.27: "Once he has begun to trace the letter shapes . . ."). Context makes the subject clear, but it is also clear because the reader recognizes the sentence as one of those transitions where Quintilian focuses on the development of the *puer.* We see this child in the abstract progressing, with the occasional reminder of his goal (1.11 substitutes *futurus orator* for the common *puer*).

His use of the term "child" is in fact rather like the use of the word "it" in recipes. In narrating a recipe, we repeatedly say "it" to refer to the developing object. So we could say add salt to it, then knead it for ten minutes, let it rise for an hour, press it down, etc., until we finally have it. The "it" is not the same throughout, but for reasons of economy, and because we tend to conflate the process with the end result, we use a single pronoun. No doubt pronouns function more widely in such a fashion. For Quintilian, *puer* functions as a virtual pronoun. The repeated use generalizes process and subsumes individuality or aberration under universality or normativity. "It" rather than Marcus or Quintus progresses nicely, neatly, in clearly defined ways. "It" is not unruly but accepts rather strictly limited epithets and predicates (the gerundives and the verbs of learning that suggest its agency is severely limited, its capacities rigorously restricted and capable of restriction) before the *puer* emerges as one trained (*instituendus*, 1.12.19) in these first studies, and soon to be the *puer maturus* or *adultus* or even *iuvenis* in the books devoted to rhetoric. Thus grammar and the child become perfectly correspondent: the child seems to be like a well-regulated word, admitting no change in its form, appearing in regular places within the text so as to guide our reading, and restricted to one field—or, in Quintilian's terms, one office. In ancient manuals, the term "child" often functions like the modern educational statistic: it is the well-governed reduction that becomes ever so easily an item of argument, preeminently a word for the ancients, a number for us.

ANIMUS PUERILIS

In his first book Quintilian presents the child and grammatical studies as perfectly congruent. The child is that stage of man disposed to grammar, and grammar is the subject and disposition fit for and productive of the free boy. In Quintilian's view the grammatical curriculum cannot summarily be dismissed as comprising those studies preliminary to the important fare of rhetoric (an attitude communicated by their name, which Quintilian does not use, *progymnasmata* in Greek, *praeexercitationes* or *praeexercitamenta* in Latin). Quintilian thinks that grammar is necessary for the growth of the child. Through grammar the child grows to *studium,* which is both zeal for literary study and zeal to excel one's peers. Without grammar the child's maturation seems unthinkable (for without education the child would be the unadorned *puer,* the slave). Here the customary rationalization for the institution of schooling is expanded to advocate a new point: Quintilian counsels that the child should not be schooled at home. He does not voice the fears of Pseudo-Plutarch about the influence of women, slaves, and freedmen.[31] Rather, homeschooling would be a species of parental neglect that would stunt the child. Quintilian can see the child's potentialities in the rough, and in sustained arguments in the first book describes how they must be fostered in the social community of the school. The idea that the child is a social animal whose capacities for further learning and adult success depend on his educational environment is remarkable. Quintilian must articulate the nature of the child mind in order to explain and establish his program.

First, in encouraging fathers to train their children toward oratory, Quintilian maintains that mankind has as its distinguishing characteristic mental activity (1.1.1; this position is taken up and refined at the outset of book 2, where he more narrowly and rhetorically defines this quality as *vox,* which signifies not merely language, but rather something like human communicative society).[32] Children are born with an *ingenium,* which comprises both a native intelligence and specific gifts toward oratory and literary study. Indeed, Quintilian does not seem to consider that there could be cognitive abilities independent of language. A child's intelligence, or literary disposition, is the promise of the future man. In Quintilian's repeated metaphor, light portends greatness. Young Geta has it: *cuius prima aetas manifestum iam ingenii lumen ostendit* ("whose early childhood already revealed the clear light of his talent").[33] The first thing the teacher is to do is perceive, *perspiciet,* the boy's *ingenium* and nature (1.3.1; the same verb is used at 1.2.16). A child's native disposition seems to be visible; its lack Quintilian also describes as visible. Those without talent are like monsters; Quintilian uses a technical term from religion that means the physically deformed, the newborn animal whose body is a composite of two species (1.1.2: "The slow and learning impaired are as contrary to human nature as are hybrid or monstrous bodies, but these are rarities," *Hebetes uero et indociles non magis secundum naturam hominis eduntur quam prodigiosa corpora et monstris insignia, sed hi admodum pauci*). Among animals deformity is corporeal, among men deformity is the failure to learn (rhetoric). Reassuringly, almost everybody seems to have a modicum of the light of talent, which can be developed by an expert teacher, *studium*, and practice (1.1.27).[34] Indeed, Quintilian encourages fathers to have the highest expectation of rhetorical success from the very birth of their sons (1.1.1).

This linguistic disposition is written on the young boy. Whereas the talentless are like beastly bodies with signs of their monstrosity, *monstris insignia*, the freeborn boy has sure signs of his talent. He has natural signs for those who can see: *Ingenii signum in paruis praecipuum memoria est: eius duplex uirtus, facile percipere et fideliter continere. Proximum imitatio* . . . (1.3.1: "The chief sign of talent in the very young is memory, which has two strengths, swift acquisition and accurate retention. The second is imitation . . . ").[35] True, he does not have judgment, the *iudicium* that characterizes *robustiores,* stronger, older youth. Choice and judgment are still beyond him, but Quintilian does not dwell on the negative characterization. The contrast with the more robust youth of rhetorical age does not denigrate the child: his capacity to imitate will ensure that he realizes the hopes of his elders.[36] The imitative quality is inherent and essential, but it is also social.[37] Thus Quintilian is quite insistent that boys go to school and not be tutored one-on-one at home.

In arguing against home tutoring Quintilian insists that the speaker needs an audience (see the discussion of 1.2.27–31 below), and at 1.2.17 has already forestalled the objection that the boy at school will be lost in the crowd, with two arguments: first, fathers should treat the teacher as an *amicus;* second, the teacher will naturally favor the student who possesses *ingenium* and *studium*. That is to say, Quintilian understands school as a Roman social community, where patronage dictates the good treatment of the student. The teacher is the father's *amicus,* dependent friend, and the student is the dependent friend of the teacher, displaying the interest and talent that every patron looks for and rewards in his clients.[38] Imitation is not simply the individual's urge to mimic, but part of a hierarchical, social nexus that ties together the (male) agents of education. School imitates society in reproducing idealized male social relations, *amicitia*. The great sign of a child's talent is of course the faithful *imitatio* that is memory. Faithful version of his father, of his teacher, and of the lessons given him, the child performs a most important, ideological virtue. Quintilian of course does not diagnose the child's imitative bent in this way. Nonetheless, his analysis reveals the potent overlay of sentiment, morality, social structure, and the institution of the Roman school.

Quintilian's instructions for the handling of the child's imitative faculties reveal the importance of this first stage. Imitation may be innate; but the child mimics for effect, and he mimics those older than he. Imitation can go wrong: Quintilian counsels that the boy can be sent to the expert reciter of comedy (1.11.1–2) but only to improve his delivery—the boy must not let any of the registers (or fun) of comedy affect his speech. Quintilian details the voices not to be imitated: woman, old man, drunkard, slave, lover, miser, and coward. Further, memory and imitation are allied. Curiously, Quintilian has defined the qualities of child memory he thinks important as ready perception and faithful retention. That is, whereas he does occasionally stress that the child is to understand what he is reading, Quintilian does not consider what a child's cognition might be like. It is sufficient to him that the child is incapable of that quality of distinction that marks the adolescent and, more positively, that he is capable of swift imitation: his lessons he quickly takes up (in imitation of the master) and then retains (long-term imitation).

While Quintilian does not despise this process as simple rote learning, he does not analyze how it works or indeed if it differs from simple rote work (he does not seem to see the connection between the processes of memory and imitation). He considers learning more effective if the child understands (and here he writes of reading, not the first step in the curriculum). The child has other innate aids to learning: he is patient of labor, and his *ingenium* is softer and more docile than that of older boys.[39] Quintilian illustrates these statements with the proof of experience: a young boy takes only two years to achieve proper enunciation, older boys take many years. He then cites the Greek term "child-learner," which was used for someone who was a "natural" at a new task. Childhood is thus the natural time to learn language. He uses a metaphor to explain the capacity for labor: as the infant can suffer a fall and not be hurt or crawl all day without knee pain, so the child's *ingenium* is equally pliable and resilient. Quintilian's metaphoric term for education at this period, *acuere ingenium* ("sharpening native disposition"), also suggests the softness of the child.

Naturally imitative, impressionable, and diligent, the child of Quintilian's pages is docile, and social. Despite presenting the boy as a soft body, one not too far from mother's milk and thus fit for the acquisition of language, by docile Quintilian does not mean passive. The desired student, Quintilian's normative *puer,* has definite *animi*—a word of considerable range: courage, emotion, and intellect. Again, there are intimations that the boy is a passionate subject and not the passive object of a curriculum. *Animi* are to be developed in a group setting. Quintilian founds his theoretical argument against homeschooling on a connection between eloquence, *animi,* and the community. These three factors are interdependent: there is no eloquence in conversation among individuals; no good education will arise from tutor and student alone. Rhetorical training and oratorical performance demand an audience; otherwise the *animi* (emotions) are fake; indeed, they are not stimulated. These points Quintilian makes in a sustained argument that begins by instructing the instructors not to overload young minds:

> Quod adeo uerum est ut ipsius etiam magistri, si tamen ambitiosis utilia praeferet, hoc opus sit, cum adhuc rudia tractabit ingenia, non statim onerare infirmitatem discentium, sed temperare uires suas et ad intellectum audientis descendere. Nam ut uascula oris angusti superfusam umoris copiam respuunt, sensim autem influentibus uel

etiam instillatis complentur, sic animi puerorum quantum excipere possint uidendum
est: nam maiora intellectu uelut parum apertos ad percipiendum animos non subi-
bunt. Utile igitur habere quos imitari primum, mox uincere uelis: ita paulatim et su-
periorum spes erit. His adicio praeceptores ipsos non idem mentis ac spiritus in di-
cendo posse concipere singulis tantum praesentibus quod illa celebritate audientium
instinctos. Maxima enim pars eloquentiae constat animo: hunc adfici, hunc concipere
imagines rerum et transformari quodam modo ad naturam eorum de quibus loquitur
necesse est. Is porro quo generosior celsiorque est, hoc maioribus uelut organis com-
mouetur, ideoque et laude crescit et impetu augetur et aliquid magnum agere gaudet.
Est quaedam tacita dedignatio uim dicendi tantis comparatam laboribus ad unum au-
ditorem demittere: pudet supra modum sermonis attolli. Et sane concipiat quis mente
uel declamantis habitum uel orantis uocem incessum pronuntiationem, illum denique
animi et corporis motum, sudorem, ut alia praeteream, et fatigationem audiente uno:
nonne quiddam pati furori simile uideatur? Non esset in rebus humanis eloquentia
si tantum cum singulis loqueremur. (1.2.27–31)

The consequence of this is that the teacher who prefers practical steps to showmanship
has the duty, when he draws out minds still unformed, not to overload at the start the
weakness of the learners but to moderate his own powers and to come down to the
understanding of the student. For just as narrow-necked jars spit back a large stream
of liquid poured over them but are filled when the flow is graduated or put in drop
by drop, similarly one must consider the capacities of young minds: for the concep-
tually difficult will not enter minds ill disposed to understanding. It is advantageous
first to have models for simple imitation, second those to be rivaled and bested. To
these points I add that tutors cannot conceive the same thought and emotion in speaking as those teachers fired by a large audience. For the greater part of eloquence rests
in emotional power: this must be experienced, this must invent representations of the
facts and must be accommodated somehow to the subjects under discussion. The more
noble and lofty this emotional intelligence, the more it is moved by greater organs as
it were, and so it swells when praised and is increased in the rush of contest and takes
pleasure in attempting something grand. There is a certain internal inhibition in slack-
ening, for an audience of one, the force of speaking prepared by such great toil: one
feels shame to rise up above the norm of conversational speech. And should anyone
really adopt before a single hearer the stance of a declaimer or the pleader's voice, the
pacing, the delivery, and finally that movement of thought and of body, the sweat, I
pass over in decent silence the rest, and the exhaustion, would he not seem to be suffering something close to madness? Eloquence would not exist in human affairs if we
spoke only with individuals.

Quintilian's first metaphor of learning, overfilling vases, suggests the rude *ingenium*
is passive (but with the slight agency of the infant, the vase spits up when overfed).
Quintilian quickly builds from this. He has warned the teacher not to overfill the
young student, then describes how praise, growth, impulse, increase, activity, and
desire will follow (*ideoque et laude crescit et impetu augetur et aliquid magnum agere*

gaudet). Thus does the child develop *animus,* which as he says is the chief thing in eloquence. In fact, Quintilian is protecting the child from being swamped, advising that he be given examples of *animus* that he can imitate, and then be led to a state that Quintilian himself likens to suffering (*pati*) high passion, where the body moves, sweat pours—Quintilian passes over with a *praeteritio* the other bodily effusions— and finally fatigue comes. All of this would be unseemly if discharged before a single tutee. Quintilian is directing the teacher on how to bring himself and the child to oratorical climax.

There is something of a mélange of imagery here, which grows worse as Quintilian turns in the next section (1.3.5) to images from agriculture, perhaps a safer and more customary way to talk of *semina* and their growth in the child.[40] When Quintilian writes here that greater organs are needed for the development of the nobler and loftier child, *organa* no doubt attempts a change in metaphorical field: *organum* is a wind instrument and not as in Aristotle the *membrum virile.* But Quintilian's prescriptions for the proper training of the child return to an anxiety about the confusion of pedagogy and pederasty: the next sentences begin with the *dedignatio,* indignity and debasement, and *pudet,* the shame felt, of the uplifted (*attolli*) one-on-one performance. The child is to imitate greater organs, namely, the great speakers of the past, before an audience. Quintilian is not here voicing direct worry about the sexual corruption of wards; he is worried about the development of virility, and speech is the mark of virility (lofty birth and commanding, masculine, heterosexual affect). A proper masculinity in the child is measured by his linguistic habits and achievements. The boy is to move from imitation to mastery (*vincere velis*), rather than, like a vessel of tight aperture, be flooded. In Quintilian's metaphors, rather than being female container, he will be more solid, with *animus, vis,* and *semina* that have grown to full fruit.[41] Thus in Quintilian's biological and physicalist model does the *puer* advance beyond grammar and on to speaking.

To define this child, Quintilian relies mostly on positive description of the apt curriculum. A cursus of studies prepares for rhetorical training, the stage of life and letters that demands judgment and that distinguishes the *robustiores* from the *pueri.* In the passage discussed above that exhorted fathers to send their sons to school, the child is theorized positively as a growth that achieves proper maturity through grammar. Quintilian also uses the prospect of the boy gone wrong as a rhetorical argument: no father wants his son to suffer shame and degradation, those consequences of homeschooling and of corporal punishment. Still Quintilian does not promise that every boy will be a star. He recognizes a variety of talent in children but entertains no idea that alternate training is required. Rather, all can improve; and while some may be more fit for one or another aspect of studies, no one escapes the whole training.[42]

The few notices of less successful students reveal a consistent and recurrent aspect of educational thought: the less successful is the less gifted. Such a child seems to be more like the neck-impaired vase and less like the sharp-tooled promising *puer.* Conversely, Quintilian does not want the boy to be too quick-witted—his description of the child begins to sound like a recipe from an experienced if inarticulate cook: do not overcook and do not undercook is seldom helpful advice, except perhaps that we are reminded of the expertise, experience, and fine judgment of the advice-monger. However, if the *puer* seems intermediate between *infans* and *robustior,* between *imbecillis* and *catus,* this is because Quintilian exploits the polar categories to reassure parents and to rationalize an elitist, difficult training. For Quintilian education must not be a simple reflection of innate talent (*ingenium*), since then training would be unnecessary. And he feared another possibility: if rhetorical education were seen as a morally neutral skill, perhaps only those with *ingenium* might succeed at it. Instead, the reader will be led to understand education as a graduated growth. This is one part of the master's grand claims for rhetoric as a moral science (the connection of maturation and the moral science of education I defer until we have finished examining the nature of the *animus puerilis*).

In his ideal central position, between excesses of tardiness and precociousness, between the home and the rhetorical school, the boy's mind requires special treatment. In its prejudgmental phase, that mind is presented with *imitanda.* These are to be retained and understood. Both the tendency to imitate and the tendency to excel are attributes of *studium,* zeal and study. The boy is not simply drawn to imitate; he wishes to impress. Thus Quintilian can imagine a bad sort of imitation where the child tries to draw attention, as we would say, by being funny, perhaps even derisible.[43]

Rivalry, both with the model texts that have been memorized and imitated and with other practitioners of oratory or literature, is one end of Quintilian's training; it was also a daily feature of the school. Quintilian has his students speak in the order of their ability. It seems that the students even contributed to the determination of this pecking order (1.2.23). Elsewhere (2.2.14) he advises that boys are not to be seated with adolescents (he fears the appearance of homosexual relations). But he also wants to develop within the lead boy (*dux*) or leading boys a mentality of excelling. This is part of the reason that no boy is to be beaten. Quintilian does not want him to take on the shame, the mentality of the slave. We have here sufficient hints of a teacher who wishes to develop the feeling of a class with its leaders. So he remarks that he disapproves of letting boys leap to their feet to applaud (2.2.9). Under such circumstances the interactive classroom has gone too far: boys now run forward *ad omnem clausulam* (2.2.12, denoting the rhythmic syllable patterns that signal the end of a sentence or clause).

PLAY AND THE YOUNG MIND

With these descriptions of the school we have advanced beyond the boy's first exercises and on to declamation or at least recitation. For young boys, the order of speaking, the approval and interaction of peers, and the praise or blame of the master were not sufficient incentives. Quintilian strongly advocated the virtues of play in a passage that, along with that inveighing against corporal punishment, has been saluted as testimony to his humanism. The directive to educate through play constitutes an essential role in Quintilian's thinking about the imitative, agonistic, and diligent tendency of the child. It is also, however, a reflection of his, and more generally Roman, thinking about the exclusive, free body (and mind) of that child. Quintilian states that the child, the type of diligence, must be given a break: respite must be granted to all both to relieve the drudgery and restore energy and because "devotion to learning depends on the free will of the student, which cannot be compelled" (1.3.8: *studium discendi voluntate, quae cogi non potest, constat*). Quintilian is again cultivating not so much a specifically childlike learning style but the latent or unself-conscious will to learn in the (prejudgmental) child. It is not the case that play liberates the mind or develops certain cognitive qualities: play spells the hard work of learning and (mis)leads the child to do what at an older age he will have the self-will to do. Play is like the honey upon the lip of the cup of bitter medicine that is *studium*—such is Quintilian's reuse of Lucretius's famous image of smearing the lip of the bitter cup of medicine with honey, when he confesses the dryness of his rhetorical material and apologizes for the lack of honey (3.1.4 [quoting Lucr. 4.11–13]: *Ac veluti pueris absinthia taetra medentes . . .*). At 1.1.20 he counsels that children are to be offered prizes, and their lessons made into games so that they will not come to hate the studies they cannot understand. Quintilian here uses the word "bitterness" of these early studies, perhaps a gesture to the Lucretian passage.[44] Quintilian's real interest lies in the later life of the student, in the age of rhetoric, when the student can understand, judge, and love his studies. For the present, the child must be offered the honey of delusion so as to prevent the development of an abiding hostility to study (just as he must not be beaten so as to avoid instilling fear and shame in him). So games substitute for judgment, self-will, and the self-conscious love of learning.

Quintilian does imagine one other use for play. The point of presenting studies as a game is to "let the child never feel pleasure at not doing his lessons; should the child ever prove unwilling, teach another child, one whom he envies, and let the first child compete and think that he is winning again and again: let the boy be drawn along by rewards also, which that age likes" (1.1.20: *numquam non fecisse se gaudeat, aliquando ipso nolente doceatur alius cui invideat, contendat interim et saepius vincere se putet: praemiis etiam, quae capit illa aetas, evocetur*). Games here also forestall a wrong passion: they prevent fear of studies and love of idleness. Quintilian somewhat begrudgingly (with a litotes "not un-useful") concedes that some games do sharpen the boy's intellect; but again he does not argue that there is something inherently useful in games. Rather, they are efficacious to the extent that they forestall the child's sense of tedium, as we have seen, and to the extent that they arouse rivalry: "Some games are not un-useful for sharpening the boys' wits, as when they

strive with one another to answer trifles of every kind posed them one after another" (1.3.11: *Sunt etiam nonulli acuendis puerorum ingeniis non inutiles lusus, cum
positis invicem cuiusque generis quaestiunculis aemulantur*).[45] He continues to make
the point that games are useful for the detection of the child's *mores*. At this young
age the child can be more easily corrected and shaped thanks to his lack of deceit
(an age *infirma . . . tum vel maxime formanda cum simulandi nescia est et praecip-
ientibus facillime cedit*, 1.3.12). A behavioral—but not an intellectual—reason directs that a child's studies be presented as a game. Games serve the apotropaic purpose of forestalling resentment and resistance, and channel rivalry. Quintilian does
believe in the joy of learning, but he does not treat games or riddles as a species of
problem solving or social learning. He records that as boys he and his peers used
to play at false geometric drawings (i.e., diagrams that must be shown to be impossible). This is play, and play at an early stage (geometry being taught concur-
rently with grammar), but receives no comment as play from Quintilian. Rather, it
is one means of distinguishing the false from the true—again a habit for life that
this elementary game rehearses (1.10.39: *Falsa quoque ueris similia geometria ratione deprendit. Fit hoc et in numeris per quasdam quas pseudographias uocant, quibus pueri ludere solebamus*). Quintilian values success at games as a sign of a swift
intellect, *signum alacritatis* (in keeping with his general view that the child is a
signum of the man). Like other signs of the child's talent, his performance in games
constitutes a diagnostic and disciplinary tool for the teacher but not a significant
medium of training.

Does the child do anything that is good in itself or productive of a mental faculty? We have considered Quintilian's repeated phrasing that *ingenia* can and must
be sharpened, and his admonitions on the careful handling of imitation.[46] Dancing and games serve their elementary purpose and will be abandoned when the child
passes to rhetoric.[47] Quintilian does describe, still in rather general terms, what
should characterize puerile education. He recommends which authors to imitate;
he confides how he encourages the youngest students (and at the same time en-
sures that they know that in the future they will have to speak differently, with greater
restraint). In his most sustained treatment of child learning, Quintilian presents the
linguistic stylization of the child as the essential, indispensable good of early education. Aside from some specific recommendations on whom to read, his directions are more metaphorical than practical. Quintilian showers upon the reader a
wealth of metaphor and simile about forming the child and his still plastic body.
These represent the speech of the young as a plump, tender infant, still close to
mother and breast-feeding. A florid, rich, milky-full style is to be encouraged. Later
this will be trimmed. Quintilian has child speech match the child body both because he sees the development of eloquence as a natural, biological growth and because he understands speech and its development in terms of imitation.[48] Bodies
and speech must suit each other. As so often, one suspects that issues of authentic-

ity and legitimacy subtend the rhetorician's account of system and practice. Like the author of the *De liberis educandis,* Quintilian seeks to produce a speaking subjectivity for a governing elite. The ability to speak is presented as a natural phenomenon correspondent to biological growth while dependent on careful nurture. It may then seem unexpected that Quintilian stresses the infantile or even feminine affinities of first training, but he sees the development of manhood and manly style as a growth away from infancy. Quintilian defends his program for boys by reminding his reader that childhood is a premature stage and cannot be judged by the stylistic criteria fit for the finished speech and the finished man:

> Vitium utrumque, peius tamen illud quod ex inopia quam quod ex copia uenit. Nam in pueris oratio perfecta nec exigi nec sperari potest: melior autem indoles laeta generosique conatus et uel plura iusto concipiens interim spiritus. Nec umquam me in his discentis annis offendat si quid superfuerit. Quin ipsis doctoribus hoc esse curae uelim, ut teneras adhuc mentes more nutricum mollius alant, et satiari uelut quodam iucundioris disciplinae lacte patiantur. Erit illud plenius interim corpus, quod mox adulta aetas adstringat. Hinc spes roboris: maciem namque et infirmitatem in posterum minari solet protinus omnibus membris expressus infans. Audeat haec aetas plura et inueniat et inuentis gaudeat, sint licet illa non satis sicca interim ac seuera. Facile remedium est ubertatis, sterilia nullo labore uincuntur. Illa mihi in pueris natura minimum spei dederit in qua ingenium iudicio praesumitur. Materiam esse primum uolo uel abundantiorem atque ultra quam oporteat fusam. Multum inde decoquent anni, multum ratio limabit, aliquid uelut usu ipso deteretur, sit modo unde excidi possit et quod exculpi; erit autem, si non ab initio tenuem nimium laminam duxerimus et quam caelatura altior rumpat. Quod me de his aetatibus sentire minus mirabitur qui apud Ciceronem legerit: "uolo enim se efferat in adulescente fecunditas."
>
> Quapropter in primis euitandus, et in pueris praecipue, magister aridus, non minus quam teneris adhuc plantis siccum et sine umore ullo solum. Inde fiunt humiles statim et uelut terram spectantes, qui nihil supra cotidianum sermonem attollere audeant. Macies illis pro sanitate et iudicii loco infirmitas est, et, dum satis putant uitio carere, in id ipsum incidunt uitium, quod uirtutibus carent. Quare mihi ne maturitas quidem ipsa festinet nec musta in lacu statim austera sint: sic et annos ferent et uetustate proficient. Ne illud quidem quod admoneamus indignum est, ingenia puerorum nimia interim emendationis seueritate deficere; nam et desperant et dolent et nouissime oderunt et, quod maxime nocet, dum omnia timent nihil conantur. Quod etiam rusticis notum est, qui frondibus teneris non putant adhibendam esse falcem, quia reformidare ferrum uidentur et nondum cicatricem pati posse. (2.4.4–10)[49]

These are both faults, although that which comes from want is worse than that from surfeit. For among small boys, perfect speech cannot be expected nor exacted: moreover, it is better to have enthusiastic talent and noble effort and a heart which for the time being essays more than what is called for. And in these years of the learner, may no superabundance ever distress me. On the contrary, I wish teachers would take this as a rule, nourish minds still tender more softly, like a nurse maid, and allow them to be sated by the milk, as it were, of a kinder teaching. For the meantime, their body will be a little plumper, which soon adulthood will draw taut. This abundant style is the hope for future strength; the infant perfectly proportioned at the outset usually presages later emaciation and debility. Let this young age dare much and discover much and take pleasure in its discoveries; do not let that age for the meantime be too dry and hard. The cure for abundance is easy; no toil repairs the jejune. In my opinion the disposition among boys least promising is that where judgment precedes talent. First off I want the supply to be fuller and more fulsome than is right. Time will decoct much, reason will file off much, some will be worn away by practice provided only that there be something that can be cut and shaped away. There will be sufficient if we have not stretched the plate too thin at the start, which the engraver, cutting deeply, will puncture. My judgment on this age will not surprise the reader who remembers Cicero's "For I want fertility to puff itself up in adolescence."

Therefore among the most important things to avoid, most especially for young boys, is a dry teacher, just as you would a dry and parched soil for crops still tender. This will render the boys humble and downcast, the sort who never dare rise above conversational style. For such boys skin and bones serve for a healthy body, weakness for judgment; and while they are satisfied with the lack of any fault, they have fallen into the fault of lacking any virtues. Therefore do not hurry along aging and do not let the vintage new in the barrel have a harsh taste: so they will age well and in their maturity be potent. Our advice is not unseemly, the talents of boys subjected to an overly severe correction during youth come to naught, for they grow despondent and aggrieved and finally hateful and, what does the most harm, they essay nothing while they dread everything. Even peasants know this: they advise tender shoots not be pruned with the knife because they seem to fear the iron and cannot yet abide the scar.

Most strikingly, Quintilian does not want the child prodigy (*omnibus membris expressus infans*). Too much man and too much virtuosity too early might suggest that teacher and teaching are unnecessary, but it is in keeping with an outlook shaped by rhetoric and the graduated curriculum of ancient education to seek stages (just as styles) in which speech and bodies correspond. Imitation is not simply a species of educational exercise or method but an underlying conceptual category. Throughout the discussions in these first two books *infirmitas* characterizes the child, and rightly so Quintilian thinks. If the child is the complete speaker and indeed shows judgment, Quintilian predicts disaster (*Illa mihi in pueris natura minimum spei dederit in qua ingenium iudicio praesumitur*, "In my experience that nature among boys offers the least hope in which native talent is consumed before [the coming of] judgment").[50] The premature stage has baby fat, mass, softness. Further, education in parallel with physical maturation follows a course of thinning, hardening, and weaning. The soft body patient of labor, the imperfect speaker with the fulsome style is completely consistent with his gendering of the child. The child is imagined as still close to the maternal body, but he must not be kept at home. The child's body is soft, patient, and impressionable, but it must not be beaten or eroticized by the older male teacher. Play will not help this body or mind mature; at best, it habituates without instilling judgment.

CHASTENING GRAMMAR: *CASTIGATIO* AND *ERUDITIO*

Quintilian's thinking about the maturation of the child rests largely on two central impulses. Mother must be replaced by teacher, and the child's closeness with the feminine must be replaced or redirected to an intimacy with the mother tongue. Biological maturation is thus recoded as mastering Latin. This is the rhetorical process of castigation (which the discussion of rhetorical *habitus*, corporal punishment, and the adolescent body in chapters 7 and 8 below describe more fully). In the preadolescent phase of grammar instruction, the lactating, natural mother loses her role to Dame Grammar or Dame Rhetoric. The personification is not explicit in Quintilian as it would later be, for instance, in Martianus Capella.[51] In Quintilian's words, the child is properly abundant, superfluous, and copious (see above: e.g., the teachers *more nutricum mollius alant*; and to characterize the boys: *lacte, ubertatis, abundantiorem;* finally, the Ciceronian tag that caps the paragraph with *fecunditas*). In this male appropriation of maternal nurture and women's social roles, the antitype to the child is not the girl—she is all but invisible—rather, the feminine is necessary but becomes displaced as a linguistic feature, a prelude in stylization. Thus the child prodigy essentially lacks this feminine rotundity: he starts too slim and will pine down to *macies* when he should grow robust. Too male too early, he will in the final event prove dry, arid, hard, and thin. Sterility is the inevitable outcome of a precocious self-sufficiency. The ideal child is thus not too quick, for he is the emblem of Dame Grammar herself, especially of all her resources, her overpowering, generative force that the maturing male will prune as his own *animus* and body harden from the promiscuous fullness of grammar and childhood.

Quintilian has presented himself as the permissive teacher of tender boys; like the students, he is not exercising judgment (or punishment) yet: "Each age has its own discipline, and work must be exacted and corrected in proportion to capacities. I used to tell boys who dared something a little bold or exuberant, 'For the time being that wins my praise, but the time will come when I shall not allow the like'; thus the boys took pleasure in their native ability and were not misled in judgment." (2.4.14: *Aliter autem alia aetas emendanda est, et pro modo uirium et exigendum et corrigendum opus. Solebam ego dicere pueris aliquid ausis licentius aut laetius laudare illud me adhuc, uenturum tempus quo idem non permitterem: ita et ingenio gaudebant et iudicio non fallebantur.*) The teacher's role here is to praise; the boys act with license, *licentius,* or as the second adverb, *laetius,* has it, fruitfully and abundantly (*laetus* is a word used to characterize style and also the act of natural, botanical growth).[52]

Quintilian returns to imagery of growth, even floral imagery, when speaking of the child's curriculum. In his second book, when discussing which authors to set boys who (though beginners in rhetoric) are ready for prose (2.5.1: *prima rhetorices rudimenta tractamus;* 2.5.2: *robusti fere iuvenes*), Quintilian imagines teachers taking one of two courses: "For some advocate the lesser authors, since they seem easier to understand; others advocate the more flowery prose styles on the grounds that they are better suited to nourishing the talents of the young scholars" (2.5.18: *Nam quidam illos minores, quia facilior eorum intellectus uidebatur, probauerunt, alii floridius genus, ut ad alenda primarum aetatium ingenia magis accommodatum*). Both choices, the lesser authors and the more florid prose, then, represent the first stage of a graduated curriculum.

The second choice (Quintilian approves of neither—he recommends Cicero and Livy somewhat jingoistically, the best first and always) corresponds not to the boys' understanding but to their *ingenia,* which we may understand here as their imitative faculties. Quintilian does not explicitly state his reasons for rejecting these approaches, but they seem to prolong childhood and the grammatical curriculum too long. A florid style is what the boys learned from the poets. Now while they have not achieved the state of judgment (Sallust, he says, is too hard to understand yet), they are ready for the style of Livy, Cicero, and other authors to the degree that they approximate Cicero (Quintilian writes more generally *candidissimum quemque et maxime expositum*).

Imitation of the florid and the fulsome style must give way to exposition and the shining clarity of the prose classics. Quintilian sounds a familiar warning: the boys must be kept from excess (2.5.21–26). Neither let them imitate the old prose authors (Cato and the Gracchi) nor the new style (he seems to be describing Seneca, although the characterization equally fits many of the declaimers preserved in the elder Seneca's collection). The potential consequences are predictable: on the one hand, reading the old authors will render the boys hypermasculine—the diction centers again on the erect, hard-muscled, emaciated: *horridi, durescere, ieiuni;* on the other hand, the moderns will send the young rhetoricians back to childhood, making them effeminate, oversoft, and overpassionate. The passage at 2.5.22 gives this warning while parodying the florid style of the moderns: "A second genre [of reading also to be avoided] quite unlike the first is the following: do not let them, ensnared as they are by the florets of this modern wantonness, be enervated by this sinful pleasure with the result that they are smitten by that oversweet genre so loved by boys for reason of its similarity to them" (*Alterum, quod huic diversum est, ne recentis huius lasciviae flosculis capti voluptate prava deleniantur, ut praedulce illud genus et puerilibus ingeniis hoc gratius quo proprius est adament*).[53] Quintilian even recommends that the reading of the moderns be put off; he fears the students will not keep the styles discrete (2.5.24: *curandum erit ne iis quibus permixta sunt inquinentur*—diction that suggests a bastard production; they will be stained by association with the wrong sort), and again warns that students have not yet reached the time of judgment (2.5.26: *ne imitatio iudicium antecederet,* "lest imitation anticipate judgment"). Children are naturally drawn to the florid and, even though they are in the hands of the rhetorician, have not graduated from *ingenium* to *iudicium,* from the generative to the manly.[54]

Quintilian has treated the child and his learning with a directness unparalleled in antiquity. Grammar is not presented as a technical subject, nor is it dismissed as a preliminary to rhetoric not worthy of the author's or a reader's regard. His justification, at a literary level, may be that Cicero had left him the topic of the early training of the student (Cicero had passed over it in the introductory remarks of his dialogue on the training of the ideal orator, *De or.* 1.23). The orator's dialogues had described the training and expertise of the *perfectus orator,* and Quintilian could now give a full account not of what that orator should be (Cicero at *Orat.* 18–19, for instance, depicts the orator as the perfect man, the man who lacks nothing) but of how he could come into being. His chief interest might then simply be as a witness to the long-standing, but little-regarded traditions of educating elite children. In fact, the child is acknowledged as a learning subject and agent whose proper development will determine an adult sense of power and authority.

Quintilian depreciates grammar as he appreciates the boy. The category of Roman childhood thus comes to trump the slighted subject of grammar (disparaged as technical and perhaps Greek). Quintilian does not name the early period of training *progymnasmata* or *praexercitamenta,* the standard term (attested later) for the prerhetorical curriculum. He does grant grammar teachers their role (they take first place, 1.4.1) and on occasion uses the Greek term for the art of grammar (2.1.4), but he seems to prefer periphrases, for example, "For Book One will treat those subjects that come before the duty of the rhetor" (1 pr. 21: *Nam liber primus ea quae sunt ante officium rhetoris continebit*), or in a similar avoidance of Greek, technical vocabulary, "the rudiments of speaking, which train the young not yet capable of rhetoric" (1.9.1: *dicendi primordia, quibus aetates nondum rhetorem capientes instituant*).[55] He refers to the topic most often by delineating the stage, not the age of the student, "the first age" (1.11.2, 1.pr.6) or, in a reference to the curriculum, "the first rudiments" (1.8.15). Quintilian thus marks grammar as preliminary without giving it a technical name or a definite age range. He also foreshortens the period of instructions—so as to introduce the boy to rhetorical training earlier and to have him overlap grammatical and rhetorical studies.

Again, his focus is on the success of the boy, not the demands or conventions of grammar. As soon as the boy can, he is to move on. The boy may pass from grammar when he is ready to read Livy and Cicero and to begin to curb the fulsome *copia* imitated, memorized, and internalized in the grammatical training. His studies are daunting, even encyclopedic, for Quintilian believes that the boy is capable of much and that the only fit training is toward that ideal orator, the man versed in all areas of knowledge.[56] Quintilian is interested in what grammar can do to move the boy along, but he also believes a natural correspondence links grammar with the child. The grammatical stage is important in that it marks the child, almost indelibly; the style of body and tongue learned here is all-important, and for Quintilian, goodness itself inheres in this style. It is not the case that grammar instruction furnishes neutral linguistic skills. Rather, the capacity for moral and manly speech takes root in the first age.

Grammar for its own sake seems a deviation and distraction. Thus Quintilian responds to the imagined objections of those who found grammar unnecessary for children or perhaps beneath the interest of the rhetorically minded: "The thought returns that some will object that what we have discussed is beneath notice and even a hindrance to students attempting something grander; and I myself do not believe one should descend to minute worryings and foolish hairsplitting, and I believe such things injure and diminish the boys' talents. But grammar will do no harm except where it is extraneous." (1.7.33–34: *Redit autem illa cogitatio, quosdam fore qui haec quae diximus parua nimium et impedimenta quoque maius aliquid agentibus putent: nec ipse ad extremam usque anxietatem et ineptas cauillationes descendendum atque his ingenia concidi et comminui credo. Sed nihil ex grammatice nocuerit nisi quod superuacuum est.*) Here grammar fails to nurture the child's talent. The child is not drawn to *eruditio*. Quintilian does not write of any natural attraction to linguistic and grammatical precision of speech or that assiduous investigation of poetic texts that marked, for instance, the learned poets Ennius and Lucilius. Quintilian's fears for the child return here (*concidi et comminui*): the ill-educated child is the broken child or the attenuated child. Too much grammar, like a beating or the overzealous imitation of the elder Cato, produces a hesitant, fearful, or thin child and style. These are moral consequences as well, since the child will not wish to study or to speak.[57]

The boy is an apprentice adult or adult-in-training whose psychology and even educational activities, but decidedly not his body and not yet his style of speaking, mimic the adult.[58] Quintilian describes carefully the qualities of this mimicry, since the boy does not have the mental capacities of the adult. The boy's motivation, his desire to outstrip his rivals, is the same as the adult orator's. Thus Quintilian, in describing the sort of student he would like, employs the vocabulary of Roman politics to enumerate the behavior of the ideal student: "Let that boy be handed over to me whom praise stirs, whom glory pleases, who when bested weeps. This is the boy who will be nourished by ambition, this the one whom harsh criticism will bite, this the one whom distinctions will stir, in this boy I shall never fear idleness." (1.3.7: *mihi ille detur puer, quem laus excitet, quem gloria iuvet, qui victus fleat. hic erit alendus ambitu, hunc mordebit obiurgatio, hunc honor excitabit, in hoc desidiam numquam verebor.*) The schoolboy is a little Cicero, not victimized by the verbal slander of Roman politics but stirred to action and revenge. Quintilian's expression here is rhetorical in its anaphora and asyndeton and in the pileup, the climax, of its abstract nouns. He has cast the Roman political landscape in miniature—little wonder then that the master does not waste words on grammar. He has described grammar's exercises for the child and thinks of grammar as a stage, but one whose importance consists in preparation of certain verbal arts and which must be used to foster an abundant speaking and writing style and a competitiveness that is at once fierce and yet emotional, responsive to failure, to criticism, and to an audience.

The life of a child is a series of engagements with texts (and audiences). A child speaks fables, reads Virgil, does not declaim. The advanced child is at work reading Cicero and Livy. The biologism of the prepubescent child and pubescent adolescent, and the social and ritual delineation of child and youth, visible at school itself through dress, are subordinated to a textually graduated, audible, and legible growth. In the process of maturation Quintilian does not draw attention to ritual, social, physical, or legal changes in the child. Admittedly, these are not his subject, but in the text of his manual they are eliminated, as the category of the child is redefined in essentially linguistic terms. Maturation is thus not an inevitable, natural process nor quite a socially prescribed rite of passage. Maturation is the teacher-led formation of speech and, through speech, of character. The able teacher can see through the rude body of the child the shape of true *ingenia*. The teacher has the tools to make these *ingenia* more and more visible until with the completed man, the orator, all the community shall acknowledge his virtues. Further, volition and judgment mark the advanced student and so divide the grammatical from the rhetorical age.

Quintilian's greatest innovation may be the articulation of the child's propensity to be educated, a disposition to docility that is both natural and social, a combination of the inborn qualities of *ingenium* and *imitatio*. What has attracted so many readers to Quintilian is his promise of *eruditio*, the process that will sharpen *ingenia* into the orator's weapons. *Eruditio*—that careful discerning of talents and shaping of them from the rough—is what the master teacher has been doing for twenty years, what he does in resisting the cries to publish quickly, and what his book will do for the coming generations.

There is a certain, stark appeal to the plan for education. Quintilian, however, never writes, as we might be tempted, following Locke's insistence on the primacy of sensation, that the child strives to differentiate and understand the stimuli coming in, tries to understand and discover his world. There is no pull to speech or to naming as there would be for Augustine. The infant is not presented in that gripping fashion that has resounded with so many readers: the child longing for speech is like Augustine and his reader longing for knowledge, for insight, ultimately for the *logos* that is God. Quintilian's child is likened to raw matter, not vicious or defective, but unformed. He is that which must be shaped. Like all human beings, his *vox* distinguishes him from the animals. He does have *ingenia*. These need sharpening. He does have desire. This needs direction (just as Quintilian's readers have desires that must be mediated by the master). And he is an imitative creature, ready to repeat—a quality that the teacher must exploit. Unshaped, passionate, memori-

ous, and imitative, the boy awaits the master's direction. Quintilian knows what to
do when in order to make this unqualified *puer* into a *vir bonus dicendi peritus.*
Quintilian writes to satisfy his readers' and the student's desire. By treating schooling as a life, a natural sequence of maturation, Quintilian excludes the other possibility, the unschooled life, as unlivable (or at least not worthy of consideration).
Fundamentally, that life could not create a moral speaking subject.

We have followed the student from home to school. The strong claim of Quintilian's text has rhetoric assert as its special function the shaping of the child into the
ideal man. At the same time, it excludes forces, institutions, and agents that any modern, and indeed many ancients, would find significant. It is a bookish claim, of course,
to insist that books shape minds (as to imply that bodies follow minds). It is also a
masculine claim to insist that the teacher's gaze can see and direct the soft child toward manhood. Both these claims are fundamental to Quintilian's new rhetoric.

I have argued that a particular valuation of the child is an essential aspect of Quintilian's conception of education. He did not put it this way. Rather, by means of definition, a rhetorical mode in itself, rhetoric is construed in a way that he meant to
be both theoretically original and a return to a native Roman tradition.[59] Thus in
book 2 Quintilian surveys definitions of rhetoric so as to arrive at Cato's *dictum* of
"a good man skilled in speaking."[60] Cato is the final member in a rhetorical climax
of definers and definitions of rhetoric. At the same time as Cato's definition subsumes the others, Quintilian insists on a moral dimension to the orator. Thus he
can imagine a totalizing rhetoric that embraces all subjects and does not cede to
philosophy or to tradition, to Greece or to *Roma antiqua,* the capacity to form the
mind and character properly. The composite account of the child-learner defines
the preadult human being essentially as *puer imitans;* like man, *vox* distinguished
him from the beasts, but his *vox* lacks *iudicium,* choice, volition, and restraint. At
every stage of his education, judgment is employed, but the puerile age requires a
father's surrogate to supply judgment, to select what is to be imitated, all the while
turning and returning the child to the labor of learning. Quintilian develops a comprehensive apologetics for rhetoric and rhetorical training through notices about
the proper development of the child and the insistence that only the good man can
be an orator. Quintilian equips Roman schooling with a finished argument for its
efficacy and indeed its very existence.

The "moral" dimension allegedly so vital to the orator is in part a fantasy of this
apologetics. Fathers and a patriarchal elite are assured that education marks the good
as good, the *boni* who are at once a social class, a moral group, and an ideal readership. But moral qualities—ethical habits, categories of people and behavior,
words and styles appropriate to different characters and different genres, the practices of moralization—are most certainly part of rhetorical training. Rhetoric is a
moral art not because Aristotle said lies were not rhetoric but because, in Quintilian's thinking, rhetoric needs a community, and in the actual exercises rhetoric imag-

ines community, human relations, and the power of speech to mediate these. Where one might speak of education as civilized and civilizing speech, Quintilian is not much drawn to theorize about the social role of rhetoric: he for the most part is stuck on the idea that rhetoric forms the individual toward a norm of speaking. Nonetheless, Quintilian's apologetics circumscribes the sphere of his institution's authority. Rhetoric defines the complete man, and so rhetorical theory thinks about virility and power as much as about appropriate or persuasive words.

Chapter 7 will address rhetorical habitus, the transformation and internalization of "judgment" as Quintilian would have it. Before we leave the manual, the prescriptive medium of child rearing and child thinking, however, I should state that I believe Quintilian was right in seeing the continuity of the rhetorical process. A convenient term to describe the rhetorician's inculcation of work habits and social attitudes may be *textualization*.[61] The next chapter addresses directly this process of textualization, the movement through the series of exercises of the Roman curriculum and the internalization of the modes of representation effected in the very composition and reperformance of the exercises.

To gauge what a student takes from his course of grammatical and rhetorical training is in fact far more difficult than Quintilian imagined. The student does not simply "sharpen his wits," nor does each student succeed in transforming himself into an orator. Not only the individual result but also the social good achieved by education can be far different from what the native participant or observer opines. Yet the claim to produce orators cannot be so easily set aside. Certainly, it represents an ideal and so is of interest as a compelling cultural fantasy, but it has also embodied and tried to instill day by day, through exercise and exhortation, definite values, habits, and routines. At least in the Roman world, before the coming of a codex culture, elite training aimed to produce speaking subjects and not primarily the more exclusively readerly and writerly subjectivity of late antiquity and the early Middle Ages. Much of what was taught and how it was taught may not have succeeded in producing a fertile *copia,* that love for traditional forms of writing, talking, and understanding. Yet insofar as fathers and sons pursued Quintilian's methods or assumed that his goals were worthy, they joined a culture. Such participants in an elite education are also practicing what they take as the defining difference of the free. The next chapters explore the subjectivity of the ancient student, both the ideal subjectivity that teacher and father and perhaps student believed the student was assuming and the practical subjectivity, the nexus of attitude and habit, that the exercise demanded.

Quintilian has certainly offered the greatest guide to this education, but he has also provided a compelling emotional and intellectual rationale for rhetorical education. The child drives him to write as that same child impels the father to educate him. Quintilian has contributed more than a synthetic pedagogics. The idea of the *animus puerilis* is new and of great consequence. The child is measured by his school activity: he or she reads, now he or she reads Cicero, at last he declaims moot court cases. In providing his field of expertise with a theoretical explanation, Quintilian has used the child as an undergirding conceptualization. He writes the child into maturity and, in a way reminiscent of Plutarch, in so doing gathers the faculties of father and mother, nurse, slaves, and pedagogue under the function of the master teacher. The child becomes a virtual imperative, demanding resources and a rigorous program and requiring and displaying the father's diligent—if delegated—supervision.

6

Grammar and the Unity of Curriculum

Describing the curriculum of a school can be like describing the plot of a novel. The successful summarist reduces the rich texture of discourse to a narrative list. Among the losses arising from the reduction: a summary list suppresses viewpoint— it is the particular, often retrospective scheme of analysis and discourse of one person—and the list of events suggests an evenly paced, progressive narrative. If a novel is not reducible to plot, schooling ought not to be reduced to that other textual list, curriculum, and, to complicate our analogy, the school is not simply a text or a series of linguistic occurrences. As with other modes of analysis in the treatise tradition, describing a curriculum as a canon of texts or as a series of task-oriented textual processes (writing sentences, reading fables, speaking theses) treats the process of education as the graduated booking of the child into the man, as if to say that child is immature when he can merely copy out lines from a book and has become mature when he can read a difficult book or speak like a book. The listlike narrative of curriculum suggests that it is the cultural equivalent of biological maturation, with discernible stages that anticipate and contribute to the final, perfected growth. In fact, accounts of curriculum contribute to schooling's narrative of order and success, although it is not at all clear that learning occurs in such an ideal, progressive, and verifiable mode.

APPROACHES TO CURRICULAR STUDIES

We live in an age in which assessment—the testing of schoolchildren, the visitation of classrooms and observation of classroom teaching, and the evaluation of schools— is politically mandated and has become an industry in itself, complete with ready-made forms, advice-mongering videos, surveys, and treatises. In addition, in the final act of rationalization, these processes of certification have become objects of academic study and debate in the university. At the heart of this complex set of practices lies a belief that the classroom, as at times the wider school, pictures the society in miniature. Consequently, the interests and the parties involved in the study of education are both earnest and varied. The scholastic microcosm is investigated with the zeal of the anthropologist amid an exotic tribe, the psychologist confronted with the nascent mind, the criminologist with derelicts in the making, and the worried parent with visions of what her child may or could be. We should not be surprised, then, that multiple methodologies are applied to schooling and the development of the young scholar. In addition, from the institutional perspective, academic research and the publishing industry share an interest in discovering and propagating new methods (and distributable forms and reports) of analysis and new cures. Schooling never pursues a single objective. The variety of interests and of ends frustrates the theorist and reformer and impels new approaches and "solutions."[1]

Certainly, the school has provided a fascinating spectacle. In need of new generations, and thus dependent on parents and on state or church authorities for the guarantee of new clientele, the school has been relatively open to inspection, admitting the nonparticipant more readily than certain courts or houses of worship. New schooling has drawn the curious; it has repeatedly been the place to view reform and the future in the making. The elder Seneca reports Roman notables visiting school speech recitals; the younger Pliny reports his invited participation in the search for a schoolteacher.[2] Yet the analyst of the school should be more than a visiting celebrity, just as his or her understanding of curriculum hopes to be more than an overview of the serial encounter of the student with distinct exercises or books. For all the observation of a class's activity, for all the generalizable data of the individually completed survey and questionnaire, the investigator of schooling hopes to verify what is an internal process—the student learning.

The following three chapters ask how the child, boy and girl, encounters and experiences, assimilates and resists, the structuring habits of the school. We still study the contents of a curriculum but without the assumption that a curriculum is a running course in which the probationary scholar hurtles past one test after another, in a progress toward a single, well-marked goal. Textbook analysis is still practiced, and not solely because of a linguistic propensity—that deeply felt belief that what is learned at school can be gauged, directed, or censored by controlling both what is read and the exercises testing or directing that reading. Modern educational research has contributed a sharp awareness of the importance of the form and context of curricular material. The set text is only the most traditional manifestation of the media of presentation, and in studying it, we examine content and strive to reconstruct the delivery of that content, the pace and manner in which it is to be learned, the description of learning that it communicates, and the sort of learning that it invites in its graphic layout, its use of tables, pictures, or drills. Such an approach, as much the result of literary and art historical studies as of cognitive psychology, hopes to uncover the norms latent in the text and in that text's use by the student. The modern researcher looks beyond (and sometimes, it has to be said, overlooks) what has been learned of, for example, algebraic equations to ask how the word problem and its schematic, illustrative presentation influenced the student's attitude toward learning, notions of gender roles and norms of behavior, and even his or her sense of self. Does the exercise communicate a concept of the normal? These questions, which underlie much contemporary educational research, tend to underestimate the artificial and abnormal qualities of the teaching exercise—the use of fantasy, of abstract and extreme settings and characters, of the monstrous, nonsensical, and humorous. The discussions below of fable and declamation try to approach characters, settings, and plots as cultural extremes.

A sensitivity to meta-learning (although I would prefer the term "the rhetoric of learning") is nothing new: Plato illustrated his theory of learning with the anecdote of a slave boy who is led by drawings in sand to realization of a geometric proof. The conclusion at the level of content is that as a slave he is unschooled and so has recollected the knowledge (thanks to the soul's prior life); but rhetorically, the message is an *a fortiori* argument: if a slave can do this, so much more should a free man (and how much more with the right guidance—yet the unphilosophical man, Anytus in this dialogue, will not learn, despite his free status). And, of course, Plato's readers are also learning to leave unasked why slave and free should not learn alike and be treated alike, and instead to view the slave as an instrument in the free man's way of life.[3]

Critical analyses of textbooks, whether the theoretical studies of contemporary America by Alan Luke or the historical studies of Latin schoolbooks in trecento Florence by Paul Gehl, follow ultimately the pioneering and much-disputed conclusions of D. Bernstein, who redescribed the school curriculum as a restricted code, in contrast to the unrestricted code learned at home. This basic observation cannot simply be reduced to the idea of a home language and a school language. Bernstein's terminology and the arguments for reform that derive from it portray the difference between home and school as artificial and arbitrary. School code is in essence a means of social distinction by which the middle class protects and replicates its language and norms. Reformers, with the aid of sociolinguists, argue that the language of an underclass is equally a language and that difficulties in achievement at school can be ascribed to the novelty and strangeness of the restricted code for those who have not learned it or its precursor at home. The efforts to teach in the vernacular, to tie learning to read to the student's current language, and to eschew a middle-class normative framework remain debated issues, but without doubt they animated a generation of teachers and researchers.[4] It must be said that Walter J. Ong, although he did not have the same influence on educators, had in 1959 anticipated the anthropological approach to the language of schooling. His study of Latin teaching in the Renaissance stressed the divide made between home and school, boys and men, and women and men through the use of Latin.[5]

In fact, the strong distinction between restricted and unrestricted codes and the reductive view that school simply tries to inculcate an agreed-upon elitist code cannot be maintained, but such research provoked scholars to consider how school language and school texts constituted codes both social and cognitive. Thus we investigate the models of social relations and interaction, the notions of agency and appropriate behavior, implicit in school exercises. Roman schooling sought to inculcate in the elite a consciousness that to them was given the privilege and responsibility of mediating the interests of all of society. This differs perhaps from modern bourgeois school texts, which have been accused of representing their society, a normative nuclear family, as representative of all society. The far less homogenizing Roman exercise, as we shall see, admits slave, foreigner, women, and freedman, as well as a variety of professions, not all respectable, that is, to be pursued by the scholar in later life, and even purports to communicate the points of view of social and political subordinates. This seems a more elaborate social apologetics, wherein division and strife are learned, and where the medium of learning establishes and anticipates the role of the governing class in arbitrating society.

In addition, the ancient exercise differs from the modern and from some medieval school materials because it is not in form a textbook.[6] Much contemporary curricular analysis attends to the ideological presuppositions inherent in the form of the textbook. The insightful work of Alan Luke, who explores both the ways the textbook models social relations and the ways it invites its reader's interaction, calls for a new form of the textbook, one that, following Umberto Eco's formulation, is an open not a closed text, that is, one that encourages its reader's engagement, embellishment, and resistance. Luke sets at the head of one of his studies this sententia of Roland Barthes: "For what can be oppressive in our teaching is not, finally, the knowledge or culture it conveys, but the discursive forms through which we propose them."[7] Having Basque or Algerian children learn French in a mode and place foreign to their native culture may be oppressive, but so is their learning the content of French history in a state school from a textbook published in Paris. Barthes's point of course was that schooling teaches a medium of knowledge, expertise, and elitism that is more formative and tenacious than the learning of content.

For the academic, the textbook is no doubt an emblem of reproduction whose form and content are outside his or her control: printed by the thousands, disseminated easily, an aide to the professional teacher but seldom authored by him or her, the textbook is one vehicle of educational standardization and censorship. For the professor, some resentment may attend the textbook: it symbolizes pre-expert but widespread instruction, the material for high schools, for introductory college courses, in short for the state of a discipline that the advanced teacher-cum-researcher often tries to deflect, moderate, and nuance. The textbook thus seems to attract interest not simply as a vehicle of education or as the lucrative branch of modern academic publishing, but as an account of an academic field that requires the professor's voice as supplement. So colleagues debate endlessly which is the authoritative or most effective textbook, a debate matched by the ambition of the publisher to issue a comprehensive version, which of course will soon need revision and republication. It is then an object for the teacher, a committee of teachers, a board of education, or a ministry of education to select from among competing sets, and, by its very ubiquitousness, its exercises, definitions, and comprehensive representations of the subject at hand, a homogenizing and labor-saving medium that frees the teacher from providing a guiding narrative. Its closedness seems endlessly normative, iterable, and a guarantor of success.

A single book usually suffices for the modern student to pass a particular stage of the curriculum (this expectation presupposes a certain kind of reading, one for the most part silent and self-contained, directed toward the specific end task of the examination and the sorts of recall and writing it requires). The ancient exercise is a more open text than the modern textbook or even the workbook. Certainly, in learning to read and write or later in the technical exercise in memory and delivery, the ancient student was required to demonstrate strict adherence to the model provided. Lines were to be copied exactly; memorization was aimed at exact, verbatim reproduction. There was much rote learning and rule following, and even when he came to declaim, the schoolboy had to adhere to the set plot of the case (the thesis). We should not imagine an open and inventive process, although as we shall see set texts were modified, abridged, expanded, and inset into larger narratives. Ultimately, the adolescent speaker worked to develop a recognizably superior and distinctive style. Yet we must distinguish a rigorous and set curriculum from a standardized one.

No ancient textbook survives because no such standard book was produced and distributed. The idea of designing a book for pedagogic ends certainly did occur, although most instances of this are from late antiquity. In ancient education, no single book replaced a course of instruction. The late antique Latin grammar manual, Donatus's *Ars minor*, comes closest to qualifying as a textbook, but the handwritten schoolbook cannot be approached as if it were equivalent to the modern printed textbook. Quintilian's book was a guide for teachers and fathers; and in the declamations attributed to him or in Priscian's account of how to teach the opening of the *Aeneid* or in the extant guides to the preliminary compositions, we have model texts, books for the teacher, parts of which were to be copied by the student.[8] True, the research methods of scholars of modern education adduce questions of the normative framework implicit in an exercise, but the model of modern capitalism, with its abundance of identical objects amid a set of choices, and in particular the modern textbook with graphics and print so voluminous, precise, and complex as to be impossible for a student to imitate, do not correspond to the school materials of the Roman world. We can and should apply categories that are current in research on the modern textbook. What survives of the ancient curricular material can be fruitfully examined in terms of story structure, types of agents, indeed notions of agency, the modeling of the importance and role of the educated, the process of identification whereby the reader-student is invited to identify with the agent of the story, and social norms and background knowledge.

In fact, the curriculum often did not require the reading for writing outcome that the textbook presupposes (where the student reads in order to write a précis or analysis or essay, and the student's writing becomes the chief mode of evaluation). Copying, memorizing, and speaking played a far more prominent role in the ancient routine of learning. Since silent reading did not constitute the medium of instruction, we need not follow the rather deterministic analysis of textbook research, which presumes the communication of a strong ideological message in a standardized written and graphic form to a receptive, passive audience of individual readers. No standardization of materials pertained within the ancient school or city, much less within Italy or the empire. Verses to be memorized, for instance, could be read from a papyrus roll or taken down on a wax tablet from a teacher's dictation; they could be copied upon a potsherd or a piece of wood. Despite the variety of material supports and the attendant varieties of reading and writing, we should not assume an impoverished schooling marked by a scarcity of books and writing materials.[9] In the Roman school, as in the Roman city, writing spaces were abundant, but not homogeneous. At a certain stage we can imagine many a student had access to a copy of Virgil's *Aeneid*. A few well-to-do students will have owned papyrus rolls. Far more would have copied on a wax tablet from dictation, and many, thanks to memory training, could have done without any material text.

A student's text in such a world is something to be embellished, condensed, glossed, recited, remembered, erased, or written over. The student's writing is a kind of practice and routine—ephemeral in comparison to the textbook; personal, not in the romantic sense, but in what I will call the authentic sense, that is, a version made one's own, even though made at times to be inspected and approved, but made also at times for no other's eyes and simply an aid to memorization or the learning of vocabulary or practice in handwriting.

GRAMMAR THEORIZED

In the examination of the first stages of schooling, where the student will encounter fable and proverb, Homer and Virgil, we will find no single text occupying as central a role as the textbook in modern pedagogy. The systematicity of first schooling arose not from any standardized textbook, but from the curriculum and rationale that grammar provided. Grammar neither encountered the disdain in which it has languished in modern pedagogic and linguistic thinking, nor had the sublime status accorded it in the Middle Ages. Paul Gehl, Martin Irvine, and G. A. Padley among others present an understanding of grammar as a cognitive system and an intellectual routine.[10] Grammar and rhetoric provided at once a rationale for learning, an explanation of the relation of language to reality and society, and the content of instruction and learning. After all, the very language of grammar and rhetoric— imitation, subordination, impersonation, the appropriate—constitutes an abstract vocabulary with which to understand the self, the group, even the political and the religious. More than merely the medium for access to culture, it was the authoritative discourse of the cultured, the rationalized network of textual practices.

This centrality of grammar was not acknowledged in antiquity. Writers of the classical and early imperial ages did not credit the achievement of their writings or the structure of their understanding to the system of grammar. Grammar was considered a complex of the rules for correct reading, writing, and speaking, and as the first presentation of literature, and was the less exalted propaedeutic to rhetoric and, for a few, to philosophy. Nonetheless, "grammar" was the formative stage in literate education. Certainly, the ancient author would have thought of himself as eloquent, trained in rhetoric, not like some schoolmaster full of grammatical detail and quibbling over minutiae. Quintilian the rhetor put grammar in her subordinate place, where she remained handmaid both to idiomatic usage and to rhetoric and was decidedly not authoritative on her own: *aliud est grammatice aliud est Latine loqui* ("And so I think it well said that it is one thing to speak Latin, quite another to speak by the rules," 1.6.27).[11]

While grammar and rhetoric constituted a continuum of training, as Quintilian saw, Quintilian's distinction of the Latin speaker from the grammatical speaker reflects a truth of ancient schooling. The educated saw themselves as speakers with a knowledge and expertise far in advance of those so unfortunate as to have only the linguistic resources of the grammatical curriculum. Yet grammar deserves more credit. In the far-flung empire, the literate elite were not all practicing rhetoricians or lawyers but writers of every stripe. The rhetorical curriculum, however, encouraged the view that the orator stood at the head of society. In fact, the correct writer was probably of greater service.

The *progymnasmata* offer the best witness to the educational program and process of grammatical instruction. The exercises, which lead the students from simple reading and writing exercises to more sustained composition, provide an explanation of their purpose and sequence, and sample texts. In reading these guides (or hearing them as the teacher's lecture), the student is inaugurated into the rationale for the hierarchy of the long series of studies.

In their excellent studies of ancient education Henri Marrou and S. F. Bonner have provided syntheses of the course of instruction. Bonner especially sifted and examined Quintilian and the writers of *progymnasmata* so as to follow the child from home learning to the grammar-school teacher and on to the rhetorician.[12] Whereas Bonner cautiously reminded his reader that particular functions could not be exclusively identified with discrete stages of teaching, A. D. Booth directly refuted the notion of a strong divide between primary and secondary education, that separating the *grammatistēs* from the *grammaticus*.[13] Marrou had noted the tendency throughout the history of education for advanced exercises gradually to percolate down to earlier stages of education.[14] Clearly, there were many ways to educate even the elite. Quintilian, for example, recommended that the rhetoricians reclaim from the grammatical teachers certain exercises.[15] In Bonner's account of the classical and early imperial periods, the child learned the alphabet and elementary reading at home; he or she practiced writing and learned to read poetry at grammatical school (and learned arithmetic there or perhaps under a special teacher, the *calculator*). Passing on to the rhetorician's school, the student exchanged poetry for prose and embarked upon the series of composition exercises known as the *progymnasmata*.

By Quintilian's day the grammarian was teaching far more, and the rhetorician had become all but a specialist in declamation. The précis of education is no doubt true to schoolboy experience, that is to say, the child is alphabetic before school, at first school he copies difficult texts that he is not meant to understand, and then he changes teachers for the final stage of learning to compose and to speak.[16] The important question is not whether we can discern the separate teachers and divisions of curriculum (such standardization is a feature of later schools, e.g., Jesuit schools or those of the cities of Renaissance Italy) but whether we can deduce the commonality of experience, method, and outlook that made the citizen of Cordoba and the citizen of Rome feel they had a liberal education. The educated man and woman started by reading Homer and Virgil, could quote from memory passages of verse, and shared a particular academic training in how to comment upon poetry, but their education should not be reduced to the least common denominator of a canon of set texts or the forms of discourse (e.g., commentary by gloss or by etymology) upon this cultural capital.

Rather, the *progymnasmata* and other directives in ancient treatises suggest the mentality that the teachers wished to produce. Teachers' wishes do not equal student practices (*credite experto*), and so the pronouncements of the theorists must be weighed against the practices of the child in daily scholastic routine. Thus, rather than redescribe the sequence of an ancient curriculum, I propose through study of a series of exercises to focus on the transformation of the child's expressive abilities. I want to emphasize three foci in these changes: textual cohesion, story schema, and categorical thinking and training in persona.

Textual cohesion means more and less than the principles of storytelling. It reflects a human tendency to try to make sense of speech, facts, observations, and even shapes. In the school exercises, it is a useful term for the goal of a process in which given elements (the barest outlines of plot or the previously learned supply of maxims, anecdotes, or rhetorical figures) are deployed as narrative building units. As a subset of the techniques of constructing narratives, the student's efforts to memorize, combine, and contextualize reported speech are particularly important. What were in origin nonnarrative *sententiae* (sayings copied and memorized at the outset of schooling) will be furnished with a specific speaker and context in the *chreia* and will in turn form the core of the stylistic recasting of fable once the student supplies two or three speakers with dueling *sententiae* and frames the dialogue with an opening or concluding moral (*sententia* yet again). This practice develops longer and more cohesive narratives. The narrative is more cohesive both because of techniques of combination and transition and because a specific, topical setting and interpretation have been added. This last quality makes clear that formal changes such as length of utterance, subordination of syntax, and the introduction of more than one speaker cannot be separated from the development of story schema itself.

Story schema refers not simply to the advanced typology or structural or thematic analysis of the narratives used in school exercises. I will use story schema to describe the learned predisposition to represent the outside world, the individual, and even the process of learning as a story.[17] Schooling, and not just schooling, has shaped the young to understand and produce certain sorts of stories. Just as the production of a story is the successful end product of the school exercise, so the child will increasingly understand story as a grammatical-rhetorical form. As nursery story and subliterary fable are to be replaced by school forms, so the child learns to prefer certain kinds of story. Both the shape of the given elements—the way certain situations and characters are liable to make a story—and the process of stylization constitute story schema. Indeed, story production does not so much mean inventing fictions of one's own as varying standard elements. To anticipate: the student learns to compose so as to remedy an insufficient treatment (the subliterary, the undeveloped) and a social or categorical impasse (the threat of violence that seems incapable of being fixed with words, like the hunger of the wolf, the aggression of the lion, or later in declamatory exercises the act of a parricide or of an uncaring and unjust father).[18]

Categorical thinking and training in persona are most directly exercised at the final stage of education, declamation, which has as its animating crisis some impasse in social, familial, and political categories that drives the student to write and speak. The student is presented with an intractable situation: the father who ransomed his son from pirates now forbids the son from marrying his deliverer, the pirate's daughter. The definition of social and familial obligations combined with fantasies of escape from the father and entrance into sexuality make a potent, unpredictable composition exercise. Simply obeying the father, repeating his *dicta* and not inventing one's own argument, will never do. The piece must be written and performed, and to do so the boy must learn how to divide the case into a set of critical issues. The training in analysis that underlies these divisions requires the student to apply abstract categories to particular plots. Faced with a seemingly clear-cut case of a guilty client, he may, for example, apply the technique of definition: Does the action fit the definition of murder? Whereas this categorical system, the stasis or status system, may appear a rigid, quasi-legal structure, in fact, it is the final application of the technique the school has trained him in all along—imitation. When he takes the given facts and re-represents them, he engages in the most sophisticated stage of paraphrase, which was both an individual exercise of the *progymnasmata* and more generally the technique that underlies all the stylization of the grammatical and rhetorical curriculum.[19] The declaimer must animate the bare exercise with voices that suit the set speakers and express their motives. As he had the lamb and the fox plead their cases in fable, now he gives the appropriate voices to stern fathers, dutiful sons, stepmothers, heroes of the state, priests, freedmen, and prostitutes. This developed training in persona compels him to express viewpoints that are internally consistent but in conflict with other characters in the case. The speaker ventriloquizes the conflicts of state and family in a way that develops his own claim to authority—the ability to speak for others and to reduce important conflicts in the family and in the state to verbal duels between men.

The present and the succeeding two chapters examine the development of textual cohesion, the qualities of the story schema encouraged by the school, and the underlying analysis by a categorical thinking about persona. The three concerns recur, although with different prominence, in each chapter. Studying model exercises rather than teacher's descriptions of the curriculum offers a better opportunity for detecting traces of students' use and practice, although the exercises are neither archival records nor the equivalent of the modern researcher's observations. In sum, the three chapters devoted to fable, sententia, and declamation examine the formation of the child as composer. I begin with fable because fable provides both the first time the child gets to tell (better, to retell) a story and a first longer writing (one that is not simply the repetition of set lines). This liberating exercise is also probably the first reward, the first time a sequence of exercises seems to make sense (i.e., has a complete outcome and one that seems substantially the student's work). Fable thus anticipates much of the justification of the difficult work of schooling: arduous obedience and routine are seen as a deferral of reward and as a practice in self-direction. This introduction to discipline comes at a moment of relearning: stories of animals, earlier the amusement of childhood, are now a medium for learning about learning. Part of this lesson is how to transform the familiar (subliterary and domestic) story or experience into a school form. After a discussion of fable, I turn back to the sententia, an earlier exercise but one that itself provides mininarratives of the movement from powerless student to powerful speaker. Understanding fable as an exercise in narrative squares well with modern approaches to first reading stories, and so I begin there rather than with the memorizing of maxims, which is customarily dismissed as rote learning or at best heavy-handed moralizing. But the world of the fable will make clear that sententia was an important element in composing a moral self, which is the schooled subjectivity that treats the self as the object and font of a moralizing discourse.[20] With the sententia the boy will adopt for the first time an authoritative persona whose speech is a series of commands. Chapter 7 explores a tremendously popular and long-lived school book of sententiae, the *Distichs of Cato,* and seeks to understand the microcosm of commands and obedience, faithful copying and study, that the schools' use of this proverbial literature encouraged. In declamation he will learn to speak other voices, but he still seeks an authority to speak as the powerful orator, a new Cato or Cicero.

THE FABLE'S LESSONS I:
ONLY CONNECT, OR TEACHING COHERENCE

When learning to read and write, the student began with the names of the letters and moved on to recognizing and reproducing their shapes, to write the simplest possible combinations of these (the nonsense syllables) and to study written sentences whose meaning or at least some of whose vocabulary was beyond him.[21] This process initiated the ancient student in the movement of education. Exercises are presented as items in a graduated, progressive whole.[22] The student need not now understand all that he does. To progress he must move up the line of exercises by demonstrating a faithful representation of the assigned lesson. In combination, the exercises themselves, the system of rewards and punishments, and the comments and assumptions of fellow students, pedagogues, siblings, and parents would have contributed to the sense that schooling is a progression from simple to greater things with an underlying coherence that will gradually be appreciated. Similarly, the *progymnasmata* set as the basic, initial sequence the series maxim, *chreia,* fable.[23] In formal terms, as a graduated progression in composition, these exercises teach the student how to make a narrative. The individual exercise creates the building blocks of the later compositions (the sort of thing to be inserted into a larger structure—where, when, how, and why would be taught later). But as an immediate sequence, occupying probably less than a year's time, the series develops smaller units into larger units. The sentence gives way to the paragraph as the unit of expression. Indeed, the later exercise cannibalistically recombines and subordinates the prior.

In practice this means that the boy first wrote and memorized a sentence: in Greek, a line from Menander, "Whom the gods love dies young," or the much copied "Work hard lest you be beaten"; in Latin, sayings like the collection attributed to Cato. Quintilian urges that one choose verses for writing practice that are moral and not frivolous (1.1.35); perhaps he meant to discourage the use of verses taken from the mimes, like the extant collection of Publilius Syrus, although that collection's alphabetical order suggests a later, nonscholastic reordering of the material. The *Distichs of Cato* begin:

> Si deus est animus nobis, ut carmina dicunt,   1.1
> hic tibi praecipue sit pura mente colendus.
>
> Since our intellect is divine, as the poems tell,
> its cultivation with purity of mind should be your special obligation.

The student receives regular encouragement to scholarly diligence and personal self-improvement:

> Instrue praeceptis animum, ne discere cessa;   3.1
> nam sine doctrina vita est quasi mortis imago.
>
> Fortify your mind with precepts; do not stop learning:
> for the unlettered life is a likeness of death.

Repeatedly, the verse imperatives direct the young student to focus on the self and his or her own words and text making:

> Cum recte vivas, ne cures verba malorum,   3.2
> arbitri non est nostri, quid quisque loquatur.
>
> Since you would live morally, do not worry about the words of the wicked;
> it is not for us to control what anyone else says.

The maxims of the elder Cato were used in schools probably before the early third century A.D.[24] Aphorisms like the austere and minimalist rhetorical advice *Rem tene, verba sequentur,* "Stick to the matter at hand, the words will come," could be directly reworked into *chreiae,* sayings stories. Thus one could append Cato's line to "When Cato was asked what he thought of fancy Hellenistic rhetoric, he said . . . " The *chreia* takes a one-liner and gives it a dramatic context, such as "Diogenes, on leaving the baths said 'No' to the one who asked if many men were bathing, but 'Yes' to another who asked if a large crowd was there."[25] The world of the *chreia* is transfused with literariness and education itself. Quintilian and Theon took their sentences from literary works. The characters are often Socrates, Isocrates, or Diogenes the Cynic; the topics often youth and education, and encounters of the educated with the uneducated. In the *chreia* the mention of the protagonist and his challenger provides a minimal setting, whereas the sentence has almost no context. The maxim's general applicability is its virtue; its difficulty, at least on Quintilian's recommendation, should come from its erudite vocabulary: with well-chosen *sententiae,* the beginning student could learn glosses as well as moral sentiments drawn from literature.[26]

The fable like the *chreia* requires a context, not "once Socrates was asked by an impudent boy," but "once upon a time there was an ass who wanted to go hunting with a lion." Just as with the *chreia,* the character type affects behavior—so the student learns types of character from reading and repeating the context given to words and then learns composition by fitting words to character (although in fable the role of the animal in the structure of the fable and not stereotypical character dictates behavior; for example, the sheep or goat is not always the victim, the fox can be tricked or disappointed in his hunting). Even at these elementary stages, composition requires a selection of registers so that, for instance, ass and lion speak their appropriate words. In practice, composition most fundamentally depends on a technique of combination that directs the student not so much to invent context as to find the right way to relate two or three snippets of direct speech, support these few speakers with a slim indication of setting, and perhaps sum up the whole with a final maxim.

The *chreia* and the fable thus share a strong formal similarity: both narrate a single episode and conclude with a sententia. In fact, the story structure of *chreia* and fable is similar: setting, problem, and solution.[27] At the level of plot, the solution may be that the wolf eats the sheep, but the writer's conclusion comes in the moralizing close—the maxim that expresses the moral and connects the fable to the world of the reader and writer. Here the writer practices evaluation of his narrative content by offering what we would call authorial comment, and this comment takes the form of the maxim.[28]

Although the ancient writers do not comment upon this, sententia, *chreia,* and fable have another formal alliance. The sententia is quite often direct, unattributed speech, examples of which the student reads, writes, and memorizes. He will redistribute this supply of memorized citations throughout his life in writings, speeches, and conversations. He will hear and know and use quotations from Menander, Sophocles, Cato, or Virgil. The first stages of the *progymnasmata* rehearse this use of speech: with the *chreia* the student learns how to attribute *dicta* and with the fable has his first practice in deploying rival, agonistic quoted speech, for the fable quite often takes a form one step more complex than the *chreia*'s structural formula of when asked A by speaker Y, speaker Z said B. The fable, after introducing animal Y and animal Z with some minimal notice of setting, has Z offer a provocative or trouble-producing remark that Y then answers (B is a more aggressive or even silencing response to A). Consider this first fable of the literary writer (not school collector) Phaedrus:

> Ad rivum eundem lupus et agnus venerant,   1.1
> siti compulsi. superior stabat lupus
> longeque inferior agnus. tunc fauce improba
> latro incitatus iurgii causam tulit:
> "Cur" inquit "turbulentam fecisti mihi
> aquam bibenti?" laniger contra timens:
> "Qui possum, quaeso, facere quod quereris, lupe?
> a te decurrit ad meos haustus liquor."

repulsus ille veritatis viribus
"Ante hos sex menses male" ait "dixisti mihi."
respondit agnus "Equidem natus non eram."
"pater hercle tuus" ille inquit "male dixit mihi."
atque ita correptum lacerat iniusta nece.
        Haec propter illos scripta est homines fabula
qui fictis causis innocentes opprimunt.

A wolf and a sheep came to the same bank,
forced by thirst. The wolf took his place upstream;
far lower was the sheep. Then, pressed on by voracious appetite,
the brigand lodged his complaint:
"Why have you muddied
the water I am drinking?" In reply his woolly fearfulness:
"Please, how could I do what you allege, Mr. Wolf?
The draught runs down from you to my tasting."
Disappointed in his suit by the force of logic,
He said: "You insulted me six months ago."
Sheep countered: "I had not been born yet."
He said: "Damn, it was your father who insulted me."
And so he seized and butchered him in a wrongful death.
        This fable is written because of those men
Who oppress the innocent on trumped-up charges.

Here we can present the story scheme as setting, problem/verbal challenge 1, response 1, problem 2, response 2, problem 3, response 3 (solution), evaluation. However, the structural scheme, the typology of the fable, fails to reveal the formal similarity of fable to earlier school exercises. The lamb speaks entirely in sententiae, the pithy ripostes that are meant to produce closure. The individual episode takes the form of a *chreia*: when asked by a wolf why . . . , the lamb said . . . (except that the fable has two speakers). Phaedrus's first fable has a more complex structure than most and is also something of a virtuoso display of dialogue. The poem strikes one as a creative-writing exercise, one of those compositions where the teacher has restricted the writer's resources: tell a story using only (or mostly) direct speech. We shall return to these formal demands of the fable, but it is important also to take note of what modern analysis of the fable makes clear: the fable mediates violence.

With *chreiae* the student learned philosophers' witty replies to challenge and to violence.[29] Now he tries responses not quite of his own invention but of his own stylistic redevising. He learns a more sophisticated linguistic treatment of violence, one of the graduated series that will culminate in the declamatory *controversia* where the worst manifestations of violence—parricide, adultery, incest, and treason—are repeatedly reopened and resutured by the adolescent declaimers. With stories of talking animals, occasions for craft and wit, the boy is assembling the first weapons of his linguistic arsenal. By composing speeches about animals in violent conflict, a child is practicing the great social good of mitigating conflict between humans without yet facing the grave reality of human conflict (and the proper, advanced linguistic means to frame the conflict).

Throughout the Greco-Roman world, fable was a genre of school practice, the student's first extended writing, and a genre of scholastic literature. We have literary collections from two first-century A.D. practitioners, the Latin of Phaedrus and the Greek of the Roman Babrius; Horace's *Satire* 2.6, on the town mouse and the country mouse, stood as an invitation to others to try the fable as a higher literary form. So Seneca, perhaps ignoring and insulting the freedman Phaedrus, recommended with a mix of flattery and condescension that Polybius, Nero's freedman and official, try his hand at the literary fable.[30] As the grammarians loved to point out, poets, philosophers, and orators used fables and sententiae. In the school, after the maxim and the *chreia* had introduced the boy to philosophers and sages, the fable offered more scope than the repetition of their terse sayings.

Roman and Greek boys and girls probably first met the fable in school as a reading and copying exercise. They would return to the fable when they advanced to the first of the *progymnasmata,* the exercises designed to lead the student who already knew how to read and write through a series of steps to full declamatory composition.[31] After *chreia*, fable, and narrative, Theon has his students advance to commonplace, description, *prosopopoia* (speech in character), praise and blame, parallel, thesis, law, refutation and confirmation, public reading, listening to lectures (and the techniques of memorizing them), paraphrase, elaboration, and contradiction.[32] Quintilian's program is not so complex, and other authorities differ from Theon in points of detail.[33] Also, the system is not so discrete as the list implies. In learning fable (or another exercise of the early sequence), the student in fact practices some of the techniques that later will receive special treatment, such as description, elaboration, and compression, and returns to the genre that was one of his first writing exercises. Quintilian wanted the *grammaticus* to teach fable, maxim, *chreia*, and etiology (explanation of causes); and only then should the rhetorician take over. Theon, however, assigns the whole series under the tutelage of the rhetorician. Clearly, what was taught, by whom, and when varied considerably.

Theoreticians have remained keen to discern divisions in the curriculum according to function, teacher, and requisite ability. It is tempting, for instance, following Piaget, to assign certain cognitive functions to certain exercises. Bonnie Fisher plots the *progymnasmata* on Piaget's map of the development of a child's cognitive abilities with the following segmentation: the first stage of egocentrism and concrete operations when the child is seven–eleven years old suits the *ludus litterarius,* where reading and repetition of the unconnected fable occupied the child to age ten. Piaget situates first abstract thinking and formal operations in the second stage (the preadolescent age of eleven–fifteen), which corresponds to the grammarian's school with its play with the form of the fable and development of point of view and sentence complexity. Piaget's final stage of classification and reflection/ evaluation would then coincide with the rhetorician's school.[34] Piaget's three stages do describe the progress, if not necessarily the process, of learning as a movement from reading and rote work to expression, from the linguistically simple to the complex. Yet the ancient schools do not have the strict tripartite division here imagined, and the learning of classifications, for instance, begins much earlier. Clearly, the exercises were understood in antiquity as a series of steps, yet neither the rather grand divisions of the exercises into abstract skills nor the overly minute and discrete enumeration of functions explains why these exercises were successful.

The key to understanding their success will come, rather, from probing the overlapping forces operating on a curriculum, including the rationalizations, some quite wrongheaded, that teachers, theoreticians, parents, and participants give to an exercise, from defining the set of skills—cognitive, physical, and social—an exercise required and promoted to, finally and more subjectively, gauging the attractiveness of an exercise, which is to say, its appeal to the student's and teacher's sense of what is appropriate, useful, and even fun. Under the last heading, the appeal of the exercise, one must take seriously the faith of the ancients that school exercises rendered the student moral.[35] The appeal of an exercise extends well beyond the moral concerns discovered in it by adults. Fisher, in her dissertation on the use of the fable in ancient, medieval, and nineteenth-century American schooling, noted the applicability of modern, child-centered research. She cited the investigation of Nicholas Turner into the characteristics of stories that children choose to read. The contemporary child is said to prefer concrete event to abstraction, unambiguous morality, simple causation, satisfactory closure, direct speech, and simple vocabulary.[36] The well-moraled fable of the school suits these preferences well, although one might want to qualify the idea of a child's preference. Children are not drawn to, nor indeed do they compose, narratives on these lines out of some natural disposition. The student learns certain forms of narrative. Because these are commonly thought of as simple, as modern teachers speak of students mastering the simple sentence or the basic paragraph, it has been easy to consider them natural. Simplicity often seems to mean an economy of language, a linearity of plot, and a consistency of motive or setting, all of which are learned skills. Each exercise arranges and presents knowledge in a miniroutine, which is not novel but related to other aspects of the curriculum and to the child's social and cognitive worlds.

THE FABLE'S LESSONS II: FABLE IN
THE REPERTOIRE OF COMPOSITION

Before we turn to what the ancient teachers said they did with fables in their school, it is important to remember that we are not examining student copies. Instead, the evidence for school fables, especially in the more advanced exercise of the ancient school, is indirect.[37] The artistic fables of Phaedrus and Babrius were turned into prose and as such became major school collections. Verse fables also passed to the Middle Ages in the book of Avianus, which in fact became part of the basic school-book, the *liber Catonianus*.[38] In addition, from a third-century A.D. account of a schoolboy's routine, we have sample fables; but again these are models for the student, even though they purport to be the work of a model child. The exercises in rhetorical composition known as the *progymnasmata* were texts for teachers, although James Butts has argued that the rearrangement of Theon's text in the fifth century represented a change in use from teacher's to student's copy (but decidedly not student versions).[39] Fables from the hand of an ancient student do survive; the so-called Assendelft Tablets, wax tablets that contain versions of fables of Babrius (and others), are the copy work of a schoolboy or girl of Antioch in the third century A.D.[40] These wax tablets come from the first use of fable as a writing and memorizing exercise. The student has probably taken these down from dictation or perhaps from the master's copy. The pupil was not doing well, for he or she made many mistakes. Perhaps this copy was not for the master's eye but for the student's own use in memorizing the fables.

The various exercises of the *progymnasmata* do not require that students compose original works. Rather, the student is required to transform language already presented.[41] The student has already learned to adapt received language at a simple level with the *chreia*. The rationale for beginning with the *chreia* was that it was short and easy to remember (Theon 64.29–30), but practice with this simple sentence did not end with a merely accurate reproduction. Given a *chreia* or a fable, the student declined them, that is, changed the case of the grammatical subject.[42] So instead of "When asked, Socrates said" or "A wolf and a sheep came to the same riverbank," the student put the subject through the various cases and numbers of the nominal declension: "The reply of Socrates was . . . ," "When to Socrates the question . . . ," "Someone asked Socrates . . . ," "By Socrates, when asked, the reply was made . . . " The accusative is easy, for the student can simply put the direct speech in indirect form. He learns to cast direct expression in subordinate syntax. So while this technique may seem mechanical, even tedious, it offers exercises in syntax that were also something of a stylistic lesson, since variation was a stylistic desideratum. Indeed, although parataxis was allowed in a simple narrative style, beginning each sentence with the same subject was not. But real esteem was accorded to one's Latin and Greek prose style when it employed complex, subordinated sentences. The sentence also becomes longer or shorter depending on transformations of the syntax to accept changes in the case of the noun (itself the rhetorical figure known as *polyptoton*). To paraphrase, to elaborate, or to compress were more systematic transformations of the model text, which extended the ability to manipulate synonyms and periphrases, which was first learned in first writing out glosses on Homeric lines.[43]

These exercises may sound like a mechanistic stylistic algorithm, but they provided practice in flexibility of expression on the very best material. Theon gives perhaps the fullest account of what models to set the student. His selections are not so much a canon as an anthology of purple patches. Tidbits of Homer, Hesiod, Herodotus, Demosthenes, and Isocrates serve as the sample exercises.[44] This sort of educational technique has been almost abandoned in modern vernacular language pedagogy, where the child learning to read is thought to be well served by language close to his expressive level; and even in contemporary teaching of the classical languages, where the modern undergraduate is said to deserve full texts. Perhaps we should remember that Herodotus has meant, for millenia of schoolchildren, the stories of Marathon and Thermopylae, as Livy has meant Hannibal and his elephants. Theon seized upon such memorable passages. And consequently the ancient student received lessons in the stylistics of the canonical authors (and admittedly not, at this stage, their structure or themes).

Each of the *progymnasmata* forms a discrete unit of argument and of composition, which can be inserted into a more extensive text. As rhetorical building blocks, they will eventually be parts of a composition, but they also share and develop pedagogic techniques. Certainly, the fable is longer than the maxim, even if less ambitious than the fully developed, literary fables of Phaedrus or Horace. Where the boy had learned the single sentence of a *chreia,* whose sentiment must fit the crusty Diogenes or rather generic Socrates, he now must recall perhaps two or three short sentences, in which the ethos of the nonhuman speaker-actor is also set by tradition. The fable can be as simple as the following from the *Ps.-Dositheana:* "A wolf came to visit a sick ass and began to prod his body and ask what parts hurt the most. The ass answered: 'Those you touch.' In this way evil men though they seem to help hurt the more." (*Asinum egrum lupus visitabat et coepit corpus eius tangere et interrogare quae magis partes ei dolerent. Respondit asinus quae tu tangis. Sic homines mali si et prodesse videntur magis nocent.*)[45] The form of question and answer, with only two parties, recalls the *chreia,*[46] but an *epimythium*—the closing moral—has been added. Perhaps in such a simplified form, the student could easily build a stock of fables: Theon implies that students will have learned "all the fables of the simple style among the ancients" (74.14), but Quintilian, Theon, and the rhetoricians have something grander in mind.[47]

Theon remarks that the fable is a multiform exercise.[48] First, in what the rhetorician calls presentation, *apangelia,* the student repeated a fable recited by the teacher. This could be a simple act of memory, but the student might use different diction (although only in the spare, simple style) and might be required to narrate the fable from the middle, that is, not in linear chronological order. At this point the student has practiced his oral memory and made modest recasting of the diction and narrative order of the fable. Declension of the fable follows, where the student varies the subject by grammatical case and number. One clue to the utility of this exercise comes from an example given by Theon. In a lost dialogue of the Socratic philosopher Phaedo, the *Zopyrus,* Socrates tells a fable about a lion in which the lion, on first mention, is in the genitive, and later in the nominative. After such practice, narrative likely seems less like a fixed text than a medium for the student's variations in the many available stylistic modes. Two strong qualities of the fable are being learned, although without being directly addressed: fables are literary texts that provide the student variety of diction within a fixed structure, and fables lend themselves readily to moralization (Theon says he considers only fables equipped with morals suitable for school use, 72.30–31). Fables are thus source material, a narrative mode, and a medium that can accommodate a particular kind of evaluation.

Later, the student learned to link fable to larger narratives. Although the composition is growing more complex, it incorporates earlier stages of the curriculum: for example, as the sententia had received a narrative frame in the *chreia,* the fable is now associated with the narrative of a historical event. With this new task, the student connects the fabulous with the real. This is most directly an elaboration of moralization—the student has hitherto joined a moral to the fable, and now he does not abstract a timeless truth but finds it, as enunciated in fable, incarnated in another, more extensive narrative. The relation of fable to sustained narrative is also important, since fable is to be used ultimately, as Aristotle directed, as an argument embedded in a larger narrative.[49] The succeeding exercises practice stylistic variation. Elaboration and abridgment add or subtract direct speech and topical description (*prosopopoia* and *ekphrasis,* both of which are later *progymnasmata*).

The next variation on the fable, *epilogos,* requires the student to add a closing moral to a fable or conversely supply a fable or fables to illustrate a given moral. The latter problem presents the greatest freedom yet encountered. The student must recall a fable from the repertory he has heard in school or frame one of his own invention. Next, *anaskeuē* and *kataskeuē,* confirmation and rebuttal, require the student to evaluate the verisimilitude and persuasiveness of the set fable. While such criticism anticipates future evaluative functions, its primary function here is to promote internalization of the criteria of composition. The student must address questions about the cohesion of the fable, such as whether the introduction given does or does not fit, and is thereby marched through basic ancient rhetorical aesthetics. He can refute or undercut a fable, as he may some day an opponent's speech, by indicating the following failures: obscurity; lack of verisimilitude (*to apithanon*) or appropriateness (*to prepon*) in the relationship of the character to the words or deeds, or of any of these to the place, time, circumstances, manner, or motives; default or excess in narrating an element of the story (i.e., omitting something necessary or including something unnecessary for the plot); violating norms of expectation (e.g., making the fox stupid); inconsistency (demonstrating that a detail does not fit with the whole); faulty narrative sequence; unsuitability, especially of the moral; nonapplicability or nonuniversality of the moral.

Having matched fables with narrative and with its intended moral, the student now directly considers the criteria of likeness. The fable was defined by Theon and others as a false story that presents a likeness of the truth. This definition will never satisfy the anthropologist, but it does address fable's central function as a compositional exercise in the ancient school. The fable comes to be understood as a fiction whose relationship to the world of experience must be carefully established while it is presented in such a way as to convince others of the accuracy and consistency of the fiction.[50]

Whether or not the precocious nine-year-old or average eleven-year-old rang all of these changes on fables, the student learned with fable to use an easy and familiar mode as a medium of rhetoric. Just as the *progymnasmata* were a graduated series, the degree of proficiency required in the uses of fable was graduated. The ancient theorists seem to have recognized both the flexibility of the early exercises and the utility in returning to the same form at different points of the student's development. Theon enjoins that the master should not correct all the mistakes at the early stage (72.4–7—just as we have seen Quintilian allow the young to have a more fulsome, less corrected style). At its most developed, the fable treats questions of violence, justice, and redress with two or more characters pleading their cases. It is little wonder that Theon compared the fable to the judicial hypothesis, in Latin the *controversia,* the imaginary courtroom case (78.11.13 and 60.6–10). But even on its own, not as an anticipation of the curriculum to come but as a discrete, compelling narrative, mastery of the fable represents a significant step toward authentic writing, by which I mean that schooled conviction that one's writing is one's own, a fresh creation to be recognized by its audience as the work of one author.

Fable lent itself especially to the first exercise in fiction because as a genre it retains a certain openness. The structure and cast of characters were relatively fixed but allowed for amplification. No fixed canon of fables precluded the efforts of young writers, and as a fictional and fantastic form, fable encouraged innovation. Fables could be presented as bare-bones plots or as virtuoso poetic texts, yet even the literary collections of Babrius and Phaedrus did not prevent augmentation. Fables encourage other fables in great part because the genre (and the teacher's or theorist's directions) encourages the reader to draw likenesses, and like jokes or limericks, in their playfulness fables dare the reader to make another. The suspension of the everyday, the use of mythic time or, better, fictive time, the interplay of generic characters, and variation in the (simple) setting are inducements to new versions. The fable can be made simple, or embellished with borrowings from more elevated genres, like the fables of the fourth-century Avianus, a staple of medieval education, who drew his diction and style from Virgil.[51]

Michel Patillon has noted that the addition of the moral to the fable breaks the narrative order of the text; a change in tense must occur even in the sparest of fables, the change from the imperfect of once-upon-a-time to the timeless gnomic present.[52] Fable thus does not stand apart from present experience; it does not have the distance or linguistic difficulty of epic. It invites the reader to relate what has been written to present experience and so enacts in miniature an attitude to texts that will recur in the student's education, especially as the student gains the linguistic skills that will diminish the difficulty of writing in grander registers. The old text is something to be moralized, and to be used for one's own argument and composition.

The ancient reading and writing curriculum employed forms of teaching texts far more varied than the modern. Most school materials were linguistically remote from colloquial language: their distinctiveness evident not only in diction (the hard glosses that the first sentences contained), but also in meter. The prosodic and rhythmic patterns of the hexameter may have facilitated memorization, but there is no evidence that they made learning to read or write any easier. The idea of beginning students with easy texts allegedly close to their experience and to their supposedly limited vocabulary is a modern one. Priscian, translating Pseudo-Hermogenes, reports that orators gave children fables first of all. In practice, no doubt, this reflects the same reality of suiting materials to young children's abilities; however, the justification for the practice is entirely different from the modern. Priscian offers a moral explanation: in some unexplained way he believes "fables easily shape the still soft minds of children to better paths of life."[53] Ease of learning was not the primary consideration, and simplicity of language does not characterize the elementary exercises beyond maxim, *chreia,* and fable.

We would replicate the ancient practice if we taught children to read by setting them a piece of Shakespeare, Milton, or even Chaucer. In first composition, in the fable, we do see language easier than the linguistically distant Homer and Virgil. And yet the very difficulty of the epic texts had advantages: at the outset of studies it would discourage vernacular paraphrase or summarization and demand instead a faithful, verbatim copying. The child begins by imitating, whether through writing or reciting or speaking, as if he were the undistorting medium for the text. Indeed, he is but a copy of the text, as much a support of reading as the papyrus or the wax that held the letters. A faultless performance, at this stage, means simply that the child reperforms the text in a fashion indistinguishable from the master's copy. The child's particular capabilities, as Quintilian described them, were a quickness to retain and a quickness to parrot what he was set. Quinitilian's desiderata do testify to the importance of memory and of oral delivery in ancient literate culture, but they are also idealizations of the child and child learning. The good student at this stage is almost invisible: that is, his performance is identical to his master's script. He leaves no mark upon the text to be reproduced. But this practice of textual performance has implications for the future. Starting a child on Homer (or with the Bible) begins the familiarization of difficult texts. The centrality of large, archaic, and complex literary works in different curricula marks their texts not simply as cultural icons but as difficult and yet daily texts, which require revisiting and reworking, and whose reading is never complete. It is decidedly not the case that throughout their various histories such complex works were given the very young for lack of other materials. The process of gaining basic literacy rehearses the future, lifelong textual practices of the student. The child may have begun writing or sounding out portions of Homer or other literary texts, and in preparing these for memorization and reading, the schoolchild punctuated, glossed, erased, and corrected. The fable, and the multiple uses to which it was put in the schools, provide an almost complete contrast. The plasticity of the fable made it the ideal medium for reading, copying, commenting, paraphrasing, composing, abridging, expanding, and reciting. The fable certainly would not displace Homer in the ancient world, but it offered great opportunity for practice and transformation.

THE FABLE'S LESSONS III:
NEW ATTITUDES TOWARD COMPOSITION

In fact, the fable provided a site for a range of textual practices different from the earlier stages of the curriculum. Like the first reading exercise, the *praelectio,* where the master read a bit and the student then tried to reproduce that bit, and where occasionally the master explained the sense or word order of a difficult portion, in making his fable the student again replicated what was given him. But as with paraphrase, practiced soon after fable, or the more advanced précis and augmentation, he has begun a different practice with a different attitude to the text. He learns to transform the text, which is a feature of language learning and of cultural learning of great importance, for here he acts not as ventriloquist for the sententious style of Cato or the hard-bitten wit of the Cynic philosopher in a *chreia,* but, like the teacher himself, he has one version of the text that he may choose to give his public in a different form.

The student has begun to exhibit expertise and not personless mimicry. In the learned play with adult speech forms, his or her practice treated language, the text received, as an object to be manipulated, altered variously, and as the stuff of play. In the recombinative technics of fable, language itself became the focus of study and of display.[54] The student has been habituated to the idea of text and apograph, the teacher's version and his or her own, lesser version.[55] Here apograph became autograph. Without the constraints of a grand literary genre, the fable invited invention and variation; it did not have the linguistic fixity of epic or of any of the canon of authors the student reads and recites; it was closest to the declamatory topic in its insistent replotting of a confrontation from a slender cast of characters and a plot. The fable did have an archetype—a mélange of plot, character, setting, speech, and moral that could be handled variously. Fable offered multiple, competing instantiations, including the prose version of the fable that the student read or perhaps had read to him, the fables he heard at home in his pre-schooldays, perhaps even his peers' versions (for the school was open, and the student could see and hear others at varying degrees of competence), and also fables embedded in Homer, Virgil, or Horace. The student probably had not yet read *in extenso* the prose texts that contained the occasional fable. But he has begun a textual practice that requires a different attitude toward the text, one that will continue in paraphrase, practiced soon after fable, and in the more advanced précis and argumentation.

Later, when the schoolboy came to versify, he may have attempted first the easiest of classical Latin meters, the meter of Phaedrus's fables, the iambic senarius.[56] Still, the appeal of fable cannot be limited to formal aspects. Fable has a breadth of applicability akin to the maxim: for every situation, for every conflict or impasse, one can summon a fable. Again and again, fable represents the literate in action, not simply because the student takes it as his first extended effort as a writer, but because the plot itself lets the clever, though at times weaker, agent prevail. Even with the most negative fables, where the fox does not get the grapes or the deer gets lured down a well, the reader learns through plot and maxim the way to avoid a mistake. The fable offers precautionary tales for potential victims, and the mentality of the reader presumed by the fable is that of a victim. The world is hostile, and its agents more powerful than we—but we can learn to be clever if we will but attend to story structure and to linguistic mastery. This cleverness has a special quality: the best protagonist is not simply the trickster but a fellow like Aesop himself who can foil a more powerful, larger foe with his innate verbal artistry. The ancient schoolchild learned to internalize the admonitory voice of school texts.

In repeating the maxims, the student adopted the persona of maxim giver and spoke in a style and tone foreign to a child's everyday speech. This first exercise inaugurated the student's identification with a powerful speaker. At its most advanced, the direct exercise in speech in character would involve specific directives to capture the tone and substance of various kinds of people. But even in this act of impersonation, the student learned to speak as the sage (male) adult, one who, like the fox or prudent sheep, has learned from experience. Ancient schooling's intensive training in literacy promised to redress the injustice that the young sense in their lack of power and worldly experience. Taking Cato's voice, the boy instructed himself to cultivate his soul, to work hard (study hard), and not to worry about those who insulted him or threatened him with harm. Fable provides the scenario for playing out the central situation of the schoolboy as child, as learner. Smaller, less powerful, but now more resourceful as an initiate into the huge world of literate culture, he may use his wit, intelligence, and concision of speech to face parents, teacher, and the writers of old, all of whom are allied against him in the daunting discipline of education. In his brief speech and writing he can deflect their authoritative accounts. The process of identification with the oppressor, involving a deflection and repression of resentment and its redirection to diligent reading, writing, and speaking, lies at the basis of schooled subjectivity.

I have stressed the subjective, attitudinal aspect of the fable, since the exercises with fables provided the first opportunity for authentic learning. The fable is not a learned form; we know of one eleven-year-old boy whose talent in composing extemporaneous verses (on a mythological theme) won him a prize, but aside from such technical, metrical brilliance, no one in antiquity would have been much impressed with the schoolboy who could recite and compose, abridge and embellish, the modest genre of the Aesopic fable.[57] The boy or girl who is competent in fable is still at an early stage in the *progymnasmata* and in rhetorical training generally. He is not yet erudite; he may not yet be able to versify; and he would not be able to answer the more arcane questions about the poets that so delighted the grammarians. Fable is an interesting stage because it stands before such erudition. We observe textual processes and attitudes but not yet the hard stuff of learning and the end product customarily equated with education: the knowledge of authors, mythology, history, and rhetoric. Like wit more generally, fable is a technique for dealing with knowledge, power, and expertise. Fable also reinforces a most fundamental feature of ancient schooling: it justifies the elite education of which it is a part. We see verbal artistry in action, mediating not simply conflict, but competing claims and discourses. As he learns to present two conflicting voices in the same story schema, the boy learns also a lexicon and rhetoric of self-correction (not simply moralizing). He has learned how to talk of deceit, cheating, and trickery, but with the specific twist of a universalizing self-address. The allegory of fable consistently exploits acts of violence as an occasion to counsel the self. The moralizing opening or close constitutes an act of interpretation that is directed to the self but also is a generally applicable conclusion. Often the direction is negative, apophatic: do not pretend to be someone better than you are, do not bother with what others say about you. The directives constitute a genre of social comfort: the reader is all right and protected from folly, his own and the world's, even if he is not yet of high status, because he is learning (verbal) self-restraint and self-reference. This is one of the high conceits of education: literature and the words of the past generation address the present reader, whose success in education is determined not simply by the accumulation of lore or technique but by the internalization of the lessons of the past. Thus education holds out the promise to be free: we shall not be victims any more than we shall be slaves. The moralizing mode is as much a routine as an attitude: as he practices reading and writing and speaking, the schoolboy learns to await with patience the achievements of pleasure, reward, and maturity. His daily labor and self-definition are bound up in this moralizing rhetoric. The young fabler is also the disengaged, evaluative observer who draws conclusions for himself and the rest of humanity from the errors, wrongheadedness, and cleverness of the wholly engaged, barely self-aware actors in the fable. The fable-making student draws him- and herself away from the dumb, unreflecting crowd.

The student has moved from copying maxims of circa eight words to the prose *chreia,* a text of approximately twenty-five words, which introduces a protagonist, a challenge, and the verbal riposte. As he turns to fable, he writes perhaps seven lines of a structure similar to the *chreia* but with an introduction (setting and possibly *promythium*) and a conclusion (*epimythium*). He has also moved from the anonymous or unattributed one-liner (save that the collection of sententiae might be attributed to Cato or Menander) to the attributed *chreia* (whose main speaker is a famous sage, while the prodding agent is usually nameless, but a character type, such as a poor student or a lazy pedagogue). With fable he repeats the more complex attribution given by his model (roles and beast characters are set and are usually two or three in number). He also writes with evaluation, an aspect of more sophisticated writing—the lazy pedagogue of the *chreia,* for example, may now be, say, the wily fox, but the boy must also communicate motivation at several levels and places, not simply with an epithet when he introduces his characters, but also in narrating and especially when concluding their conflict.

This increasing differentiation of role and motive requires that the boy's attitude to his writing (and speaking) also change. In copying *chreiae,* he was to believe that Socrates or Diogenes or Cato really said the words he repeated. With fable he recasts a story, one by definition fictitious, whose nonfacticity creates space for his own version and implies a need to comment, to modulate in what sense the story is true. He is moving from truth telling to the processes of attribution, as, for instance, the modern undergraduate writes of what Homer meant, but the graduate student learns greater obliquity: he writes of what others have said Homer meant, and is most concerned with learning an advanced mode of attribution and evaluation. In the ancient curriculum, the fable begins the process of attribution whereby competing narratives are compared and contrasted, their plausibility subjected to vigorous, systematic evaluation, even as declamation deals with at least two narratives arising from the same minimal "facts." In both the rudimentary and the advanced exercises, the student takes the given, underexpressed material as facts, and his function is to represent these as truth through the techniques of augmentation and stylization taught him.

When the fable may have more than one episode, the student must provide transitions as well as introduction and close. Narrative making is here especially a matter of coherence. Two or more characters are introduced, their hierarchy signaled by place in the animal kingdom and by reference to the genre of fable. They must be brought to a single crisis. The grammarians do not stress unity of place, for at this stage theoretical prescriptions are kept to a minimum. The student learns the shape of a story from the models provided. Temporal order is also observed and importantly is signaled. The maxim is timeless; the *chreia,* while an episode, has no strict indication of its time. Despite the historicity implicit from the name of the speaker and interlocutor, the situation is general and iterable. Indeed, often it does not seem to matter whether Diogenes or Socrates is the subject. So "Cato" can take over a number of sentences from "Menander." The fable has of course "once upon a time," and though this is abstract compared to the scene setting the boy shall learn from his future reading of history or political speeches or even from his master's commentary on the poets, it is internally coherent. Notices of time help to articulate what is narrated as an event. In point of style, this means that the student will use an opening formula (especially the indefinite adverbs or pronouns, "once upon a time" and "a certain . . . ") and without further ado bring on two characters.[58] The speech of the two characters, separated by a sentence to advance the narrative, and brought to closure with a concluding sentence and/or the *epimythium,* forms the sum of the structure. At times the mere mention of an animal and the imperfect tense suffice as opening formula: for example, for Phaedrus (who uses comparatively few introductory markers) *Lupus arguebat . . .* or *leporem obiurgabat passer* (1.10.4 and 1.9.4 respectively). Certain temporal formulas feel like a familiar stage. "Once upon a time" or "A certain farmer" represents the lifting of the curtain: the audience is primed for the entrance of the characters. Extremely brief notices of occasion add the scenery and tone. Thus from "It was winter" the reader can expect that scarcity and famine are going to be the backdrop for a provident and a spendthrift character, and so on comes the ant (Babrius 140 begins: *Kheimōnos hōrēi*). The literary fabulists Babrius and Phaedrus use temporal clauses or a movement from the perfect to the imperfect tense and participles to express relations, sequence, and causation.

The style of the fable is for the most part paratactic (encouraged by a striving after compression and brevity that favors the genitive or ablative absolute or the use of participles rather than conjunctions and complex, subordinate constructions), and the lines are often end-stopped (the unit of sense thus corresponds to the line). But the young reader and imitator of these collections learns some syntactic subordination. The simple sentence of the maxim has been reworked to the more complex formulation of "When X said, Y said" or "When X saw, X said," where an initial subordinate element (more often the absolute participial expressions or a past participle agreeing with the subject; both are simpler versions of the subordinate clause, which in Greek and Latin often requires a nonindicative mood) communicates the setting and the challenge. And where the causation and motivation of the *chreia* may be riddling, requiring the reader's decoding of the underexpressed, terse saying, the fable is comparatively overexpressed, redundant at times with opening advertisement to the reader (the *promythium*), plot, notices of evaluation, and final moral (the *epimythium*)—the *chreia* being more like a riddle or a punch line, the fable a more sustained story-joke. In its completeness, the fable does not ask for the hearer's interpretation, nor need we supply a setting or names to the words expressed. As readers we are coming closer to aesthetic appreciation: when we laugh or admire the wit of the fox or the author, we are confidently in the know, not making an interpretation but accepting the one we are invited to share. The story's wholeness allows us to attend to other features, those of style and language. Part of the value of a set curriculum comes from the scope granted to stylization. This is why *inventio* is so restricted in the writing exercise (up until declamation). The process of finding material must not be an additional task. The repertory furnished by the list, whether of maxims, anecdotes, or declamatory categories (types of status), and the mental crutch of memory contribute to *inventio*. So too should the student's reading—this is why Quintilian and Plutarch encourage wide reading, so that the student will excerpt and have ready for use a stock of maxims, exempla, and rhetorical figures. The fable for the first time allows the boy or girl to redeploy his or her small stock, and to compose and be evaluated on a stylistic plane.

School practice with fables taught the student to compose by joining, augmenting, and elaborating discrete smaller blocks and parts. Good writing then required a technique of appropriate subordination and recombination of learned forms. In rewriting fables the student also learned notions of causation and linear order. Transforming the sententia into a fable changed received information into an object to be studied with a view to embellishment or reconfiguration. Such transformations reinforced in students the consciousness, initially acquired in the glossing of difficult texts, that words are manipulable objects. In addition to a self-consciousness about language, the student learned specific uses of language. Most immediately, excellence in language was rewarded by progress along a graduated curriculum, but language was used within the plots of the exercises to model conflict. The student learned verbal skills of attack, pacification, resolution, and deferral.

The ongoing practice of stylization leads ultimately to declamation. While there were several intermediate exercises, I shift our focus directly to declamation because we have extant samples close to school practice, whereas for narrative or exemplum we have nothing so close to an actual exercise, but we must rely instead on the theorists' directives and the literary collector's near-encyclopedic efforts. Sententia, fable, and declamatory speech clearly manifest the thread of moralizing composition that wove together the school curriculum. Of course, the extant collections are more whole than the actual practice of the schools. We have no interruptions, no bad examples, no failures of memory or lapses of taste (except in the criticisms recorded by the elder Seneca). Further, school collections invited an omnium-gatherum inclusivity. After all, writing is being encouraged: maxims, fables, and exempla are the sort of thing every scholar is to collect and memorize for himself. Fable is a magnetic and agglutinative genre, inviting each collector to revise and even occasionally to fabricate wholesale. As these forms invite collection and reproduction, they ascend from the practice of the ancient schoolroom and become valuable collectibles in themselves, gathered in books meant to be read as literary productions in their own right and not as a helpmeet for the maturing speaker. Even if we could win our way back to some archetype, the master who wrote sample exercises would have made them better, more consistent, polished, and integrated than those he delivered or had his students deliver in a packed and noisy room. The decontextualization involved in putting them into book form brings attendant changes in the form of the fable (so Phaedrus, no doubt following the lead of the poetry books of the Augustan period, takes great care over thematic unity, programmatic initial and final poems, guides to the reader, and variety of beast fable and anecdote). And as the master collecting and writing up fables or exempla did not strictly replicate his teaching role, so too the reader is far more than a student. We do not take in the fable by listening or copying it onto our wax tablet. Far more like the scholar of late antiquity, we live in a world where school curriculum and associated texts form a literature of their own, especially when in the large book (codex, textbook, monograph). Still I will ask the reader to play the voyeur, to consider several exercises in detail, exercises that would not have filled up a codex but would cover only a few pages or tablets. These briefer exercises, treated below in chapter 7, are the collection of maxims called the *Distichs of Cato* and a Greek-Latin learning aid with the unwieldy title of *hermeneumata,* the ancestor of the glossary and the colloquy. The final chapter devoted to declamation charts the development sketched above in the context of the fable, the sequential progress to a fluency of expression, which brought with it an attitude of mastery, dominion over self, over style and speech, and over those for and to whom the student spoke. Now I return to the maxim, since we have a collection that was actually designed for students' use (unlike the collections of fables), and since, after a description of the formal lessons of the fable, we can better appreciate the exercise's imaginary, the world it imagines for its young practitioner and the roles it presents and requires in its own execution.

7

The Moral Sentence

In 1605, the great classical scholar Joseph Scaliger reedited a text that had been very successfully edited by Erasmus, the *Distichs of Cato*. This third-century A.D. Roman school text had lost none of its appeal, but Scaliger's sense of the popularity and utility of the work was striking. In his edition of the *Distichs*, he remarked: *Est vero iste libellus non solum pueris, sed et senioribus factus. Et ego mihi conscius sum, multos gravissimos et doctissimos viros non puduisse, iam provectos aetate, haec disticha memoriter discere.*[1] ("In fact this is a book not only for boys but for their elders. And I myself am well aware that many deeply serious and learned men, in their old age, felt no shame in learning these distichs by heart.") That old men, in an era of increasing literacy, should pick up a printed copy of a Latin reader and not only read but learn by heart, and take to heart, a series of maxims supposedly written by the archetypal Roman old man some two thousand years before displays remarkable confidence in the efficacy of the text. The flourishing publication history of the text attests that generations found it believable and valuable—but why, with all the printed and handwritten texts in circulation at the beginning of the seventeenth century, should any reader, much less Scaliger himself, have turned to a pagan, traditional, and slight collection of verse maxims that were not the work of the Roman censor Cato, whose name they had held for fourteen centuries, but a schoolbook that was common, even ubiquitous, throughout the Middle Ages?[2]

The classical scholar should perhaps be especially sensitive to the impulse to literacy, since in the West this has so often taken the form of a longing to know Greek and Latin. Shards of pottery, bits of wood, and reused papyri scribbled over with the ancient student's efforts show the diligent labor and desire to write, to copy, to spell, even to leave his or her own version; and while at times we may have visions of the dull schoolmaster droning on with the paradigms of the dead languages, the history of the learning of Greek and Latin has far more vibrant images. Petrarch's model epistles would teach us all to write and converse with the ancients (indeed as the ancients). The Neoplatonist physician of the fifteenth century Marsilio Ficino had a near-mystical faith in the power of Greek letters. Influenced by the Cabalists, he imagined that the very sound of Greek promised insight. The Renaissance fascination with the *Distichs of Cato* reflects a faith that the classical text will make the reader's thought and language authentic—that is, concordant with ancient canons of style and with ancient wisdom.[3] The *Distichs* may have contributed to humanists' sense of the importance and seriousness of ancient texts, but the allure of the *Distichs,* and their role in encouraging virtue and Latin, are not limited to the Renaissance. As a favored text, the *Distichs* are something of a special case: they were consistently used in elementary education and their precepts both direct and depict the young learner moving toward mastery. The *Distichs* promise access to the world of literacy and commanding speech.

Scaliger himself in his prefatory remarks recognized something different about this text. It is appealing. One wants to memorize the maxims, and these maxims lead us on a distinctive, attractive path.[4] Scaliger's preface proclaims that the *Distichs* are useful and moral (as had other writers, with some Christians in the Middles Ages going to bizarre lengths to square the ethics of the text with proper dogma).[5] Let us not dismiss the faith of so many readers in this text: the *Distichs* is a thoroughly, purposively moralizing text that makes a deep impression upon its user. It imagines its young reader as an agent in need of moralizing, and it imagines that the maxims themselves will set the young on the path to virtue. It does not prescribe a philosophical program nor cleave to any sect: its dogma, if one can even use the word, is entirely commonplace, even self-contradictory, as proverbs can be. Yet the *Distichs* assure their young reader that by attending to the verse itself he will learn life skills that, though now slender, will grow to become the means to cultivate his soul, harm his enemies, and help his friends. The *Distichs* confirm that the students of Latin shall become liberal, humane, educated men, proper Romans like old Cato. No doubt, the *Distichs* is an especially successful species of educational self-justification and protreptic, one of the ways that the institution of the school maintains its value and initiates its practitioners.

The present chapter begins by considering the educational imperative in this set of verses: the overt directions and the implicit habits that arise from practice with this text and encourage a way of reading and of life. After a review of the place of the maxim in Hellenistic and Roman education, the figure of Cato the educator and the relations of his sententious writings and persona to the surviving *Distichs* demand attention. Then the chapter turns to a close analysis of the *Distichs* so as to reveal the system of agents, problems, and processes that they imagine. Thereby we get at the heart of the imaginary of the text, the way it communicated the educated life and process.

THE EDUCATIONAL IMPERATIVE

In form the distichs are two hexameter lines, which usually have an imperative, often negative, exhorting the student (always presented as a boy, although girls would have used the same text) to some course of action. Many reflect on the process of schooling:

> Instrue praeceptis animum, ne discere cessa,   2.31a
> nam sine doctrina vita est quasi mortis imago.

> Fortify your mind with precepts; do not stop learning:
> for the unlettered life is a likeness of death.[6]

A number express an ethics of restraint, familiar in its commonplaces but directed to the future fame of the student:

> Luxuriam fugito, simul et vitare memento   2.19
> crimen avaritiae; nam sunt contraria famae.

> Flee opulence, and remember to shun too
> the accusation of greed; for they are inimical to good repute.

More pointedly, several of this class focus their ethical advice on how to deal with friends, especially slights from friends:

> Si tibi pro meritis nemo respondet amicus,   1.23
> incusare deos noli, sed te ipse coerce.

> If no friend treats you as you deserve,
> do not reproach the gods but check yourself.

> Gratior officiis, quo sis mage carior, esto,   4.42
> ne nomen subeas, quod dicunt, officiperdi.

> Be more grateful for services rendered, that you may win greater affection,
> and that you may avoid the title, as the saying goes, of a favor vacuum.

The *Distichs* do exhibit an economy of themes and situations, but perhaps their strongest binding tie comes from the repeated urging to the user to practice verbal self-control. The imperatives counsel when to speak and when to keep silent, and this phatic and apophatic response shapes the coherent ethics of the exercise.

The imperative is a mode that characterizes this exercise, stage of schooling, and the student's life. The first distich established this imperative mode as programmatic: the new life of the scholar derives the imperative to study from literary authorities and must internalize it as a form of self-improvement (with shades of philosophical self-purification).

> Si deus est animus nobis, ut carmina dicunt,   1.1
> hic tibi praecipue sit pura mente colendus.
>
> Since our soul is divine, as the poems tell,
> you must especially cultivate this with a pure mind.

The third-century Roman student who first copied out these lines never imagined he was inaugurating the greatest schoolbook in the history of Western education. Probably he would not have thought that the practice in verse maxims was so important; perhaps he longed to be reading prose, the speeches of Cicero, and not the Virgil on which he had learned to read and write and to receive his master's explanations. Perhaps he longed for the day when as an advanced student he would declaim, counseling Cicero not to burn his writings no matter what the evil Marc Antony threatened. Poetry was decidedly not the height or end of schooling, and the hexameters bearing Cato's name were scarcely *carmina*, poems. Whatever a schoolboy might have thought in the early third century A.D. as he learned some hundred of these sayings, he would not have thought of his copying and memorizing as something innovative or epoch making. He was repeating maxims as Greek and Roman schoolboys had for centuries.[7] He would have believed that he was repeating the words of the elder Cato, the censor whose fame grew even as his genuine writings receded from circulation. The teacher who collected and versified these sayings would have known that they were a hodgepodge, that they did not represent the *verba ipsissima* of the old Cato. I doubt that the anonymous master was trying to work a fraud. He too was simply writing out of a tradition, both the tradition that used sentences to communicate literacy along with an ethical point of view and the tradition of impersonation. Greek schoolboys learned sentences of Menander, some of which the poet never wrote, as surely as with the *chreia* young Greeks and Romans learned verbal ripostes of Socrates and Diogenes that the philosophers had never uttered. In the dynamic and living schooling in the verbal arts of attack and defense, genuineness was not as important as authority and impersonation.

It may have seemed unremarkable to its practitioners, but what sort of learning did the copying of *Si deus . . .* launch? To try to answer what one piece of a curriculum achieves is often difficult. Even if the exercise is designed for a set purpose or in the course of years of practice has come to be administered at a particular stage in the student's life, its effect on the student is not guaranteed; what students take from an assignment is often far different from what their teachers desire; and the exercise may show its effect only years later, especially if it contributes to a set of skills whose integration may pass without notice until the student believes he has (suddenly) mastered a new task. But to analyze the exercise we need not believe in its efficacy, immediate or deferred, nor are we reduced simply to attempting to recapture what its maker or administrator meant to do with it. Neither of these approaches, the impulse-and-reaction or the describe-the-intent line of interpretation, shed much light upon the literate process that school composition often represents; both methods are ultimately linear (conceiving of schooling as a straightforward communicative transfer: teacher or exercise, the one with more knowledge is giving that knowledge to the unfilled vessel) and so miss that relationship of reading,' writing, memorizing, and speaking the text that involves several agents, places, and even media. Thus we shall try to measure the utility and point of the exercise by reference to the ongoing process of education. We need to discover both its affinities to other aspects of the curriculum and to ask how it shaped the student in his relation to his own education.

The *Distichs* prompt such an approach in part because they direct the reader to act as an educated man and in part because they are assembled from pieces of the curriculum, phrases and sentiments from poetry, rhetorical figures whose names and use will be taught later, and lines that can be developed into a fable or even a declamation. From the start, the collection seeks to make the student conscious of a new difference: he has a duty, indeed a natural impulse, to educate himself. Were we simply tracing the technical affinities of pieces of the curriculum, we might say that *Si deus . . .* prepares the schoolboy for the syllogism, not the strictly logical argument but the proposition that takes the form of a conditional sentence based on received ideas, the rhetorical enthymeme. Cicero, and after him Macrobius, show how such a slender beginning should be built into a proper philosophical syllogism. Cicero sets the scene as the oracular pronouncement of the authoritative grandfather to his grandson (*ille* is the Roman general the elder Scipio Africanus; hence Cicero is composing a speech in character, a prosopopoeia).

> Et ille: Tu vero enitere et sic habeto, non esse te mortalem, sed corpus hoc; nec enim tu is es, quem forma ista declarat, sed mens cuiusque is est quisque, non ea figura, quae digito demonstrari potest. deum te igitur scito esse, siquidem est deus, qui viget, qui sentit, qui meminit, qui providet, qui tam regit et moderatur et movet id corpus, cui praepositus est, quam hunc mundum ille princeps deus; et ut mundum ex quadam parte mortalem ipse deus aeternus, sic fragile corpus animus sempiternus movet.
>
> Nam quod semper movetur, aeternum est; quod autem motum adfert alicui, quodque ipsum agitatur aliunde, quando finem habet motus, vivendi finem habeat necesse est. solum igitur, quod se ipsum movet, quia numquam deseritur a se, numquam ne moveri quidem desinit; quin etiam ceteris, quae moventur, hic fons, hoc principium est movendi. principii autem nulla est origo; nam ex principio oriuntur omnia, ipsum autem nulla ex re alia nasci potest; nec enim esset id principium, quod gigneretur aliunde; quodsi numquam oritur, ne occidit quidem umquam. nam principium exstinctum nec ipsum ab alio renascetur nec ex se aliud creabit, siquidem

necesse est a principio oriri omnia. ita fit, ut motus principium ex eo sit, quod ipsum a se movetur; id autem nec nasci potest nec mori; vel concidat omne caelum omnisque natura et consistat necesse est nec vim ullam nanciscatur, qua a primo inpulsa moveatur.

Cum pateat igitur aeternum id esse, quod a se ipso moveatur, quis est qui hanc naturam animis esse tributam neget? inanimum est enim omne, quod pulsu agitatur externo; quod autem est animal, id motu cietur interiore et suo: nam haec est propria natura animi atque vis; quae si est una ex omnibus, quae se ipsa moveat, neque nata certe est et aeterna est. hanc tu exerce in optimis rebus! sunt autem optimae curae de salute patriae, quibus agitatus et exercitatus animus velocius in hanc sedem et domum suam pervolabit; idque ocius faciet, si iam tum, cum erit inclusus in corpore, eminebit foras et ea, quae extra erunt, contemplans quam maxime se a corpore abstrahet. namque eorum animi, qui se corporis voluptatibus dediderunt earumque se quasi ministros praebuerunt inpulsuque libidinum voluptatibus oboedientium deorum et hominum iura violaverunt, corporibus elapsi circum terram ipsam volutantur nec hunc in locum nisi multis exagitati saeculis revertuntur.

Ille discessit; ego somno solutus sum.   (*Somnium Scipionis* 18)

And he said: "Exert yourself and reckon thus: you are not mortal, but this body is; for you are not that which your shape describes, but the intellect of each man is that man, not the shape that a finger can trace. Know therefore that you are a god, seeing as a god is that which lives, perceives, remembers, plans and which rules and directs and moves that body whose charge it has, just as the chief god does the universe; and just as an immortal god himself moves a universe which is in part mortal, so an eternal mind moves the perishable body.

"For that which always moves is eternal; moreover, that which imparts movements to another body and which in turn is incited by an exterior source, since it has a terminus to its movement, necessarily has a terminus to its life. Therefore only the self-moving object since it is never abandoned by itself never ceases even to be moved; as for the rest of moved objects this is the spring, this the first beginning of movement. A beginning has no origin; for all things arise from a beginning, but it can be generated from no exterior thing; nor could that be a beginning which is born from a different source; but if it never arises, never does it set. For a beginning once quenched will never be reborn from another object nor will anything else create it, seeing as all things necessarily arise from the beginning. So it happens that the beginning of motion is an essential of the self-mover, that cannot be born or die; otherwise of necessity all of the heavens would collapse and all of nature come to a halt nor encounter any force to communicate the first impulse of its movement.

"Since therefore it is clear that the eternal is that which moves itself, how could anyone deny that intellects possess this nature? For everything driven by an external force is without intellect; moreover, that with intellect is moved by its own, interior motion: for this is the essential nature and force of intellect; and if of all objects this is the single thing that moves itself, certainly it was not born and is eternal. Exercise this in the best pursuits! Moreover, these are the most diligent safeguarding of the fatherland; stirred by and trained in these, the intellect will more quickly fly to this seat, its own home; it will achieve this all the more readily if even in the time of its enclosure in the body it passes out-of-doors, and in contemplation of those things which lie outside, it draws itself away from the body to the highest degree possible. Indeed the intellects of men addicted to bodily pleasures, who have made of themselves a display as servants to those pleasures, and who on the prick of lusts heeding those pleasures have violated the laws of gods and men, once they have slipped off their bodies flit about the earth and do not make their return to this place until age gives way to age of their relentless harrying."

He departed, and I was released from sleep.

I have quoted this famous ending of Cicero's *De republica* in its fullness because it represents the stylization, the rhetorical embellishment, of the first distich. Note in particular that the structure is simply the enthymeme (the rhetorical syllogism) about the immortality of the soul/intellect capped by an imperative: *hanc tu exerce in optimis rebus!* Cicero continues, as will the *Distichs,* to make clear what those best, liberal pursuits are. On first reading the *Distichs* the student will have no hint of philosophical-rhetorical stylization, yet he will learn the very basic shape of the argument. So if years later the argument for the immortality of the soul fills him with excitement, the philosophical breakthrough may seem to depend on the inevitable logical sequence of tenets.[8] The educational historian will, however, see the vast background knowledge (the *carmina* studied from first schooling, the aphorisms memorized and internalized), the attuning of the student to this shape of argument (and the substance of the argument, which presents the young student as a developing and special agent), and the disposition of education to mask its agglutinations—that habit that presents material and ideas as new and self-dependent whereas in fact schooling often involves a sequence of increasingly complex forms whose dependence on earlier lessons is not signaled. More immediately, by beginning with this distich, the boy is learning that he has a special duty to his self: education is decidedly not the acquisition of skills, the rote adoption of a severe, paternalistic code; it is his own act, an act of self-improvement, although in the Latin, without any such enlightenment term, *colendus* implies a stronger imperative, one to self-worship; in fact, it directs the boy to see the routine of schooling as a personal ritual.

Antonius in Cicero's *De oratore* (2.147–48) says the three most important things for *inventio* in speaking are talent, theory, and diligence.[9] Talent may be the most important, but the one most under our control, most able to be improved, and of best use in pleading cases is diligence: *Haec praecipue colenda est nobis.* The second line of the first distich simply puts this into verse. A tag from Euripides, *o nous hēmōn estin en hekastōi theos* ("In each of us our *nous* is a god"), well known in the schools, has been combined with an exhortation from Cicero on the virtue that is best for producing speakers.[10] The writer of *progymnasmata,* Theon (103.3 ff.), explained how the line from Euripides should be commented upon—that is, how to confirm it with illustrations of its truth and nobility. The rhetorically trained student would have recognized Cicero's expansion as a grand treatment of a commonplace. In the *De oratore* Cicero's diligence, exemplified in the careful attention to the opponent's words and in imbuing the mind with commonplaces (*pervolatur animus,* 2.149), is transformed into care of the self, where perhaps his example of what the *animus* is to do has shaped the thought of the composer of the distich. The first distich contains another Ciceronian expression. At *Pro Milone* 61, Cicero somewhat boldly characterizes his client as *pura mente et integra.* The writer of the *Distichs* found the *pura mente,* I believe, in a famous, lost work of Cicero, the *Hortensius.* At *Tusculanae Disputationes* 1.65 Cicero had written: *animus ut ego dico, divinus est, ut Euripides dicere audet, deus, et quidem si deus aut anima aut ignis est, idem est animus hominum.* ("The soul, as I put it, is divine, as Euripides dared to say, a god, and indeed if god is a breath or fire, so is the soul.") The next paragraph is a quotation from the *Hortensius,* which characterizes the prime mover. The last sentence describes that *deus* as *mens soluta quaedam et libera, segregata . . .* I suggest that the succeeding passage further described god as *pura mente,* and that it was from this passage that Macrobius took it, in his commentary on the *Somnium Scipionis* (*Comm.* 1.14.17: divine bodies *de pura mente constare;* cf. 1.17.12 *purissima mente*). The first distich is thus a Ciceronian pastiche of passages where *animus* was discussed, based directly (including even the syntax) on the *Tusculans* passage, with a second line modeled on the injunction in the *De oratore,* and with diction imported from the *Hortensius.* It is quite possible that the *Hortensius* had both *pura mente* and a sustained passage similar to the *Tusculanae Disputationes.* Certainly, the preteaching or intimation of grander styles and subjects to come is a central feature of the lessons of the *Distichs.*

The *Distichs* do not continue to theorize or expound the elevated view that describes schooling as an ongoing and self-directed process nutritive to the individual soul. This is not their point. Rather, they are introductory or initiatory and instill a sense of distinction within the student through an interconnected mode of reading, writing, and reciting imperatives. They work by a sort of unobjectionable sameness: "Cultivate your soul" means "Be a good student," and this imperative soon seems indistinguishable from "Don't worry about what others say about you" or "Don't believe another too quickly." In their metrical regularity and common diction, the fields of activity—reading and studying, being a good friend, knowing when to talk and when to hold your tongue, deferring the impulse to immediate revenge— take on a certain homogeneity and interconnection. Studying, indeed the mundane tasks of writing and memorizing, thereby become a moral act. Like the Greek sentence "Work hard [i.e., be a student] lest you be beaten," *Si deus . . .* was a favorite writing exercise. In a Corbie manuscript of Statius we find it carefully copied: it has become the exemplar of writing, something everyone has written and thus a comparandum to measure one's calligraphy.[11] This distich has in miniature all the qualities of the whole; it communicates the conviction that the student is engaged in a

higher calling as he begins an integrated curriculum, which is to be understood as
a self-realizing writing act: self-cultivation is chaste (*pura mente*) reading and writing. Part of this chaste writing is the proper orthography exhibited in the boy's copying of the maxims. Herein lies a clue to the allure of the collection. It promises that
we too can write, can learn, and can win our way to distinction (the recurrent *fama*
of the distichs). Equally importantly, it invites our use: here is something valuable
that we can make our own and that will serve us well, if we only heed its imperatives.

This directive to heed and use the text was recognized, theorized, and made memorable by the maxim with which the introductory prose letter concludes: *legere et
non intellegere neglegere est* ("To read and not to comprehend is to neglect"). Here
we have the first mark of use upon the collection, for the opening epistle is an addition, an ancient addition certainly, unlike the (medieval) metrical prefaces to books
2, 3, and 4.[12] The epistle marks the first augmentation we can detect; it also marks
the beginning of the text as a book, something read together and something whose
shape, whose physical format, is becoming more fixed (rather than being a model
or resource for the student's own use). The epistle shares with the later additions—
respectively the prefaces, the short prose imperatives, and the surreptitious distichs—
a desire to encourage the student to read the book and a desire to add maxims. Like
many of the distichs, it relies on the wordplay known to the rhetoricians as paronomasia, where different words sharing the same root are brought into close contact
(which almost inevitably in the *Distichs* is crafted to maximize assonance). Equally
scholastically, it employs the rhetorical figures of definition and of *figura etymolog-
ica*. Again, the young reader finds and takes samples of techniques whose names and
uses he will not learn until much later. He hears the almost singsong formula of the
line, which helps him memorize, while he need not know that he is also collecting
examples of verse form: the regularity of word placement, caesura, and metaphorical diction will form a sort of substrate, which will prove useful when he returns to
the study of poetry (the regularity is achieved by such features as common formulas and formulaic verse design; twenty distichs, for example, end with *memento*, all
but one of these with an infinitive preceding). What this reader, intermediate between the decoding of syllables and words and the grammatical study of poetry,
should appreciate is that his reading is not a mechanical process but an act of understanding, and also a moral act. Proper reading is, in short, conceived of as a virtue,
a personal virtue that will distinguish the reader who understands this epistle from
those who have the skill only to decode the syllables of the *Distichs*.

THE STUDENT'S WORLD

Part of the point of a preface is to construct an ideal reader. Thereby the author hopes
to guide the use of his book. Like the courteous or gentle reader of some Elizabethan
text, the intelligent reader of the schoolbook is a projection of the author's desires:

the present reader will be such if he reads the present text properly. The preface like-wise inscribes an ideal relationship of reader and reading that is both a disposition toward and a result of the text. The *Distichs* are meant for the maturing reader, one ready to turn his back on the mechanical process of reading. So they are serious in a way that even fable for all its moralizing is not: the sentences draw from and point to the adult world. Fable does not make explicit the immaturity of the reader, al-though the sentence of the *promythium* or *epimythium* points beyond the narrated text to life. In the *Distichs,* fantasy is present only in that the young reader is made to imagine at times that he is an adult.

Like fable, however, the young writer still identifies and puts at the center of his composition a victimized, threatened self. More concretely still, individual distichs exhort the student to diligent study and make clear the consequences:

> Cum tibi sint nati nec opes, tunc artibus illos   1.28
> instrue, quo possint inopem defendere vitam.
>
> Since you are a father but not a man of means,
> give them a liberal education as the means to escape the pauper's life.
>
> Instrue praeceptis animum, ne discere cessa;   3.1
> nam sine doctrina vita est quasi mortis imago.
>
> Fortify your mind with precepts; don't stop learning:
> for the unlettered life is a likeness of death.

The text represents the student as on a lifelong, soul-cultivating mission where learn-ing is equated with wealth and resources; it is the very stuff of life. This theme may be implicit throughout the work, but it is clearest at the beginning and end. After *Si deus . . .* came a distich advising the student to sleep less (*Plus vigila . . .*). Occa-sionally, the distichs connect the exhorted speech or action to the boy's special sta-tus as an educated man. One variation on the theme that the boy is to hold his tongue imagines him at a dinner party:

> Inter convivas fac sis sermone modestus,   3.19
> ne dicare loquax, cum vis urbanus haberi.
>
> At banquet make sure you restrain your speech;
> do not earn the name of a chatterbox, since you wish to be known
>   as a man of culture.

Here the text makes clear the ambition of the ideal boy: he wants to be urbane, a man known for his wit and superior language, a man like Cicero. While this is the aim, he is not yet there. He is still worried about being called names (cf. *officiper-dus*). Where the preface forecast a performance of intelligent reading, the body of the text suggests he is on his way to, but not arrived at, the destination of mature speaking and reading. For all the imagining, he is still a schoolboy and a son:

Verbera cum tuleris discens aliquando magistri,   4.6
fer patris imperium, cum verbis exit in iram.

Since in your student days you suffered the master's blows,
put up with a father's rule even when in his wrath he moves beyond words.

In a scenario typical of the school, the boy is and is not an adult. He is being given greater freedom (and resources) to speak, indeed to issue the imperatives that he is learning by heart, and yet he is firmly reminded of his limitations, that is, he is still the object of the imperative, at best the youth on the margin of the adult male dinner party. The distichs entice the boy to further study by promising and postponing reward, and vengeance upon his present detractors. He gets to imagine attending the adult party, yet even in this make-believe version must learn to keep his tongue. Those distichs dedicated to education itself, which most closely mimic the boy's actual station, reiterate the need for deference and deferral: the boy does read and write and speak of himself as an immortal intellect to be cherished, as a man of liberal education, even as a stern Roman censor, but he remains the potential victim: a pupil or child to be chastised, a friend to be betrayed or maligned. Freedom from restraint and from misappraisal of his worth lies just in the future. This is the state of *puer educandus.*

With this lesson comes the imperative to be educated. The close of the collection makes the point forcefully:

Disce aliquid, nam, cum subito fortuna recessit,   4.19
ars remanet vitamque hominis non deserit umquam.

Learn a profession, for, when fortune takes her sudden leave,
skill abides and in the course of life takes no reprieve.

Exerce studium, quamvis perceperis artem: 4.21
ut cura ingenium, sic et manus adiuvat usum.

Practice your art, whatever profession you choose,
As diligence fosters talent, so work aids experience.

Disce sed a doctis, indoctos ipse doceto: 4.23
propaganda etenim est rerum doctrina bonarum.

Learn (by all means) but from the expert; yourself teach the inexpert:
for knowledge of the liberal arts must be sown.

Discere ne cessa, cura sapientia crescat: 4.27
rara datur longo prudentia temporis usu.

Do not stop learning, let wisdom grow from diligent care:
expertise rarely comes from the long run of trial and error.

> Cum tibi contigerit studio cognoscere multa,   4.48
> fac discas multa vita nescire doceri
>
> Since by chance study has introduced you to much,
> Make sure you learn much: only the fool learns from life.

With these last three we witness the boy being included in the community of the learned. In a contrast characteristic of ancient schooling, art is the alternative to practice. The boy does not learn from experience; what the fool or the uneducated learn from life the boy attains by study.[13] Herein lies his superiority. We cannot conclude that every or indeed any ancient student was smitten with the message. Even from the diligent copy and use of the *Distichs* that their very survival indicates, we shall not know, as Scaliger indicated of his contemporaries, that the maxims quickened the devotion of the ancient student. Again, the direct, moral efficacy of the text lies outside our grasp as examiners of school curriculum; rather, we overhear how the process of education was conceived, how it tried to differentiate itself from other pursuits, and how its special claims of its own usefulness were inculcated through the medium of the instructional text. So we cannot conclude by rating the relative importance of different encouragements to be educated, as, say, today we are concerned with the images of education in film, television, and politics, with the economic and social and legislative incentives to stay in school, and with the ways that schooling encourages its own institutionalization and special status. In ancient terms we shall not know whether a schoolboy experienced 3.6 beatings a month and whether this was a greater help to memory than the form of the *Distichs*. But we can see the rationalization of schooling and the particular nexus of issues brought to the attention and to the daily practice of the ancient schoolboy. And where the repeatedly apophatic (negative) imperatives and the frequent mentions of disastrous consequence attending the lazy scholar may seem to the modern a harsh mode and a mode destined to fail for reason of its negativity, it was effective—not in terms of the quick access to basic literacy favored by modern states but in the highly selective (discriminatory) mode its own society valued. Its wide use and many additions and versions intimate that Scaliger was right: it was also a source of pleasure.

CATO AND CATONIANISM: THE HISTORY OF A MODE

From the 1605 edition of Scaliger to the laborious and detailed critical edition of Marcus Boas (published posthumously in 1952), the *Distichs* have not changed as much as they had in their long course from their recording in the late second or early third century A.D. through their dissemination and translation in the Middle Ages and Renaissance. Boas's edition has returned the text to a close proximity of its archetype, while also providing a valuable archaeology of this text by indicating the strata of additions and accretions. I would like to go back farther still so as to suggest why this text was associated with Cato's name. Cato and sententiousness were almost synonymous at Rome, and the schools sustained and recreated this association and this mode each generation.[14] The mode is more performative and generic than genuine, which is to say we are not tracing the real words of Cato but following a mode of impersonation that inextricably joins the personality of the Roman censor to the Latin reader.

If we put aside for the moment the inconvenient limits of human biography, we find that Cato wrote numerous works in the second century B.C., then a collection of sayings in the second or third century A.D.—the *Distichs*, whose manuscripts often begin: *incipit dicta Marci Catonis ad filium*. An introductory epistle was added not too long after. Then the work was carved into four books, with the prose epistle left to introduce book 1, while verse prefaces introduced books 2, 3, and 4. The short sentences, some translated from the sayings of the Seven Sages, some modeled on themes of the hexameter distichs, may already have been added to the beginning of the growing schoolbook. Schoolchildren in the eighth century read fables and maxims from a *liber Catonianus*. In the ninth to tenth century a fifth book was added: three poems of Eugenius Toletanus, bishop of Toledo (647–57), "Against Drunkenness," "Reminder of Human Mortality," and "Against Overindulgence in Wine." With this act we may well be dealing with a different if allied phenomenon, the magnetic pull of manuscripts, which draws like material but which is not composition in persona. Later still an epitaph was added for Cato's son; in a few manuscripts there follows an eleven-line poem on the names of the Muses. The work is now spinning its course as a schoolbook, and perhaps with the epitaph the manuscript is filling up as a book, drawing biographical comment and filler. In the ninth century, the *Distichs* were regularly bound with Avianus, later regularly with Donatus, Avianus, and Priscian; later still (thirteenth and fourteenth centuries), Theodulus would replace Avianus as Cato's companion.[15] Throughout this tradition Cato keeps writing to his son, because schoolboys are copying him and learning his precepts by heart. The circulation of this text is greater still, as it is translated many times, and the vernacular versions added proverbs.[16]

Catonian personality has been a part of first writing and reading from at least the third century on to the modern period, thanks to the many versions of the *Distichs*. This tradition is actually longer and may have a connection to the genuine Cato. Cicero knew of a collection of Cato's sayings used in school (*Off*. 1.104), and Plutarch refers to a collection of his sayings (*Cat. Mai*. 2.4), yet the *Distichs* show little stylistic affinity with the old censor, aside from the reliance on the imperative. From the evidence of Cicero's notice, either there was a collection of sentences that anticipated the *Distichs'* pretense to be Cato's or, before the era of the Augustan poets and their transformation of the curriculum of the schools, a work of Cato had survived. To the schoolchild, questions of authenticity did not matter. The trecento

Tuscan schoolboy read before his Cato a "Donadello," his elementary grammar, which has inherited only the name, not the text, of Donatus. School texts could circulate *sub nomine auctoris veteris* without any significant relationship to their titular author.[17]

The *Distichs* have an additional feature to complicate their authenticity. The genre of sayings does not lend itself to rigorous, clear-cut authentication. We cannot, following the principles of stemmatic criticism of manuscripts, compare variants among proverbs and confidently declare we have deduced the stemma of transmission. Like the *chreia*, sayings could be declined by the schoolboy, and Cicero himself will vary a quotation (or the historical *exemplum*—these are in the ancient mind figures of speech, forms of argument, not inviolable historical kernels) either from a slip of memory or to suit his context. Texts of proverbs and sayings need not have the fixity often imagined for classical texts. In the modern hunt to attribute words to a historical figure, the most advanced gymnastics have come from New Testament scholars in debates about the sayings of Jesus. The methodologies have been sophisticated if misguided; one of the most involved stratagems declared authentic only those sayings that fit neither ancient Judaism nor later Christian theology— thus the sayings that did not reflect contemporary Judaism or the early church could be deemed the genuine words of Jesus. The circularity of the argument— the genuine Jesus was neither Jew nor Christian but man of genius and thus unique, revolutionary—seemed preferable to the criteria of the form critics.[18]

We should take the broader view that in various ancient cultures the sayings of wise men have been a fertile genre, and that sayings are in essence not a fixed genre but rather one that encourages various literary productions. In the case of Cato, we could adopt formal techniques and strike out all sayings that do not exhibit the marks of mid-third-century B.C. Latinity, but since copyists and citers did not always have a modern sense of linguistic precision, they would regularize forms or rearrange word order as they quoted from memory or for the purpose at hand. On a strict hunt for archaism, we could well miss much that is genuine. We also would be following on the heels of the grammarians, who have preserved much of the old Latin but did so only because a line of an early tragedy or of Cato's prose had some obsolete form. Thus, like them, we would have a distorted sampling of the old language. In addition we encounter the difficulty that the chief sources have necessarily distorted the form of the sayings: Plutarch's biography of Cato was written in Greek; the *Distichs* are in dactylic hexameters.

A thematic and ideological approach, on the other hand, has its special perils. The picture of Cato arises in great measure from the later tradition: to square his sayings with this picture simply repeats the understanding of Cicero or, perhaps worse, of Plutarch. Still, one could exclude everything that does not reek of a mid-republican business-agrarian ethics; but, as we shall see, the historical Cato had an extraordinary range of interests, and of speeches and writings.

I shall follow a different course by starting from the observation that Cato's writings to his son were misunderstood in antiquity,[19] and then suggest that after Cicero's notice, the genuine sayings were replaced or substantially reworked in a school setting. The form of the replacement, I suspect, was the extant *Distichs*. In essence, we have a Cato to fit the new poetry curriculum that included Horace, Virgil, and Ovid.[20] To demonstrate these points I need to reconsider what Cato had in fact written in his educational writings to his son and then to consider the affinities of the extant work to an Augustan poetics. This should illumine the circulation of *dicta Catoniana,* in time, in the school, and in the process of composition.

Cato wrote precepts addressed to his son. Alan Astin, in an appendix to his fine book on Cato, sorted out the *testimonia*. He wisely saw that scholars, on the spur of Cato's alleged anti-Hellenism, had elevated the varying notices of the title to an encyclopedia of Roman education. He disbelieved Cato's rabid anti-Hellenism and disbelieved that Cato wrote a systematic work.[21] Ancient authors quote from a letter to Cato's son, precepts to his son, a history, a work on agriculture (arguably not the extant *De agri cultura*), and a work on medicine (Plutarch says a notebook). Astin whittles away at these alleged works, showing that there is no consistency in the titles assigned, beyond the term *ad filium*.[22] Astin further noted that Cicero never refers to a work on oratory by Cato. This argument from silence is especially convincing because Cato was such an authority, a figure to be cited if one could. And he is a figure of great prominence and importance in Cicero's *Brutus*. As a matter of principle one should not argue from the noninfluence of a work to its nonexistence, but Cato makes a special case, especially for the late republicans who were looking far more carefully into their first literature. If not Cicero, the hard-core antiquarians Varro and Nigidius Figulus left no stone unturned. In addition, Cicero's very fictional program in his dialogues—the *Laelius de amicitia,* the *Cato de senectute,* the setting of the *De oratore,* the early Roman figures in the *Brutus*—was made possible by silences in the record. Varro had restored much of the old words, monuments, places, and practices in his voluminous writings. Cicero could still read some of Cato's speeches, but he could not read, nor could the encyclopedist Celsus in the next generation, any systematic work by Cato on oratory or medicine or old age for that matter. A convincing division of the genuine works of Cato must include the *Origines,* the *De agricultura,* the speeches, and then writings to his son.

The *testimonia* that refer to the lost works repeatedly connect the work in question to the son. In 1850 O. Jahn had argued that Cato wrote a set of books to aid the education of his son (the elder, Licinianus, not Salonianus).[23] This is a deduction from the titles in the *testimonia* and from a passage in Plutarch (*Cat. Mai.* 20.7), who writes that Cato wrote a history in big letters for his son. Two other notices of Cato's distinctive and public treatment of his family are significant here. According to Plutarch (*Cat. Mai.* 20.3), Cato declined to have his son educated in the school of his freedman Chilon, on the grounds that it was not right for his son to be subject to a slave. The second notice also comes from Plutarch (*Cat. Mai.* 33.4), who notes that Cato wrote a handbook (*hypomnēma*), in his own hand, for the dietetic treatment of his *familia*.[24] Astin rightly noted that this was not a medical handbook. *Hypomnēma* and its Latin equivalent, *commentarius*, were used for the unstylized narrative that the historian used in making his history. Plutarch may have used the word simply to reflect its lack of polish. One suspects that large sections of Cato's *De agri cultura*, with its embedded recipes, agricultural and managerial directives, and prayers, which lacks the stylistic consistency of, for instance, Livy's appropriation of archaic material, would have struck Plutarch as *hypomnēmata*. The writing to his family may have been made public by Cato himself, who clearly thought his household management (of slaves, children, and wife) and his own writing practices of public merit and who thought it important to contrast polemically his writing practices with those of other Romans and their Greek clients. Cato objected to the opulent display of slaves, but he publishes on the proper management and care for slaves, both in the *De agri cultura* and in this lost work on diet. Cato's *De agri cultura* testifies to the fact and the necessity of delegation.[25] Indeed, it is a text where oversight, administration as we would call it, is more the *disciplina* than agriculture itself.[26] Cato wants his Roman audience to conclude that the great man and his family do not need a medical, rhetorical, or agricultural *technē* or educational texts in Greek; his family is in itself an agricultural and oeconomic script for the rest of Rome.

Cato's most famous notices of his own writing dramatized the process of composition and revision; in a speech demonstrating that he has not profited personally from public office, he directs his slave on what among his good deeds to include and what to exclude. He is decidedly not writing in his own hand. Instead, as Fronto preserves for us, he tells his slave to strike out this and that part of his sterling record of service to the Roman people.[27] This portion of the speech, purporting to be the unself-conscious report of the man's actual life, a bit of unedited montage, is in fact a magnificent, staged rhetorical performance, a *praeteritio* and a recreation of dialogue. Together with the notices that he wrote a school text for his son in big letters and that he wrote directives for the physicking of his family, his composition on his composition reminds us that Cato knew the value of the display of writing practices. He presents himself not surprisingly as a self-sufficient writer. He has no poets as clients (although apparently early in his career he may have tried: he brought Ennius to Rome when returning from Sardinia in the Second Punic War).[28] In the *De sumptu suo* the slave scribe is present only as the instrument of his deletion and self-control. The contrast of free author with the slave's (mechanical) role recurs in another notice of Cato's writing, the record that he wrote school texts for his son. Perhaps he had to write for his son because he would not let him go to Chilon's school (presumably with the rest of the sons of Cato's circle). Here we must be careful in taking the biographical notices too simply. He did not write an educational manual, but that does not mean he wrote school texts solely for the use of his son. As with the publication of his speech, we overhear and oversee the process of Cato's composition; we are let in on the private document, the directives to his *vilicus* and the schooling of his son. With the latter the *testimonia* indicate individual *Latin* exercises, not some grand or theoretical treatment: in sum, a history in big letters and *praecepta*. To anticipate: these were what the Greek curriculum and perhaps the Latin curriculum could not provide—a prose history of Rome and prose maxims to correspond to the Greek gnomologies. Ennius and Naevius are reported to have taught in both languages (Suet. *Gramm.* 1.1); and while we have no notice of their curriculum, their poetry and that of Livius Andronicus could have provided a Latin version for much of the traditional fare of the grammar school, but not prose maxims or prose history.

What were these *praecepta*? The *testimonia* do not agree upon the topic. The extant sayings touch upon medical, agricultural, and stylistic advice and have led scholars to identify lost treatises on these topics. Yet quotations "from" these lost works seem to have been recycled—at times it seems that ancient authors were not reading Cato but larding their works with familiar quotations. Astin argued that the work to Cato's son was in fact a collection of precepts, sententiae.[29] Now, Livius Andronicus had provided a first poetic text for the Roman schoolboy; perhaps even in his lifetime this was replaced by the hexameter version whose fragments we have; indeed, Ennius and Naevius, we can imagine, would have preferred the hexameter and their own hexameters to the Saturnian verses of Livius or their reworking as hexameters. Cato's precepts were the Latin correlate for an ubiquitous Greek first writing and reading exercise: the *gnomologium*.[30] This miscellany form explains the variety of topics found in quotations that then led later Roman authors to misattribute the quotation and invent works for the founding figure Cato.

Extant Greek *gnomologia* indicate a continuous tradition like that of the *stephanos,* the miscellany of verse. John Barns has demonstrated that the prose-writing exercise was ethical, divided in subjects, in turn sometimes divided into sections pro and contra, on the theme of marriage or women in general, for example.[31] Perhaps what truly appealed to Cato (the military and political Roman would not have found appealing Greek poetic ethical material with its insistent musing on fortune and her injuries) was the form of the prose *gnomologium*: gnomic advice written in the persona of the paterfamilias. Photius's summary of Stobaeus makes this authorial stance clear: *Septimiōi idiōi uiōi . . . sullexamenos epi tōi ruthmisai kai beltiōsai tōi paidi tēn phusin, amaurotaran ekhousan* ("to his own son Septimius . . . having excerpted for the management and improvement of the child's nature, which is somewhat dim").[32] The gnomology had the double attraction for Cato of communicating the perspectives of a traditional paternalism with a display of writing in his own voice and hand to his family. It also offered him the opportunity for recycling his own sententiae, for the kind of self-excerption we see him practicing elsewhere. The gnomology appealed as writing in a familiar mode: a version of writing not as the delegated duty of a client or as a systematic manual but as a disciplinary instrument of the father himself. Like the handbook for his slaves' care and like many of the passages of the *De agri cultura,* the precepts were a list of imperatives to be remembered. Again, he writes with a father's industry and care in a parsimonious, terse mode to insure industry, thrift, and profit, this time in his son.

The extant distichs provide a view of the qualities of paternalism, imperatives, and traditionalism that helped shape the attitudes and practice of the young writer, but only in this generic sense are they the legacy of the historical Cato. In the opening letter, where Cato tells his son, "I shall teach you how to compose the moral foundation of your soul" (*docebo quo pacto morem animi tui componas*), the lesson of self-composition has no doubt been retrojected from the first distich, *Si deus . . .* Nonetheless, the real Cato has triumphed in a way: every Latin schoolboy is his son, and his son is not going to Chilon's school. Cato has furnished an ongoing Latin tradition for the early reader.

THE IMAGINARY OF THE TEXT

The anonymous scribe and teacher who penned for Cato the opening letter of advice to the young student had read the *Distichs* well. He responded to the underlying promise of the verses—education is a prize worth our sacrifices, and the series of directives in the text lying before us, waiting to be read with our newly won skill, will launch us upon the course of self-composition.

The following pages inquire into that self-composition. Despite the enthusiasm of the preface writer, the child is not a passive vehicle waiting to be filled up by Cato's directives. While the individual by the very act of schooling adopts socially approved behaviors, the mode of acquisition is not so simple as the model of a dictating text and its larger allegorical correlate, the replicating society, suggest. Thus the process of use must interest us as much as the virtues or patterns of behavior abstracted from the school text. Like the introductory letter, the *Distichs* invite the child to direct his own life of learning. In part as the reader learns, copies, and speaks imperative, he identifies himself as Cato (even if he is a schoolgirl). At least within the play parameters of the school, the child now gives the orders. This seems a powerful act of subjectivity, a milestone in the co-constitutive acts of culture, learning to read and write, where the initiand is directed by texts and teachers and the experience of so many who learned to read before, and yet who by reading and in reading may feel free, arrived, and powerful.

The child assumes the voice of command and makes the text his own by reading, writing, memorizing, and reciting the distichs. In treating the text no longer as the ciphers of a script but part of his daily, lived routine, the student internalized the Catonian mode, to which he might often return, as when in full-scale declamation he speaks as the severe father and, if needed, as the errant or penitent son. Now his practice is more imitative, and meditative—in the Latin sense of practicing and recasting a set model. The meditative mode lies between the early imitative and the future compositional modes. In distinction from the verbatim reproduction of the model, the student practices with his model. He had practiced in a meditative manner when he "declined" the *chreia* by taking the set formula "When asked . . . , Socrates said . . . " and varying this sentence by changing the grammatical case from the nominative. Similarly, in composing his fable, the boy might have recast a verse fable as prose. As with fable, the reader is easily tempted to invent maxims on the lines of those he has read. As a mode of moralizing and as training in sententiousness, the maxim is an endlessly productive genre that values pithy expression of sentiment about a recurring set of themes rather than rote recall of a model. Indeed, the verse form of the distich implies a variation on the original prose of Cato. In addition, the genre is agglutinative, not exclusive. Various sayings are drawn to it. The genre acts like a supermagnet for wit and eagerly, indiscriminately, takes strips of context and ascribes to Cato aphorisms of other historical figures, even turns of phrase of the Augustan poets. Persona, style, and meter rather than a single source unite the *Distichs*.

Certainly, the meditative mode trains the student in verbal variation, but also in the cohesive stance of persona. When declining a *chreia* the student varied the grammatical case of "Socrates" and attended to the consequent syntactic changes. Such stylistic play has an importance beyond the immediate, technical training in a flexible relationship between grammatical and topical subject; it encourages a realization of the shape and mutability of language. The student learns that language is an object—not a sacred object to be preserved, chanted, written, and rewritten—but an object of and for one's fashioning. The declension of maxim or *chreia* comprises the first step in the process by which the student learns that his practice with texts fashions a relationship among the written text, a persona, and a performance. The meditative mode begins by breaking the rapport between writer and reader. The written no longer constrained the reader-copier. The paratexts to the *Distichs* (epistle, prefaces, insertions, epitaph) reiterate the relationship of the text and the boy. He is no mere drudge; this is not dictation. Rather, at the grandest, it is self-composition. The boy is doing more than reading or writing (so *intellegere*, not *legere*); and as the epistle writer promises, following the lead of the first distich, he is doing more than learning or even composing words (*morem animi tui componas*). When we begin to imagine that the text will affect us, we have entered the meditative mode. When we believe it will have permanent, improving effect, we have adopted not simply the persona of the teacher but the essential ideology of the social institution. More simply, at this point we believe we are schooling ourselves, not being schooled.

The paratexts try to dispose the student to a definitive sort of reading and use.

Although decidedly not transparent indices of an identical use of the text through time, they intimate expectations about the text. The idea that Cato, the writer of the distichs or his stand-in, the teacher, will compose the *mos* of the student's *animus* arises from a reading of the *Distichs* themselves, with their encouragement to study and the promise that the student's forces will grow until he is a man, a master of his speech and action. The diction nicely collapses the technical and the moral (just as had the maxim *legere et non intelligere neglegere est*). Neglect is a moral category, a failure to do what one should, and *mos* is not simply customary observance, convention, but convention sanctioned by Roman tradition as right, estimable, and imitable. Thus the prefatory epistle instructs its ideal reader that the mind and learning have a moral life and routine. Further and most significantly, this routine can be shaped just as surely and apparently as one's writing. In sum, according to a rhetoric of educational training, a system of compositional rules and practices renders discourse efficacious and the self moral. And these seem to be the same thing. In Quintilian's terms the good man is the man skilled at speech.

The *Distichs* present a series of roles and relationships that help create the imaginary of the text. The imaginary springs from the amalgam of the fictitious situations and agents presented in the various distichs, but is also shaped by the uses to which the text is put. In turn, the paratexts seek to enshrine certain uses of the text, to direct the imaginary of the text by positing an ideal reader and reading practices. At its most heavy-handed, scholarly commentary on a text attempts to fix meaning for future readers. From an equally schoolmasterly impulse, the writing of an opening epistle or the adding of simplified versions attempts to guide future readers in their use of the text. Like fable, the collection of sententiae seems to invite such embellishment—without the fixity that the commentator on a classic may try to impose. Some unknown early user has prefixed to the two-line verse distichs simplified versions. Again, like the epistle, these lines are not "authentic"— were we to persist in whittling down the schoolbook to an ur-manuscript. However, the short sentences found between the opening exhortation and the body of the exercise show an authentic, ancient embellishment of the *Distichs;* they form a direct link with the old, Greco-Roman tradition of the gnomology (they include Latin versions of the Greek sayings of the Seven Sages, part of Greek school sentences).[33] The imaginary of the *Distichs* has repeatedly spurred readers to fill up the text, to provide it with paratexts—prefatory passages that replicate educational exhortation, titles, and even an epitaph—and to add sentences of their own, both short sentences and spurious distichs. These short sentences present one rewriter's distillation of the longer precepts. They seem less objectionable, slightly bowdlerized versions of the *Distichs,* since they do not refer to the student's aggrieved position: there is no friend who has offended. Indeed, *invidia,* ill will and rivalry, has no place in this rewriting. Instead the unobjectionable advice works (rapidly) from god downward:

deo supplica	Worship god
cognatos cole	Love your family
datum serva	Preserve what is entrusted to you
foro pare	Obey the laws
cum bonis ambula	Keep good company
mundus esto	Be neat
saluta libenter	Be prompt to salute
maiori concede	Give way to your elder
magistratum metue	Honor the magistrates
verecundiam serva	Preserve your modesty
rem tuam custodi	Guard your patrimony

This set of virtues includes as venerated elements god, family, law, and the social superior. Indeed, the imperatives inscribe the reader in a series of hierarchies, often set in the public sphere, a number of them in the street, where the boy must behave appropriately toward magistrates and fellow citizens. In the school curriculum, the colloquies imagine these scenes as developed dramas of encounter. In addition, economic activity, beginning with the third sentence, has a prominent place, where the general message is not "Make money" but "Preserve your patrimony." Principal seems if not as important, certainly a similar *venerandum,* an object of diligent care like the gods, a social superior, or one's own reading and writing.

mutuum da	Loan money
cui des videto	Be careful to whom you loan
conviva raro	Party seldom
nihil temere credideris	Credit no one without deliberation
aleam fuge	Avoid gambling
alienum noli concupiscere	Don't covet another's possessions

Finally, the educationalist has his customary instinct for self-preservation and perpetuation:

libros lege	Read books
quae legeris memento	Remember what you have read
liberos erudi	Educate your children
litteras disce	Learn your letters
liberalibus stude	Study the liberal arts

In this primer of Roman virtues, god, family values, and study form a somewhat rough trinity. The thematic similarities of a set of prescriptions reveals what one abbreviator and subsequent readers made of the long text. For future readers, the short sentences would be one of several preliminary exercises. Again we see the customary form of simple model and later expansion, another instance of a graduated reading, writing, and speaking curriculum. We also see conceptual fields, united as themes of the imperatives and set in a simple hierarchy: god at the outset, then family and social values, school at the end.

Did the imperatives have their intended effect upon the student? No doubt, some Romans loaned badly, ran through their patrimony, and did not supplicate god as surely as memorizers of the Ten Commandments have coveted their neighbor's ox. The historian, faced with a text of moral imperatives as with so much other evidence, may have to be content with describing social attitudes (or the material and cultural conditions that underlie the formation and communication of such attitudes). The relation of attitudes to behavior has seemed to some historians unrecoverable. Certainly, it will be so if we think of the text, even these simple commands, as transparent and efficacious. Not all readers and writers became lifelong literary soul cultivators, as the *Distichs* advise. A better heuristic tool may well be found in routines of use. One examines what the text invites, not moral action in the abstract, but habits of speech and writing to mediate social, familial, and personal relations. In their brevity and moral earnestness, the *Distichs* seem to need no interpretation; they pose as the irreducible *dicta* of the old Cato, but the reader's task is more than learn and repeat; it is one of use: memorize and apply, refashion and recast.

THE WORLD OF THE *DISTICHS*

Although not with the economy of the short sentences, the two-line imperatives do present a self-contained world. The brief sentences had presented a short course in *pietas* by dictating essential relations to the gods, family, and the state, with the school as another realm for diligent devotion. The two-line verse precepts present their own imagined world; yet while the *Distichs* lay down resolutions for problems in social conduct and in daily routine, they do not constitute a clear ethical system. One early precept demonstrates the situational quality of the collection:

> Clemens et constans, ut res expostulat, esto: 1.7
> temporibus mores sapiens sine crimine mutat.

> Be lenient or severe as the situation demands:
> The wise man suits his ways to the times without fear of recrimination.

This distich sets responsiveness above abstract virtue: it advocates the virtue of prudence over noncontextualized principles of right action. Others do spell out what to do in certain situations:

> Nil temere uxori de servis crede querenti: ·   1.8
> semper enim mulier, quem coniux diligit, odit.

> Don't just believe your wife when she complains of the slaves:
> For a woman always hates whom her spouse loves.

These and others like them offer rhetorical virtues: whose speech to believe, whose to distrust, when to speak, when to keep silent, again and again how to avoid *crimen* (verbal attack), how to seek *fama* (verbal support). The recurrent structure of verse form and verbal mood (imperative) and this underlying thematic contribute to the cohesion of the text. In addition, restatements of the educational ideal justify the hard course upon which the schoolboy is set:

> Instrue praeceptis animum, ne discere cessa,   2.31a
> nam sine doctrina vita est quasi mortis imago.

> Fortify your mind with precepts; don't stop learning:
> for the unlettered life is a likeness of death.

The life to be lived, this mind cultivation through precepts, is the coherent whole of which the precepts are a part and to which they invite the reader. The internalization of the precepts, both taking them to heart and acting upon them, renders the text cohesive—any contradiction stems from our failure to understand. If this defense of a lack of systematicity seems cultish, it is because both cult and school depend on shared experience for their rationale. The preface admonished that reading should not be mechanical. Reading then demands exegesis, but the explanatory system is not expounded, since it belongs to lived experience and will arise from the master's explanations of ambiguity in various texts, from the internalization of the maxims, and from the application of these to life. This text, like other sapiential literature, does not teach dogma but the promise of maturity and wisdom. Part of this promissory didacticism is the text's notices of its partiality (it offers directives but no explanation of, for instance, how to respond to circumstance) and the reader's incomplete understanding (the reader is in need of the text's directives and is imagined as the young student, one intermediate between *legere* and *intellegere*).

Admittedly, the life imagined by the text seems liminal, at times even a little nasty. The reader/copier/memorizer is always a *tu,* a second person singular. He and she are always a boy. The boy does not get to write in the first person. The ancient early writing exercises were not narratives in the first person. The schoolchild was not taught the familiar modern sequence where the "I" is gradually sequestered, even censored, until one is said to be writing objectively, that is to say, in the alleged impersonality, distance, and supposed narrative cohesion of the third person, where pronouns often function anaphorically to bind the text together and not deictically or self-referentially. The ancient student would get to use "I," but later when that "I" is totally fictionalized, when he speaks in the persona of another in some declamatory theme. There he must reinsert the "I" into the spare third-person narrative that is the thesis of the declamation. In the *Distichs,* however, the reader is always the "you" directed by an imperative (even if this imperative is the so-called third person, the imperative of law).[34] This second-person subject is part of a hexameter line; most often the subject comes at the end of the line in the form of the imperative; and the most frequent form, twenty-three times, is *memento*. So the student hears father Cato talking to him and must imagine himself as the memorious son. What he imagines doing, aside from remembering, is a series of bodily actions or states—stay awake, stay silent, stay cool:

> Officium alterius multis narrare memento,   1.15
> at quaecumque aliis benefeceris ipse, sileto.
>
> Remember to spread abroad the news of a good deed done to you,
> but speak not at all of the services you have rendered others.[35]
>
> Ne cures, si quis tacito sermone loquatur: 1.17
> conscius ipse sibi de se putat omnia dici.
>
> Don't worry if someone whispers:
> The self-conscious man thinks everything is being said about him.
>
> Si tibi pro meritis nemo respondet amicus,   1.23
> incusare deos noli, sed te ipse coerce.
>
> If no friend treats you as you deserve,
> don't reproach the gods but repress yourself.
>
> Servorum culpis cum te dolor urguet in iram,   1.37
> ipse tibi moderare, tuis ut parcere possis.
>
> When indignation at the faults of your slaves drives you to violent anger,
> control yourself so that you can spare your property.

The situation of the distich, the danger from which your trained disposition delivers you, can be simply *res* or *tempora,* which we might treat as the calque for *tukhē*—that agent ubiquitous in the Greek *gnomologia* and anthologies. But the *Distichs* seem more concerned with the unrewarded self than any musing on misfortune. The greater world, teachers, parents, and peers have not recognized the misfortunate "you," who must, despite all injustice and resentment, learn to keep silent. The unfaithful friend makes a frequent agent or stimulus. He offends verbally, by not praising you, for instance. Praise and blame swirl about in the tempest that is the world of the *Distichs*. Amid this circulation, fear of verbal criticism stings the most (it is the most frequent stimulus; see 2.13, 2.19, 3.2, 4.16, 4.29):

> Luxuriam fugito, simul et vitare memento   2.19
> crimen avaritiae; nam sunt contraria famae.
>
> Flee opulence, and remember to shun too
> the accusation of greed; for they are inimical to good repute.
>
> Cum recte vivas, ne cures verba malorum,   3.2
> arbitri non est nostri, quid quisque loquatur.

Since you would live morally, don't worry about the words of evildoers,
it is not in our power to control what someone else says.

Utere quaesitis opibus, fuge nomen avari: 4.16
quid tibi divitias, si semper pauper abundes.

Use the resources you have stored up; flee the title of a miser:
what good are riches to you if ever-parsimonious you store them up?

Sometimes the "you" is a master (*dominus*, 3.10), an old man (*senex*), a witness (*testis*, 3.3), a bridegroom, a husband, even the flogged son (4.6). In 1.28 you read that you have no wealth; in 1.30 you read another role you are growing into:

Quae culpare soles, ea tu ne feceris ipse: 1.30
turpe est *doctori*, cum culpa redarguat ipsum.

What you find fault with in others, do not commit yourself:
for it disgraces a learned man when a fault convicts him.

Impecunious and on the way to being a scholar, imagining through literature future courses of life, now you know that you are in the academy. In all these male roles the *Distichs* impart what you should attempt, mostly in negative fashion. To the quietism and self-restraint of the "you" slighted by friends (1.23: *te ipse coerce*), 1.14b adds another instance of the dissimulation of hurt:

Dissimula laesus, si non datur ultio praesens: 1.14b
qui celare potest odium, post laedere quem vult.

If you have been injured and no means of immediate vengeance is at hand,
    conceal your feeling:
the man who can hide hatred can take his vengeance later on anyone
    he desires.

You are in a perpetual state of denial and of lack:

Ne tibi quid desit, quaesitis utere parce, 1.24
utque quod est serves, semper deesse putato.

Use sparingly what you have stored up so that you do not fall into need,
and to preserve what you have, imagine you are ever in lack.

The student is not simply presented with states of absence; he is told to imagine them. Instead of physical violence or even verbal remonstrance, the aggrieved "you" turns to a mental activity: remembering and deferring and so imagining that the present state will one day soon come to an end.

A mental state of lack and denial marks the student, both in the initiatory moment (when he comes to school, when he comes to literacy) so well developed in the *Distichs* and through the graduated stages of the curriculum. It is no accident that the diction of the last distich cited is taken from a fable in Horace.[36] The poet represents a later stage in the curriculum, when exegesis will return to rationalize the state of lack that the poems of Horace so often advertise. Ultimately, at the highest level of exegesis, although this may not appeal to contemporary literary sensibilities, the poet's literary deference will be explained by the scholiasts in biographical terms (by his subordinate relations to Augustus and Maecenas, by his "preference" of a Sabine farm to city life, and politics, at Rome) and by the philosophers in terms of Epicurean tenets. Then reading of Horace will be led back to tenets, but the *Distichs'* lines anticipate the more advanced play with the text. So 1.37,

> Servorum culpa cum te dolor urguet in iram,
> ipse tibi moderare, tuis ut parcere possis,

is modeled on Horace *Epistulae* 1.2.59–61:

> qui non moderabitur irae,
> infectum volet esse, dolor quod suaserit et mens,
> dum poenas odio per vim festinat inulto.

> The man who fails to control his anger,
> will wish undone what his aggrieved passion has concocted
> when he jumped to violent retribution and his hatred knew no vengeance.

The *chreiae* present anger at slaves as the crucial test of one's manliness and education: "Zeno, on seeing a student's young slave bruised from a severe beating, said to his student, 'I see the traces of your anger' "; and "Plato, when angered by a gluttonous and disgusting slave, summoned Speusippus, his sister's son, and said as he was leaving, 'Beat this slave, for I am too angry.' "[37] In the distich only the foolish man believes his wife when she complains of slave behavior. Formally, then, distich 1.37 makes the sparest epitome of the Horatian lines. It prepares the student for the sentiment of restraint, for the crucial vocabulary of self-control, and for the exposition of ethical themes in verse.

Equally, it is but one form of school play with two lines from Horace, which the student could expand into a developed fable. As a preliterary form, the *Distichs* give the moral of poems or parts of poems. In fact, they teach that a poem can be fragmented, its pieces reused and recombined to other forms and even purposes. But notice of the formal affinities of the verses does not do justice to the complexities of this distich as an intertext, for it intersects with school discourse about the slave and the self, and their crucial distinction. While drawn from Horace, the connection of the distich remains invisible until the student has learned lyric or satiric poetry. Then he may realize the source of the simplified verses, but he will also realize that Horace himself, the authoritative classic, can be varied, reworked. A tag leads to Horace (indeed, a training in compressed maxims probably made the reading of that difficult poetry easier), but equally a complex poem can be reduced to tags. Further, the boy would surely feel the connectedness of his reading and of his intellectual life. Again we should stress that this does not mean he will love Latin lyric or the ironies of Latin satire. Horatian poverty will be hard to embrace except in textual play. Yet several distichs share with moralizing exegesis of Roman comedy and satire the imperative to preserve his patrimony. All of this moralizing may well contribute to a sort of social comfort, where the student learns to meet grievance and injury not with violent reaction but with deferral or even textualization. Writing, more reading, and exegesis may be the proper responses to a sense of injury. These practices constitute the *meditatio* to which the Roman reader will return again and again.

In fact, at least according to the rhetoric of the exercise, the young student pens his way to a sort of quietism, a species of self-control and denial (1.23 and 1.24). While not preaching pacific virtues (see 1.14b), the *Distichs* practice a displacement of violence with the boy learning to write his revenge. At the head of the virtues, according to the *Distichs*, stands patience (suffering and perseverance), but patience is only a virtue because it is the means to the end of vengeance and superiority:

> Quem superare potes, interdum vince ferendo,   1.38
> maxima enim morum semper patientia virtus.

> The man whom you will one day best, conquer for now by suffering:
> for the greatest moral virtue is always patience.

In the world of the *Distichs* the child wants to excel: his motivation hardly needs to be named. Of course, the child wants to beat his peers. There may be joy in learning one's lessons, pleasure to be found in literature, and the *Distichs* do name the cultivation of the self as the worthy end of schooling and declare as the tangible result of education a profession and an inalienable livelihood, but the child is moved by the desire to beat his peers and to be known for the triumph. Quintilian would be proud. In such an agonistic world, the division between those whom you can harm and those you cannot is both a sign of your progress and a crucial skill, not to be misjudged. Patience qualifies as a virtue because she serves the boy toward his final victory. No doubt, school thrives on this controlled competition, which feeds and redirects an aggressive rivalry and spreads the passion to win games to an ethical habit. Successful schooling, in a system that prizes elitism, will not mean that everyone is a winner; it will mean that the boy has internalized the desire to excel, or, put more negatively, the threat of the schoolmaster has been replaced by self punishing self. So distich 4.40, while directing all blame to the self, also internalizes the sequence of error, punishment, and renewed effort:

> Cum quid peccaris, castiga te ipse subinde:
> vulnera dum sanas, dolor est medicina doloris.

> If ever you blunder, punish yourself immediately:
> in the course of doctoring the wound, pain will be the cure for pain.

The distichs that champion self-coercion and self-chastisement subsume all error and all offense into failures of self-management. Grief, *dolor*, is thereby not the condition of someone aggrieved by an agent who must be punished but the self-inflicted inducement to greater mental labor. Again a common diction and strategy collapse various fields of human activity: social relations, family roles and behavior, and the world of the school. The elimination of external agents aims at a certain subjectivity, where the self is not an object directed, injured, or sickened by forces outside the self. This training would dispose the student to more advanced, contemporary thinking about the self (Stoicism in particular). In addition, by idealizing an approved routine, the training can return to the individual any failures to realize that routine. If a child is bothered by the taunts of his peers or if a ten-year-old boy cannot sit still or lacks the motor skills to write smoothly or perhaps even articulate all the sounds of his language, these behaviors are marked as problems of self-management.

Educational thinking ranks bodily actions by labeling some as immature, servile, or effeminate. Thus the boy is presented with bodily, physical, visible differences by which he can measure his progress. In this learning of routine, the boy casts himself as the chastiser, the one who makes his body chaste, who has, as the first distich advised, a pure mind. Discipline, which is to say, the learned life and not physical punishment, checks and redirects bodily urges. Such anyway is the mentalist rhetoric to be learned from the *Distichs*. The boy must become not the squirming child or the irate man who beats slaves but, as in 1.9, the advice giver who directs a friend resistant to counsel or, as in the next distich, the sage and terse speaker who persuades the verbose. In his rhetoric to the friend or to the talkative, he will have the distichs themselves as his weapons of persuasion. Through these scenes the text models both ideal behavior and ideal reading—the boy has internalized the roles of the school exercises and can use them as his own. Of course, the friend reluctant to heed advice and the friends prone to chatter are alter egos of the maturing boy. The ideal ego is that of the paterfamilias in training.

In contrast to these negligent self-composers, the successful boy develops the habit of reducing, excerpting, expanding, and moralizing the text. At the same time he learns to imagine himself in that text, to identify with its ideal type, and to reproduce and recast its words as his own. The *Distichs* exert a pressure to internalize the lessons of the imperatives. Certainly, the student in this early exercise was to reproduce the verse lines exactly, but the lines encouraged self-composition in the mode of Cato. The boy adopts an outlook toward his self and his community but also toward his current and ongoing practice, education. The *Distichs* provide an emerging sense of self: the child composed and consoled by this text is different from his peers; he is aggrieved but full of promise, just waiting for his seniority so that he can be recognized, so that he can excel. A state of expectant mastery describes the boy's disposition toward textuality. Amid all the strictures of a strongly supervised curriculum, the boy in the *Distichs* seems to sense his own progress from mechanical ventriloquism to rhetorical improvisation and impersonation, from simple reading to true understanding.

We should not underestimate the force of the feeling of improvement and achievement. Of course, it does not arise exclusively from this or any text. Rather, in the course of schooling a child is struck and told his speech or reading or writing is inferior, flawed, perhaps even puerile or servile. Another child or the same at another moment is praised for his speech or writing. It is worthy of a free man, true to the teacher's model, Cato's directives, or much later to Cicero's style. He may speak and write without fear. As he advances in the curriculum, he is told that his exercises are his own. As Quintilian would say, they show his judgment. The best declaimers are models for the other boys to emulate and perhaps to push from first place. The text of the *Distichs* contributes to an interrelated practice of physical and verbal punishment, daily speaking and writing exercises, oral directions and the student's performance. The boy is learning to position himself in a fluid economy of praise and censure; thus he becomes a citizen in a community that grants status to good performances and can rearrange its hierarchy of the approved. He is becoming both performer and critic and thereby escaping the child status of object and victim.

Faced with the sheer slowness, the attrition, the ideological severity, and the technical drudgery of this system of education, we may little wonder that literacy was not widespread. In a typical elitist claim, the school's spokesmen—teachers, theorists, exercises—maintained that they produced free men not basic literacy, and the blazon of their success was the great speaker or writer (a truly accomplished reader was not impressive—slaves performed this role). The *Distichs* have allowed us a look into the process of this education. They may also be useful if they have prompted a realization that ancient education was different in kind. If one views composition as a basic end of education, it is tempting to identify with the schoolchildren of old. Perhaps we can be as enthusiastic as Scaliger and imagine ourselves as young Cato learning to read and write. Like learning to read, composition seems a neutral, technical, even ahistorical category. These blanketing terms, especially reading, have been challenged, since the processes involved vary from time to time and culture to culture; more importantly, they ignore the different material conditions of their production and the very different subjectivities of their agents.

Perhaps the present study of fable and maxim should bring to mind a better comparandum than our own schooling: Roman elite training in composition may have been more like a technical and creative craft apprenticeship, as if the Roman student were like a Renaissance sculptor or painter in training, first copying traditional forms until he could shape the material like his master. Indeed, the apprentice's hand becomes so like the master's that modern connoisseur-critics debate vigorously whose work is whose. Thus one could argue that rhetorical training developed a series of technical exercises in composition and performance that led to the *suasoria* and *controversia* of declamation, which may be likened to the apprentice's or journeyman's trial piece, the performance that advanced him to master. In the *suasoria* the boy practiced a mature ventriloquism wherein he spoke as the advice giver to some famous figure. Imitative and derivative, combining the various building blocks of composition at which he has been so thoroughly rehearsed, the boy may, within the narrow confines of the plot set him, speak his own piece. Perhaps such composition begins to sound like a caricature of mannerist art, where tradition, genre, and technique determine all, and meaning (allegedly) has receded in favor of a rivalry of formal virtuosity. Comparisons with the graphic arts serve to remind that a traditional, labored, imitative apprenticeship, while restricting the number of practitioners, does manage to maintain a tradition and produce a few outstanding artists. It also sustains an audience. The limited social end of a difficult education may seem clear: for a hierarchical society so interested in the accumulation and distribution of status, schooling performs the diligent rivalry, removed from physical violence, of a class of peers seeking both their own and their master's praise. But mannerist art may provide a more significant point of comparison for Silver Latin and imperial schooling. Both worlds were saturated with art, in the sense of a widespread appreciation of traditional modes and the ability to work, judge, and communicate subtle variations or combinations of these modes. Rhetorical schooling produced an audience of connoisseurs, a far wider group than the restrictive strictures suggest, who used, valued, and judged a system of communication, identity, and display.

This chapter began by seeking Cato, or the practice of the little Catos who used "his" book to start them off on the course of education and maturity. The encounter with Cato brings the reader face-to-face with *verba prisca,* the world of the Roman sentence, which is not the hard, genuine place of the real Cato or modern lexica and lexical or stylistic studies but the fluid, creative, lived place of a Roman tradition that was a great recyclery of old words and old styles. In this world, words travel and are fixed and travel again, changing from prose to verse, even from Greek to Latin. Studies in the curriculum and canons of the school often treat the Roman school as a sort of transfer station where a common stock of examples and sayings and treatises and poems passes through the shadowy way station of the Middle Ages before being reclaimed and recleaned as good, lost freight. In fact, the *Distichs* formed part of a creative world in which style followed many demands, where the old and genuine Catonian tag *rem tene verba sequentur* was a daily, routine imperative, where stylization, speaking as Cato, was more important and more common than encountering and miming the *verba ipsissima* of the censor of the second century B.C.

The reader's encounter with a paternal and atavistic language instruction contributes to a premise that every generation is the same, sitting at the knee of old Cato, learning that hard, marble thing that is Latin. At this stage the syntax is not difficult; the forms of the language are poetic but not archaic. The student is not yet faced with the difficulty of full-scale composition. He has a sure guide; so the maxims attest with their initiatory enthusiasm. Still he reads a school language and is encouraged in school activities, part of which is the sentiment instilled by the *Distichs:* Cato's language and directives are for you. Every generation can then be self-legitimating, the same in its mimicry of the old. This experiencing of the past elevates the child's play with speech and style to markers of identity and exclusivity. In what may be the grand fiction of learning Latin, the exercise ushers students into a complete world with the promise that the child will therein become an adult, a masterful self-composing agent who has developed an ethics of self-address, self-chastisement, and ultimately triumph. Control of the young self, the rhetoric of the school counsels, will provide redress. Here too the school gives voice to what the child feels or is meant to feel. Reading Cato, the young boy learns that his wrongs have been felt before, indeed that they are not peculiar but categorical and that redress lies in a schooled maturity.

Not all students would have read Cato as I have described. We have only to read the scholiasts to witness how differently students and teachers have understood classical texts through their long reception history. My reading has tried to reconstruct the experience of reading this text in a Roman school. This depends on a consideration of the techniques of ancient instruction described by other texts, the ancient visions of what Cato represented, and the internal pressures of the *Distichs*. The last comprise the text's explicit directives to the reader and the patterns of use encouraged by the text. Authorial pronouncements of intent are not so useful, especially with a text written in persona, except that these prefaces are rather paratexts, signs of use left and recorded by various readers of this text.

In the following chapter, the final devoted to exercises, I apply a similar investigative technique to two other exercises. To the culminating performance of Roman schooling, declamation, I have juxtaposed a far less grand example of early bilingual training. I fear that otherwise, like many an account of education, the rationalization from within the institution pirates our understanding. The abstract categories provided by the educational system are thereby taken as the raison d'être of the curriculum. Ancient education is then described as the progressive mastering of a formal system of argument and persuasion. With declamation, the formal teleology of figures learned and compositional strategies mastered seems to indicate that the student has reached the final means to argue and persuade. There is some truth in this, but it does ignore the developing subjectivity of the student. A humbler exercise shows us not simply the workshop of the rhetorical artisan but the continuities in subject matter, attitudes, and practices that shaped the subjectivity of the educated.

Rhetorical Habitus

Declamation was the final practical performance training in speaking of the Roman school. In outline, the exercises are simple. Finished at last with the preliminary exercises (the *progymnasmata*), the adolescent male gets down to intellectual wrestling that mimics the strife of adults through the pretense that the boy is the head of a household, a lawyer, a magistrate, or an adviser. First in the *suasoria* (which girls too might have spoken, since it was taught in the grammarian's school), he is a counselor to some great man, trying to turn the tide of history. Should Numa accept the kingship offered by the Roman people? Should Alexander set sail upon the ocean? The *suasoria* offers an easier situation than the *controversia,* the second exercise of declamation, because the composer has to manage only one voice, but, as in the *controversia,* he speaks in competition, to win the praise of his teacher, to affect his rank in the class, and on special occasions to impress the other boys and fathers, even aficionados who have come to hear the talent. In both cases, as one suspects of his future career, the coin of prestige and status must be won from an approving audience.

The *controversia* presented a more challenging structure and a more complex (imaginary) audience: the declaimer now pretends to plead in the law courts. His teacher has provided a few sentences describing the (bizarre) situation and a law that stipulates dire punishment. The declaimer must compose and deliver a speech attacking or defending the allegedly chaste prostitute who wants to be a priestess or some young man who has run afoul of a severe father. Quintilian indicates that grammarians had quite often taken on the *suasoria,* and that many rhetoricians specialized in the more advanced *controversia.*

The verbal pyrotechnics of the declamation have long impressed or distressed readers.[1] Take up the beginning of the excerpts of the elder Seneca and you will find fast-paced prose, with short sentences, interspersed with apostrophe and sententiae. At times it is hard to follow, perhaps because we do not have the full version but certainly because the declaimers strove for surprise and pungent expression. It would have been easier to grasp in person, with gesture and expression to help one understand the changes in focus and address. Here is a sample. The plot is complex (one of two brothers has a son; the brothers fall successively in and out of poverty; the son moves from one house to the other, supporting the one and getting in trouble with the other) but typical for the genre and similar to many examples of New Comedy. Porcius Latro, Seneca's friend and favorite, had the son speak thus:

> What is your reproach against me? Extravagance, I suppose. All my excessive expenditure had been lavished on supporting two old men.—When my father told me not to, he said: "*He* wouldn't support me if *I* were in need." Now he was in such a plight that his last hope of support lay in the house where there lived the son he disinherited and the brother who hated him.—Suppose he dies in poverty? What will you do? It will cost you more to bury your brother than to feed him.

It does go on and on. Here is more melodrama with the sort of twist in outlook that the declaimers loved:

> My parents, who quarrel on every other topic, agree only in censuring me. Happy sight, if I can reconcile the two of you! And I shall do it—even your expressions encourage me. Rise, fathers, attend, judges: one of my parents has been saved—the other needs to be saved.

Somehow the great type for the instability of fortune is dredged up: "Who would believe that Marius, as he lay in the gutter, had been consul—and would be again."[2] Certainly, the speaker relies on antithetical expression and conjures the scene with a heavy hand. How do the expressions of the father and uncle encourage the speaker? They are both scowling and so united in their hatred, as Latro has just argued. The unrelenting quality of outrage would have been leavened with such mininarratives as descriptions of places and historical exempla. Still, obscurity is easily hit upon when each speaker tries to trump the prior, but from Seneca especially one gets a taste of the speed and fun of the performance.

The ancient denigrators of declamation did not appreciate the usefulness of adolescent boys reflecting on stepmothers' actions, on fathers' drastic measures, or on sons' divided loyalties. In antiquity, declamation was taken as an index of the vice of the age. All the complaints of its fatuity and overblown phrasing, its striving for wit, and its isolation from real life and real law have as an unexpressed premise the understanding that it is a newcomer, decidedly not part of the traditional education. This is accurate only in part. The elder Seneca believed declamation had grown up with him at the end of the first century B.C. Admittedly, public performances of declamation marked the literary culture of the capital in his day, not in Cicero's, and the education of Cicero or his son was more varied than the system that would spread with the establishment of an imperial government. Seneca does not seem to have realized the connections of the exercises with prior forms, and he does not seem to have known much of the school of Plotius Gallus, which had tempted the young Cicero with its practice declamations in Latin.[3]

For all the criticism of the style of declamation, this was the education recommended by Quintilian, a master of Latin prose style himself, and of course declamation had been a fundamental part of the education and literary sensibility of the great authors of the early empire from Ovid to Lucan, Pliny, Tacitus, and Statius. Complaint about the style and melodrama obscures the technical demands of this composition and misses the larger lessons of declamation. Despite the impression arising from the critics and from the state of the evidence (Seneca's collection especially), which prizes the excerpt, the declaimers relied on a rigorous structural undergirding, which their audience was likewise trained to appreciate. It might be expected that the schoolteacher Quintilian would laud structure, but Latro also, the declaimer most celebrated by the elder Seneca, stressed division, which is both the argumentative structure of the speech and the reduction of the case to an essential issue or issues (in the declamation where a candidate for a priestess-ship happens to have been a [supposedly nonparticipating] prostitute, and the law stipulates that the priestess must be chaste, the declaimer asks: Is chastity simply virginity or the company one keeps? And does the present case fit the spirit and not simply the letter of the law?).[4]

This chapter will present a more positive picture of the methods and effects of declamatory training. First it considers the intellectual debts of declamation, its continuity with ancient rhetorical teaching and even with ancient philosophy. Then it discusses declamation as a training in persona. As with so much of the ancient curriculum, we cannot be sure that an educational practice remained the same over centuries of use. The chronological limits of declamation are the end of the republic and the end of the empire. To take just Latin examples from the late empire, the future emperor Gratian was said by his teacher, the professor-poet Ausonius, to have been a fine student in grammar and rhetoric, and the sixth-century bishop Ennodius has left model declamations. Jerome refers to his frequent declamation as a boy.[5] But it is unlikely that Ausonius had the same aims as the first-century A.D. master Quintilian. The growth of the grammarians amid other changes suggests that education became more concerned with written than oral skills. The best evidence for declamation comes from the first and early second centuries A.D. This chapter considers especially the evidence left by two great literary figures of the early empire. Seneca the Elder left a record of the virtuoso treatments of professional teachers and (higher-status) advocates, the *Oratorum et rhetorum sententiae, divi-*

siones, colores. Quintilian's great treatise and the declamations associated with his school reveal more directly school practice.

The *suasoria* and the *controversia,* though the last of the series of compositional exercises, could employ any of the earlier exercises, especially description of places, speeches in character, fictitious interrogation, and apostrophe. In addition, the student declaimers had prepared well. They had listened to model declamations from their teacher, had received his advice, the *sermo,* on the particular declamation, and had been collecting in notebooks the noteworthy bits of other declaimers and famous passages from literary authors. They might also have access to systematic collections, like the elder Seneca's extracts, Otho's book of *colores* (see Sen. *Controv.* 1.3.11; and cf. 1.pr.11 for written or forged declamations then in circulation), and Valerius Maximus's nine books of exempla. Seneca said that Latro needed no *codices,* that he wrote everything in his mind (*Controv.* 1.pr.18). Indeed, Seneca writes as a champion of memory, recalling both the mnemonic system at which he excelled and the great treatments of prior declaimers.[6] But most declaimers would have been more like Seneca's readers and less like Latro: they would have written down the bon mots they had heard, and read all the manuals they could find. The declaimer Votienus Montanus is making an unremarkable generalization when he says: "In preparing a declamation, one writes not to best [a courtroom opponent] but to please [an audience]" (*Controv.* 9.pr.1: *Qui declamationem parat, scribit non ut vincat, sed ut placeat*), and Quintilian refers in passing (2.11.7) to the *commentarii,* the notebooks, of children, in which they set down the bits of declamation they admired. All this preparation was brought to bear on set speeches, in part because the declaimers were playing at the grandest role in Roman society, not that of the emperor (which was not an ambition to acknowledge) but that of the orator, the man who speaks to defend his friends, reunite the family, repair society, and champion Roman values. As little Ciceros, the speakers place themselves at the apogee of an imaginary Roman society, in a sort of idealized, frozen republicanism where the chief virtue and the end of life is the doing of *beneficia* to clients through speech to the acclamation of the society at large. The good society imagined through declamation is not political in the sense that stories of tyrants slain might arouse animosity against the emperor or even nostalgia for some lost political republicanism. Rather, Roman sons compete in an euergitism that solves such fundamental issues as the relations of fathers and sons, all in the ludic setting of the school and its occasional performances.

THE INTELLECTUAL ROOTS OF DECLAMATION

Among the exercises considered in this book, declamation offers broad evidence of the history of the use of an exercise over time and at the hands of variety of practitioners. Although declamation offered the most advanced training in rhetoric, it may well disappoint the enthusiast of rhetorical theory. If one were to present the history of ancient rhetoric as devolving from a tension inherent in Aristotle's relation to Platonic thinking, where rhetoric seems now grandly the art of persuasion, of psychagogia, now more humbly the science of language, or even more mundanely the practice of speech training, declamation would come in at the bottom of the diminuendo from philosophy. Ancient rhetorical investigation embraced all three tendencies—investigation into the psychology of consent, into the structure of linguistic and textual form, and into the formation of a speaking subjectivity. Declamation is not a watered-down, Roman and hence antitheoretical version of the last. It is rather a species of topical argument and thus belongs to one of the strongest strains of the rhetorical tradition.

It is difficult to label this strain, since it is both ultimately pre-Aristotelian and, in its fully enumerated form, the work of the first-century B.C. Hermagoras of Temnos, who simplified and systematized Aristotle's thinking on topical invention. The reader may have to suspend what he has learned of ancient rhetoric in order to appreciate this influential system, for, unlike the modern, the ancient student did not learn his rhetoric from reading Aristotle's three books on the subject. The ancient teacher might well impart that there were three kinds of oratorical discourse: forensic, deliberative, and epideictic. The divisions of a speech would be described, but the properly Aristotelian rhetorician should argue with syllogistic logic. Indeed, according to Aristotle, all argument is syllogistic, but for Aristotle an orator usually argues using enthymemes, not fully expressed syllogisms. An enthymeme is an incomplete syllogism usually consisting of only probably true premises, which often leaves unexpressed a single premise or the conclusion of a syllogism. A classic illustration is "Socrates is virtuous; for he is wise," whose premises, as George Kennedy explains, "are only probable and the universal major premise, 'All the wise are virtuous,' is assumed." An audience does not have the patience for full logical proof, and thus the orator admits the expression but not the substructure of logic.[7] The young declaimer, were he to follow the full philosophical mode, might have treated the law, which his teacher had set him in the outline of the declamation, as the major proposition. The essential challenge is to present the particulars of the case as the minor proposition to the major proposition of the law. However, Hellenistic and Roman schoolchildren, rhetoricians, and orators did not operate this way. Nor did they proceed in an anti-Aristotelian mode; they pursued a course to which Aristotle had contributed, though in a separate, earlier work, his *Topica*.

In the preparation of orators, perhaps it had never been important to distinguish the three branches of oratory. Rare was the speaker who would have addressed the assembly, the law courts, and ceremonial displays. It is little wonder that a mock forensic form, the *controversia*, comes to be the ultimate exercise, since legal writing and speaking were of the greatest importance for the Romans. The simplification of rules for oratory can be glimpsed as well in the manual *Rhetorica ad Herennium,* where three styles of discourse have replaced the three types of speeches as the composer's main directives. Of these two triads, the first is occasion-based, the second content-based. Topical argument is more concerned with the audience, not as a particular body but as human makers of judgments. Perhaps as rhetorical training came to be more a system of universal education and not so specifically the preparation of elite youth in city-states, the new audience came to affect rules of composition—the larger the audience the more occasion and content will recede as controlling influences, and a tendency to homogenization of method increases as a wide readership, and not a specific set of auditors, becomes the default target of reception. While declamation subsumed deliberative, forensic, and epideictic oratory in its show speeches of advice and legal conflict, it expressed its theoretical underpinnings in terms of topical argument.

Topical argument was a branch of invention, one of the techniques for producing proofs to sway an audience. It came to be, after Hermagoras in the first-century B.C., the rhetorical substructure of the persuasive section of a speech. The main narrative of the speech proceeded by a topical investigation. The term *topos* was perhaps always ambiguous. It had been current prior to Aristotle, who himself uses the term variously and indeed rethought significantly, in the *Rhetoric,* how arguments should be made. Subsequent users of the term often vacillate between two meanings: a familiar place in a text (and especially the set piece that fills that place) or a kind of argument. Declamation is topical argument both because it rejoices and abounds in these familiar places and because it proceeds by Hermagoras's modification of Aristotle's system.[8] According to Aristotle, every speaker needs to learn how to reason dialectically, which means to apply the theory of what can be affirmed. The speaker must move from generally accepted norms or propositions to a particular end. All predications fall into one of four categories: definition, genus, property, and accident. Dialectical reasoning examines ethical, logical, and physical propositions that arise from what is acceptable to a majority of the audience. Aristotle imagines that human language is interested always in moving from point A to point C, where B has been unexpressed. In its fully developed stage in the *Rhetoric,* this entails finding the middle piece of a syllogism. A student learns from the *Topica* the general kinds of reasoning that underlie all propositions. The restriction of the source of predications to four categories directly ties Aristotle to the subsequent rhetoricians and their influence on the schools. In practice, one can see, from Aristotle on, the tendency to structure inquiry about a series of general, often markedly ethical questions. Thus the Aristotelian speaker will be prone to introduce the following sort of reflection: should one do good to one's enemies? Dialectical reasoning leads to the answer no by three steps. First, it is a generally received opinion that we should do good to our friends. Second, we arrive at the contrary (which of course is false or inconsistent): we ought to do good to our enemies. The contradictory of the contrary to a common opinion will be probable: in other words, one now negates the contrary and can say: we ought not to do good to our enemies. The reasoner is here employing *topoi* and a logic of opposites so as to test whether the proposition fits a known *topos*. Topical argument at this level enlarges the stock of general judgments. The declamatory speaker will employ similar consistency-based thinking but with a handier scheme.

Aristotle had implied that the student should make a copybook of opinions under the headings that are the *topoi* of the *Topica*. In *Sophistic Refutations* Aristotle indicates that the Sophists had set their students exercises that were generally reproducible (see also Cic. *Brut.* 46). The Roman rhetorician of the early empire could also have consulted the *Topica* of Cicero. I introduce this for reason of the light that it throws on the milieu of rhetorical education immediately preceding the flourishing of declamation.

Cicero maintains that he wrote his *Topica* in seven days from memory while en route from Velia to Rhegium.[9] The work has never pleased students of Aristotle because Cicero treats *topoi* as means of invention rather than as an analytics of argument, and because he mixes in status theory. In both these regards, he anticipates the practice of the declaimers and no doubt reflects Hellenistic practice. At *De oratore* 2.162 Cicero described *locus* as the house of proofs (language and an approach that Boethius will emulate).[10]

Cicero and the Hellenistic rhetoricians were not getting their Aristotle wrong. They were proceeding in an eclectic way to codify the means of invention, and, practically speaking, putting arguments into prose works means subjecting the facts at hand to set sorts of questions (Can I define murder to exclude my client's actions? Can I draw arguments from the qualities of my client's person?) and recycling set pieces already collected in notebooks or memorized (perhaps I can include the philosophical question, Should one do good to one's enemies? in the case before me).[11] The listlike qualities of both aspects of invention must have had a strong appeal to the schools. Students could memorize four categories and reams of examples and be taught gradually to weave these together.

The greatest impulse to such tapestry came from Hermagoras. He devised a strategy for the invention of arguments of an elegant, memorable simplicity. It is perhaps good to remember that while this system of questions, *stasis* in Greek, *status* or *quaestio* in Latin, came to affect all sorts of literary compositions, it was designed to supply the speaker in a legal case with material for his eristic speech. The Hermagorean student knows to put the facts of his case to one of four reflections. He will found his pleading on one or more of these issues: did the alleged event happen, does it fall under the terms defined by the law, what was the motivation behind the event, and should the present court be hearing the case? In the memorable brevity of school Latin, conjecture asks *an sit*, definition *quid sit*, quality *qualis sit* (as for the last, competence, in Latin *translatio,* as we shall see, the student, follow-ing Cicero and Quintilian, did not use).

Hermagoras also subjected the law to four questions: letter and intent, ambigu-ity, contrary laws, and analogy. The declaimer, however, was not treating real laws. The system would come to influence Roman law, but the declaimers did not follow this aspect of Hermagoras's system. They had, of course, learned to treat ambigu-ity and obscurity and to consider the personae of the characters of their composi-tions. Armed with the questions *quid sit* and *quale sit* and the contrast of *littera* and *voluntas* (where equity could be summoned to counter a strict legalism), one would be able to declaim.[12] *An sit* was of course of vital importance for a real case, as was competence, but the student is being trained in compositional artifice not forensic method (thus the so-called inartificial proofs, such as oaths and witnesses, are neg-lected). And of course it would be all too easy to invent contrary laws or conven-ient witnesses to escape the unpleasant facts of the case set for declamation. None-theless, while declamation avoided conjecture, it explored the chief subdivisions of conjecture—did the accused have the capability and the desire to do the crime?[13] *Potestas* and *voluntas* are explored in the development of persona—for example, the case of the blind son found in his murdered father's bedchamber, which requires arguing from signs and from persona. Could a blind man do the deed? Would a son act so? are the general, topical reflections that arise when the declaimer prac-tices his systematic invention.

Declamation as a training in topical argumentation did not make clear its the-oretical debts to rhetoric or philosophy, except in the emphasis given *divisio,* the division of the speech into a series of questions (based ultimately on Hermagoras).[14] In fact, declamation belonged to a long tradition of practice oratory, whose first ex-tant exercises are the mid-fifth-century tetralogies of Antiphon. Like Roman decla-mation of the empire or the cases pled in Plotius Gallus's school in the late repub-lic, the student presents mock judicial cases (although Antiphon's reflected the course of a real Athenian case with four speeches: contra, pro, contra, pro). Aris-totle and Theophrastus are said to have introduced the philosophical thesis to the schools (which proposes a general case; the hypothesis supplies names or a specific occasion or time). Philostratus maintained that Aeschines, driven from Athens by Demosthenes (330 B.C.), initiated the Second Sophistic movement, which used hypotheses with the characters the poor man, the hero, and the tyrant, who recur in later declamations.[15]

Roman declamation drew on these intellectual strains through the medium of the Hellenistic schools and particularly the Greek scholars who came first in the third century B.C. from all parts of the Hellenistic world, some simply from south-ern Italy but others from Greece, Asia Minor, and Egypt, to change the course of Roman schooling. At Rome the early use of the verb *declamare* (often in the derogatory sense of overloud delivery) and a late gloss of *declamatio* as Greek *anaphonesis* indicate an original meaning of voice training.[16] The word could simply mean "to practice or rehearse": Marc Antony and Pompey are each said to have "declaimed" in private as preparation for important cases. Cicero declaimed in Greek up to his praetorship, in Latin for all his life. He draws attention to the novelty of the word and refers humorously to his retirement practice of philosophizing in Greek as *senilis declamatio*. Cicero was out of step or sympathy with developments such as Plotius Gallus's school (early first century B.C.), which modeled exercises on Roman cases and whose speakers were faulted for loud delivery. It was under Augustus that declamation began to flourish.

While born of the school, declamation's popularity as adult entertainment is well attested. Augustus, Agrippa, and Maecenas visited one performance (*Controv.* 2.4.12). Seneca the Elder recalls as performing or making comment a who's who of the Roman literary scene: Asinius Pollio, Cremutius Cordus, Valerius Messala Corvinus, and Ovid with his fellow poets and friends Cornelius Severus and Albinovanus Pedo. The leading orators and philosopher (Fabianus) appear.[17] Seneca the Elder presents snippets from the contests of professionals and from the performances of famous teachers whose schools were open to visitors. The audience mercilessly pounces upon slips of taste, plausibility, or Latinity. The declamatory milieu emerges as a verbal culture of extreme competition for the performers (whether schoolboys or the freedmen, provincials, and some equestrians who were the professionals) where aristocrats such as Messalla or Pollio could make or break a reputation with their pithily worded put-down.

THE APPEAL OF DECLAMATION UNDER THE EMPIRE

To be good at declamation demanded an intelligence disposed to wit, especially to that verbal play that bests an opponent. Roman declamation required facile role playing and advanced literacy skills. The importance of these for Western education, as for literature and law, is significant. Nonetheless, no inevitable factor forces education to be competitive, fantastic, and verbally aggressive and agile. Roman school texts helped socialize the student into an elite man. School composition and declamation communicated definite social values about the values of different sorts of people, institutions, and actions. No doubt, rhetorical education aided in the creation of a communicative class—not a class that can be rigorously described in positivist, sociological terms but a class or mode that communicants adopted on tombstones when they paraded their literacy and culture; in letters to patrons, magistrates, or even the emperor; and in talk among their fellow citizens and to visitors, but also to superiors and subordinates.

A great deal of the success of this education cannot be explained in a strictly functionalist manner. The exercises, however daunting or inefficient and exclusive by modern standards, encouraged the student to think of her- and himself as ascending the pinnacle of Roman society, becoming a master of persuasive speech, another Cato or Cicero. Roman declamation, in particular, but also earlier parts of the curriculum, encouraged the last stage of impersonation. The student took on the speaking role of his father. The boy plays at an adult's role, but this is not a simple impersonation. He speaks in the persona of the aggrieved, as in real life a patron or paterfamilias would on behalf of his client or social subordinates. In declamatory cases, he might speak for the freedman accused of ingratitude, the son accused of rape or patricide, the stepmother accused of poisoning, or the military hero accused of desertion. In addition to learning how to think categorically, the young man considered the various plots that could trouble the home or the city, the breaches of loyalty of social or familial order.

Declamatory plotting was more than a projection of patriarchal anxiety or filial fantasy; it explored social and familial relations quite frequently by imagining and animating the situation, sentiments, and even words of the victimized. Speaking on behalf of the prostitute who applied to be a priestess or the rape victim who hesitated between choosing the death of the rapist or marriage with him did not prepare the youth for a similar situation in adult life or necessarily inculcate an empathetic point of view.[18] It did naturalize the speaking rights of the freeborn male elite.[19] Conflicts were to be decided by a contest of his and his peers' speech; the problems of the freedman, the poor client, the wronged wife, the impetuous son, were available in an intersecting schema of set themes and expansions on these formulas. It is true that social problems sound like so many talk-show routines, resolution so many sound bites. Yet this was a desideratum. Such school exercises with their projection of idealized social and family order are a kind of social comfort, a reassurance to and from the elite as well as a linguistic training of that elite.

Declamation also prepared students for Roman law and especially inculcated the idea that the law needed interpretation, that written law would not adequately solve problems, and that educated men could plead to affect its application.[20] In reading these school exercises we can overhear the schoolboy rehearsing the needs and demands of all who might be clients for the future father. Victims abound, since declamation mimics law cases first of all in its claim to redress the breakdown of social order. Father-son relations are a frequent topic. Themes do vary in the different collections, from the elder Seneca to those from the school of Quintilian and later still of Calpurnius Flaccus and even the sixth-century bishop of Arles, Ennodius. And yet there is a great continuity of technique and of focus.

A comparison of the fictional situation imagined by declamation with that of an earlier exercise elicits a role familiar from the *Distichs of Cato*: the boy was learning to command. His educational practice rehearses him in the role of slave owner, father, advocate—in sum, of the paterfamilias. The plots of the exercises determined the identity of the persona and suggested the general line of his attitude, but the declaimer was free to invent a psychology—emotions, motivation—for this character. The treatment of the aggrieved son or of the imperious father made use of other taught material, all the arsenal of rhetorical figures and compositional method. Among these techniques were several that explicitly impersonated his characters: *fictio personae* (the presentation of a character), the comparison of characters, *sermocinatio* (the imagined direct speech of these characters), and lastly *color*—which is the twist given to the plot, the innovative interpretation of the given theme.[21] It is, however, a technique allied to those others of impersonation because the young advocate imagines the *animus* of his client—the motives that may ameliorate the harsh-looking evidence. This is where spin is added to plot.

Roman school texts rely especially on the figure of *fictio personae*.[22] Quintilian noted the vital role of persona: the commonplace becomes a real speech by the addition of the defendant; the thesis becomes a *suasoria* by the addition of a persona (*Inst.* 2.4.22). Speaking a declamation is an exercise in persona, and the master of the declamatory collections that emanate from Quintilian's school repeatedly directs his students in the choice and treatment of persona. Persona writing is a kind of ritualized composition where stereotypes are called out for new service or renewed service in a conflict that itself is a remanifestation of a familiar problem. The place, the setting, and the facts are given in the statement of the theme; the student must now animate the scene and redirect this harsh outline of a plot by filling it up with characters and supplying their motivation. He spins the formulas of the themes into narratives.

Prosopopoiae in ancient literature have charmed modern readers into treating each instance as a sort of literary character. It is debatable that ancient readers and auditors, themselves trained in the technique, invested the rhetorical pieces with such autonomy. The effect on the speaker does not seem to have been considered. *Fictio personae* may be understood as a master's trope. Roman school practices chart the identification of the young reader as the commanding Cato to the skilled youth as declamatory advocate for the injured. The rhetorical fashioning of the self and others constituted a technology of the self—to use another gloss on *fictio personae*—with definite material, social, and ideological contexts. Declamatory training in this particular rhetorical figure is important then on several levels: it involved the adolescent in the assumption of roles of social subordinates; it offered imaginative play in the attitudes and words of adults; and it mirrored and affected the changing roles of the adolescent.

The well-figured, well-scripted voices of freedmen, slaves, women, and children that one meets in the school exercises of imperial Rome are not straightforward expressions of Roman attitudes but rather something more like social protocols—the virtuous and villainous ways of fathers and sons, slaves and stepmothers. Despite being recognizably fantastic, idealistic, or unreal, these voices provide an opportunity for a contest and judged discourse about the proper relations among men, women, children, freedmen, and slaves.[23] The declaimer did not sustain the voice of the subordinate for the duration of his speech; he was an advocate. But he did imagine the woman's or the slave's words and feelings (as at times he would those of his opponent), and the shift from advocate to subordinate persona is quite easy and frequent.[24]

In trying to understand the schoolboy's assumption of intersecting attitudes about speech, his roles, and his community, I consider two intensive exercises of speech training in persona: first declamation and then the *colloquia* of *hermeneumata*. Both afford an excellent opportunity to glimpse the student at work making distinctions. The craft of where to place various *personae* and what words and sentiments were appropriate to them distinguishes the students of liberal education. Exercises such as the *Distichs of Cato* had helped begin this distinction and had as well communicated a vision of this distinction: the schoolboy was reminded that he was to sacrifice now so as to be eloquent later. Now, the role playing of declamation trained the adolescent in a sort of situational ethics. To a degree the student learned how others, specifically those denied the right to speak, might speak and feel in some period of crisis.[25] This is not the same as a sustained novelistic technique of representation. The speakers of declamation appropriate voices in the particular context of a major grievance where freedman or woman or even the son himself transgresses the usual ethic of silent obedience to speak his or her mind.[26] The boy's appropriation of voice thus bridges the impasse. This sort of transgression is no doubt fun, and much humor, and not simply comedy, depends on the disjuncture of person and speech type (register). To speak with paternal authority, to castigate, to act the *laudator temporis acti* had become trite and, perhaps more to the point, involved no crisis of categories. The father's part that offers great challenge is the speech on behalf of the father who would marry his daughter to his freedman. Thus declamation trained its pupils intensively in the hard part of advocacy. More generally, declamation trained a young Roman in a sympathy of viewpoint, emotions, motivations, and speech that he would need in treating his future clients. Sympathy is, of course, a humanistic interpretation, one that downplays the practice of social order and social comfort that arises from representing the elite as the conduit for subordinate expression, complaint, and resolution.

Roman declamation put the finishing touches on a visible and audible social distinction—the young men of this school could be seen and heard performing as the important, even governing adults they would become. Yet play is many things, a rehearsal of skills for later "life," an expression of anxieties, a changing developmental stage. The developmental context of declamatory training is illuminating, for the progression from *suasoriae* to *controversiae* has an analogy in stages of child development described by modern researchers: in Erikson's terms the ego task "I am what I imagine I can be" changes at eleven to twelve years to "I am what I learn" (as the psychosocial stage passes from industry vs. inferiority to identity vs. role confusion). The adolescent is "primarily concerned . . . with the question of how to connect the roles and skills cultivated earlier with the occupational prototypes of the day."[27] In Piaget's terms development is the continued reorganization of mental structures—this is essentially what the teaching of rhetoric offers, provided it follows the grammarian's school. The concrete mental operations (what Erikson termed "industry") of ages seven to eleven become by age twelve more and more formal. Rhetorical training and its specific exercises in *divisio,* which are the particular formal challenge of the *controversiae,* are exercises in theory building.[28] Quintilian says simply that the *controversia* is harder than the *suasoria,* but how is it harder? In the demands of *divisio* and of role playing. The student must now play more roles than the counselor advising x or not x. Now he disputes whether x occurred, what it was if it did occur, whether x fits the spirit or only the letter of the law. The declaimer also learned—and the master of the declamations from the school of Quintilian repeatedly points out—what persona to adopt, how to represent *animus* (intention, psychology). The student constructs a narrative that explores the psychology of action and agent. Theory building may devolve from the variety of perspective demanded by declamatory plots. In addition, theory building may necessarily depend on thinking about that which is not, in considering the extreme expression of classes, or in entertaining various explanations at the same time.

Clearly, declamation exercised the young in issues of identity and status, role confusion and resolution, as at the same time the young man learned figured speech. Declamation provided the face-saving distance from the adult world to train, retrain, and to display category making. And the young man could talk, indeed had to talk when it was his turn to declaim. Seneca the Elder has colored our picture of declamation with his focus on adult performers. Within the schools, interruptions, the mud-slinging repartee of one-liners, applause, and hissing were absent, or at least they were under the benevolent tyranny of Quintilian.

Mastery of speech, virility of style, demanded that the young man speak as *patronus* for those denied the right to speak.[29] The minor declamations of Pseudo-Quintilian offer the best evidence to gauge this training in persona. Often, what is said of declamation derives from the theorist Quintilian or from his ambitious fellow Spaniard Seneca the Elder.[30] The minor declamations are far closer to school practice.[31] The manuscripts preserve what seem to be notes taken at the school of Quintilian. Each declamation has a title, then the facts of the case in a plain Latin, quite often then the teacher's advice on the division of the case and the persona to be used, and finally excerpts from the declamation. These vary in fullness, sometimes with samples from both sides of the argument. The divisions are not that complex; Quintilian himself was not impressed with academic overrefinement in this area. Frequently the cases hinge on definitions or on the spirit versus the letter of the law. The fact is seldom denied, for this would require witnesses; and the declaimer is not being trained in court procedure but in categorical thinking and a supporting, deft fluency of expression.

The case can still be complex. A mother who has lost her son is accused of treason under the following circumstances.

272. ORBATA PRODITRIX

QUI CONSILIA PUBLICA ENUNTIAVERIT, CAPITE PUNIATUR. Ad colligendum filii corpus nocte processit mater. Comprehensa ab hostibus et torta indicavit auxilia venire; quibus oppressis de vinculis effugit et nuntiavit cuniculum agi. Oppressis hostibus rea est quod consilia publica enuntiaverit. CD.

272. THE BEREAVED MOTHER TURNED TRAITOR

THE PUNISHMENT FOR DIVULGING STATE PLANS IS DEATH. A woman went out by night to recover the body of her son. She was caught by the enemy and revealed, under torture, that relieving troops were on the way. These were caught and crushed. She escaped and warned her city that a mine was being dug. The enemy was defeated. She is accused of divulging state secrets. SHE IS DEFENDED.

The speaker then makes a defense that demonstrates well the variety of techniques grounded in sexual differentiation: the speaker successively eliminates the possibility that a woman is a speaking subject. He argues that a woman cannot have anything to do with *publicum consilium* ("state secrets," the term from the law); her action was *confessio* not *enuntiatio* ("divulging," again from the language of the cited law). Of course the declaimer is proceeding by definitions of the public sphere and public language, but he is also defining a woman, in negative terms and in terms that, like his very speech, exclude her from public speech. Her speech cannot be significant, actionable. The speaker began with mock incredulity that a woman can be tried on this charge. The opening paragraph moves from this suggestion that the court has no jurisdiction to consideration of the language of the law. In formal terms, he intimates that the *stasis* could be *translativa,* but instead will deal with the *stasis legalis* by definition. In fact, throughout the disclaimer and the definitions, he is concerned with the persona of a woman. The categories do not leap to mind like different codes tried on a puzzle; the woman puzzles his categories. She puts the system, not of status theory alone but of public speech, to the test.[32]

This is not an exceptional case; nor is the treatment of feminine speech peculiar to the needs of this single advocate. Advocacy is here a learned and learnéd skill. By his very training the schoolboy enters into *publicum consilium;* his speech and its categories become differentiated from those of Latin speakers who have not been to rhetorical school and from the woman categorically silent. In the *sermones,* the formal guidance that the instructor gives to his students before their competitive declamations on a set theme, the schoolmaster takes special care to indicate what personae are to be assumed, when, and in what matter. All of this he says is crucial to the audience's reception.[33] The mimicry of a woman's role, of her speech, grievances, emotions, and motivation, is part of the mimicry of adult male speech. The "femininity" of this training was clear even to the Romans, and not simply in the satirists' and moralists' complaints about effeminate style. Juvenal associates *color* and woman in his sixth satire. He can, humorously, present *color* as equivalent to feminine psychology. The natural response of the adulteress caught in the act is to call for Quintilian to produce an exculpatory *color* (6.279–80: *sed iacet in serui complexibus aut equitis. / dic, dic aliquem sodes hic, Quintiliane, colorem*). Training in persona was effective declamation, itself ostensibly a training for oratory. Thus declamation could be understood as a grade in elite male speech; still somewhat feminine and childish, its odd preoccupations, its strongly gendered and classed stereotypes, were mystified as the only eligible choices for the solution of conflict and for male verbal display.

The instructors put a high value on the handling of persona, in part because such sustained fiction (being "true" to a character whether on the stage or in a novel) requires the difficult suppression of extraneous comment, gesture, and viewpoint.[34] This process of composition and performance resembles the teacher's advice to write in the third person and to stay there. More than a gesture of anonymity or objectivity, such a compositional voice represents a (repressive) training in a new mode, decidedly unlike the way children tell stories and unlike the way the student wrote his composition last year at an earlier grade in school. In Roman declamation much care was needed in the handling of persona because the conflict at the heart of a case often depended on the crossing of categories, on one person fitting or assuming two personae: the prostitute who would be priestess, the stepmother who would be kind, the military hero who seems to be a deserter. In the case of this hero the crossing of personae is especially complex and instructive. Here in *Declamationes Minores* 246, the declaimer does learn, at some formal level, how to spread the applicability of the charge. In American political terms he is learning how to smear— how to use prejudice to produce a plot. This is the case of the *Drugged Military Hero Who Was a Stepson* (*Soporatus fortis privignus*). Briefly: a military hero on the eve of battle was given a sleeping potion by his stepmother.[35] He was accused of desertion. Acquitted of that charge, he accuses his stepmother on a charge of poisoning. The declaimer's first task is to redefine poisoning to include drugging. Again the declamation works by definition, and it works out a conflict—the brave man accused of desertion—but shifts the blame to the stepmother.

This exercise offers training in associative thought: cowardice, poison, and woman are associated, but do not dismiss it as a typical exercise in misogyny. In this case we are to understand that the stepmother acted out of love for her stepson, protecting him, keeping him from battle. This is a case of categories set upon their heads: the soldier who sleeps, the stepmother who loves, the well-loved son who denounces. Yet through the role playing, through the inversions of natural and actual behavior, runs the strong yarn of rhetoric about women's language and the possibility of speaking for them. *Declamationes Minores* 306 is a miniexposition of a woman's ways, presented as a finite set of oppositions: the speech contrasts her characterization to that of a young man; reconstructs what a clever, deceitful woman would have done; describes a woman's motivation in terms of avoidance of gossip (*fabula*); and imagines the speech of a *mulier privata*. These extremes of plot test the applicability of the rhetorically constant and the commonplace. The speaker practices the commonplace arguments, the tactics and treatments, that are suitable when the motif woman, poisoning, or cowardice arises. In the drugging of the city's hero, public crime is brought back to domestic irregularity. And the rhetorician is to be guided by persona: to convict this aberrant persona (the good stepmother), the schoolmaster tells his students to note that the father had not done this and the mother certainly would not have.

The comparison of personae is a technique he recommends elsewhere. Through such a normative practice, a stepmother is denied her speech, smothered by comparison with the dead mother. Invoking the dead to silence a woman is not a new technique. Cicero had done it mercilessly and brilliantly by exhuming old Appius Claudius to taunt Clodia in the *Pro Caelio*.[36] Declamatory Latin repeatedly, indeed insistently, veers away from giving women a voice. The Roman schoolboy was trained in stock characters, and these provided him the tools to speak for women, among others. A number of rhetorical techniques, often centering around persona, and the segregated rhetorical school itself contributed to the construction of a feminine speaking part: herein role playing and role projection coincide so that only the male can speak. Following his teacher's lead, the schoolboy learns and defines when and what a woman can speak. He not only acts as her advocate but imagines for his audience's benefit her words and presents these through the filter of *sermocinatio* and apostrophe. He may cut and paste her quotation, he may address her, but above all he comes to fill up her silences.

Declamation thus does not simply mimic gendered speech types but represents the right to speak in gendered terms. In supplying voices for the physically wronged and the socially dispossessed (and this is a significant collapse of categories), declamation equates itself with the possibility of speech. Within the declamation, the snippets of speech given women are carefully controlled to forestall the plot from descending into *fabula*, gossip, rumor, woman's prattle. The division of the theme into distinct questions and the rhetorical stylization help make adultery, parricide, and other anxieties of the father something more than, other than, *fama* and *fabula*. Thus declamation makes no romantic quest for genuine voice; rather, it speaks for those denied expression, not to recover their voice but for the male elite to joust for the right to speak. What stands against this high style is not some other genre or register, woman's speech or servile, vulgar frankness, but the silence imposed by paternal speech and violence.

At the outset of his speech, the declaimer often denies that his case is a familiar one (one that has already been adjudicated or one unfit for adjudication). In technical terms the declaimers argue that there is no *praescriptio* applicable to their case. Their case is still oral, not bound by the existing written formula, and so still litigable. Of course, the attempt to deny the speaker his case, the forestalling of speech that is *praescriptio,* never succeeds in declamation. Each successive declaimer can rework the categories and reimagine motivation. This is essential to the verbal dueling of declamation; there can be no scripted presolution, for then there would be no performance, no display of manly speech. An inherent resistance to law and father's speech embellishes declamatory plotting, performance, and even style. At the same time, paradoxically, the declaimer maintains he is speaking like an adult advocate, on serious matters in a serious style in a serious contest.

Declamation takes its start from a denial of *praescriptio,* for as a genre it arises from the gaps of the litigated or performed past. So in *Declamationes Minores* 254 (The Exile Accuser and the Divided Judgment), the persona comes to a theme already treated and tries to break this impasse. In addition, the speaker sits astride two categories—his right to speak is suspect; he must justify his very speaking. Declamation repeatedly casts itself as a court of appeal, reconsidering not simply stock themes and character, but in its very plots representing judicial impasse and re-resolution. Like some real cases, declamation argues that it deserves to be (re)heard, that it is unique, that it is not the same as the definitive decisions of the past. In this replay, stock subjects restrict the field of variables, allow novelty to be identified and isolated, and make possible the representation of social, familial, and gender conflict as verbal and categorical options on the verge of resolution. *Praescriptio* arises not as a serious procedural issue (with which declamation is repeatedly unconcerned) but as a manifestation of the threats to take away voice. Otherwise conflict would go unresolved, that is, declamation would be denied its performative and reflective roles. Loss of voice threatens the disowned son, the wronged husband, the abducted, the raped, the cuckolded, and also the declaimer, who will be robbed of the chance to gain status if he is denied speech. Providing voices is associated with resisting the script of the law and asserting there is something more to be said at the same time as it displaces more serious injury and injustice. This makes for an expansive (social) reflection on the law and on social roles and categories.

The subjects of declamatory speech are not neutral fodder for the practice of rhetorical technique. At the least, like other childhood games, declamation taught competition and rule following and inculcated habits of stratification and distinction.[37] Verbal games in particular, as play with language, seem to teach an awareness of form. Thus nonsense games or nonsense words imitate the form of language, and so perhaps teach an awareness of language as language, as play. No doubt Roman declamation has this connection with the nonsense songs learned by children, but it too has specific social stimuli and consequences.[38] As a creation of categories and of role playing, it was a part and not a reflection of social practice. It intersects significantly with the social construction of gender and does so in ways overtly concerned with the possibility and appropriateness of speaking by and for women. Like the declaimer, who had to speak on behalf of a prostitute seeking holy office, the schoolboy playing adult advocate often took up the petition of one whose profession, status, dress, and perhaps sociolect prohibited her from legal speech. In a display of manly style the speaker redefines what woman or what kind of women can be defended, that is, granted a patron's voice. The violence that is done to women, provided it fits certain categories, qualifies as the right of men to speak. Should the declaimer slip, he can be accused, as declamation repeatedly was, of effeminacy and corruption. He speaks on the verge, not a speaker of legal age himself, yet molding himself and being molded by his male teachers and peers into a speaking male adult.[39] The declaimers are constantly concerned with the propriety of their own speech and of their imaginary clients: What should the chaste prostitute have done?[40] But action seems to be interpreted as speech: Should she have spoken up? Should she be petitioning? Similarly, were the bereaved mother's words treasonous speech or private, feminine confession?

Like so much melodrama, declamation reads as a strange fusion of the Attic stage and the Hellenistic comedy: parricide, incest, kidnapping of children, sons' abandon, and fathers' severity endlessly return. Characters shuffle in and out of the house, without the assistance of the wily stage slave but with the more mundane stage technique of the rigged plot: kidnapping, abdication, adoption, are all in the script. In short, declamation rehearses familial and social injury.[41] Perhaps more concretely than Roman comedy, Roman declamation considered the conflicting calls of public and private life. The comic son has erred and is gradually won back to the house by the verbal ruses of the slave. The declamatory son confronts his father not simply as the errant, spendthrift lover but as a military hero, as a ransomer of his imprisoned father, as a rival lover, as the son adopted into another family and now his father's protector, or as the prosecutor of his father for insanity.[42] The schoolboys were investigating *pietas,* the social practices owed the state and father at a time when they emerged (in declamatory terms) from the *voluntas* but not the *littera* of the law of *patria potestas.* The speeches of declamation consider the stance to be taken toward paternal authority and speech. The themes play at undermining his *dicta:* his injunctions, his wills, his legislation. The speakers' division attempts to isolate social roles that in fact are not separate, since, for instance, the *filius* can also be *sui iuris,* the woman can be daughter and wife. We witness the conflict of categories, a conflict perhaps not for the father at the top of the hierarchy but for those entering a midposition in that society. The liminal quality of both speakers and subject needs to be emphasized.[43] These boys or adolescents, probably wearing their adult toga, put on about ages twelve to fourteen, and a decade away from marrying, were becoming like dad, acting like men by a rehearsal in speaking for others—at the safe distance created by school and by declamatory topic and style, all evidently ludic versions of adult practices.

A humanistic interpretation of this social practice would posit that such role playing through participation as performer and audience member might broaden the child's perspectives.[44] Yet the young student's growing mastery of speech depends on the exclusion of any speaker not of the status or gender of the young practitioners. And declamation abounds with examples of those figures who prompt speech but will never be admitted to civil speech: freedmen, slaves, women. Here too rhetorical schooling practices government—the right to speak for others and to define their interests becomes a recognizable, laudable, and enviable talent.

Mastery is more than a metaphor or some idealized hope or trope of the governing class, as a completely different school exercise indicates. Among the late antique school exercises that have survived, the most interesting are brief writing exercises in Greek and Latin, most likely deriving from early third-century Gaul, which have as their subject something the boy could readily imagine, his daily routine. In these descriptive terms, the *hermeneumata* sound like elementary exercises in bilingualism, or perhaps spelling and writing exercises, practice in orthography—though the orthography is quite unclassical.[45] The boy's schoolday is narrated from the start: he wakes, washes, has breakfast, goes to school, has his lessons, comes home. In fact, my description of the exercise parallels what you will find in histories of education and wherever historians mention such minor texts. Keith Bradley, however, has suggested that such texts show the socialization of the young into mastery, into the position and attitude of a slave owner. We can specify the skills reinforced by this writing exercise. Perhaps these taught a certain amount of vocabulary. But morphologically and socially, they taught the imperative.[46]

The narrative of the day is in fact a series of imperatives: starting with the dawn the boy orders his slave to wash him. Clothe me, feed me, and so on. He dismisses his slave for lunch. This is practice in social and grammatical imperatives as the boy takes his slave out of his home, through the streets, where he encounters another pupil with retinue, and into the school. A second social speech act, the *salutatio,* punctuates these imperatives. The boy greets his teachers (and we hear of his progression through a hierarchy of teachers); and when he returns home for lunch, he greets the whole *familia* and is greeted by them. Thus he learns (to write) or rehearses the names and positions of slaves and free in the family, and of teachers and pupils in the school.

The *colloquia* present a number of lists: these can be vocabulary exercises (the narrative of the day pauses while the student writes out all the words having to do with writing materials), parts of the body for the slave to dry, morphology practice. These work by various principles of expansion. The clearest are the thematic, where the topic directs the choice of words.[47] But words are often generated by doublet (phrasal variation), by change in tense, by change in grammatical gender (*nutrix nutritor*), or by change of preposition.[48] Within a larger narrative, the student then practices pausing and expanding his writing.

The hierarchies within these deviations from narrative order are very important, as is the fact that scribal practice organizes experience and language. At the proper stage in his own day, the student rehearses canons of authors (the reading list) and of professions. Writing, social order, and memory are inextricably connected—and practiced in the *hermeneumata*.[49] Indeed, the reported speech events of the *hermeneumata* contribute to a sort of social grammar. The student reports that he prayed for the good outcome of his entire day (Dionisotti 1982, 14). Then he writes of that idealized day. He speaks in order, and the good speakers are distinguished from the poor by teacher's praise (Dionisotti 1982, 39).

Other colloquia report verbal strife: the student disputes with a peer about who spoke first (*Monacensia* 2, p. 646 Goetz). Real verbal conflict and abuse, the opposite of social order, is narrated, but in scenes outside the school and home (*Harleianum* 15–18, pp. 641–42 Goetz). The boy seems to call his enemy a slave, but this is an insult, as the repartee makes clear: *Ego enim ingenuus omnibus notus et pater familias. Apparet a facie tua* ("I am a freeborn citizen known to all and a paterfamilias." "You sure look like it"; *Harleianum* 23, p. 643 Goetz). One of the striking correspondences with declamation (and one of the ways this exercise anticipates and naturalizes the future practice of declamation) is the representation of verbal conflict within the plot. In writing and speaking these exercises, the student plots a verbal dueling. Extra school activity is given a school form. The relearning of fable as a literary form provides a parallel and is likewise a textual, intellectual version of violent confrontation. The schoolyard fight (in Roman terms the encounter in the street) is written and learned as a verbal duel. Such reading, writing, and reciting refracts and domesticates "real" intraelite struggle, of the boys in the classroom, of the boys' families in the city. In the street, for instance, the student encounters one who owes him money and refuses to pay. The debtor who denies his debt is no true paterfamilias (hailed as such at *Harleianum* 23, he is called *fraudator,* but the scene closes with *Modo bene, et controversiam facere non est bonum libero homini et patri familias,* "Very well, it is not good for a free man and the head of the household to have a dispute"). Verbal abuse attempts to cast the offending peer as a slave, but physical violence is avoided. Only within the school can the elite engage in *controversia*. Here all may be *patres familias,* and there is no gibe about servile look (although vulgar speech and *verba sordida* are castigated, as in the elder Seneca's report of what the great critics thought of various speakers).

The other social conflict in these exercises, aside from orders to slaves to be quick, also involves a simple hierarchy of the socially abject and the socially correct. In a scene at the forum (Dionisotti 1982, 104.74) a thief is condemned *as he deserves,* whereas the succeeding vignette of the unjustly accused man of high status has *dis-*

erti viri, eloquent speakers, deliver him from his detractors. Between the thief and the aristocrat delivered comes this set of skilled speakers. We are told that each man litigates and succeeds according to his *facundia.* Not innocence or guilt but learned eloquence distinguishes, saves, and ranks this middle class of characters.

Through the school's exercises, speaking and writing of daily experience becomes part of daily practice, just as the prayer rehearsed and routinized the day's activities. The *hermeneumata* work a piece of Roman socialization through writing and recitation, with a firm emphasis on the speaking and writing roles of a freeborn son.[50] When, in a scene strangely disjointed from the rest of the *hermeneumata,* someone reproaches the narrator, this castigator reminds him that he has not acted the part of a paterfamilias.[51] Within the text the student is reminded that he dresses the part of a *filius familias* (10); that he changes upon returning to his home into cleaner or fancier clothes while his slave waits.[52] Like his trip to school or recitation of exercises, these scenes enact social practices supported by slaves that distinguish the young master from his slaves. The boy learns along with his writing, which is inextricably bound to that social distinction, morphological and social imperatives. His training in literacy skills becomes part of the power to utter a command, one that grows unambiguous and efficacious in its iteration. The exercise is a repetition of interconnected routines: what had been speech at home to slaves is now written down, and delivered orally before a critical schoolmaster. This routine turned into writing is expanded morphologically and phrasally, and of course translated insistently into Greek. While the young master once seems to towel himself off, he does not have much to do but to speak and to write.

The master of language thus emerges, at least within school forms, as the powerful, subordinating, and ordering agent in his society. Declamation presents various subordinate voices, from the disreputable to the victimized, which are better understood as norms and counternorms than transparent indices of behavior. Whether or not we can recover general attitudes to marriage or rape or pirates from these exercises, we can see the process of the socialization of the boy into an idealized speaking role. Declamation is all the more potent a genre of social fiction to the degree that the subject comes to treat the act of ventriloquism as his right. The final fiction considered, the boy's life, also conflates socialization and maturity with the right to speak and write for others. Declamatory role training casts slave or freedman or woman as the foil—present but silent, the source of conflict, the goad to speech; but rather than attribute the construction of these categories to elite texts— a move that replays the conviction that texts can write for others—we should stress that these educational texts intersected with and contributed to larger social practices, larger oppressions, and resistances.

Social and textual practices do not necessarily neatly overlap. I have written throughout of the boy and Roman education's shaping of that boy or adolescent. I follow the silences of the exercises here. The great historian of ancient education,

Henri Marrou, assumed that girls were present in elementary education. We do not now, thanks especially to the work of Alan Booth, believe that the Roman schools were the graded system of the post-Napoleonic nation. As with many other societies, there was great variety in schooling practices, including age gradations. Should we conclude that girls were present? Certainly not in the rhetorical schools, but what of the earlier schools? This is not the same question as whether Roman girls were literate or what percentage of them were literate; it is a question of schooling practices. Marrou and others have taken the occasional notices of girls being in school (from the poets Martial and Ausonius) and generalized from this.[53] I offer an old piece of evidence—a few notices from the bilingual exercises—so as to reconsider the textual practice of writing about women's education. In the opening of the *Hermeneumata Leidensia* the writer declares his audience as *omnibus amatoribus loquellae latinae* (to take just the Latin half from this bilingual text). The preface of the *Monacensia colloquia* reports that it is the first of three books, written for small boys wishing to speak Latin and Greek (*parvulis pueris incipientibus erudiri*).[54] Even if we imagine that girls were lovers of Latin speech, the exercises repeatedly address the *puer,* and it is a *puer* who responds to the father's or schoolmaster's orders and who in turn commands his male slave.

An analogy: reading American primers and textbooks the historian would find, until very recently, starkly white texts and might conclude that no person of color was present in the classroom or in any classroom. School texts do not mimic the classroom but seek to shape it, and do so with a rather rigorously exclusive modeling. In some schoolrooms the girl was present, but we have no evidence she was given an exercise that imagined her daily routine. We do not read of her giving commands or of her movement about the house, to school and back, not following the boys to the forum. She learned reading, writing, and perhaps reciting as a mimicry of male behavior.[55]

Supplying personae shares with many aspects of education the intention to form a student in a particular fashion—giving him specific values, skills, and conceptions and idealizing these as the educated way. Persona building is thus a political enterprise, one at the heart of the training of the literate classes who wrote and read Latin literature. The most advanced general training in the appropriation of personae came from rhetorical schooling, where girls were absent. Its final manifestation comes from an even more advanced phase of Roman imperial linguistic expertise—the law, where the original stage mask of persona in all its variety is reduced to a verbal fiction, degendered as it is used to mean the male right-bearing citizen.[56]

Conclusion

A liberal education, on an ancient and a modern understanding, promises freedom from want, from ignorance, and perhaps from convention, although this last claim especially merits strict questioning. The idea that education changes something essential about a person, even that it liberates the self, remains strong. Plutarch and Quintilian, however, as we have seen, were not writing Enlightenment essays about the self tearing itself away from its own society's institutions. They were adapting and explaining the system of education that had spread across the Mediterranean in Hellenistic times. They might have believed, as Cicero did (*De or.* 3.127), that the curriculum of studies could be traced to Hippias of Elis, a Sophist remembered for his banausic and academic knowledge—showman of the liberal arts, he had also made his robe and ring. Among the Sophists, Hippias was remembered as something of an eccentric. Plato in turn had helped distinguish the self-sufficient man as the philosophical man, whose knowledge decidedly did not extend to the manual arts. The virtuosity of the Sophists, especially the ability to speak on any subject and the suggestion that there was an intellectual method to mastering the important areas of knowledge and expertise, left a strong mark on Hellenistic education. Education was believed to move students toward self-sufficiency (not necessarily novelty) of thought and expression.

The Roman "liberal arts" could trace their ancestry through the Hellenistic and classical Greek schools to that fertile period of intellectual investigation embodied in the Sophists. Yet centuries of institutionalized schooling had tamed the unconventionality of a Hippias or a Socrates while at the same time schooling remembered these figures and promised an enlightenment and expertise distinct from that of the workaday world. In the service of its elite class, education distinguished culture holders from those deemed less fully human, the illiterate and the less literate. At the same time, following Hellenistic culture, the Romans came to theorize liberal education as the literate culture that defined the Roman man. Pieces of this culture, according to some authorities, could be granted to women, and slaves could well be the best professionals and literally liberate themselves.[1] The role of public speaker, that ideal type of the civilized man, would, however, not cross the barriers of class and gender.

The high value set upon the ancient speaking subject has been emphasized and even reinforced by later scholarly tradition, which knew antiquity chiefly through texts and which saw its own activity in considerable part as a return to those ancient masters of language. Friedrich Nietzsche, professor of ancient rhetoric long before his writings ensured his place as a philosopher, asserted, preposterously and perhaps ironically, that speech was the chief concern of classical culture.[2] With this claim Nietzsche adopted one of the most compelling fictions of Western society: a culture aims at rational, ordered, civil discourse, and at one *persona*—the author-orator, the governor of his tongue and, by a metaphorical, corporal, almost sympathetic-magical logic, consequently the citizen worthy to govern others. According to the rationalization that envisions society as a culture of speech, speech other than the approved is not culturally mainstream, is deviant, and is marked so by its manifest affinities to one socially inferior subset (women, slaves, the mob). Effeminate, servile, or vulgar style supposedly cannot express, much less attain for its speakers, the high and free ideals and order that are best for the culture as a whole. In ancient terms speaking well, *eu legein,* is the orator's ideal, and the laity are left *eu phēmein,* which idiom means not what it says, "to speak well," but by the original euphemism, "to keep a reverent silence." Horace repeats the expression as an imperative: *favete linguis.* All are to be silent, not simply before the priest but before the poet. Like Virgil, Horace offers an ideal of communication, that of the vatic poet, rival to the statesman-orator. Roman education will appropriate both the classical poet and the classical orator as models of *eruditio,* the skill at oral and written language that defines the good men of education. Plutarch, as we have seen in chapter 3, develops an argument that eulogics, the science and practice of educated speech and reading, overlaps and reinforces eugenics. Education thereby rises triumphant as the sole labor suited for men, while the worrisome thought that education is a Greek import imperiling the father's heirs and house recedes as so much slander that the educated man will know to suppress.

As a social institution, ancient education developed compelling modes of reassurance, no doubt responsive to the unusual network of interested parties—teachers, parents, students, civic authorities. Such reassurance ranged from a grammarian's explanation of the purpose and value of an exercise to the great treatise of Quintilian and even to legislation. Inevitably, educational ideology was implicated in ideas and practices of the wider society. Perhaps the most direct challenge to the time-consuming practice of education was to articulate the rationale for having elite children do no labor, and this laborless activity had to be defended as the right of the freeborn, indeed the qualifying characteristic of their right to rule. Consequently, in defenses of education, notions of agency are particularly important. To its credit, the institution of education was trying to create a specific social actor. In order to impart a sense of social and educational distinction, the materials and procedures of the classroom had to vaunt the end product—that wonderously articulate governor who could solve ethical, familial, social, and political disputes—and to range against him various rivals and foils. Here schooling manifestly reflects key attitudes of the elite, but in doing so it does not simply replicate social norms (preeminently, the natural right of the free to govern the unfree, the poor, and the female) or mystify them (as a mental freedom different from the impulses that drive the noneducated) but modulates them so that schooling itself rises as a social desideratum. Beyond what one may term the wish ideology of the institution, such educational ideology encourages in the student a sense of distinction and subjectivity. The skills of a school exercise can also be techniques of identification. In reading, writing, memorizing, explaining, and recasting the proverbial material of the *Distichs of Cato*, a student comes to take on the identity of the wise old man. All the school's methods can thus be strategies of participation (even where that participation is compelled). If the *puer educandus* thinks of himself not as the victim of tasks, threats, blows, precepts, and sermonizing but the agent, writing, reading, speaking, and fashioning his own style, delivering his own imperatives, saving the family and the city from the threat of pirate, rapist, and adulterer, this boy becomes a Roman adult. Others can be whipped or even caned; the educated boy has escaped from being an object of education by speaking of and for the wronged. He tells the stories of the raped girls and maimed boys or men (the blinded, the handless males) and restores what is right. He thus distances himself from those who would only repeat the *dicta* of fathers, which, whether the unexplained proverb or the unembellished statement of inflexible declamatory law, are his starting point.

The display of stylized speech involves more than class solidarity or a contest among the elite for distinction, since reflections upon the proper use of language, both those within and outside the school, practice a kind of social testing and idealization.[3] The mechanisms that train children how to produce and how to evaluate language help police an elite. In this organization of power, elite and nonelite are to a degree complicitous. The freedmen teachers of the Roman schools, like the freedmen who have left their tombstones, were proud of their literacy and their culture. Roman education practiced speaking about and for them, too; they were a part of liberal education much as girls participated in an education that presented the student as the *puer educandus*. It is not the case that the nonelite or the female was invisible in liberal education; rather, their participation had an obliqueness that left the commanding voice to the freeborn male. Their presence, as pedagogues and teachers, as fellow students, and as characters in composition exercises, impelled the boy to speak. Such a training prepared all the participants of the school for the society's adult systems of patriarchy, patronage, and imperial bureaucracy.

In detecting freedmen's pleasure in their status as citizens or the schoolchild's satisfaction in his or her growing literate capacities, we are not simply witness to the strength of Roman institutions—formidable though they were—in winning allegiance and ensuring social replication. To have faith in education is not to be a dupe to the patterns and structures of a society's ideology. Roman declamation reveals, and not simply to the scholar two millennia removed, the violence at the heart of familial, social, and political relations. Imagining what is not and what should be can be potent—not with the inevitable consequence of social or political reform but with the probable consequence that an individual's way of understanding the world will change. To consider how someone different in important social ways may think is a step toward a theory of mind—the understanding that other subjects think and hence act differently from oneself.

Imagining appropriate sentiments and penning convincing characters are not the same as ethical action. Imagination and schooling remain ludic activities. In declamation the Romans imagined a society of law where the occasional tyrant threatened justice, but no emperor held sway. In Roman reality no emperor was swept from power, no republic restored, on the goad of declamatory indignation. Yet Romans would continue to speak, write, and think of themselves and their society in the categories of free men, freely speaking, deciding through law and equity how to maintain the great achievements of their ancestors. Equity is a most important category; for if declamation imagines a society of law, equally it imagines that law cannot govern all situations and all peoples. It needs humane administrators and champions. To speak of law and justice, to know the ancestors' code, and to pity the aggrieved are the way Roman men govern—even, ideally, the essential way Roman men conduct themselves.

A genuine pleasure comes with gaining literacy, not because the child is hoodwinked by the theorists' claims and the schoolmasters' practice. Growth in communicative competence and in the analysis of emotions and motives brings delight, a sense of change, of improvement. Most immediately, the adult world is more responsive to these modes of communication, and so the child has accomplished more than winning the praise of teacher or parent. He enters into the discourse of adults. Training in role playing leads to an understanding of the subject's developing roles. Contriving speeches and plots, like reading literature—especially where that "reading" tends to probe the morality of individual characters' actions, to require the reader to memorize speeches, and to compose similar speeches in character—also has the pleasure of fantasy and creation. The Roman schoolchild's identification with the Aeneas or Ascanius of Virgil's epic is thus of a different order from that of the modern, silent, hurried reader.

Certainly, education in all its proscriptive modes prods and tugs the child to act and learn in set ways, and to value the process of education. Yet education's successes do not follow unhesitantly from the series of teacher's measures: statement of learning goals, curriculum designed to enact these, application to student. The student's resistance is customarily treated as a stage to be overcome. Even those theories that treat education as a vehicle of social replication seem to neglect the difficulty of learning—as if social norms are learned passively or unproblematically. Identification of a student or reader with a character, theme, situation, or even a formal feature of a written or oral text is a complex process, which no doubt changes the interpretation and use of a text as well as the student's outlook or self-assessment. Roman education was not an easy process, and students' resentment and resistance are clear. No doubt, frustration and anger were inseparable from the gradual formation of subjectivity this book has tried to describe. The act of learning to write, first of making letterforms in wax that mimicked the master's, was not as easy as our own. The writing of lists of nonsense syllables or the copying of epic verses, composed in a Greek at least eight centuries out-of-date, does not have the ease or allure of writing stories in language customarily used by the eight-year-old. One suspects that the child was not the waxlike, memorious, and imitative *animus* of Quintilian's pages nor the sturdy growth of Plutarch's essay. When the young Lucian was out of his teachers' sight, he scraped the wax from his tablets and modeled little cattle, horses, and men (*Somn.* 2). Saint Basil advises: "Don't be like thoughtless children who out of anger with their teacher break his tablets"; he then relates an incident that perhaps shows as much about the resiliency and optimism of children as about their piety or attitude to school: the children were happy to be let off school in order to join prayers for the relief of a famine.[4]

The ancient school could be more gruesome. In Egypt, a precocious Coptic beginner, Synphronios, whose writing excelled that of a boy who had started reading, had his thumbs broken.[5] In late antiquity, grammar was personified and equipped with a *scalprum* for scraping pupils' tongues and throat to perfect their pronunciation.[6] These and similar stories attest to a knowledge that the school disciplined the body. The educated body was different and had suffered to achieve this difference. Resistance and revenge might come in subverting the school materials to objects of play, or to weapons of abuse. The stylus that carved Virgil in wax could also mark the school's walls, as at Pompeii. Or in the sweet revenge of fantasy and school exercises, violence could become the stuff of schooling. Prudentius, the Christian poet of the fifth century, would become one of the great school poets. In his *Liber peristephanon* (Crown of the Martyrs) he reports a story of schoolboys' revenge.[7] Cassian of Imola had been a teacher of shorthand to a school of one hundred boys. At times he had spoken harshly. He was a Christian and was condemned by the Roman magistrate (these judges tend to have a declamatory flair: they twist Christian language or interrogate in a most declamatory manner). At Imola the judge set the boys on their master. They come styli in hand to practice their writing upon the master, asking if he can read their writing now, have they dug their letters deeply and clearly. Prudentius, who, curiously, viewed the severe teacher as the hero of his piece, had the story explained to him by a local guide after he had seen a lurid painting at the martyr's tomb.

Roman students did not have to wait for Prudentius for violent tales of retribution. Their education thematized (literally reduced to themes for the student's analysis and composition) conflict with rivalrous students, with teacher, and with father. Violent themes abound in school exercises. Greek children from the fourth century B.C. (perhaps earlier) could analyze culpability in the case of the boy who was accidentally killed by an errant javelin throw in the gymnasium. From fable to declamation, the protagonists evade violent threats and at times work their own violence. The utility of violence in promoting students' participation seems well established by the longevity of such forms of school exercise. The appeal to the adolescent of plots of patricide finds a ready explanation in a range of modern psychology. Yet whether or not socialization of the young male in a patriarchal society requires such fantasy, Roman education offered a playacting of the move from powerlessness to power and of resistance not simply to father, authority, the state, or law but to the state society cast youth in: more than unenfranchised, the student was without voice and was subject to the voices of parents, pedagogue, and teachers. The exercises seem both productive of resentment (with their harsh depiction of the boy's state and their call for him to put off revenge) and the means to escape that resentment. A vital part of those means was the control of violence, the ability to control one's own violent impulses and the ability to depict and mediate violence through story.

The control of physical and verbal violence in this slave-owning culture, where slaves are subject to their master's whim and yet are part of his household, important for his reputation as well as his finances, was rehearsed in the school plots that depended on the student imagining himself as the mediator of violence. At the same time, such an education encouraged the pleasures of the violent tale. Despite the talk of the orator as the ideal citizen, Rome was still a martial, if not quite a warrior culture. Verbal display of violence occurred in epic, drama, satire, even love elegy. The spectacle of punishment, the public games, drew some censure from the elite, but perhaps this too is so much verbal comment on a socially given, ineluctable theme. This elite complaint often seems to proclaim not the importance of reason but the social, cultural, and intellectual distinction of the reasoner. A liberal education did then treat serious issues, not the bombast of far-fetched cases, but the growth of the Roman man. His capacity to speak developed from the traditional, recurring challenge of ending violence in the house. The plots equate the ending of violence with the restoration of familial, social, and civic roles, all of which depends in turn on the student "speaking well." To reach such a state of eloquence, to become like Cato or Cicero of old, took great preparation. It was a great *ponos, labor,* for those who had no need to work, for those who—in the conceit of the governors—deserved naturally to govern and had but to speak to win consent.

NOTES

INTRODUCTION

1. Marcus Cicero wrote his father's freedman Tiro, perhaps because he did not dare ask his father for any additional funds or resources (*Fam.* 16.221, no. 337 Shackleton Bailey). See also Plut. *Cic.* 24. Trebonius wrote to Cicero pater on May 25, 44 B.C. (*Fam.* 12.16, no. 328 Shackleton Bailey); he proposed having young Marcus visit him in Asia but was murdered in Smyrna by Dolabella. On the course of young Marcus's studies, see Abbott 1909; and Daly 1950, 49–53. Dyck (1997, 11) suggests that Cicero hoped this work on ethical responsibilities would inspire his son to mend his indifferent educational ways.

2. See the fine exposition of this bilingual school exercise in Dionisotti 1982; and the discussion in chapter 8 below.

3. On Augustine's education, Brown 2000, 23–28, provides a beginning. On Augustine's practice as a reader of the classics, see Hagendahl 1967; and Stock 1996.

4. Kramer 1958 and 1963 provide a basic introduction. Gesche's study (2001) of Babylonian education in the first millenium B.C., based on 5,000 unpublished school tablets from the British Museum, is of great importance and a valuable source of bibliography (see pp. 6–8 for important caveats regarding modern ideas of education). The attitudes the Egyptian scribe should hold are described in the *Instruction of Khety* (also known as the *Satire of the Trades,* translated in Simpson 1973). On scribal education, see Brunner 1957/1991; Quirke and Spencer 1992, 122–23, 131–32, 136, 140–41. See also Ray 1986. On the possible influence of Demotic (Egyptian) education on Hellenistic schooling, see Morgan 1998.

5. It is noteworthy that in describing this early education, Bonner (1977, 3–9) began his first chapter by referring to the Romans' hardy neighbors, the Sabines, and then turned to the Augustan poet Horace's evocation of ancestral ways. This evidence attests to the attitudes of Romans in the classical and early imperial periods toward a lost era of simplicity and virtue and does not constitute reliable evidence for early Roman education. On Italic literacy and culture, see chapter 1 below.

6. On the exclusion of freeborn Romans from the profession of teaching, see De Robertis 1967, 81.

7. The early history of education in Greece was reconsidered by Bolgar (1969).

8. See now Too 2001 and 2000; Too and Livingstone 1998; and Morgan 1998.

9. Replacing such works as Ziebarth 1913 and Gwynn 1926 are Marrou 1948/1956 and Bonner 1977. In addition, a series of articles by Booth are important: 1976; 1979a and b. The reader may also consult Clarke 1971, but now especially Robb 1994 and Morgan 1998. See also Vössing 1997. Corbeill 2001 explores Roman education as citizen training. On Greek education in Egypt, see Cribiore 1996 and 2001. For a thorough if necessarily brief review of Roman education, with special emphasis on the various participants and their relationships, see Rawson 2003. On the figure of the grammarian: Kaster 1988. See also the various essays in Beard et al. 1991; Frasca 1996a and b; Legras 1998. Griffith 2001 offers a valuable account of the complexity and variety of early "Greek" education. Marrou 1948/1956 overemphasized the structural and institutional systematicity of Roman education. The systematicity of the Roman curriculum has been long recognized; see Murphy 1990, 159–62.

The social function of grammar has been explored by Irvine 1994; Gehl 1993; and Amsler 1989. The study of the Roman grammatical arts has received welcome impetus from Kaster's detailed study of the grammarians (1988). For fuller bibliography and discussion, see chapter 5 below. Morgan (1998) and Cribiore (1996 and 2001) have given special attention to the processes of learning to read.

In addition to a number of the general studies of ancient education cited above and the numerous studies of individual late antique and medieval authors and their relations to classical culture, see especially Roger 1905; Riché 1975; Curtius 1952, 36–42; Kühnert 1960; and Marrou 1958.

I am indebted also to contemporary approaches that stress education as social replication (Bourdieu among others) and to investigations of the relationship between the forms of instruction and subjectivity. Donald (1985) outlines an interpretation of schooling as the formation of subjectivity (against or at least alongside the view of education as socialization).

10. It is with some trepidation that I have made the experience of education and contemporary evaluations of this experience my focus, but along with trepidation, I must express grateful appreciation to my teacher, Ramsay MacMullen, who so clearly set the importance and difficulty of such an approach. In his wide-ranging reflection on the practice of ancient history, MacMullen observed: "In people's feelings toward each other and toward each other's general behavior lie the most difficult questions for exploration" (1990, 10).

11. Girls did not attend this rhetorical school. Philosophy might be studied later, and an Epicurean teacher recommended that girls be taught as well, whether in school or at home we do not know. In the late republic the well-to-do sent their sons to Athens or other famous cities of learning for further study. Medicine, law, or architecture could also be pursued.

12. The study of ancient children and childhood has been a particularly fruitful area in ancient social history. See Golden 1990; Dixon 1992; Wiedemann 1989; and Rawson 2003. Bradley's exploration of family sentiments and relations can be found in such studies as "The Social Role of the Nurse" in his *Discovering the Roman Family* (1991); for a sharp response: Garnsey 1991. For a succinct account of the socialization of the Roman child, see Saller 1994,

142–52. Kleijwegt (1991) took some to task for confusing ancient and modern ideas of education, notably Emiel Eyben; see Eyben 1993.

13. For a useful and perceptive survey of Roman school texts, see Gianotti 1989.

14. See, for instance, among theoreticians of narrative, Newton, who stresses not the direct efficacy of texts in producing ethical subjects but rather the representative force of texts: "Certain kinds of textuality parallel this description of ethical encounter in several obvious ways. Cutting athwart the mediatory role of reason, narrative situations create an immediacy and force, framing relations of provocation, call, and response that bind narrator and listener, author and character, or reader and text. . . . In this sense, prose fiction translates the interactive problematic of ethics into literary forms" (1995, 13).

15. Bonner (1977, 61, fig. 10) has an image of a wax tablet from Egypt inscribed with repeated *philoponei*.

1. IN SEARCH OF THE ROMAN SCHOOL

1. A sketch of Rome's first teachers and schooling can be found in Bonner 1977, 20–27; a full account in Kaster 1995. On Spurius Carvilius, see Gianotti 1989, 426. See also McNelis 2002, 67–94. See Morgan 1998, 26–27, for the lack of an educational program at Rome.

2. How many young Romans learned to read and write at any one time is a controversial issue. Harris (1989, 16) maintains: "The school systems of Graeco-Roman antiquity were for the most part quite puny." Without entering into the ongoing debates about the extent or quality of literacy (a number of scholars revise and extend the debate in Beard et al. 1991), I note two relevant features of ancient education: it was never interested in what historians of literacy following Lawrence Stone take as either a desideratum or a benchmark, that is, mass literacy; and secondly, literacy was a marker of high status. Schools were widespread but not numerous, well distributed horizontally but not vertically, in the cities of the Mediterranean cultures. Pliny made a letter of the request and his diligent effort to find a teacher for the citizens of Comum (*Ep.* 4.13). Harris (1989, 15–21) analyzes the conditions impeding widespread literacy.

3. A synthetic and compelling explanation can be found in Gruen 1992, chap. 6.

4. The effects should not be confused with Roman judgments about trade. See Andrew Wallace-Hadrill, "Elites and Trade in the Roman Town," in Wallace-Hadrill and Rich 1991, 241–72. Wallace-Hadrill takes as his point of departure D'Arms 1981, which treated such attitudes as something of a social fiction, unlike Finley (1985, chap. 2), who saw them as more straightforwardly normative.

5. Likewise, as I have discussed in chapter 2 of *Latinity and Literary Society at Rome* (Bloomer 1997), Suetonius dated the beginning of philology to the embassy of Crates in 168, on which he broke his leg in the Cloaca Maxima. The injured philosopher recuperated at Rome, giving well-attended lectures (on his reception, see now Goldberg 2005, 27–28, with bibliography). For similar enthusiasm among a contemporary Roman audience, cf. the story of Carneades' lectures, which impressed and repelled the elder Cato; subsequent generations at Rome seem to have had a positive impression. Thus Lactantius cites Lucilius and Cicero as testimony to Carneades' rhetorical powers (*Inst.* 5.14 f.). Carneades had come on

an embassy with Critolaus and Diogenes (154 B.C.), all of whose lectures were well attended (Pliny *NH* 7.112; Gell. 6.14.8–11 and 17.21.48); cf. Cic. *De or.* 2.155, *Acad.* 1.46; Plut. *Cato Mai.* 22.1–5). The technology of rhetoric had its showmen: e.g., Carneades, who spoke one day in praise of justice, the second day contra (Cic. *Rep.* 3.9); but the show was not so new as these accounts suggest: the envoy of King Pyrrhus, Cineas, a student of Demosthenes, had impressed the Romans in 280 B.C. by greeting by name the senators and citizens surrounding the senate on his second day in the city (Sen. *Controv.* 1.pr.19; Plut. *Pyrrh.* 18.4; Pliny *NH* 7.88). His wit and flattery seem to have been successful: among other diplomatic coups he managed a return of prisoners of war without ransom. His *sententiae* were remembered: e.g., "The Roman senate is an assembly of kings"; "Fighting with Rome is like battling a hydra"; see Plut. *Pyrrh.* 19.6; App. *Sam.* 10.3; Eutrop. 2.13.3.

6. Bonner (1977, 115) wrote with dispiriting honesty: "There is scarcely any part of the study of Roman education in which precise information is so difficult to obtain as that which concerns the localities and premises in which teaching took place." See note 13 below on the various forms and places of the Roman school. Scholars' difficulty in describing the place of school does not simply derive from an evidentiary difficulty. Hamilton (1979, 1) sets the historian a challenge: "Any description of classroom activities that cannot be related to the social structure and culture of the society is a conservative description."

7. Garcia y Garcia (2005, 58–70) reviews the evidence for schools at Pompeii. A fourth-century school with walls inscribed with a teacher's lessons has been excavated in Egypt: see Cribiore, Davoli, and Ratzan 2008.

8. See, for example, the often-reproduced Attic red-figure cup in Berlin (no. 2285) and similar scenes conveniently published in Beck 1975, pl. 10. A scene of a Roman teacher talking to his students can be found in the commentary on the grammatical primer (*Ars minor*) and sustained grammar (*Ars major*) of Donatus written by the African grammarian Pompeius (late fifth or sixth century). This *Commentum artis Donati* has been abused as derivative of Servius. As Holtz (1971, 50) has remarked, Pompeius does afford the best picture of the classroom. Kaster (1988, 158–61) has rightly objected that the addressee of Pompeius's pages—the "you" directed by his text—is in fact another teacher. Nonetheless, the qualities of lecture and commentary, student and teacher questioning, and mistakes and corrections are well illustrated by Pompeius.

9. The relief, reproduced by Bonner (1977) as a cover illustration and as figure 9 (p. 56), was first published by Hettner (1903, 21). The round-backed chairs are seen also in a scene of family dining, which suggests that this chair was common in Trier or that it suited the sculptor. It is not then specifically a school piece. The dining scene is reproduced as plate 20a in Wightman 1971. On the distinction between caning and whipping, see Saller, "Whips and Words: Discipline and Punishment in the Roman Household," in Saller and Shaw 1994, 133–53. For a succinct review of known pedagogues (including four women), see Rawson 2003, 165–67.

10. Philodemus *A History of the Stoics,* cols. 66, 70, cited by Dirk Obbink in his introduction to Gigante 1995, vii.

11. A most elaborate map is described as being planned for a school; but, as Sundwall (1996, 619–22) notes, Dilke's work has demonstrated the "almost total lack of map consciousness" among the Romans. Dilke 1985, 54: "The rhetorician Eumenius, born c. A.D.

264, writes of a map which he is planning for the school at Augustodunum (Autun, France): 'Also let the schoolchildren see it in those porticoes and look every day at all lands and seas and every city, race or tribe that unconquerable emperors either assist by their sense of duty or conquer by their valour or control by inspiring fear. There you have seen, for educational purposes, visual aids to supplement what is difficult to absorb merely from being told about the situations, areas and distances of all places. Their names are written in, the sources and mouths of all rivers are indicated, as are all coastal indentations, and the parts where the ocean either encircles the world or makes an inroad into land masses.'" The Latin text can be found in Mynors 1964, IX (IV).

12. On the physical process of reading a papyrus roll, see Birt 1907, 2–19.

13. See Bonner 1977, 115–25. Schools on the street: Dio Chrys. 20.9; at the juncture of streets: Justin 21.5, implied by Quint. 1.4.27 and Hor. *Epist.* 1.20; under or near a portico: the Pompeii painting was originally published by Helbig 1868, no. 1492 (see also the seated teacher in no. 1499), reproduced by Bonner (118, fig. 11); near a temple: Suet. *Gramm.* 15; a rented shop: Marrou 1948/1956, 362; in a pergula which, as Bonner (120–22) argued, was the room (a loggia) above a shop, which itself was an arcade; see also Bonner's discussion of balcony rooms (121–22), and see Platner and Ashby 1927, 504–5. School at the teacher's home: Suet. *Gramm.* 7; Cic. *Brut.* 207; Gell. 16.8.2.

14. Laurence 1996, 25–26.

15. See Richardson 1992, s.v. *Athenaeum;* Palmer 1990; and Coarelli 1993.

16. Rémondon 1964, a virtuoso reading of a single sentence—cited and celebrated by Bagnall 1995, 33.

17. On the identification of schools from graffiti, see Della Corte (1959), whose conclusions have been shown by Gigante (1979, 23–34) to be overconfident. Indeed, Della Corte's identification of another Pompeiian structure as a gymnasium (1924, 44–60) had already been doubted by Delorme (1960, 229–30).

18. See Andrew Wallace-Hadrill, "Elites and Trade in the Roman Town," in Wallace-Hadrill and Rich 1991, 248.

19. See Pavolini 1987. See also Harris 1989, 236–37. On slave training in literate skills, see Mohler 1940; Booth 1979b; and Rawson 2003, 187–91.

20. On the Greek grammar school, see Marrou 1948/1956, 144–45.

21. Bonner 1977, 57. See now Corbeill 2001, 277–78.

22. Cicero writes Atticus (*Att.* 8.4.1) that he will tutor his son Marcus and his nephew Quintus, rather than find a new teacher (*meo potius labore subdoceri* implies Cicero is teaching them at home). On tutors, see Rawson 2003, 160–62.

23. Jameson (1990), in his insight that the Greek house did not segregate the genders but regulated the flow of visitors, provided the impetus to what has become a more nuanced understanding of the experience of ancient architecture. Nevett 1997 offers a succinct review of scholarly approaches to the interpretation of the house and takes as a starting point for all future research a dialectical relationship between social and spatial organization (i.e., architecture reflects and informs lived experience). See also Nevett 1999; George 1997; Alison 1993; and Wallace-Hadrill 1994. On the overlapping public and private qualities of the Roman house (and daily experience), see Treggiari 1998. On the interpretation of rooms in the Roman house as multifunctional, see now Hales 2003, 3–5, with bibliography.

24. Cooper 1996, 21, supplies a parallel: if there were schools in ancient Israel like Ko-ranic schools, they would have left no archaeological traces (since they were held in a room of the teacher's house or in a public corner).

25. Horace contrasts a poor schooling among centurions' sons to his father's diligent care for his education (*Sat.* 1.6).

26. Quint. 2.1.2.

27. Sen. *Controv.* 9.2.23.

28. Quintilian disapproved of random seating (2.2.12) and approved the custom of seat-ing by ability, which he had learned from his own teachers (1.2.23).

29. See Bloomer 2001; and chapters 5 and 8 below.

30. The evidence for recitation was usefully collected by Dalzell 1955. For a reassessment of the performance of speech that stresses social and ludic qualities, see Dupont 1997.

31. On the places of declamation, see Bonner 1949, 39–40; and chapter 6 below. Latro blundered by referring to ingrafted nobility when Agrippa, in the audience with Augustus, was on the verge of having his sons adopted by the emperor (ca. 17 B.C.; Sen. *Controv.* 2.4.12–13). Gnipho's school: Suet. *Gramm.* 7.

32. Cic. *Nat. d.* 1.15 depicts such a scene of debate and discussion; *Fam.* 7.23.3 discusses appropriate statuary. On the development of spaces of culture in the Roman villa, see Clarke 1991.

33. For both the Romans' understanding of the effect of what they took to be Greece's superior culture and modern estimation of Greek cultural and institutional influence, see Beard and Crawford 1985; and Gruen 1992.

34. Macrob. 3.14.6–7 (*ORF* p. 133). See Bonner 1977, 44, on music and dancing schools at Rome and the bibliography there cited, especially Mountford 1964; Wille 1967; and Raw-son 2003, 170–72.

35. On Cato's relation to Greek intellectual culture, see Astin 1978, 157–81; Gruen 1992, 52–83; and Letta 1984. For an insightful study of the particularly Roman influences on and interests of Cato's writing, see Sciarrino 2004. More generally, for the process of Helleniza-tion at this time, see MacMullen 1991.

36. On the issues of the origin, influences, and phases of the Roman alphabet, see Pros-docimi 1989. The material evidence for learning to read and write from this early period is thoroughly presented in Pandolfini and Prosdocimi 1990. Against the view of Harris 1989, Cornell (1991) argues for a widespread use of literacy. Cornell (17) notes that the evidence indicates both Greek and Etruscan transmission of the alphabet.

37. Val. Max. 1.1.1. See Wardle's comment on this passage (1998). Cf. Cic. *Div.* 1.92; and on the *Etrusca disciplina,* Thulin 1909. Even if Roman youths were learning religious lore in Etruscan cities, this does not mean that schooling came from the Etruscans or exclusively from them. Even where Etruscans exerted an unmistakable influence on the Romans, in mat-ters of religion, scholars rightly stress an Italic religious *koinē* (see Pandolfini and Prosdocimi 1990, 51–57). For a tentative redating of the education of Roman youths in Etruscan cities (to the second century B.C.), see Thulin, *RE* 7: 2437; and for a judicious review of the anec-dotal evidence of Romans learning Etruscan, see Adams 2003, 166–68, 293.

38. See Brendel 1977, 408–9, and 344, for indications of Etruscan literary culture. On the fragment attributed to Licinus, see Courtney 1993, 82–86.

39. For an overview of the relations of Rome with Etruria, see Pallotino 1991, 80–105; 1984, 195–99 and 244–60.

40. Nevio Zorzetti (1990) has reinterpreted what Niebuhr took to be a Latin epic tradition, the lays of Rome, as rather the Romans' memory of a native song culture. See also Cole 1991a; and Phillips 1991. Habinek (1998, 34–45) argues for "a revolution in the sociology of literary production" at Rome in the third and second centuries B.C.

41. Pandolfini and Prosdocimi (1990, 4) conclude from the variety of types of inscribed objects that these were not meant for educational purposes. Writing this early on was a mark of the aristocratic, mercantile class (Pandolfini and Prosdocimi, 6; and cf. Cristofani 1987, 25–37).

42. Pandolfini and Prosdocimi 1990, 6–7. See also Cornell 1991, 23–24.

43. Artifacts from the Puglia excavation are on exhibit in the Museo Archeologico "Gaio Cilnio Mecenate" of Arezzo.

44. On the history, distribution, and phases of these objects, see Pandolfini and Prosdocimi 1990. The inscribed alphabets seem often to have had magical resonance: Lejeune 1952, 199–203; and Bonfante 1990, 15. On the interpretation of the formulas of early inscribed objects, see Agostiniani 1982, 21–24.

45. The Venetic material is analyzed in de' Fogolari and Prosdocimi 1987. Prosdocimi claims with good reason that these tablets are "the most important documents for the teaching of writing in ancient Italy" (363).

46. De' Fogolari and Prosdocimi 1987, 264–65, 271–74.

2. FIRST STORIES OF SCHOOL

1. The history of education is part of the history of the contact of Rome with Greek culture. The fundamental study remains Momigliano 1971. Momigliano's sketch of the coming of Greek and Greek experts under Roman sway firmly set the issue in the broader context of the contacts of the major civilizations of the Hellenistic era. Subsequent Roman historians have taken up the challenge to describe in detail the lives of these experts. See especially Bowersock 1965, chap. 3, pp. 30–41; and chap. 10, pp. 122–39; for the later period: Bowersock 1969. Rawson 1985 is especially useful.

A judicious snapshot of the expert *familia* of a Roman aristocrat can be found in the appendix to Treggiari 1969, 252–64, which lists and describes Cicero's freedmen and slaves. Cicero, one of the most philhellenic of his generation, had by Treggiari's count twenty slaves and freedmen. Another ten, belonging to friends and relatives, were "in Cicero's occasional or permanent employ." Rawson 2003, 154–55, provides a sketch of the activities of one such freedman, Apollonius, who served his former master, the son of the triumvir Crassus, but also visited Caesar and Cicero. Kaster 1988 catalogs educational instructors. See also Christes 1979.

Mohler (1940, 262) began his important study with the reminder "that a large proportion of the brain-workers in ancient society were of servile status." See also Treggiari 1969, chap. 3, "Careers," esp. section iii, "The Learned Professions and the Fine Arts," pp. 110–41. Booth (1979b, 11–19) considers the specific question of slave training.

2. On the relation of encomium to Plutarch's biographical project, see Wardman 1974, 12–18.

3. On these figures in Greek literature, see Kleingünther 1933; and Murray 1989.

4. Diod. Sic. 12.12.4.

5. The stories of Romulus and Remus are certainly as important cultural myths for the Romans as those of Achilles and Chiron were for any Greek community; see Wiseman 1995. On Numa's instruction from Pythagoras, see Gruen 1990, 158–70; and Ferrero 1955. Hus (1965, 15 n. 5 and 27–28) discusses the lack of legendary or divine instruction among the Romans.

6. See Kennell 1995; and Griffith 2001, 48–51.

7. The latter at Xen. *Lac.* 2.13. For the institutions of homophilia, see Griffith 2001, 61–66.

8. Booth (1978, 123) doubts the accuracy of Valerius Maximus's statement (4.4.1) that the Gracchi attended the school of a *grammaticus*. See Booth, 123 n. 22, for Greek scholars as tutors within the household.

9. His son, the younger Africanus, notably followed suit upon Hasdrubal's surrender: see the discussion and references in Astin 1967, 76 (for Paulus, see Polyb. 29.2; his triumph: Livy 45.35). On Paulus as an educator, see Plut. *Aem.* 6; also Astin 1967, 15; and Walbank 1979, ad Polyb. 31.22.4.

10. Suet. *Gramm.* 2 (and see Kaster 1995 ad loc.). I have discussed the peculiar shape of the anecdote (Bloomer 1997, 38–40).

11. A useful overview of Greek philosophy at Rome: Garbarino 1973. Kaster 1995, 59–60, considers the evidence for the date of the embassy.

12. Suetonius is not alone in "forgetting" or simplifying the debt of Rome to Greeks; see Petrochilos 1974; and for a corrective to the impoverished view, Gruen 1984, 250–60. On Crates at Rome: Kaster 1995, 61–63. A rich account of the Hellenistic experts at Rome, including Crates and Carneades: Rawson 1985, 66–99. The ancient evidence well presented: Hillscher 1892, 355 ff. See also Christes 1979. The enthusiasm for Carneades' and Crates' lectures: Gruen, 258 n. 41.

13. The first two chapters of Hopkins 1978 (pp. 1–132) describe the economic and social consequences of (continual) conquest for the developing empire.

14. Astin had thoroughly refuted the older view in his valuable two biographies, *Cato the Censor* (1978) and *Scipio Aemilianus* (1967). Building on such work, Gruen (1992) has reconsidered from a wider cultural perspective Roman relations to Hellenism in the second century (see also Gruen 1984 and 1990).

15. Astin 1978, 104 ff.

16. We do not know what form the school took, but in 184 B.C. Cato bought two houses and four shops (Livy 39.44.7), which, as Wallace-Hadrill (1991, 262) argued, were probably "like the standard Pompeian pattern of a house flanked by two shops." Among the shops or businesses in these four *tabernae* or their *pergulae* could well have been the school.

17. Polyb. 31.24 recounts the moment Scipio turned to him for guidance; he advises the young man that a host of Greek experts in education are in Rome. Books were more plentiful, at least for him, than at any time. Aemilius Paulus had given his sons King Perseus's library (see Walbank 1979, ad Polyb. 31.23.4); see also Plut. *Aem.* 6.8; and Astin (1967, 15), who, for independent evidence of Scipio's Greek education, directs the reader to Diod. Sic. 31.26.5 and Cic. *Brut.* 77. Cicero there relates that Aemilius's adoptive father, Scipio, had written short speeches and a history in Greek. From Cicero's diction (*oratiunculae* and *Graeca*

scripta dulcissime) it seems these were school exercises. My interpretation here is at odds with those who have seen in the choice of Greek more serious and formal purposes: e.g., Gelzer (1933, 129), who argued that the Greek history was directed at a Greek-speaking audience or simply that Latin was not yet suitable as a historical medium; and cf. Peter, *HRR* 1. 118 (both cited by Douglas 1966 ad loc.). Cicero's diminutive and his "charmingly written" point to the work of a child. See also Walbank (1979, on 31.25.2), who notes that only Diodorus maintains that Polybius educated Scipio in philosophy and that this notice is an addition in a passage drawn from Polybius, without any independent corroboration.

18. Skutsch 1985, 1 n. 1.

19. On the interest of the third- and second-century B.C. Roman aristocracy in literature, see Habinek 1998, 34–68; pp. 60–68 stress the symbolic value and selective adaptation of Greek literary culture for Roman ends.

20. The conflicts in Cato's articulation of a nativist, agricultural ideology with contemporary social, economic, and political realities have been ably discussed by Gabba 1989 (in passing). We have only small pieces of Cato's depiction of his own life, including fragments of the speeches "On His Consulship" and "On Censorial Legislation," *ORF* frs. 50 and 122. Of course, the various (?) works to his sons, and his account of agriculture and of warfare, communicate a picture of the ideal Roman and his activities, where the Roman reader may read his duty from the example of Cato and his family.

21. The children were also related to him by his adoption: they were the grandchildren of his adoptive father.

22. ἐπεὶ δὲ ἤρξατο συνιέναι, παραλαβὼν αὐτὸς ἐδίδασκε γράμματα, καίτοι χαρίεντα δοῦλον εἶχε γραμματιστὴν ὄνομα Χίλωνα, πολλοὺς διδάσκοντα παῖδας· οὐκ ἠξίου δὲ τὸν υἱόν, ὥς φησιν αὐτός, ὑπὸ δούλου κακῶς ἀκούειν ἢ τοῦ ὠτὸς ἀνατείνεσθαι μανθάνοντα βράδιον, οὐδέ γε μαθήματος τηλικούτου [τῷ] δούλῳ χάριν ὀφείλειν, ἀλλ᾽ αὐτὸς μὲν ἦν γραμματιστής, αὐτὸς δὲ νομοδιδάκτης, αὐτὸς δὲ γυμναστής, οὐ μόνον ἀκοντίζειν οὐδ᾽ ὁπλομαχεῖν οὐδ᾽ ἱππεύειν διδάσκων τὸν υἱόν, ἀλλὰ καὶ τῇ χειρὶ πὺξ παίειν καὶ καῦμα καὶ ψῦχος ἀνέχεσθαι καὶ τὰ δινώδη καὶ τραχύνοντα τοῦ ποταμοῦ διανηχόμενον ἀποβιάζεσθαι. καὶ τὰς ἱστορίας δὲ συγγράψαι φησὶν αὐτὸς ἰδίᾳ χειρὶ καὶ μεγάλοις γράμμασιν, ὅπως οἴκοθεν ὑπάρχοι τῷ παιδὶ πρὸς ἐμπειρίαν τῶν παλαιῶν καὶ πατρίων ὠφελεῖσθαι·

23. Astin (1978, 341–42) also notes that the contrast with Cato's education of his second son may have reflected Cato's attitudes toward slaves, not toward Greek education.

24. *PW* no. 5.

25. Indeed, the story had already been reduced to a *sententia* (or at longest an *exemplum*) by Pomponius Rufus in his *Collecta*, where Valerius Maximus found it and recast it as an exemplum (by A.D. 31; see my discussion of the passage, 4.4.pr., in Bloomer 1992, 143). Plutarch then included it in his life of Phocion (19.3). A similar story is attributed by Plutarch to an Ionian woman who boasted of an expensive piece of her own weaving. Her Spartan hostess pointed to her four sons, very handsome and well behaved (κοσμιωτάτους), and instructed the Ionian: "These should be the handiwork of a good and noble woman, and she should take pleasure and boast of these" (Plut. *Lacaenarum Apophthegmata* 241.9, repeated by Stob. *Flor.* v. 47). See Barnard 1990; and López 1998, 98–121. The association of sons and mother had a lively political future. Letters were manufactured in which Cornelia reproved Tiberius Gracchus for his political program (see Instinsky 1971). The memory of Cornelia continued to be

manipulated at Rome for political ends: a statue modeled on Phidias's seated Aphrodite was erected in the portico of the enemy of the Gracchi, Q. Metellus Macedonicus, with Cornelia named as mother of the Gracchi on the inscription on the base (*CIL* VI 10043; and see Plut. *C. Gracch.* 4; and Pliny *NH* 34.31). The phrase was later augmented with notice of her as daughter of Scipio Africanus. Coarelli (1978, 13–28) argued that the rewriting was the work of later enemies of the sorts of reform associated with the Gracchi (see esp. 19, 23–24). The site of the statue was itself renamed in honor of Augustus's sister Octavia, and the statue became a type (see the summary treatment with illustration: Fantham et al. 1994, 265).

26. Suetonius writes (*Aug.* 44.3) that the emperor took it upon himself to teach his grandsons reading and writing, swimming, and the elementary curriculum and took the greatest care that the children imitate his own handwriting. Quintilian (1.1.28) stresses the importance of students writing in their own hands. Delegating the task to slaves is clearly disapproved. Augustus wrote and corrected his own letters (Quint. 1.7.22; Suet. *Aug.* 71). So too Fronto reminds the emperor, his correspondent, that he has written in his own hand (*Ad M. Caes.* 2.4 and 2.10.1).

27. See, e.g., Rawson 2003, 36–38 (and 97), on the children of Germanicus and Drusus and their importance as a marker of general civic well-being.

28. Fraenkel (1922, 376) described the prominence of education in New Comedy, which is interested in "man as a social being, an ethical agent, subject and object of paideia." Pedagogues, for instance, appear often as characters (listed in Schmitter 1972, 27).

29. Plautus likes to joke about school and schooling. The young masters are chastised for not paying strict attention to the lessons of the wily slaves (*Pseudolus* 1193 identifies the wily slave who gives his name to the play as "Your professor, who taught you this trick," *Praeceptor tuus, qui te hanc fallaciam / docuit*). The courtesan is an adept schoolmistress in her proper faculty. At *Bacchides* 163–65 the pedagogue complains to his wayward charge: "A worse teacher has taught you these things, not I. You are a student far too attentive to these subjects than the course of study I set you, where all my labor is lost." (*peior magister te istaec docuit, non ego. / nimio es tu ad istas res discipulus docilior / quam ad illa quae te docui, ubi operam perdidi.*) Plautus has certainly taken much of this from his Greek original (as the references just above this passage to Hercules, Phoenix, and the music master Linus suggest), but he delights in the material, as did his audience no doubt. Hus 1965, 17–22, provides a short review of the use of *docere* in Plautus.

30. This was not the case in the Hellenistic city of Pompeii, which had both a version of the Greek ephebeia and a palaestra: Marrou 1948/1956, 243, citing Conway I, 42.

Although the gymnasium and ephebeia were not adopted at Rome, Romans began traveling to Greece to complete their studies. The first Roman name found among the lists of ephebes at Athens dates from 119–118 B.C. (Marrou, 247, citing *IG* II², 1008). On Romans traveling to Greece, see Daly 1950, 42–58. On the Romans' opposition to athletics see Marrou, 248–49. It used to be said that the Romans were shocked by the nudity and ensuing (!) homosexuality of the gymnasium. The Roman cities already had their own practices and institutions for the acculturation of young men. The (coveted) technology of Greek education was adopted within the (private) system of the Roman family and patronage. Architectural motifs from the gymnasium also entered the private site of culture, the villa and elite house. The scope of the Roman public baths may have been influenced by the great gymnasium complexes, but as Marrou pointed out (249), the palaestra was a subsidiary space in the public bath complex. On the lesser importance of the palaestra in Roman bath complexes, see also Delaine 1988, 16–17. Yegül 1989, 21–24, traces the tendency to add hot baths to gymnasia from classical Athens through the Hellenistic era.

31. On the social symbolism of the Roman house, see Wallace-Hadrill 1994, 4–16.

32. *Disciplina* is a favorite word in the elder Cato's writings. In addition, the cluster of family value terms in Plautus corresponds well with Cato's lexicon, e.g., Cato apud Festum 281.23 Müll. s.v. *repastinari: in parsimonia atque in duritia atque industria omnem adolescentiam meam abstinui, agro colendo.* In particular, *parcus* becomes a traditional term (*frugi*, not so used in Cato, is frequent in the classical period): Cic. *Cael.* 36: *patre parco ac tenaci; De or.* 2.287: *optimus colonus, parcissimus, modestissimus, frugalissimus* (reminiscent of Cato's famous *bonus colonus* at the outset of the *De agricultura*); Hor. *Sat.* 2.5.79: *donandi parca iuventus;* Ter. *Ad.* 1.1.20: *parce et duriter se habere;* cf. also Cic. *Verr.* 2.2.3: *res familaris conservatur diligentia et parsimonia;* Plaut. *Trin.* 4.3.20: *veteres mores veteresque parsimoniae.*

33. *Agr.* 1. Courtney points out that Cato uses a sententia here and at 2.7 to conclude or emphasize his point (1999, 54 and 55 ad loc.).

34. It cannot be known whether Cato's *De agri cultura* was written and read by the time of the play's production. Still, Cato and his sententia would have been well known. He was one of the most prolific speakers, not simply through his political speeches but in all the lawsuits that he invariably won. His advice to delay building: *Agr.* 3.1. Astin (1978, 190–91) reviews the slim evidence for dating Cato's work and concludes that a date of composition in the later years of Cato's life is "plausible but is not securely established."

35. Similarly, the father of Plautus's *Captivi* values his son above all capital, or so he says before condemning his unrecognized son to heavy labor. In comedy this protocol seems expressed when father or son is absent; it belongs to soliloquy not to actual dialogue of father and son. Thus it is marked all the more as fiction.

36. The *probus* Roman is one who keeps faith. The word certainly can describe a witness (Plaut. *Trin.* 1096) but denotes a broader social virtue; e.g., Plaut. *Mostell.* 408: *Pluma haud interest patronus an cliens probior sit.* See the discussion of the term and these and other examples in Hellegouarc'h 1963, 494–95.

37. On Plautus's addition of Roman ideas and practices, indeed whole semantic fields, especially in his jokes, see Williams 1968, 285–91.

38. Görler (1974, 51–62) discusses Cicero's habit of presenting contrary philosophical viewpoints. Further insight into what one might call Cicero's dialogics, which emphasizes the implication of the (Roman) political or cultural with the (Greek) theoretical, has been presented in two studies on Cicero's *De divinatione:* Beard 1986 and Krostenko 2000.

The corrective to the old view of a Scipionic circle and a reassessment of the period's cultural agents and movements: Astin 1967, esp. 294–306, "Appendix 6: The Scipionic Circle"; and 1978. Gruen (1992, 197–202) reminds that Terence was an established playwright by the time of the production of the *Adelphoe,* while the members of Scipio's circle were in their youth—hardly the great patrons aiding a young poet. For further bibliography on the history of the question of the Scipionic circle, see Gruen, 224–25.

The arguments for an allegorical reading of the two fathers in Terence's play are sketched in Grilli 1979. Ramage (1959) has collected ancient testimonia relevant to the concept of *ur-*

banitas. Quintilian believed that Marsus's depiction of the *homo urbanus* was the elder Cato (Quint. 6.102–12). On the claims made in the name of pure Latin, see Bloomer 1997, 1–17, and on *urbanitas,* 58–59.

39. Gratwick (1987) contrasts the philosophical opposition of the Greek original (the brothers as Epicurean and Cynic or Stoic: 22–23) with Terence's downplaying of Micio as an Epicurean (28). Gratwick notes Terence's further complication of the dramatic stereotypes (e.g., 30): Micio's speech (*Ad.* 679–96) is untypical of the *senex lepidus.*

40. Hor. *Epist.* 2.1.69–75. For the hexameter replacement of Livius Andronicus, see Courtney 1993, 45 ff. The original version of Livius was not simply a translation or a school aid—see Mariotti 1952. In the first century A.D. a translation, in fact a version, the *Ilias Latina,* was made (see Grillo 1982 and Scaffai 1982).

The first sign of the displacement of the old poetry is a notice in Suetonius's biographies of the grammarians (Cicero had already drawn attention to changes in the curriculum when he remarked that his generation had memorized the Twelve Tables, "which no one nowadays does," *Leg.* 2.59). Q. Caecilius Epirota, a freedman of Atticus, was a school reformer: Suetonius (*Gramm.* 16.3) describes him as the first to dispute in Latin (*disputasse*) and the first to use the Augustan poets for grammatical-literary exposition (*praelegere*); see Kaster (1995, ad 16.3), who argues that dispute signifies a more informal instruction with give-and-take from Epirota's older (adolescent) students.

41. Suetonius records epigrams of Julius Caesar and of Cicero that praise Terence's stylistic achievement: *puri sermonis amator* and *solus lecto sermone.* See the assessment of Terentian style in "The *purus sermo,*" chap. 7 in Goldberg 1986, 170–202. On Terence's reception, see Duckworth 1952, 396–433.

42. For the anecdotal evidence of Latin speakers using and understanding Greek, see Adams 2003, 9–15.

43. Gratwick 1987, 22, although he notes (citing Vischer 1965, 60–88) the integration of such attitudes into Roman political ideas.

44. Rawson (2003) begins her authoritative book by asking how welcome a Roman child was, and proceeds to trace the representations and recognitions of children in Italy from the first century B.C. to the second A.D. She notes (e.g., 25) the lack of interest in children in the art of the late republic.

45. The educational notices, while commemorating the family, do not emphasize the triad of father, mother, and child, familiar from later tombstones, for which see Saller and Shaw 1984, 124–56.

3. THE SCHOOL OF IMPUDENCE

1. This joke book is now available in a Teubner edition: Dawe 2000.

2. Aristotle uses the word in this sense at *Rh.* 3.14.6: ἐν δὲ προλόγοις καὶ ἔπεσι δεῖγμά ἐστιν τοῦ λόγου, ἵνα προειδῶσι περὶ οὗ ὁ λόγος καὶ μὴ κρέμηται ἡ διάνοια. ("In prologues and epic poetry there is a foretaste/sample of the speech so that the audience may know ahead of time the subject of the speech and the mind may not be kept in suspense".)

3. For the picture of Socrates painted by Xenophon, see Vlastos 1991, 99–106, and for Socratic irony, see chap. 1.

4. Rhetorical training was long and difficult, but the theorists and practitioners emphasized its difficulty in part to justify its pursuit as a manly activity. See Brody 1993, 3–15.

5. Cramer (1954, 235), writing of the temporary, occasional nature of the edict, concludes "that it lapsed quietly on December 31, 139." Suolahti (1963, 444–45), in surveying the relations of the two censors, while not downplaying their disagreement, stresses the illness of Crassus as a factor in his resignation. The censors did manage to appoint the *princeps senatus*. Having failed to perform the *lustrum* and complete the census, these two censors left important business for the next censors to do (whose election was delayed until 89 by the Social War), business more compelling apparently than an edict against rhetoricians.

6. Cramer 1954, 233.

7. Cramer (1954, 52) celebrates these five for the successful, swift introduction of Hellenistic philosophy to Rome.

8. Badian (1972, 151–99) reviewed the subject of the early poets' relations to upper-class Romans. See also Jocelyn 1969, 32–47. Goldberg (1995, 30–37) takes issue with the scholarly consensus that the poets were of low social order and suspects that later Roman prejudice against the theater has colored scholars' judgments.

9. Archias was the client-friend of Cicero's educational patron L. Crassus. Archias wrote poems praising Marius and Lucullus, but not Cicero, who had defended him against the prosecution of Gratius, the agent of Pompey in this attack upon Lucullus's client.

10. See the life vignettes of teachers in Suetonius's *De grammaticis;* Suetonius's ideological leanings are discussed in Bloomer 1997, 67–71.

11. On Cicero's exaggeration of Crassus's opposition to Hellenism in the *De oratore,* see Gruen 1992, 264–66.

12. MacMullen (1966) applied the phrase to Roman history. The chief source for the Bacchanalian affair is Livy 39.8 ff. See Gelzer 1936, 275–87; and the discussion with extensive bibliography in Gruen 1990, 34–78, chap. 2, "The Bacchanalian Affair." For a review of alleged anti-Hellenism in second-century Rome, see Gruen 1992, 258–60. For Cato's opposition to astrologers, see *Agr.* 1.5.4.

13. Cramer (1954, 44–58) analyzes the adoption of astrology by the Romans of the mid-Republic (in the context of the transfer of other Hellenistic religious practices). For the important role of astrology in the politics of the early Roman empire, see Cramer, 81–145; and for the various official forms of expulsion, 233–47. The second emperor's lifelong fascination with astrology is discussed (at times with an almost novelistic recreation of motive and scene) in Hayes 1959, 2–8, but see esp. Potter 1994, 158–62. The ancient testimony for the praetorian edict for the expulsion of astrologers is Val. Max. 1.3.3. See also Cramer 1951.

14. In addition to the letter of the law, the official speech against luxury included the speeches of censors; see Gruen 1992, 54, for a brief review of Cato's various actions, and 69–71 (with bibliography) for a broader discussion of the ineffectiveness of such "legislation."

15. Hillscher 1892 provides a still useful digest of the evidence, but see Christes 1979; on individual figures, see Treggiari 1969; Gruen 1992; Kaster 1988 and 1995.

16. Cornelia set the type for the Roman (widowed) mother as educator. Tacitus takes it up in the biography of his father-in-law, Agricola, whose widowed mother, Julia Procilla, moderated his passion for Greek philosophy (*Agr.* 4).

17. Gruen (1990, 179) emphasizes strongly that the edict censured but took no steps to

disband the school. The edict is preserved at Suet. *Gramm.* 26. The reference in Gell. 15.11.2 probably derives from this passage. Tac. *Dial.* 35.1 refers to Cicero (see *De or.* 3.93). See the commentary of Kaster (1995, 271–97). Rawson (2003, 147–49) briefly discusses the edict. Narducci (1989) interprets the actions of the Latin rhetors as an effort to spread what had been an aristocratic privilege to a broader segment of Roman society.

18. Suet. *Gramm.* 25.2; the translation is from Kaster 1995, 30–31.

19. See also Treggiari (1969, 117), who compares other passages illustrating Cicero's insistence that Greek studies were necessary (*Opt. gen. or.* 18, *Part. or.* 1 ff., *Brut.* 310, *Off.* 1.1; and cf. Suet. *Gramm.* 2).

20. Bonner 1949, 18.

21. Gruen 1990, 180–84, with bibliography. Marrou (1948/1956, 252–53) had already warned not to construe the incident as an aristocratic check on Marian interests but to see Gallus's school as a less expensive route to the skill in speaking that aristocratic youths learned by apprenticeship in the forum. Bonner (1977, 72) had noted that the marriage of Crassus's daughter to Marius's son argued against a political interpretation (Gruen 1990, 182, suggests the marriage occurred between 95 and 90). On Crassus and Antonius in the *De oratore*, see also Gruen 1992, 264–68.

22. Cicero tells us nothing of his early education (although the old poets whose quotations pepper his rhetorical and philosophical works would have been learned under the *grammaticus,* and he does say he learned the Twelve Tables by heart as a boy, *Leg.* 3.59); characteristically, he does tell stories when there is a connection to Rome and its leading citizens: he and his cousins attend the scholarly discussion at L. Crassus's house (*De or.* 1.191 and 2.2). He relates both that Crassus dissuaded him from Gallus's school and that he studied Crassus's speeches (*De or.* 3.93 and *Brut.* 169; see also *Brut.* 164 and *De or.* 1.225 for Cicero's admiration of the most famous of Crassus's speeches, an admiration, like his criticism of Gallus, voiced late in life). Plutarch (*Cic.* 2.2) tells the story that the parents of Cicero's schoolmates came to school to hear the young prodigy. Finally, Cicero chose to "attend" professional Roman orators, e.g., Cotta and Hortensius (*Brut.* 317; cf. *Sen.* 29).

23. Elizabeth Rawson's biography of Cicero offers a judicious discussion; see chapter 2, "At the Foot of the Ladder, 90–77 B.C.," in the revised edition (1983, 12–28).

24. A sketch of a probable course of Cicero's studies, which makes the interesting suggestion that the poet Archias was Cicero's early teacher at Rome, is Clarke 1968, 18–22. The tendentious qualities of the *Brutus* as a history of Roman oratory and as a presentation of the author (the work concludes, 301 ff., with a comparison of Hortensius and Cicero) have been recognized by, e.g., Rathofer (1986), who argued that Cicero hoped through the dialogue to anoint Brutus as his political and oratorical successor. Sumner (1973) offers amplification and corrective to the details of the lives of the individual orators mentioned by Cicero. The presence of Cicero in the work (his style, his life, his *animus*) was nicely put by Johnson (1971, 62): "The *Brutus* is a book about the disintegration of a style and the loss of an audience."

25. See Plut. *Cic.* 3; and Cic. *Amic.* 1.

26. See Rawson 1983, 15; and Nep. *Att.* 1 and Cic. *Leg.* 1.13.

27. Contact with Greek philosophers at Rome in the 80s: Diodotus the Stoic lived with Cicero (*Brut.* 309, *Acad.* 2.36.115); in 87 B.C. the head of the Academy, Philo of Larissa, came

to Rome and greatly moved Cicero (*Brut.* 306; Plut. *Cic.* 3.1); contact with Epicureans is probable, although references come from Cicero's visits with Atticus in Athens (*Fin.* 6.1.3), when Cicero studied with the new head of the Academy, Antiochus (*Brut.* 315 and Plut. *Cic.* 4.1; cf. Cic. *Leg.* 2.14).

For the political import of the speeches *Pro Quinctio* (81 B.C.), *Pro Roscio Amerino* (80 B.C.), and *Pro Aretina*, see the reservations of Rawson (1983, 22–25). Leeman (1963, 95–103) discusses Cicero's development at this time, including Cicero's first contact with the teacher Molo (see Davies 1968, 303–14; Cic. *Brut.* 312; Val. Max. 2.2.3). Caesar was captured by pirates on his way to study with Molo (Suet. *Iul.* 4.1; Plut. *Caes.* 3.1).

On the date of the *De inventione*, close to the edict, see Kennedy 1972, 106–10. Gruen (1990, 185) follows the traces of an earlier Roman tradition of such works (Quint. 3.1.19; Victorinus, in Halm, *Rhetores Latini*, 308) but notes Astin's skepticism that Cato had written such a work (Astin 1978, 333–34; and see below chapter 5). Uncertainty about the date of the *Rhet. Her.* (possibly even in the 50s: see Douglas 1960) precludes using it as evidence for the tradition. On the history of speech exercises at Rome, see Clarke 1951; Kennedy 1972, 91–92; and Schmidt 1975.

28. Plut. *Cic.* 3. Years later Cicero took pride in his *Pro Roscio Amerino* as an attack upon Sulla (*Off.* 2.51). For the factions agitating with Cicero against Sulla, see Ward 1970, 127–29.

29. On the physical regimen of speech training, see Rouselle 1988, 11; Dugan 2001, 400–28; and Gleason 1995, 103–30.

30. Cicero on his reasons for leaving Rome: *Brut.* 313. See Daly 1950; and for Cicero's son: Abbott 1909; and Daly, 49–53.

31. Treggiari 1969, 128: "The most eminent of the rhetors were not the freedmen who taught in Italy, but free Greeks in the great centres of culture in the eastern empire, while much of the work which might have been done by freedmen in Rome was taken over by practising Roman orators, who took pupils into their households as Scaevola did Cicero and Cicero did Caelius, and by treatises based on Greek teaching such as the *Rhet. ad Her.* and the works of Cicero himself." Later Cicero would have a series of teachers for his son: Tyrannio, Paeonius, and Dionysius (*QFr.* 2.4.2; 3.3.4; and *Att.* 4.8–15).

32. See Treggiari 1969, 117.

33. Cicero concludes the *Brutus* with an account of the weakness of his constitution as a young man, which he attributes to his violent, loud delivery. Friends and doctors counseled him to give up oratory. *Brut.* 313: *erat eo tempore in nobis summa gracilitas et infirmitas corporis, procerum et tenue collum: qui habitus et quae figura non procul abesse putatur a vitae periculo, si accedit labor et laterum magna contentio. eo que magis hoc eos quibus eram carus commovebat, quod omnia sine remissione, sine varietate, vi summa vocis et totius corporis contentione dicebam.*

34. For Cicero, a knowledge of Greek is indispensable. Indeed, in giving a sketch of the development of oratory at Rome, he ties its final success to a knowledge and synthesis of Greek expertise (*scientia*): *De or.* 1.4.14–15; see Treggiari 1969, 117; cf. Cic. *Opt. gen. or.* 18; *Part. or.* 1 ff.; *Brut.* 205, 310; *Off.* 1.1.

35. Cicero's own practice should be understood against the background of Roman use of Greek rhetoric and rhetorical training. Suetonius was ill-informed on the topic: he quotes the senate's decree of 161 against philosophers and rhetoricians, the censors' of 92, and then

passes on to a notice that Cicero attended a school of declamation even during his praetorship (*Gramm.* 7.25). In fact, the earliest fragments of Roman oratory (second century B.C.) contain rhetorical figures (Kennedy 1972, 91); see Bonner 1949, 16–26, for a sketch of practice at Rome before the age of Sulla. Cicero lists a number of speakers who practiced exercises (apparently at home): Caius Papirius Carbo, Marcellus, and his son-in-law C. Piso (*Brut.* 105, 249, and 272). At *De or.* 1.154 Crassus says these consisted of reading passages (a) by the speaker; (b) by Ennius; © by C. Gracchus. The young Crassus practiced Latin versions of the Greek orators (*De or.* 1.155; see also Clarke 1951).

Cicero describes his own early practice at *Brut.* 310: *commentabar declamitans—sic enim nunc loquuntur—saepe cum M. Pisone et cum Q. Pompeio aut cum aliquo cottidie, idque faciebam multum etiam Latine, sed Graece saepius;* he practiced more often in Greek for two reasons: it offered a greater stylistic challenge, and the best teachers did not know Latin. On the connection of paraphrase and translation, see Roberts 1985, 8–9.

36. Fantham (1978a, 109–10) notes that Quintilian (10.2.5) disagrees with Cicero's opposition to paraphrase of a Latin model and that Quintilian has better appreciated the importance of assimilation that derives from study and practice with model texts.

37. At *Tusc.* 1.7 Cicero playfully calls his new habit of talking on philosophical topics to his friends in the privacy of his villa his "senile declamation." The serious challenge of writing philosophy in Latin: Leeman 1963, chap. 8, "The Styles of Philosophical Writing in the Republic," 198–216; and Poncelet 1957. Cicero avoided using Greek loanwords but was forced in the philosophical works to coin neologisms (*Tusc.* 1.8.15, *Fin.* 3.2.4–5): see Laurand 1965, 78–81.

38. Murphy (2001, 29) describes the dialog as "the last major objection against the well-organized, discourse-centered teaching program."

39. On Cicero as a translator and the consequent enrichment of Latin, see Powell 1995, 273–300. See also Cicu 1991; and Dubuisson 1989. A very brief corrective to the view of Cicero's principles of translation as primitive: Gee 2005, 40. Fuller comments and appreciation: Clausen 1986; Morford 1967; Soubiron 1973, with much older bibliography; and Kubiak 1981.

40. See Gentili 1979; Mariotti 1952; and Traina 1970.

41. Schoek 1966 (based on the 1570 text); for a brief discussion and bibliography of Ascham's method of imitation, see Schoek's introduction, pp. xx–xxi; see also Harding 1961, 93–94.

42. Kennedy (1972, 84–96), while noting that Cicero does use Crassus as a mouthpiece (6), treats the Crassus of Cicero's *De oratore* and *Brutus* as historically reliable. For a nuanced argument regarding the persona of Crassus in the *De oratore*, see Leeman 1963, 112–13.

43. A senator could be asked for his sententia in a formal *interrogatio* in the senate; see *OLD*, s.vv. *sententia* 3 and *interrogo* 3; and for the complex evidence of the sequence and procedures: Talbert 1984, 240–49, 276. *Probare* was a verb used of the censors' actions: e.g., *censores hasce aras probaveront, CIL* 1.2439; *censores villam publicam in campo Martio probaverunt,* Livy 4.22.7 (these examples from *OLD*, s.v. *probo* 3; and cf. Quint. 4.pr.3: *probaverit sanctissimus censor*).

44. Bonner (1977, 73 n. 50) cited in support of the older meaning of the term the following gloss: *declamatio/anaphonesis* (*CGL* 3.351.65). Stroh (2003) offers a thorough reap-

praisal of the history of the term *declamation*. He demonstrates in particular Cicero's pejorative, nontechnical use of the term and the term's range of meeting, from the loud delivery of a practice text to the school and performance *controversiae* and *suasoriae* of the time of the elder Seneca.

45. Quint. 2.4.41–42: *His fere veteres facultatem dicendi exercuerunt, adsumpta tamen a dialecticis argumentandi ratione. nam fictas ad imitationem fori consiliorum que materias apud Graecos dicere circa Demetrium Phalerea institutum fere constat. . . . Latinos vero dicendi praeceptores extremis L. Crassi temporibus coepisse Cicero auctor est quorum insignis maxime Plotius fuit.*

Varro *Sat. Men.* (p. 157 Riese): *quod aput Plotium rhetorem bubulcitarat;* (p. 186 Riese): *ille ales gallus, qui suscitabat aitharum Musarum scriptores? an hic qui gregem rabularum?*

Cic. *De or.* 1.202: *non enim causidicum nescio quem neque clamatorem aut rabulam.*

Cic. *Orat.* 47: *non enim declamatorem aliquem de ludo aut rabulam de foro sed doctissimum et perfectissimum quaerimus.*

Quint. 12.9.12: *si a viro bono in rabulam latratorem que convertitur.*

Suet. *Claud.* 2.2: Claudius maintained that he had been kept under a pedagogue who was a barbarian and ex-muleteer (*barbarum et olim superiumentarium*).

Speed of movement and loudness of delivery were traditionally the marks of the demagogue: preeminently, of Cleon in Thucydides. Demosthenes censured swift movement and loudness (μέγα φθέγγεσθαι) as characteristics of the envious man. Cf. his criticism of swift movement and loud talkativeness at *Contr. Steph.* 77. These references are given by Holden (1894), ad Plut. *Per.* 5.8; Pericles was the archetype of the best orator, restrained in movement, speech, and expression. Another antitype to the demagogic and the vulgar was Aristotle's great-souled man, whose movement was βραδεῖα. Plutarch draws on Pl. *Phdr.* 270A for his depiction of Pericles' severe and unlaughing composure.

46. *De or.* 2.86: *clamare contra quam deceat et quam possit, hominis est, ut tu, Catule, de quodam clamatore dixisti, stultitiae suae quam plurimos testis domestico praeconio conligentis;* cited in this context by Bonner (1977, 73).

47. Castorina (1952) argued that Cicero's attitude toward style changed, but not necessarily his practice (remarks on Asianism and Atticism here are too schematic). On Cicero's changing practice, see Davies 1968 and Johnson 1971. On the charges against Cicero's style, see now Dugan 2001: 422–25.

48. *De or.* 1.83, 1.105; Val. Max. 2.2.2; Juvenal 3.74; Pliny *Ep.* 5.20.4. Seneca the Elder (*Controv.* 4.pr.7) seems to praise Haterius for being the only Roman to transfer the *facultas* of the Greeks into his declamation. But the next sentence identifies this as speed of delivery, a fault in Latin, censured by Augustus himself.

49. See Cic. *Brut.* 325 on the speed of Asianists. For Cicero's approval of youthful richness, see *De or.* 2.88. Antonius's treatment of the appropriateness of *copia* to the young orator is picked up by Quintilian (2.4.4 ff.). But speed of delivery had already been grouped as a fault with agitated delivery (perhaps to be associated with demagoguery) by Lucilius (ca. 115 B.C.): Nonius 21.18 preserves a fragment (nos. 273–74) cited to illustrate the idiom *quiritare* ("to shout," i.e., like a politician who constantly calls upon the citizens, *Quirites*): *Haec inquam rudet ex rostris atque heiulitabit / concursans veluti Ancarius clareque quiritans.*

50. Plut. *Ti. Gracch.* 2.4–5: by name Licinius, "a not unintelligent household slave."

51. See Treggiari 1969; note 30 above (the teachers of Cicero's son and nephew); and Rowland 1972. More than a few Greek experts disappointed Cicero: in addition to the failings of some teachers, the poet Archias failed to write propaganda on his behalf; his brother's scholar-freedman Philologus set the assassins on his trail. More positively, Tyrannio and others of Atticus's experts helped him organize and refit one of his libraries (*Att.* 4.8). Cicero draws readily on Atticus's entourage, e.g., asking Atticus's help through "his friend, clients, guests, freedmen, and slaves" to get the library given him by Papirius Paetus (*Att.* 1.20.7).

52. Gruen (1990, 185–87) argued that what irked the censors was the establishment of the school of rhetoric and not instruction in Latin per se. Grammarians had taught in Latin before the 90s. Suetonius tells us that the early grammarians offered instruction in rhetoric (*Gramm.* 4). L. Aelius Stilo probably taught rhetoric (as well as composing speeches for Roman orators: cf. Cic. *Brut.* 169, 205–7; Suet. *Gramm.* 3; cf. Gell. 1.18.2). Antonius's pamphlet on oratory, published without his consent, was presumably used in rhetorical training (Cic. *De or.* 1.94, 1.206, 208, 3.189; *Brut.* 163; *Orat.* 18; Quint. 3.1.19). On the date of this work, probably between 102 and 91, see Calboli 1972; and Manfredini (1976, 138), who argued that Plotius Gallus essentially taught shortcuts, and cited in support the anecdote at Quint. 2.22.1, in which a professor, challenged to define *schema* (figure) and *noema* (thought), responded he did not know, but if they had anything to do with the subject they could be found in his declamation; Manfredini remarked: "The professor may not have been Plotius Gallus, but the position is similar."

53. For complaints about declamation, and for its champions, see chapter 8 below.

54. Cicero's judgment of the *De inventione* as immature: *De or.* 1.2.5. The older, but essential bibliography and discussion of the relationship to Cicero's *De inventione* is conveniently found in Caplan 1954, xxv–xxxii. Leeman (1963, 25–42) offers a judicious summary.

4. THE MANUAL AND THE CHILD

1. Abbott (1980) provides an extensive philological and literary commentary. However, Abbott's assertion that the treatise lacks originality and literary merit slights its political, social, and educational ambitions.

2. Fifty years ago, scholars argued from the apparent noninterest of the ancients (and of medieval culture) that there had been no childhood before Rousseau, and early modern Europe. They were right only in the sense that Ps.-Plutarch, like many others, did not see childhood as a symbol of a beneficent nature or as a stage to which one should want to return. Nonetheless, the author of the *De liberis educandis* does envisage stages; for instance, he divides children from adolescents by the quality of their faults (12B) and says everybody knows this difference. Children have school faults, trivial things like not listening to their pedagogues; youths commit more serious offenses (gluttony, sex, theft, misuse of patrimony).

Ariès (1962) maintained that childhood was not recognized as such until the sixteenth century. Kleijwegt (1991) has argued a similar case for antiquity, without convincing the majority of social historians. Orme (2001, 3–5) reviews scholars' reception (and increasingly the refutation) of Ariès's views. Orme's work is itself a thorough recuperation of the experience denied by Ariès (and others). On the lack of interest displayed by ancient literature in preliterate children and the early stages of development, see Morgan 1998, 241–44.

3. For a lucid discussion of the program of Xenophon's *Oeconomicus,* see Johnstone 1994, 219–40.

4. Roman treatises on agriculture: Fuhrmann 1960, 156–59, 162–64. On the first extant Roman work on oratory, the *Rhetorica ad Herennium,* and the earlier Roman tradition, see above, chapter 3, pp. 50–52; also Fuhrmann, 41 with notes. Conte has written of the encyclopedic urge that directed the elder Pliny's reading and writing (1994, chap. 3, "The Inventory of the World: Form of Nature and Encyclopedic Project in the Work of Pliny the Elder," 67–104). Della Corte (1946) provides a brief review of the principal encyclopedists from Cato to Cassiodorus.

5. Vitruvius (7.pr.14) had noted that a work on architecture was among the nine (grammar, dialectic, rhetoric, geometry, arithmetic, astrology, music, medicine, architecture). See Dahlmann's comments in *RE* (s.v. Marcus Terentius Varro, Suppl. Band 6.1256–59).

6. See the Teubner edition of *Iulii Frontini Strategemata* (Ireland 1990). The unknown author of the *Rhetorica ad Herennium,* writing ca. 86 B.C., declared that he might write about military science and the administration of the republic (3.2.3).

7. On the interest of the intellectual culture of the Augustan and early imperial periods in compendia of culture, see Rawson 1985, 117; Beagon 1992, 2–15; Bloomer 1997, 38–71, and remarks on the elder Seneca, 111–12.

Fuhrmann's valuable book (1960) traces the development of books of *technē* from the Sophists and Plato through Hellenistic times and up to the Roman *agrimensores* and the collectors of Roman law. For technical writing, see Formisano 2001; and Kullmann, Althoff, and Asper 1998. On Vitruvius, see now McEwen 2003.

8. Antonius had treated *inventio* in the second book of the *De oratore,* and the Roman reader could have read of *inventio* in Cicero's own *De inventione* or in the *Rhetorica ad Herennium.* The same works offered discussions of arrangement and style, as did Quintilian and others; e.g., Sen. *Ep.* 114.15 picks up the subject of the arrangement of words. Discovery, arrangement, and stylization were with memory and delivery a ubiquitous description of rhetorical science. The *Ad Herennium* (1.3) begins with these five. Memory and delivery are less important as literature becomes an increasingly written form—as rhetoric comes to define literary aesthetics more broadly and not simply oratory. On the individual terms, invention, arrangement, and style, see the entries in Sloane 2001.

9. LSJ defines the word as (1) "dagger"; (2) "handle"; (3) "manual, handbook"; and notes that it was the title of works by the Stoic philosopher Epictetus and others. The Latin *manuale* is used to refer to the handbook by the jurist Paulus (but with no sense of a weapon): *OLD,* s.v. 2.

10. Babbitt 1927, xxviii.

11. On the popularity of the *De liberis educandis* in the Renaissance, see Babbitt 1927, xxviii. The treatise influenced a variety of texts, not simply educational manifestos. Francesco Barbaro, for instance, draws on the advice for child rearing in his *On Wifely Duties,* presented to Lorenzo de Medici and Ginevra Cavalcanti on the occasion of their marriage in 1416. There is much special bibliography: e.g., M. H. Shackford, *Plutarch in Renaissance England with Special Reference to Shakespeare* (1929; Norwood, Penn., 1977) and Isabelle Konstantinovic, *Montaigne et Plutarch* (Geneva, 1989)—the reception of Plutarch's *Lives* has been more studied than his *Moralia.* The French translation of the *Lives* by Jacques Amyot (1559) and Thomas

North's translation of this into English (1579) began this imbalance. The great essayists Michel de Montaigne and Francis Bacon ensured the influence of the *Moralia* (again after translations into the vernacular). For a brief survey of Plutarch's reception history, see the chapter "Readers" in Lamberton 2001.

12. As Berry (1958, 387) wrote, "Muretus (1559) first cast doubts on the Plutarchan authorship and Wyttenbach (1820) after a careful analysis decided that it was not the work of Plutarch." See Berry for discussion of the similarities of the *De liberis educandis* to Plutarch's works and for further bibliography on issues of authenticity and alleged sources for the work. Wyttenbach's arguments are found in vol. 6 of the revised (Leipzig) edition of *Opera moralia* (1820, 29–64). On the inauthenticity of the work, see also Albini 1997, 59 n. 2. For a brief review of stylistic methods of dating Plutarch's works, see Ingenkamp 1971, 116–18. I am not completely convinced that the work is not Plutarch's. Hein (1916, 13) noted Plutarch's practice of revising his works. The *De liberis educandis* might be an unrevised work or an auditor's copy of his lecture or an enthusiast's composition in the mode of Plutarch.

13. Abbott 1980, 2: "P gives notice that he subscribes to the ideals of 'liberal' education appropriate to the sons of free citizens who are not subject to the necessity of training for a trade or occupation"; also, Abbott, 3: "P shares the classical assumption that education properly so called can exist only for the free citizen (cf. Grasberger II p. 3; Mauch pp. 11–14; M. Pohlenz, *Freedom in Greek Life and Thought*, tr. C. Lofmark (Dordrecht 1966) pp. 102–105)."

14. The Latin title is anticipated in one of Varro's *logistorici*, the *Catus de liberis educandis*. These prose works may have been dialogues. The chief speaker at any rate was a contemporary Roman delivering his wisdom and expertise; in this case the Roman *catus*, sage or wise man (correlate of and perhaps rival to the Greek *philosophos*), may be the jurist Q. Aelius Tubero. Extant fragments treat the early familial care of the boy (e.g., naming) but suggest the work described his training to adulthood (Dahlmann in *RE*, s.v. Marcus Terentius Varro, Suppl. Band 6.1262–64).

15. The answers: teachers of the wrong sort pilloried, 4B; corporal punishment inappropriate, 8F; education for the rich alone, 8E.

16. And to a Horatian delight in displaying a resourceful accommodation to limited means. Horace's father's role in his education: *Sat.* 1.6.71 ff.

17. On household slaves, their numbers and functions, and prominence in literature, see MacMullen 1990, 243–44.

18. Veblen devoted chapter 3 of his *Theory of the Leisure Class* (1899) to leisure, and chapter 4 to consumption.

19. Abbott (1980, 2–4) deems the educational aims of Plutarch primarily moral rather than intellectual.

20. On the idea of prescriptive texts, see Foucault 1990, 12. For the Roman idea that the teacher was a surrogate father, see Kaster 1988, 68.

21. Athenian ideas of manliness (including women and slaves as defective males), and especially the economic and social underpinnings and consequences of this ideology, are well discussed in Cohen 2003.

22. *Habitus* in Bourdieu's modification of the Aristotelian term is an embodied social structure, a social categorization manifested in materialist, often bodily practice. Bodily disposition does not simply reflect social status but creates and repeats social divisions. See Bour-

dieu 1984 for his influential argument about elite taste and its social replication; and for a corrective to the schematism of this approach from an anthropological perspective, see Throop and Murphy 2002.

23. Crito had urged Socrates to escape, in part so that he might tend to the education of his sons (*Crito* 45C8-D6)—an argument without effect. Plato's indifference or resistance to the argument of a strong, essential bond between father and son can be seen in the *Cratylus;* see Rosenstock 1992.

24. See Zanker 1988, 156–59 (Augustus and family legislation), 193–210 (the family mythology of Augustus, including treatment of him as *pater Aeneas*). Within the schools, the *Aeneid* may have been the strongest impetus to such concerns.

25. Emerson 1880, 137–38.

26. Berry (1958, 389) distinguishes the philosophy here advocated, a kind of education in traditional Greek literary culture, from Stoicism. Berry continues to describe the debt of the *De liberis educandis* to Xenophon. On philosophy as the goal of Plutarch's education, see Westaway 1922, 170; Berry, 389. For a detailed discussion of the classical and Hellenistic conception of philosophy as a way of life as opposed to an academic career or set of dogmas, see Hadot 1995.

27. Nurse: 3C, 3E, 3F (the last cites Pl. *Rep.* 377E as authority that nurses should not tell chance stories to children); servile mother: 1A-C; slave: 3C (mothers are better than wet nurses), 4A (list of wrong sort of slaves for pedagogues), 5F (delineation of what makes a good slave age-mate); bad teachers: 4B; base men (*ponēroi*): 12D. *De audiendis poetis* 36E contrasts what the boy hears from mother or nurse or even father or teacher with the precepts of philosophy. The *De liberis educandis* seems to represent then the penultimate stage in education, where the boy is still under a father's care. Slave influence would continue to worry parents and educational moralists; see Leyerle's discussion of John Chrysostom (1997, 5: 262 n. 133 [children to be protected from disedifying stories of slaves]). On Roman attitudes to surrogate mothers, see Meurant 2004; Bradley 1986 and 1994a.

28. For additional comparisons of the child to wax, see Leyerle 1997, 265 n. 159.

29. The encyclopedist Stobaeus preserves a fragment of the New Comic poet Philemon, which comes from a play called ὁ Ἄπολις (The Man without a Country), fr. 11, line 6 (Edmonds 1961) = Stob. *Flor.* 2.4.10.

30. Berry (1958, 391) notes that the essay begins with the theme of eugenics and credits Jaeger (1948, 246), who traced the theme to fourth-century interest in the subject. I disagree with Abbott (1980, 5), who states that "birth" in the *De liberis educandis* "is strictly outside his [Plutarch's] scope."

31. I use the text and translation of the Loeb volume of Babbitt 1927. The original for his "A goodly treasure, then, is honourable birth" says, more literally, "Free birth is the honorable treasure chest of free speech." The original Greek reads as follows:

καὶ σοφὸς ἦν ἄρ' ὁ ποιητὴς ὅς φησιν
ὅταν δὲ κρηπὶς μὴ καταβληθῇ γένους
ὀρθῶς, ἀνάγκη δυστυχεῖν τοὺς ἐκγόνους.
Καλὸς οὖν παρρησίας θησαυρὸς εὐγένεια, ἧς δὴ πλεῖστον λόγον ποιητέον
τοῖς νομίμου παιδοποιίας γλιχομένοις. καὶ μὲν δὴ τὰ φρονήματα τῶν

ὑπόχαλκον καὶ κίβδηλον ἐχόντων τὸ γένος σφάλλεσθαι καὶ ταπεινοῦσθαι
πέφυκε, καὶ μάλ' ὀρθῶς λέγων ὁ ποιητής φησι
    δουλοῖ γὰρ ἄνδρα, κἂν θρασύσπλαγχνός τις ᾖ,
    ὅταν συνειδῇ μητρὸς ἢ πατρὸς κακά.

32. See Whitmarsh 2001, 6 and 41 ff., for the sense of belatedness in the literature of the empire.

33. The complexities and ideological qualities of "nature" as a concept used in relation to education are well discussed in Fantham 1995.

34. Loraux 1982; see also Johnstone 1994, 219–21. On the Cynic and Stoic backgrounds to Musonius's thinking, see van Geytenbeek 1962, 40–50; and Berry 1958, 392; cf. the Cynic point of view in Diogenes Laertius's life of Diogenes in a passage praising training, askēsis, at 6.70.

35. Loraux 1982; see also Johnstone 1994, 219–21.

36. The (often self-conscious) role of ancient paideia in making men is described and analyzed especially for the imperial Greek world in Gleason 1995. Whitmarsh (2001) explores the relationship of writing Greek literature and Greek identity under Roman rule. See now also Connolly 2003; and Swain 1996.

37. Cribiore (1996, xiv) uses the expression to conclude her preface; see p. 127 on the use of φιλοπόνει in teachers' model texts for student copying. The exhortation appears in Hellenistic inscriptions as a heading for a contest in the gymnasia. Cf. Men. Monost. 422: ὁ μὴ δαρεὶς ἄνθρωπος οὐ παιδεύεται, "Without beating, a man is uneducated."

38. The connection of free birth with freedom of speech, although often identified with classical Athens, certainly antedated Greek democracy. Noble bodies are expected to speak nobly, with Thersites as the epic antitype. Speech is often understood as an extension or reflection of the body of the speaker. Teucer reassures Ajax in Sophocles' play that "no one will say you have spoken a suppositious (bastard) word" (482). The scholiast explains: "It is necessary that he say such words because he speaks freely because of his free status" (Αἴαντα· δεῖ οὖν τοιουτους λόγους <λέγειν> ὅτι διὰ τὴν ἐλευθεριαν παρρησιάζεται; Papageorgius 1888, ad Aj. 485). Here the scholiast responds to the lines of Teucer but may have been influenced by such tags as the one attributed to Demosthenes by the collector Stobaeus (Flor. 13.17 = Dem. 13 fr. 21): Οὐδὲν ἂν εἴη τοῖς ἐλευθέροις μεῖζον ἀτύχημα τοῦ στερέσθαι τῆς παρρησίας, "There is no greater misfortune for free men than the loss of freedom of speech."

39. Bourdieu (1984) relates cultural preferences to the indices of gender, locale, and class; see, e.g., 105 and 114–25 for, respectively, the relation of variation in cultural practices to geographical variation and the relation of the distribution of economic and cultural capital. The interest of the social institution of education in replicating qualifications and restrictions is well discussed in the various essays in Cook-Gumperz 1986; see also Apple 1982.

40. Abbott (1980, 119) observes that the relationship between nous and logos remains obscure throughout the text. He translates nous and logos as "mind" and "reason" respectively but notes that Wyttenbach 1820 translates logos as "speech" and indicates that Glaeser considers this view.

41. The tripartite terminology may derive from Chrysippus; see (pro) Dryoff 1897, 239

ff. and (contra) Pohlenz 1955, 76. Van Geytenbeek (1962, 29) cites these scholars and also a fragment (*SVF* III, 214) that attributes to Aristotle the dependence of *aretē* on *phusis, ethos,* and *logos* (*askēsis* is used as a synonym for *ethos* in Stoic and Aristotelian writers).

42. Musonius Rufus fr. 3. Plutarch wrote a treatise advocating the education of women; Stobaeus preserves a few fragments, *Flor.* 15.125–27. On possible relations between Plutarch and Epictetus, see Opsomer 1997.

43. The term is ably explicated by Hellegouarc'h (1963, 484–50). See also the valuable discussion of the criteria, process, and agents in the Roman aristocratic practice of *existimatio* in Habinek 1998, 45–60 and n. 50.

44. By so doing, he was justifying a Greek habit of thought. Dover (1974, 88–95) details the application of the term *phusis* to an individual's traits and character and notes that the term need not apply to inherited (genetic) qualities.

45. On archaic Greek texts' use of a language of metals to represent a hierarchy of values, see Kurke 1999, 41–60 and 101–11. Carson (1990, 158–60) describes the Greek imagination of women as polluting and polluted. Ps.-Plutarch's diction here (1B) is *anexaleipta oneidē,* indelible disgraces. They are stains, smears (the meaning of the root *lip* is "fat, oil"), that cannot be removed. Isocrates writing to King Philip (5.71) had used the adjective of the honors that Philip would enjoy in perpetuity. Ps.-Plutarch may have had this diction in mind (the adjective is rare in Greek); the irremovable reproaches of the bastard are then set against the famous king's irremovable honor.

46. According to Lucian (*Conv.* 8), at a Greek wedding feast a child distributed bread to the guests, repeating: "I have fled *kakon,* I have found the better." Carson (1990, 162) interprets this element of the rite as a preperformance of the marriage's redemption of the bride. Women of the family who prove unchaste are reintroducing the evil, *kakon.* Characteristically, the *De liberis educandis* depicts the consequences of the father who cannot keep to his precepts, who is not rightly educated, in terms that stress his femininization.

47. The author had demonstrated the importance of having a free mother and a free father with the authority of Euripides by citing *Hipp.* 424–25 at 1C: "A man, though bold, is made a slave whene'er / He learns his mother's or his sire's disgrace" (Babbitt's trans.). The father's faults receive the author's attention. Just as he had warned against marriage with chance women, the author repeatedly prescribes a father's actions. The father is imagined as the good planter: 2B (the conceit is continued at 2E). The student takes on this role when he culls passages from his reading like a farmer reaping his harvest (8B: συλλογὴν κατὰ τὸ γεωργῶδες—"a harvest agriculture-wise"—agricultural metaphors are ubiquitous, e.g., 13B: challenging the student with too onerous tasks is like overwatering plants). This book (papyrus roll) of excerpts he then calls a tool, an *organon* (thereby explaining his own simile).

48. The adjective *spoudaios,* a favorite in this text, helps to unite the fields of the metaphors: fathers and planters are serious / zealous, and so are seed, studies (5C: *agōgē* is *sp.;* 1A: the point of the treatise is to find the system of education that will make children *sp.* in their character; 9A: *spoudē* is all serious pursuit, activity, in life, as opposed to rest and relaxation (cf. 11E); the adjective is used at 2B of seed; 3E: nurses must be *sp.;* 4B: men use their *sp.* slaves for their farmers, sailors, merchants, household managers, stewards, yet most important is to have a pedagogue who is *sp.;* 4E cites Socrates' words from *Cleitophon* 407A

that men put all their *spoudē* into the making of money rather than the care of sons). Berry (1958, 391) points out Xenophon's use of *spoudaios*.

49. The cultivation of his son is thus another aspect of the *ponos* of a father. When he engaged in sexual intercourse for the sake of children, the Greek father worked. The activity of the marriage bed is *ponos;* his other erotic behavior is *eros*—a distinction elucidated by Carson (1990, 149) (citing Xen. *Mem.* 2.1.11). Carson also discusses here the agricultural language for male, married intercourse.

50. At 2E the term is used in a sustained illustration meant to demonstrate the point that labor is necessary in education. He turns to agriculture and arboriculture, and says that even good earth requires cultivation. Trees left alone will grow crooked; they require *paidagōgia* to become straight and productive.

51. The exemplum has more resonance because of Spartan training of boys (indeed, it could well have served as an etiological explanation for these practices). In the *pheiditia,* clubs with common meals, the fare could be improved by hunting. Grouped into *ilai,* packs of boys had to forage or steal their food (Plut. *Lyc.* 17; Xen. *Lac.* 2.6–11). Older boys belonged to *krupteiai* (Xen. *An.* 4.6.14; Pl. *Leg.* 633C). The custom became a commonplace, e.g., the exemplary story of the boy who hid a stolen fox and when the rightful owners came to inquire said nothing while the fox chewed through his side (*Apophthegmata Laconica* 35 (234 A); Plut. *Instituta Laconica* 12 (237 D 12); Isocrates, *Panathenaicus* 214; Heraclid. Pont. fr. 2.8 [Karl Müller, *Frag. Hist. Graec.* vol. 2, p. 211]). The artistic future of "Plutarch"'s story of Lycurgus would prove remarkable. A dog eating from a dish occurs frequently in Dutch art of the sixteenth and seventeenth centuries, alongside depiction of children or of the well-ordered family table (the parable of Lycurgus is itself only directly depicted once, in the ca. 1600 Lycurgus of Caesar van Everdingenen)—see Bedaux and Ekkart 2000, 19–20; and Franits 1993, 148–60. The artists, in depicting the exemplary family and upbringing, knew of Lycurgus's pup as the emblem of appetite.

52. See the discussion of Theoc. 18 in Carson 1990, 151.

53. The author here engages in typically Plutarchan argument. Plutarch treats breast-feeding in the *Consolatio ad uxorem* 609E and wrote a treatise on the subject (the *Tittheutikos,* listed at Lamprias 114). See Albini 1997, 62–63, for additional passages in Plutarch and bibliography.

54. See note 1 above.

55. Plutarch is steering a course between the overzealous and the neglectful father and recommends that fathers test their sons every few days. He continues to say that teachers will do better if they know a *euthunē* is coming (9E). Here his diction echoes the end-of-year accounting the Athenian magistrate owed the people.

56. For a discussion of Greek medical attitudes to the female body (and its liquids), see Hanson 1990.

57. ἔτι μέντοι signals the specification of the general point ("still however"). It is a cluster of particles used in later Greek. Plutarch has it only twice (here and at *Sol.* 18.6) and had sufficient precedent in, e.g., Dem. *De cor.* 58.5. For ancient awareness and characterization of the distinct speech of children, see Golden 1995.

58. For the idealized behavior of the wife as within the house, see Carson (1990, 156), who cites Woodbury 1978, 296–97. The father who fails to heed such advice brings contagion to his family, i.e., he acts like an unchaste daughter or an adulterous wife.

59. Stadter 1999, ad 24.8, notes that *sunoikein* is "a normal word for married to"; so too LSJ.

60. The most famous son of chance is Oedipus—so he thinks at any rate (*OT* 1080).

61. The opposition is found in a fragment of Menander (fr. 722, lines 9–10) and reflects a sentiment dear to Epictetus: "Freedom and slavery . . . are both works of choice" (*Gnomologium Epicteteum* sent. 31, in Henricus Schenkl, ed., *Epicteti dissertationes ab Arriano Digestae* [Stuttgart 1965], 485). Compare this gnome of Plutarch, from his lost work *Parallels*: "Because of the dignity of lofty thinking, men desire to be free and because of the nobility of choice, they are least attracted to slavery" (διὰ φρονήματος ἀξίωμα φιλελεύθερον καὶ προαιρέσεως εὐγένειαν ἥκιστα ἐθελόδουλον; preserved in Cassius Dio [*Historiarum Romanarum Xiphilini Epitome,* ed. Dindorf-Stephanus, p. 31]).

62. Dover (1974, 52–53) describes the popular application of moral terms (e.g., *kakos, mokhthēros*) to spheres of material comfort.

63. For instance, Abbott 1980, 194–95.

64. In Cicero's dialogue *De divinatione* (79), C. Aurelius Cotta makes the same excuse for his passion—the philosophers condone love for boys. For the variety of attitudes toward homosexual practices among the Romans, see MacMullen 1990, 177–89. Abbott (1980, 256–57), in noting the author's awkwardness in treating the topic of homosexuality in relation to education, concludes: "Nowhere else in the book does P, normally so dogmatic, appear so unsure of his ground." The author here too reflects a Plutarchan attitude. Mossman (1997, 134) notes the dialogue's "deliberate omission of homosexual themes and its substitution of heterosexuality into the traditional *symposion* context."

65. 10B: ταῦτα δ᾽ ἐστὶ τὸ τὸν βιον ἀτύφωτον ἀσκεῖν, τὸ τὴν γλῶτταν κατέχειν, τὸ τῆς ὀργῆς ὑπεράνω γίγνεσθαι, τὸ τῶν χειρῶν κρατεῖν.

66. Abbott (1980, 127, 160) argues, citing 7C5 and 7D2, that the author privileges philosophy over rhetoric, but more emphasis should be placed on Plutarch's reliance on the Isocratic conception of the philosophy of education. Muir 1998, 14, represents the consensus that "Plutarch, Cicero, and Quintilian all adopt the Isocratic idea of liberal education in conscious opposition to Plato and Aristotle. (Hadas, 1962, p. 37–38, p. 53; Finley, 1975, p. 199; Curtius, 1953, p. 37; Kennedy, 1980, p. 31; Oakley, 1992, p. 48)."

67. For the tradition that celebrated the philosopher as impervious to insult, see van Geytenbeek 1962, 134–42. Westaway (1922, 200) notes the particular, personal interest of Plutarch's concern with emotion: "Even the social aspect of his morality has a characteristically personal turn. In his essay on anger, for example, he is less concerned with the effect of a man's anger on his victims than with its effect on the angry man himself—the distortions of his face, his loss of dignity and self-respect, and even possible self-inflicted injury to his person."

68. LSJ "up to 7 yrs.," citing Hippocrates (as quoted by Philo in the *De opificio mundi* 105; a most schematic arrangement—Hippocrates named seven stages of a man's life). In the *De liberis educandis, paidia* refers once to slaves (3F), once to nursing babies (9A), and once to children who are of an age to be taught first table manners (5A). τὰ παιδία are then preschool-age children or young slaves, both of whom have no *paideia* ("education, upbringing" to be contrasted with "nurture, feeding," τροφή; see LSJ s.v. παιδεία). ἡ παιδιά are childish things, games, play. παῖς, in Hippocrates' reckoning a child of eight–fourteen years, is the customary term for a school-age child and a slave of any age.

5. THE CHILD AN OPEN BOOK

1. Two books of rhetoric were published under Quintilian's name (recorded by note takers, without his approval). See Quint. 1.pr.7-8; and the discussion of identity of the work in Winterbottom 1984, xii–xiii.

2. Colson (1924, lxv) noted the fit of the two works and their joint effect on the humanists (Guarino's translation of the *De liberis educandis* ensured its wide influence).

3. The new beginning need not be respectful. Rousseau, for instance, takes direct aim at the rhetorical educational tradition in his manifesto for the natural man. See France 1995.

4. Colson (1921, 152 n. 7) noted: "It is a complete error to suppose that Q.'s influence on education only begins with Poggio's discovery of the complete text in 1416." Appreciation of Quintilian has been steady: e.g., Fantham 1998, 23: "No one has ever doubted that Quintilian was a superb teacher." Dissenting judgments are marked as extreme: the satirist Juvenal in full misogynistic rant (6.75) alleged that women would love comic actors, singers, etc., but not our author (*An expectas ut Quintilianus ametur*). Kennedy (1962, 132), however, judged Quintilian's work a failure. He is well answered by Johnson 1966. Harding 1961 offers a summary account of the (positive) reception of Quintilian in England, chiefly from the Renaissance on. See also Colson 1924, xliii-lxxxix; Kennedy 1969, 139–40; and Cousin 1963, xcvi, cxvii. On Jerome's use and Augustine's probably indirect knowledge of Quintilian, see Roberts 1985, 66. For Quintilian in the medieval period, see Lehmann 1959; Boskoff 1952; Coulter 1958; and for a detailed study of a particular use (transforming Quintilian into sententiae): McGuiness 1999.

5. More judiciously, Johnson (1966, 80) observes: "Quintilian's monument . . . is this combination of literary Classicism, the set text, the technique of *praelectio*, prose composition and Ciceronianism."

6. Poggio exaggerated the mutilations of the pre-1416 texts. See Colson 1924, lxiv-lxxxix; and Johnson 1966, 93. The greatest enthusiast may well have been Lorenzo Valla (or Petrarch, who addressed a letter to him, *Fam.* 24.7; or perhaps Erasmus); see now López 1999. Petrarch had a manuscript of Quintilian in 1350 (Ullman 1973, 131). On Poggio's discoveries, see the entry on Quintilian in Reynolds 1983; cf. Winterbottom 1967.

7. It must be said that the first two books have not always engendered admiration. With their complaints the critics seem to replicate Quintilian's own embarrassment about discussing grammar and the early curriculum (expressed several times in 1.4 and 5 and following Cicero's lead at *De or.* 3.48). Nettleship (1886, 202, 208–11) faulted the structure of the two books as an imperfect melding of sources (Remmius Palaemon and Pliny's *De dubio sermone*). Von Fritz (1949) defended Quintilian and argued that his conception of grammar was directed not to linguistic theory but to stylistic prescriptions for correct speech—a topic of paramount importance for an educator.

8. For a list of ancient works dedicated to sons, see Roos 1984, 200. Gianotti (1989, 437) discusses the dedication to a son as a sign of inscription into the familiar mode of transmission of synthetic works in substitution for or support of schoolwork.

9. Kennedy 1969, 43.

10. Reinhardt and Winterbottom (2006) observe that education for Quintilian was deeply moral. They note: "[Teachers] used their authority not merely to teach the syllabus

but, consciously and unconsciously, to inculcate values. Quintilian wrote, and no doubt said, much that tended to the establishment of maleness. Effeminacy, in all departments, was frowned upon. . . . The *Institutio*, though, went far beyond this. Quintilian's concept of the orator was deeply moral: the first part of *uir bonus dicendi peritus* was as important as the second" (xxvi).

11. Seneca the Elder attributes the definition to the elder Cato (*Controv.* 1.pr.9), as does Quintilian in the declaration of his great purpose: *Sit ergo nobis orator quem constituimus is qui a M. Catone finitur, vir bonus dicendi peritus*. Winterbottom (1964) argued that the historical experience of political informants, the *delatores* and their trumped-up suits so· memorably castigated by Tacitus, had blackened the name of oratory, and so Quintilian writes to redeem rhetoric. On the social implications of the term *bonus*, see Hellegouarc'h 1963, 484–500; and for the social ideology underpinning Cato's conception of the judgment of men as good (the ancestors' *existimatio* of a good man as a *bonus colonus* and the textualization of this process): Habinek 1998, 46–50. See also MacMullen (1990, 13–24), who begins with historical instances of the reverse phenomenon: the social judgment that a man is not a *vir bonus*. On the *vir bonus* as an ideological formulation of the authoritative speaker, see Gunderson 2000. Walzer (2006) rightly recognizes Quintilian's ambition to have rhetoric do the work of moral philosophy, and stresses Quintilian's devaluation of philosophy in contrast to Cicero. The contrast between Cicero's and Quintilian's vision of the ideal orator is discussed in Classen 1986. See also Brink 1989, 502–3, appendix 4, "Quintilian and Tacitus on Cicero's Encyclopedic Approach to Oratory." Quintilian is hardly unique in trying to found the practice of rhetoric on virtue. Cicero's character Crassus lauded the Stoics for such an effort but saw their project and the style they might adopt as impractical (see Atherton's discussion of *De or.* 3.65: 1988, 401). The beginning of Cicero's *De inventione* presents eloquence as the single factor responsible for good government. Atherton (1988, 395 n. 10) notes the possibility that Stoicism influenced the famous definition: "Its totemic rôle may be another, small illustration of the happy coincidence between (some) of the principal tenets of Stoic ethics, and Roman ideology as developed in the face of Greek culture"; and describes Quintilian's distancing of his ideal orator from Stoic ideas (Atherton, 423–24). For Quintilian's relation to Stoicism, see also Colish 1985, 327–29. Reinhardt and Winterbottom (2006, xlv) remark: "Diogenes of Babylon was the source from which Quintilian and Aristides got their Stoicizing conception of rhetoric, taking into account the similarity of views and the apparent wide circulation of Diogenes' works. It would, however, be wrong to think that the central views on rhetoric as present in Quintilian 2. 14–21 and 12 on the one hand and Aristides on the other were peculiar to Diogenes within the Stoic school."

12. The child is often understood as passive, but Quintilian grants him more agency than Ps.-Plutarch, who had used the metaphor of wax receiving an impression: "For just as seals leave their impressions in soft wax, so are lessons impressed upon the minds of children when they are young" (*Lib. ed.* 3F, Babbitt's trans.). Plato (*Rep.* 377B), writing of the malleability of the young, and the lasting influence of this molding, seems to have in mind a signet ring marking wax. The image recurs in John Chrysostom *Inan. glor.* 33.440; for this and other plastic images used by Chrysostom, see Leyerle 1997, 265 n. 159.

13. The diction and the figure recall Seneca the Elder's preface to his work on current

oratory, the *Oratorum et rhetorum divisones, colores, et sententiae,* which survives in truncated form (text and translation: Winterbottom 1974).

14. Cf. Cic. *Nat. d.* 2.9.23: *refrigerato et extincto calore.*

15. The *topos* of the author reluctant to part with his work was most famously made into a poem by Horace (*Epist.* 1.20). Martial shared Quintilian's bookseller and uses the same verb (*exigo*) in a wonderful epigram, *Exigis ut donem nostros tibi Quinte libellos, / Non habes, sed habet bibliopola Tryphon . . .* (4.72). Three centuries later Ausonius could still weave a dedicatory letter and verse preface from the *topos* of the much-importuned author, e.g., *Bissula* 4: *tu molestus flagitator lege molesta carmina.*

16. Quintilian nicely has the diction for his friend's literary passion echo a Horatian line (*amor flagrans, Carm.* 1.25.13). The application of *flagro* to study becomes a conventional expression, e.g., the student of Augustine, the commentator of Cicero's *Somnium Scipionis,* Favonius Eulogius, ends his work with a complimentary salutation to his dedicatee: *flagras ardore discendi* (*Disputatio de somnio Scipionis* 28). Quintilian like Horace was influenced by Cicero's own usage: the perfect orator burns with zeal for literature: *studio flagrare* (vel sim.) is used four times in the *De or.* (1.115, 135, 3.125, 230). The last passage is in all likelihood the most influential, for it comes at the very end of the dialogue in a memorable close. Cf. also Hor. *Epist.* 1.108–9: *calet uno / scribendi studio.*

On the structure and formulas of the prefaces in Quintilian's work, see Ahlheid 1983; and much more briefly, Janson 1964, 50–60.

17. The relations of Cicero and Varro amid the tug and pull of inscribing each other as character or dedicatee make an interesting case study of literary dedications as public gestures of politeness and respect; see Bloomer 1997, 53–55.

18. There has been much (unnecessary and anachronistic) worry concerning Quintilian's apparent capitulation. Peterson (1891, x) called it a stain on Quintilian. Clarke (1967, 35–36) is far more sympathetic. According to Jerome's *Chronicle* (ann. Abraham. 2104 = 88; the date is wrong: Clarke, 30–31), Vespasian had granted Quintilian an annual allowance. Suet. *Vesp.* 18r reports that rhetoricians received from the emperor a salary of 100,000 sesterces. On the literary patronage of the Flavian emperors more generally, see Woodside 1942; and Fear 1995.

19. Bradley (1985) presents the evidence for educators of the imperial family (and others, of senatorial and equestrian rank; see Bradley, 491–94, for educators of children of servile rank).

20. 4.pr.1: *Adhuc enim velut studia inter nos conferebamus . . . contenti fore domestico usu videbamur.*

21. There is a slightly declamatory quality to Quintilian's grief (which is not to say that it was not genuinely felt or meant), but, as with the rest of his writing, Quintilian is exemplary. So here he presents a mini-lament on *vulnera orbitatis* (a phrase twice used and a *topos* for the declaimers). The thought and expression of the wife who escaped further *cruciatus* by death are declamatory, too.

22. The theme of bereavement in the proems is well brought out by Leigh (2004) at the outset of his article, where he compares the restrained grief of the great general Aemilius Paulus at the deaths of his sons with the emotional account of Quintilian.

23. See above, note 1.

24. Brink (1989, 473 n. 10) notes of this passage: "The retirement, *quies,* cannot have been very quiet. He suffered great personal misfortunes—the loss of his young wife and his two sons (*I.O.* 1 pr. 6). He was appointed tutor to Domitian's great-nephews (the emperor's intended heirs (Suet. *Dom.* 15.1)), scarcely a sinecure."

25. The gerundive is often used in this final sense. Quintilian's expression is like the common idiom *operam dare* with dative of gerund or gerundive: Allen and Greenough, *A New Latin Grammar,* 505; see also Ernout and Thomas (1953, 279b), who suggest that the more frequent use of such final dative gerunds and gerundives in imperial literature is a literary response to the change in the spoken language that favored *ad* with the accusative.

26. As the entries in Lewis and Short make clear, Cicero used *erudire* as one half of his characteristic verbal doublets; so *erudire* and *docere* or *erudire* and *instituere* mean "educate."

27. *CIL* I, 2.1214: *docta erodita omnes artes.*

28. On such iconography, see Bagley 1990.

29. The pairing of the gerundive with the boy often marks important transitions—in the life of the boy and in the structure of Quintilian's book. In the first two books the boy is modified with the following gerundives: *erudiendus* (1.pr.1, 1.pr. 6); *instituendus* (1.1.12, 1.1.15, 1.10.1, 1.12.19); *alendus* (1.3.7); *monendus* (1.3.13); *dandus* (given to the *comoedus*; 1.11.1); *mittendus* (to the teacher of declamation; 2.1.3); *tradendus* (to the teacher of rhetoric; 2.1.7 [cf. 2.1.13: *abducendus*], 2.2.1, 2.3.1, 2.3.11).

Less frequently, "boy" is replaced by the desired end: *orator instituendus* (1.pr.25, 1.1.21, 1.3.18); *orator educandus* (1.pr.6); *orator informandus* (1.pr.23). Other synonyms for "boy": *excitanda mens et attolenda* (1.2.18); *aetas formanda* (1.3.12); *aetas emendanda* (1.4.14); *animus tractandus* (1.3.6); *animus intendendus* (2.2.12); Quintilian reports Chrysippus thought the minds of infants had to be formed, *formandam* (1.1.17).

30. Giuliano (1978, 33) notes that puberty is described in Latin as *aetas perfecta.* Quintilian certainly shares this valorization of adulthood, but he avoids strictly age-grade or biological designations.

31. On occasion Quintilian finds faults with fathers; it is they who encourage the bad habit of their sons' frequent declamation (2.7.1). On parents' potentially damaging role, see Cousin 1935/1967, 17.

32. In the Roman tradition Sallust anticipates Quintilian in distinguishing man from the animals by the *ingenium animi,* mental capacities. See the notes of Davis 1967. The idea that the divine creator distinguished man by means of *logos* stretches back to Isocrates. See Fantham 1995, 125–26. Sallust perhaps follows the lead of Cicero, who at the beginning of his youthful work, the *De inventione,* has voice distinguishing man from beast and inaugurating human society. The Roman version of the Greek *logos* emphasizes speech rather than reason.

33. Cf. 1.1.2: *elucet spes; spes* again at 1.3.2 and 2.4.7.

34. *Quapropter ei cui deerit ingenium non magis haec scripta sint quam de agrorum cultu sterilibus terris. Sunt et alia ingenita cuique adiumenta, uox, latus patiens laboris, ualetudo, constantia, decor, quae si modica optigerunt, possunt ratione ampliari, sed nonnumquam ita desunt ut bona etiam ingenii studiique corrumpant: sicut haec ipsa sine doctore perito, studio pertinaci, scribendi legendi dicendi multa et continua exercitatione per se nihil prosunt.*

35. In the *Republic,* Plato's educational theory, especially for the young, is based on the

observation that the soul imitates and becomes what it imitates. In the *Metaphysics* Aristotle outlines the relationship between memory, images, and art. The faculty of memory retains images of things perceived by the senses. From repeated impressions of a certain thing, we gain experience of that thing. Aristotle, following Polus, says that "experience makes art," for, briefly stated, out of many similar experiences a universal judgment is formulated. The precondition for experience, and thus art, is memory (980b21—981a10).

36. In book 10 Quintilian returns to give a more theoretical account of imitation, in which he distinguishes the early imitation of the child from the theoretically informed activity of the teacher (10.2.2; and see Fantham 1978a, 104).

37. Reinhardt and Winterbottom (2006, xxvii) indicate that imitation of oratorical models goes back to Isocrates, who advised that the teacher should present himself as a paradigm of imitation to his students.

38. 1.2.15–16: *"Nec ego tamen eo mitti puerum uolo ubi neglegatur." Sed neque praeceptor bonus maiore se turba quam ut sustinere eam possit onerauerit, et in primis ea habenda cura est ut is omni modo fiat nobis familiariter amicus, nec officium in docendo spectet sed adfectum. Ita numquam erimus in turba. Nec sane quisquam litteris saltem leuiter inbutus eum in quo studium ingeniumque perspexerit non in suam quoque gloriam peculiariter fouebit.*

39. 1.12.7–14: *Quarum nos una res quaelibet nihil intermittentis fatigaret: adeo facilius est multa facere quam diu. Illud quidem minime uerendum est, ne laborem studiorum pueri difficilius tolerent; neque enim ulla aetas minus fatigatur. Mirum sit forsitan, sed experimentis deprehendas; nam et dociliora sunt ingenia priusquam obduruerunt (id uel hoc argumento patet, quod intra biennium quam uerba recte formare potuerunt quamuis nullo instante omnia fere locuntur: at nouiciis nostris per quot annos sermo Latinus repugnat! Magis scias si quem iam robustum instituere litteris coeperis non sine causa dici παιδομαθεῖς eos qui in sua quidque arte optime faciant) et patientior est laboris natura pueris quam iuuenibus. Videlicet ut corpora infantium nec casus, quo in terram totiens deferuntur, tam grauiter adfligit nec illa per manus et genua reptatio nec post breue tempus continui lusus et totius diei discursus, quia pondus illis abest nec se ipsi grauant: sic animi quoque, credo quia minore conatu mouentur nec suo nisu studiis insistunt sed formandos se tantummodo praestant, non similiter fatigantur. Praeterea secundum aliam aetatis illius facilitatem uelut simplicius docentis secuntur nec quae iam egerint metiuntur: abest illis adhuc etiam laboris iudicium. Porro, ut frequenter experti sumus, minus adficit sensus fatigatio quam cogitatio. Sed ne temporis quidem umquam plus erit, quia his aetatibus omnis in audiendo profectus est. Cum ad stilum secedet, cum generabit ipse aliquid atque componet, tum inchoare haec studia uel non uacabit uel non libebit. Ergo cum grammaticus totum diem occupare non possit, nec debeat ne discentis animum taedio auertat, quibus potius studiis haec temporum uelut subsiciua donabimus? Nam nec ego consumi studentem in his artibus uolo: nec moduletur aut musicis notis cantica excipiat, nec utique ad minutissima usque geometriae opera descendat; non comoedum in pronuntiando nec saltatorem in gestu facio. Quae si omnia exigerem, suppeditabat tamen tempus; longa est enim quae discit aetas, et ego non de tardis ingeniis loquor.*

Cf. 1.12.1: *Quaeri solet an, etiamsi discenda sint haec, eodem tempore tamen tradi omnia et percipi possint. Negant enim quidam, quia confundatur animus ac fatigetur tot disciplinis in diuersum tendentibus, ad quas nec mens nec corpus nec dies ipse sufficiat, et, si maxime patiatur hoc aetas robustior, pueriles annos onerari non oporteat. Sed non satis perspiciunt quan-*

tum natura humani ingenii ualeat, quae ita est agilis ac uelox, sic in omnem partem, ut ita dix-erim, spectat, ut ne possit quidem aliquid agere tantum unum, in plura uero non eodem die modo sed eodem temporis momento uim suam intendat.

40. The turn to agricultural imagery leads to Virgil's *Georgics*, which Quintilian cites as an authority for sparing the rod: 1.3.13: *adeo in teneris consuescere multum est* (*G.* 2.272).

41. For the aesthetic of *imitatio* and *aemulatio* in Silver Latin, see Reiff 1959.

42. 1.1.2: "*Praestat tamen ingenio alius alium.*" *Concedo; sed plus efficiet aut minus: nemo reperitur qui sit studio nihil consecutus. Hoc qui peruiderit, protinus ut erit parens factus, acrem quam maxime datur curam spei futuri oratoris inpendat.*

Cf. 2.8.12: *Inbecillis tamen ingeniis sane sic obsequendum sit ut tantum in id quo uocat natura ducantur; ita enim quod solum possunt melius efficient.*

43. Without judgment, the child will simply imitate the wrong things; see 1.11.1, 2.5.22 ff.

44. *ne studia qui amare nondum potest oderit et amaritudinem semel perceptam etiam ul-tra rudes annos reformidet.*

45. Quintilian is, of course, full of advice that he is sure will sharpen boys' *ingenia* and strengthen their *animus*. Reading Homer is especially good for the latter. For the approved early reading list, with advice to postpone those authors who contribute to *eruditio* but not strengthening, see 1.8.

Quintilian does say that geometry is useful for sharpening boys' wits and arousing their minds in 1.10.34, a passage whose sentiment and diction is taken from Cic. *Rep.* 1.30: geom-etry and astronomy are of value only *ut paulum acuant et tamquam irritent ingenia puero-rum, quo facilius possint maiora discere.*

46. The diction *ingenia acuere* is taken from Cicero (see the passage from *Rep.* 1.30 cited in note 45 above). The elder Seneca described the wretched contemporary state of education as an effeminized softening of wits (Sen. *Controv.* 1.pr.8: *Torpent ecce ingenia desidosae iu-ventutis . . .*).

47. Dancing: 1.11.18–19. Studies for the very young are to be presented as a sort of game (1.1.20), but Quintilian does not recommend play except as a vehicle for communicating ac-ademic content or generating academic enthusiasm.

48. For a sympathetic appreciation of Quintilian on imitation, see Clark 1957, 144–76. On imitation in Cicero, see Fantham 1978b; and in Quintilian, 1978a; see also Fantham 1995; and Morgan 1998, 251–54.

49. Cicero supplies Quintilian with some of these metaphors, but Quintilian serves his reader a more concentrated dose. Here he has quoted Cicero's "For I want fertility to puff it-self up in adolescence" from *De or.* 88. *Brut.* 288 (*quasi de musto ac lacu fervidam orationem fugiendam*) lies behind Quintilian's language (as does *De or.* 3.103, which provided the com-bination of austere and decocted in another image drawn from winemaking). In the *Brutus* Cicero had been talking of avoiding unfermented speech, an image that Quintilian transfers to the person of the young speaker and the need for his slow maturation.

50. Quintilian prefers joy and *ingenium* to *iudicium* in this age; e.g., 2.4.14: *Aliter autem alia aetas emendanda est, et pro modo uirium et exigendum et corrigendum opus. Solebam ego dicere pueris aliquid ausis licentius aut laetius laudare illud me adhuc, uenturum tempus quo idem non permitterem: ita et ingenio gaudebant et iudicio non fallebantur.*

51. In the third book of *De nuptiis mercuriae et philologiae*, Martianus Capella person-

ifies the seven liberal arts as the servants of the goddess Philology. Grammar appears, rather like a Roman doctor, with a scalpel to excise the faults of the young. See Bagley 1990 for the influence of this image.

52. *Laetus* is used of style to mean "abundant, fertile, rich." Cicero uses it so (*De or.* 1.81), and Quintilian follows him, e.g., of Homer *laetus et pressus* (10.1.46). The reading of Lucretius and Virgil no doubt kept current the overlapping application of the word to poetry and to agriculture.

53. Quintilian's warning that one should not teach children poetry that is either too soft or too forceful is reminiscent of Plato's poetic education of children in books 2 and 3 of the *Republic*. In these books Socrates argues that children ought to imitate poetry that is harmonic in rhythm and beautiful in imagery so as to develop a moderate and courageous soul as opposed to a soul that is disordered by the excesses of licentiousness or graceless severity.

54. *Iudicium* is associated with *inventio*: see 3.3.5, 6.5.1; and Cova et al. 1990, 25.

55. Quintilian rejects the use of the calque *oratoria* or *oratrix* for the Greek *rhētorikē*, and *litteratura* for *grammaticē*, at 2.14.1–4. On his use of Greek technical vocabulary, see Cousin 1935/1967.

56. So while he recognizes students will have different aptitudes, he argues against giving them rein to pursue their best subject. They must learn everything so as to fill up the deficiencies left by nature: *Quod mihi (libera enim uel contra receptas persuasiones rationem sequenti sententia est) in parte uerum uidetur: nam proprietates ingeniorum dispicere prorsus necessarium est. In his quoque certum studiorum facere dilectum nemo dissuaserit. Namque erit alius historiae magis idoneus, alius compositus ad carmen, alius utilis studio iuris, ut nonnulli rus fortasse mittendi: sic discernet haec dicendi magister quomodo palaestricus ille cursorem faciet aut pugilem aut luctatorem aliudue quid ex iis quae sunt sacrorum certaminum. Verum ei qui foro destinabitur non in unam partem aliquam sed in omnia quae sunt eius operis, etiam si qua difficiliora discenti uidebuntur, elaborandum est; nam et omnino superuacua erat doctrina si natura sufficeret* (1.8.6–8).

57. Quintilian disapproves of the pedantry of grammarians (1.8.18–19), which will only impede the children's *ingenia* (*et detinet atque obruit ingenia*).

58. Cova et al. (1990, 173–81) directly address the idea of rhetoric in Quintilian as psychology and the psychology of the child (for the latter, see also Bianca 1963, 102).

59. *Pace* Kennedy (1962, 140), who finds Quintilian as an educator and rhetorician "unadventurous" and faults the author for not excoriating the empire for the collapse of oratory. Fantham (1978a) offers a sophisticated analysis of the relation between Quintilian's thinking about the decline of oratory and his theories of imitation. On Quintilian's own claims for originality (often expressed with a deference typical of Silver authors—so, in straying from Cicero's focus, he refers to his *temeritas*, 12.pr.4), see Logie 2003.

60. Friedrich Solmsen, "The Aristotelian Tradition in Ancient Rhetoric," chap. 8 in Rudolf Stark, ed., *Rhetorika: Schriften zur aristotelischen und hellenistischen Rhetorik* (Hildesheim, 1968), 285–311 (reprinted from *AJP* 61 [1942]: 35–50 and 169–90), can stand as representative of the expert approach to Quintilian that reconstructs Hellenistic sources for the theories and treatments of rhetoric in the *Institutio oratoria*. Atali (1995) argues for a specifically Stoic influence on Quintilian's definition (thus denying innovation to the Latin rhetorician). Direct Stoic influence on Quintilian's concepts has been overstated, since Stoic ideas were part

of the philosophical *koinē* of this period. An apposite instance is the treatment of nature in Quintilian: see Fantham 1995. Cousin (1935/1967, 11–14) had sketched Quintilian's development of Cato's definition of the orator and the Stoic background to the origin of oratory (165–66). Morgan (1998, 226–34) discusses the qualities that Quintilian's good man and orator should have.

61. The closest term in Quintilian's text for this disposition may be *facilitas,* which he argues in book 10 comes from the combined practice of reading, writing, and speaking. He treats it as a disposition necessary and ancillary to formal instruction (*praecepta*): *illis firma quaedam facilitas, quae apud Graecos nominatur hexis acceserit.* It is a calque for the Greek *hexis* (as an Aristotelian term, more frequently translated as *habitus*).

6. GRAMMAR AND THE UNITY OF CURRICULUM

1. Donald (1985, 216) connects the multiple functions of education to its insistent variation.
2. Pliny *Ep.* 4.13. For broader questions of patronage of schools, see Fear 1995.
3. Scott 1995 offers a wide-ranging discussion of the *Meno* and its thinking.
4. See Bernstein 1964. For the reception of these ideas and subsequent directions in the sociology of education, see the various essays in Richardson 1986; Cook-Gumperz 1986; Dale, Esland, and MacDonald 1976; Apple 1982; and Giroux 1983.
5. See Walter J. Ong, "Latin Language Study as a Renaissance Puberty Rite," *Studies in Philology* 36 (1959): 103–24, reprinted in Ong 1971, 113–41.
6. Cribiore (1996, 52) has observed that while *technai* were used in the schools from the first century A.D., "the exercises show that no individual, standard manual was adopted in the schools" until perhaps the fifth-century adoption of the grammar of Dionysius Thrax.
Research on the textbook is extensive; see Apple and Smith 1991; Baker and Freebody 1989, 1987, 1988a and b; Luke 1988 and 1989.
7. Barthes 1982, 476 (cited by Luke 1989, 53).
8. Patillon (1997, xix) remarks that Theon's work was meant for teachers. The English reader is now well served by Kennedy 2003; see also Roberts 1985, 6–15, with bibliography.
9. See Cribiore 1996, 57–75, chap. 5, "Writing Materials Used in Schools."
10. Irvine 1994; Gehl 1993; Padley 1985; Amsler 1989. A more generous interpretation of the meaning and influence of grammar is not simply a current of contemporary scholarship but a reflection of ancient and medieval usage. Robbins (1998) notes the difference between *mikra* or *palaia grammatikē* and *megalē* or *neōtera grammatikē*, viz., the teaching of reading and writing and stylistic excellence in written and oral language and the interpretation of literature.
11. Cicero had provided the model for distinguishing the appropriate, general learning of the orator from the abstract expertise of the professional philosopher (*De or.* 218–25). The philosopher, the actor, and the recondite lawyer all serve as foils to his ideal orator.
12. Unlike the stages of the curriculum, the connections of the curriculum have received little comment. Bonnie Fisher noted that Roman education was unified by the "repeated exposure to a select body of material at progressively higher or advanced stages" (1987, 13); she describes this aspect of the ancient curriculum as recurrence not repetition, i.e., the return to material after a period of time and with some change of practice (44). Fisher also re-

alized that the stated goal of ancient education, to prepare speakers, did not square with the actual processes (16). On the *progymnasmata*, see now Webb 2001.

13. Booth 1979a. Marrou (1948/1956): 429 had remarked that the divisions were not always made "very rigorously." A brief review of teachers and the curriculum, with illustrations of the six-year-old Marcianus going to school and of the teacher Furius Philocalus, can now be found in Rawson 2003, 158–84.

14. Marrou 1948/1956, 172.

15. Morgan (1998, 199–203) summarizes the papyri evidence that shows some students completing only a portion of the *progymnasmata*.

16. Rawson (2003, 158–59) cites examples of six-year-olds being educated. Children are said to go to grammar school at seven (Bonner 1977, 35). This seems a deduction from Quintilian (1.1.15–19), who is in fact not writing of sending children to school but refuting the view that children younger than seven years should not be taught to read.

17. A useful introduction to research on the shape of children's narratives: Peterson and McCabe 1983. Norman (1982, 81–95) explores the relations between learned routines and new learning.

18. Adrados (1999, 132) has aptly used the term "agonal fables" to describe these plots of violent confrontation. Perry's lengthy edition of the fables and their *testimonia* with full discussion (1952) should be used only with Adrados's cautions and in the light of his discoveries of the ancient traditions of fable collection. A second important volume is van Dijk 1997. See also Holzberg 2001; and Henderson 2001. Mann (1996, with bibliography) presents the complex medieval Latin traditions of fable in judicious and brief terms.

19. Roberts (1985) writes, correctly, in the first paragraph of his useful book: "Histories of ancient education largely ignore the paraphrase." He notes (2) that Thraede's list of paraphrastic techniques is incomplete (viz., *amplificatio, exornatio, variatio, additio,* in Klaus Thraede, "Epos," *RAC* [1962]: col. 1025). Roberts remedies this neglect in his chapters "The Paraphrase in Rhetorical Theory" and "The Ancient Practice of the Paraphrase" (5–36 and 37–60). See also Reiff 1959.

20. Webb (2001) argues persuasively that the *progymnasmata* often relied on themes from epic and tragedy and (like declamation) trained the student in values of social order.

21. The ancient *testimonia* describing the processes of learning to read and write are succinctly set out by Cribiore 1996, 139–44. Her ensuing discussion of the actual exercises is highly valuable. See also Cavallo 1989; Johnson 2000. The bibliography on learning to read and write grows apace. Four important historical studies: Darnton 1991; Sherman 1995; Saenger 1997; and Reynolds 1996. A valuable introduction to the processes of reading: Just and Carpenter 1987. On learning to write: Kress 1994. General issues of development of a child's language: Romaine 1984; Elliot 1981.

22. Quintilian assigns this duty to the teacher (7.10.8–9: *Praeceptoris est in alio atque alio genere cotidie ostendere quis ordo sit rerum et quae copulatio, ut paulatim fiat usus et ad similia transitus*).

23. Perplexingly, Marrou writes that the list of *progymnasmata* "was always the same: fable, narrative, 'chria', aphorism" (1948/1956: 173). This is not Theon's order. The confusion is not helped by Marrou's vocabulary: he calls a paraphrase a fable and discusses the *chreia*, "what we should call a fable" (174). See Schussel 1933; Granatelli 1995; and Webb 2001, 296–300.

24. Cicero knew of a collection of the censor's sayings (*Off.* 1.104).

25. I begin with Diogenes the Cynic because Dio Chrysostom said that everybody could tell a *chreia* of him (as Hock and O'Neill [1986, 7] retail, citing Dio Chrys. *Or.* 72.11). Krueger (1993) discusses the *chreia* tradition of Diogenes in late antiquity; see especially his remarks on the *chreia* in the school curriculum (31–33). Krueger reports the estimate of the number of Diogenes' *chreiai* from Fischel 1968, 374. This *chreia* is told by Diogenes Laertius (6.40). I use the translation of Hock and O'Neill (29).

26. Quint. 1.1.35–36.

27. Gibbs (1999, 1) defines the fable as "brief and witty negative exempla based on the correction, punishment, or prevention of a mistake." While we need not limit fables to "animal stories," we must recognize the difference in status of the agents, the threat of violence, actual physical harm, and the frequent inversion worked by craft and especially wit. Gibbs was correcting van Dijk's formulation (1997, 72) of the fable as "a fictitious, metaphorical narrative"—a definition generic in many senses. For an exhaustive treatment of definitions, ancient and modern, see Adrados 1999, 17–47.

The relation of proverb and fable was recognized in antiquity; see, e.g., Quint. 5.11.20 and Adrados's discussion (205–6).

28. Most scholars call this an *epimythium;* Theon uses the term *epilogos.*

29. Cf. the *chreia* about Socrates and the young taunter who kicked him, deployed by Ps.-Plutarch in the *De liberis educandis* (10C; and cf. above, chapter 4, pp. 78–79), where the philosopher, when threatened with physical injury or when tempted to inflict physical injury, turns instead to words.

30. See Sen. *Dial.* 8.3; and Postgate 1919.

31. Theon believed that these exercises provided the skills in, e.g., narrative, refutation, and confirmation, which were necessary for students embarking on the *hypothesis,* the speech on a set but specific topic (60). Theon sees the *progymnasmata* as the fundamental training in discourse, for poets, historians, writers, and orators (70.26–30; and see Patillon 1997, xvi–xix).

32. On the original order (as indicated by the Armenian MSS), see Butts 1986, 12–18.

33. The chief sources for *progymnasmata:* Aphthonius (fourth cent. A.D.), Nicolaus (fifth cent. A.D.), Ps.-Hermogenes (third cent. A.D.), Theon (second cent. A.D.). The earliest testimony is from Rome: Quint. 2.4.1 and 2.10.1; Suet. *Gramm.* 4.7 and 25.8. The famous orator Libanius composed model *progymnasmata*. Further bibliography in Patillon 1997. In the preface to his edition of Theon, Patillon discusses the positions of Theon, Suetonius, and Quintilian (with useful charts, and see his remarks on Theon's additions to the traditional exercises, pp. xxix–xxxi). On the identification and dating of Theon, see Patillon, who departs from the tradition, stemming from Wilamowitz, of putting Theon just earlier than Quintilian, for which see Butts 1986.

34. Fisher 1987, 45–51. An analysis of the shape of children's narratives, more critical of Piaget: Peterson and McCabe 1983.

35. Exercises seem to moralize the child through imitation, as if by learning the words of the ancients, children adopt their manners. In rhetorical terms, imitation is imitation of words and of persona. Theon writes of the *chreia* that it imbues the boy both with technical skill at speaking and with morality (*ēthos*), "since we are being trained by the sayings of the

wise" (60.19). On the moral purpose of the fable, see Ps.-Hermogenes 1.7–9, Nicolaus 17.16–20, and the discussion of these passages, and others, in Patillon 1997, xix–xx. Patillon notes the interest some of the *chreiae* had for young men, both the puritanical (Sophocles finally freed of the tyranny of lust) and the tabloid (the adulterous flute player Didymus hung by his name/testicles—a pun in action).

36. Tucker 1981, 9–14, discussed by Fisher 1987, 35.

37. Marrou (1948/1956, 173) quotes a fourth- to fifth-century schoolboy's fable, Fayum papyrus [Babr.] 437. In this instructive and popular composition, a son has killed his father and fled to the desert, where, climbing a tree to avoid a lion, he is bitten by a snake and dies (see Cribiore 1997, nos. 230, 231, 232, 314, 323, 409, 412). For additional papyri *progymnasmata*, see Marrou 1948/1956, 174; Zalateo 1961 (e.g., no. 273, a rather perfunctory effort at *ethopoiia*; no. 355 in Cribiore 1996, 52 and 262); Morgan 1998, 221–22. For a full analysis of and commentary on a late third- or early fourth-century A.D. Egyptian student's Latin translation of a fable of Babrius, see Adams 2003, 725–41.

38. After a useful review of the evidence and scholarship (including A. Cameron's influential interpretation of the prose rhythm of the dedicatory letter) that demonstrates the affinity of Avianus to late antique Latin, Gaide (1980, 27) concludes that one cannot establish the date of publication. The sequence of fable following *sententia* described by the writers of the *progymnasmata* can be seen in practice in the Carolingian world. The text of Avianus's forty-three fables adjoins or is in close proximity to that of the *Disticha Catonis* in three early manuscripts: Trier 1093 (tenth cent.), Leiden Voss. Lat. Q 86 (ca. 850), and Vat. Reg. Lat. 1424 (tenth–eleventh cent.). Later the two texts become part of the *Auctores octo* (see Boas 1914).

39. Butts 1986, 20.

40. See Adrados 1999, 106, 115–17; Hesseling 1892–93; also van Leeuwen 1894. On the use of wax tablets, see Rouse and Rouse 1989; and Cribiore 1996, 65–69; Preisendanz 1930, 11 ff.; 1933, 153 ff.; on wax tablets with guide letters incised, Haarhoff 1958, 184 n. 7.

Of course, much has survived in boys' and girls' hands from the ancient school, particularly in Egypt, and especially from the earlier stages of literacy training. The patricidal, desert-seeking, lion-avoiding, snake-bitten boy of the papyri (cited above, note 37) is a rather simple fable. A master's schoolbook survives (Collart 1926) that originally included alphabet and syllabarium, then the extant lists of one-, two, three-, four-syllable words, sentences ascribed to Diogenes, a prologue to fables, and postscript by the student. Marrou argued that the *PBouriant* was a master's model text (1948/1956, 154–55). Thus, like Priscian's *Partitiones*, it describes how one teacher thought the schoolroom should operate. A model text for the young reader and writer of the third century B.C.: Gueraud and Jouguet 1938. For this text and the rich materials on learning to read and write Greek in Egypt, see now Cribiore 1996.

41. Roberts (1985, 29–30) has connected the important role of tautology, the rewriting of an earlier author's version, in ancient literary composition to the school practice of paraphrase.

42. Marrou (1948/1956, 172) argued that other declension exercises, including simple morphology drills, belonged to secondary-school education.

43. Homer had provided first writing exercises (Marrou 1948/1956, 162–63), and Quintilian had recommended using this exercise to learn hard words. Under the grammarian the student returned to Homer and to glossing, by preparing his text by making a

vocabulary list (see the example and discussion in Marrou, 166–67; and the discussion of papyri glosses of Homer in Roberts 1985, 40–44). The list making is, of course, an aid to understanding the archaic language of the epic, but it also reprised textual practices (preparing, annotating, punctuating so as to make a text one's own; having a shadow or double version to the plain text).

44. Theon 65.30 ff.; and compare Marrou's discussion of Greek literary authors used in the schools (1948/1956, 162–64). Marrou calls Homer, Euripides, Menander, and Demosthenes the four pillars of Hellenistic education, all the while reminding that these four predominated but did not exclude others.

45. Goetz 1892, 45. The Latin *si et* makes no sense as Latin but translates verbatim the Greek ει και, "even though." The Greek means: "Thus evil men, even though they seem to do good, actually do harm."

46. Fables can be made from *chreiae*; see Adrados 1999, 511–13.

47. Under the grammarian, students would have read a prose collection of fables or would have treated verse collections as prose—Babrius's iambs are copied out as prose in the *Ps.-Dositheana*. There seem not to have been verse collections before Phaedrus and Babrius. On the fourth-century B.C. collection of Demetrius of Phalerum and the subsequent, complex history of fable collections in Hellenistic times, see Adrados 1999, 410–42 and 585–99.

Suetonius, who in recounting the development of rhetorical study at Rome, notes that before the rage for declamatory training rhetoricians set their students various exercises, among which he lists fables and singles out their utility for various modes of presentation (*Rhet.* 1 [25]). For the rhetoricians' discussions of the fable, see Perry 1952, 236 ff.

48. Roberts (1985, 59) treats the literary and school paraphrases of fables including the papyri *PGrenf.* II 84 and *CPL* 38.

49. *Rh.* 2.20; and cf. Cicero (*Part. or.* 40), who notes somewhat diffidently that fable can be an argument. Cicero does not himself use fables in his speeches.

50. Fisher (1987, 31) has described the pedagogic utility of the fable as fundamentally a compare-and-contrast exercise.

51. Avianus's metonymy in particular is redolent of Virgil and Ovid (and of course the training in poetic language and figures prepares for the reading of those more advanced school authors).

52. Patillon 1997, lii.

53. Prisc. *Praeexercitamina* 1.1: *Ideo autem hanc primam tradere pueris solent oratores, quia animos eorum adhuc molles ad meliores facile vias instituunt vitae.* Priscian is here writing of the practice of *oratores*, teachers in rhetorical school, and is translating Ps.-Hermogenes (see Courcelle 1969, 322–30).

54. The student may not consciously realize or reflect on the mutability of language. At times students no doubt blundered on without understanding the changes they were making, as, for instance, the writer of the Assendelft Tablets wrote Babrius's verses out as prose. The routine does presuppose (and inculcate, one assumes) attitudes toward the school matter.

55. The papyrus from Egypt show a mixture of student's and teacher's hands. See Cribiore 1996, 97–118.

56. Wilkins (1905, 74–75) lists the ancient testimonia for the learning of versification in early schooling. Roberts (1985, 70) doubts that versification was a standard school exercise

but notes (65 n. 19) that a number of the poems in the *Anthologia latina* are versified *pro-gymnasmata*. Poetry was an essential of the orator's education. See North 1952.

57. In a contest in Rome in A.D. 94, Quintus Sulpicius Maximus spoke in the persona of Zeus reprimanding Helios for loaning his chariot to Phaethon. The boy's parents recorded this and appended the winning verses to the funerary notice (Dessau, *ILS* 5177).

58. Avianus in his forty-two fables uses *quondam* six times, *olim* once; *forte* serves four times. Other formulae: *fertur* thrice, *fama est* once. Phaedrus prefers *olim* to *quondam* (five times—one restored by Iannelli at Perotti 5—to twice) and uses *forte* five times, *dicitur* and *narratur* once each. Given the number of Phaedrus's fables, these figures are comparatively low. Babrius, however, has "once upon a time," ποτε, nineteen times but prefers by far the indefinite pronoun τις, which he uses thirty-six times. He has ἔτυχε, the equivalent of *forte*, once; λέγουσι and φασι twice each.

7. THE MORAL SENTENCE

1. The preface of Joseph Scaliger's 1605 Paris edition was often reprinted and is perhaps most easily found in Arntzenius 1754.

2. On the manuscript and printing history of the *Distichs*, see Boas 1952, vii–lxvii. Although he does not treat Scaliger's editing of the *Distichs*, Grafton (1983, 1993) offers a sympathetic account of the debts of method and the achievements of Scaliger's criticism. In addition to editing the *Distichs*, Scaliger translated them into Greek. Scaliger had printed the *Distichs* (along with Publilius Syrus) with notes and his own Greek versions of some of the distichs in 1598 in Leiden (Bernays 1855, 286–87).

3. On images of the classical languages and belief in their transformative power, see Waquet 2001; Farrell 2001; and Bloomer 2005.

4. *Pace* Fantham 1998, 28 n. 18: "It is somewhat horrifying to realize that these undistinguished couplets and one-liners were still being used for education in the early sixteenth century when Erasmus 'edited' the Distichs and Publilius with other improving excerpts for the use of his friends teaching in English schools."

5. Scaliger also echoes the diction of the *Distichs*: compare *his ego mihi conscius* to 1.17: *conscius ipse sibi*. On the fortunes of the *Distichs*, see Boas 1952; and Wells 1994. The bibliography on this school text, its translations, and influence on medieval literature is large. In addition to Boas and Wells, see Skutsch 1905; and, e.g., Hazelton 1957 and 1960.

6. The second line seems a version of Socrates' maxim "The unexamined life is not worth living for a human being" (*Ap.* 38a), accommodated to a grammar-school setting. Part of the value of the *Distichs* is that they will be reused and relearned later in a student's career.

7. For the history of collections of gnomai, see Barns 1950a; and Morgan 1998, 120–23.

8. The *Somnium* was a school text, at least by late antiquity, when Macrobius wrote his commentary, and the student of Augustine, Favonius Eulogius, wrote his *Disputatio de somnio Scipionis*.

9. On the history of this trio of ideas (a commonplace well before Cicero's time), see Shorey 1909.

10. The author of the *Distichs* preserves the (memorable) grammar of Euripides' line by translating *nous* as *deus*. Of course, it means what Cicero glosses it to mean, "divine." *Nous* in

Euripides is a mental faculty. See the discussion of *nous* in Sullivan 2000, 44–54. Women, children, and slaves can have it. An old man can lose it. A citizen and a leader need but do not always have it. At *Trach.* 652 Andromeda says that *nous* has been her worthy teacher (*khrēstos didaskalos*). Though at home, she had not listened to women's speech but relied on her own *nous*. For Anaxagoras, *nous* was a divine principle, and Plato wrote in *Leg.* 897A that *nous* is god in the correct sense and that intelligence possesses self-motion (898A). Eur. fr. 1018 is the immediate source: ὁ νοῦς ἡμῶν ἐστιν ἐν ἑκάστῳ θεός ("In each of us our *nous* is a god").

11. Boas 1952, 35: "In Statii codice Puteano folio ultimo (ex monasterio Corbei) hoc distichon ut exemplum scripturae exhiberi monet O. Müller (*Woch. f. Klass. Phil.* XX (1903): 195)."

12. Boas 1914; 1934; 1952, 95–96.

13. Παθὼν δέ τε νήπιος ἔγνω, "Only the fool learns from experience" (a tag from Hes. *Op.* 218), means also: "Only the child (the one without words) learns from experience."

14. Cicero noted the existence of a collection of Cato's sayings, among others (*Off.* 1.104: *Multaque multorumque facete dicta, ut ea quae a sene Catone collecta sunt, quae vocant apophthegmata; cf. De or. 2.271*). Cato was not the only third-century figure remembered in the schools: see Roos (1984, 53) on Appius Claudius Caecus as a gnomic poet, and on the connection of *sententiae* to the archaizing movement (183–84). At *Gramm. lat.* 1.310 (Diom.), Cato is given Isocrates' sentence about the roots of literature being bitter, which is then "declined."

15. On MSS with Avianus and with the later additions, see Boas 1914, 24 and 42–43 respectively.

16. For vernacular versions, see Roos 1984.

17. On these Tuscan school texts, see Gehl 1993.

18. There is an ample bibliography on the topic; see esp. Sanders 1985.

19. See Astin 1978, 332–40.

20. Q. Caecilius Epirota, a freedman of Atticus, was the first to teach Virgil and "the other new poets" (Suet. *Gramm.* 16.3). The demise of Ennius and the older poets, who had such a vibrant hold on Cicero, would seem to stem from the schools' canonization of the Augustan poets.

21. Astin (1978) perhaps downplays the interpretive tradition that saw Cato as anti-Hellenic (as opposed to the historical fact of Cato's familiarity with Greek culture); so he doubts that readers interpreted the two fathers in Terence's *Adelphoe* as Cato and Lucius Aemilius Paullus. Astin does not blame Cicero, but I will—the Ciceronian lens has a built-in refractory defect: philosophical schools, political factions, even famous dead Romans, often fall into pairs with Cicero as the true Roman mediating the destructive poles. In his history of Roman oratory, the *Brutus,* Cicero has made Cato into a convenient foil for himself. Cato is the point of origin, the pure native, whence Cicero, after the history of figures narrated in the text, arises as the apex of a Greco-Roman culture.

22. Astin 1978, 338.

23. Jahn 1850.

24. Gigante (1995, 17) distinguishes *hypomnēma* and *hypomnēmaticon* as final and first drafts. Bömer (1953) describes in detail the tradition of the *commentarius / hypomnēma* as the notes that the historian must then stylize so as to make history of them. The Latin expression is in origin "ganz unliterarisch" and as the suffix *-arius* indicates, practical (Bömer, 211–12).

25. On the large number of Cato's slaves, see Astin 1978, 261–62.

26. On the ideology of this remarkable text, see now Reay 2005.

27. Fronto *Ad A. Imper.* 1.2.9 = *ORF,* Cato fr. 173. Cato orders his slave to produce the book in which was written the speech from a suit against M. Cornelius. From this he cuts and pastes into the speech he is working on, the *De sumptu suo.*

28. Cato's relations to Ennius: Skutsch 1985, 1.

29. Astin 1978, 339–40.

30. Following Horna (1935), Barns (1950a) distinguished the literary *stephanos* from the educational *gnomologium.*

31. Barns 1950b. For examples of such papyri, see Berl. KL. Texte V. 20 A and B (P 9772, 9773); cf. Stob. *Flor.* 76–74; and the second-century A.D. *Disticha Argentinensia,* in *Archiv für Pap.* 2 (1903): 185 ff.

32. Cited by Barns 1950b, 3. For the debt of τύχη in the gnomai to Euripides, see Barns, 3 n. 3. Morgan (1998, 133–34) connects the theme of patience amid misfortune in the maxims to Hellenistic philosophical quietism.

33. As with fable, it was Demetrius of Phalerum who collected these sayings for school use. See Diels 1954, 73a. As Marrou (1948/1956, 404) pointed out, the first literary notice of the Seven Sages comes from Plato (*Prt.* 343A).

34. The Latin imperative in *-to* urges an action "envisaged as non-immediate, either in a temporal or a conditional sense" with either definite or indefinite subjects (Risselada 1993, 122). The use of the future imperative in conditional sentences made it a favorite of legal and instructional texts. See notes in Dyck 2004, 100.

35. The Latin expresses a social relationship: an *officium* is a service done for the patron by a subordinate, a *beneficium* is the patron's act—unrequired—benefiting a subordinate. Thus in the distich the "you" is superior both as an actor of *beneficia* not *officia* and as one who praises others not himself. Compare 4.42, which likewise counsels the boy to display his appreciation for the services done him: *Gratior officiis, quo sis mage carior, esto, / ne nomen subeas, quod dicunt, officiperdi.*

36. Hor. *Sat.* 1.1.37–38: *non usquam prorepit [formica] et illis utitur ante quaesitis sapiens.*

37. Diog. Laert. 7.23; and Plut. *Lib. ed.* 10D. I use Hock's translations (Hock and O'Neill 1986, 4 and 33). For the theme of the refusal to beat, cf. Socrates unmoved by his tormentor at Plut. *Lib. ed.* 10C.

8. RHETORICAL HABITUS

1. Quintilian mounts a (qualified) defense of declamation at 2.10. The most prestigious ancient critics in antiquity: Petron. *Sat.* 1; Tac. *Dial.* 34–35 (in fact this work offers both a proponent and a critic of the new style in general), and the lost work of Quintilian, *De causis corruptae eloquentiae* (see Reuter 1887; Brink 1989). For discussion of the various ancient criticisms, see Cousin 1935/1967, 127–29; Kennedy 1969, 50–53; Caplan 1970; and Berti 2007, 219–47. Gunderson (2000, 1–4) has pointed out the declamatory quality of ancient complaint about criticism (and its insistent repetition). Fantham (1978a, 105) notes that Quintilian (10.2.11) faulted declamation qua fiction—as an imitation, it must necessarily lack the vitality of real forensic cases (see the discussion of Reuter 1887, 26–27). See also my dis-

cussion of perhaps the most famous ancient complaint, the declamation teacher Agamemnon in Petronius's *Satyricon* (Bloomer 1997, 212–14).

2. Seneca the Elder 1.1–3. Translations from Winterbottom 1974.

3. For Seneca's misunderstanding of the history of declamation, see Fairweather 1981, 124–31; and Berti 2007, 110–14. At the end of his life Cicero came, somewhat reluctantly, to adopt the term: Fairweather, 128; Bonner 1949, 26–31. On Quintilian's account of the origin of declamation, see Brink 1989, 500–502, appendices 1 and 2, "Demetrius of Phalerum and Fictitious Themes," and "'*De causis*' on provenance of declamation"; and Granatelli 1995, 152–55. See also Kaster 2001.

4. Berti (2007, 45) describes well that Seneca has presented Latro as the ideal declaimer.

5. See Jerome *Ep.* 81.1.3. Ausonius describes his teaching of Gratian at *Praef.* 1.24 ff. His praise of his student comes in the *Thanksgiving for his Consulship* 15 (and is in keeping with the hyperbolic qualities of his imperial ward, who as a boy could run faster, jump higher, etc. than everybody else).

6. Gunderson (2000, 30) discusses the importance of memory in Seneca's understanding of his project. On Seneca's possible written sources, see Sussman 1978, 75–83; and Fairweather 1981, 39.

7. Kennedy 1991, 42.

8. On rhetorical theory before Aristotle, see Cole 1991b. For the commonplace in Aristotelian thought, see esp. De Pater 1968. For the later traditions: Green-Pedersen 1984, which includes Boethius, but see also Stump 1988.

On Hermagoras of Temnos, see Barwick 1964; and Nadeau 1959. A concise introduction with bibliography: Hohmann 2001, 741–45.

9. For Cicero's account of the composition, see Cic. *Top.* 1 and *Fam.* 7.19.

10. Boethius (A.D. 480–524 or 526) echoes much of Cicero's treatment (the art of discourse is finding and judging arguments, viz., topics and analytics) but provides clues of the tradition between Aristotle and Cicero (there is additional if slim evidence from the commentators: e.g., Alexander of Aphrodisias in his commentary on Aristotle's *Topica* (book 2, p. 67 Wallies) gives Theophrastus's definition of a *topos* as the first principle or element from which we take the first principle of particulars, defined in its outline, undefined as to its applications).

11. Quintilian (2.11.7) alludes to students keeping notebooks of the good material of other declaimers.

12. The division between letter and intent strictly belongs to a legal status. See Berti (2007, 86 n. 3) on *voluntas* versus *littera,* and more broadly his appendix (115–27), which treats the kinds of status used by the declaimers of Seneca's collection.

13. Berti (2007, 115–17) lists the few cases that do invoke a question of fact. Such declamations do not introduce new facts or witnesses. They argue from ambiguous signs, especially in hard-to-prove cases such as poisoning (*Controv.* 7.3 and 9.6).

14. On the term *divisio,* see now Berti 2007, 27, and the analysis of particular divisions at 81–99.

15. A certain amount of caution is called for since the sources indulge in an easy schematism—the real orator drives out the lesser, who turns to school—and that vice of ancient intellectual history where every development is granted a famous name. Theophrastus and

Menander were interested in a similar variety of ordinary people and extreme character types. On the tyrant in declamation, see Tabacco 1985.

16. Fairweather (1981, 124–31) provides a judicious account of the history of the term and of the institution at Rome. See also Bonner 1949 and Kaster 2001.

17. Berti (2007, 36–39) succinctly reviews the elite who appear in Seneca the Elder's pages.

18. Kaster (2001, 328) perceptively remarks that rape in declamation does not lead to an exploration of the psychological state (of attacker or victim); it is rather a "social mess" that the speaker must then redress.

19. The association of the learning of theory—the principles of rhetoric—and speaking for others is not accidental. For this aspect of totalizing theory and the reaction against essentialist scholarship, see Richlin 1993, 276, with bibliography.

20. Some modern scholars have lamented that declamation was poor preparation for the law, since it was so different, so fantastic. Quintilian, quite sensibly, notes that the laws in declamation were easier to learn than the real thing (*Inst.* 7.4.11). Cicero describes a similar practice: at *De or.* 2.100 he notes that in school children are given easy cases that require no knowledge of the law. The melodramatic, even bizarre quality of many of the cases is essential to the learning and testing of categorical thinking, as the strange but memorable cases taught in American law schools attest. For some of the similarities of argument and situation in declamation and the Roman jurists, see Dingel 1988, 2–3.

21. On *color,* see Sussman 1978, 41; Schönberger and Schönberger 2004, 13–14; and Berti 2007, 27–28.

22. *Fictio personae* translates the Greek προσωποποιία. See Quint. 9.29 ff. for an extended discussion (also 3.8.51 ff., a remark on the declaimers' practice). He notes the possible distinction of this figure (representation of speech of humans, *sermocinatio*) from that of nonhuman speakers, e.g., a city speaking. But he is not much impressed by such distinctions and further recognizes the connection of these figures to apostrophe and ethopoeia (the representation or description of character). See also the recommendations of the Master in the *sermo* of *Decl. Min.* 260.

Russell (1983) began his study of declamation, the most penetrating and complete analysis of the phenomenon, with a realization of the importance of *fictio personae* (1: "Pretending to be someone else, and composing imaginary speeches in character, is an essential part of most literary activity") but turned from this to emphasize firm organization as the defining difference of declamation. Russell also notes (11), of the school exercises before declamation: "The most important of the *progymnasmata* was naturally the one that approached most nearly to the *meletê* itself," *ethopoiia*—the representation of character.

23. The palpably full and difficult expression of declamatory style has its own ideological functions. Thorstein Veblen pointed out that the leisure class speaks in a "cumbrous and out of date" fashion because such usage implies waste of time, and the freedom from the need for direct, efficacious speech (cited in Burke and Porter 1987, 6).

The unreality of declamation also served an educational need. Luke (1989, 64–65) describes the importance of alternate worlds projected by narrative text: "The capacity of text to convey fantasy and thereby to take the reader beyond lived experience is a primary educational effect of text." The school exercise has to be fantastic to free the student from his present view of the world, of roles, and especially his relations to these.

24. As Winterbottom (1984, 301 ad 247.7) notes, insertions of direct speech need not be marked. In this oral medium a shift in persona could be marked by a shift in tone or gesture; see, for example, *Decl. Min.* 299.5 and Winterbottom's note ad loc. (p. 425), citing Håkanson, where the declaimer makes it clear that it is the girl who speaks the offending *color*.

25. Greek theorists laid down the conditions by which the declaimer had to speak not in the person of the defendant but in that of the advocate (see Russell 1983, 14, citing Hermogenes' *Peri methodou deinotētos*, p. 436 Rabe)—e.g., a speaker who has had his tongue cut out (Libanius *Decl.* 36). Most often it is not the literally maimed male but the female who requires a speaker, but see *Rhetores graeci* 8.344 for cases of women speaking for themselves; also Winterbottom 1984, 309 ad no. 250.1. *Decl. Min.* 360 seems to present two women speaking in competition (a widow quarrels with her daughter-in-law about the dowry): the first *sermo* introduces a declamation for the daughter-in-law (*nurus dicet*); the second concludes the plea and then skips to the argumentation of the mother-in-law (*Contra illa dicet . . .*).

26. In the plots the verb *tacere*, "to be silent," often means "not to bring a suit" (e.g., *Decl. Min.* 368: *Ob hoc abdicata tacuit*). The *rapta* then speaks by having her advocate sue. The declaimers of Seneca's collection in speaking of a tortured wife repeatedly say of her *tacet* (*Controv.* 2.5.4–6). Silence is always a thing of the past in declamation. A declamation can turn upon a woman's words, as the adulterous wife's *non es meus* must be explained in *Decl. Mai.* 23, and the riddling *ante morietur, quam illi nubat* uttered by the mother about her daughter will be variously explained in *Decl. Mai.* 40. Sussman (1987, 143) of *Decl. Mai.*, citing parallels in declamation and in Ovid, calls the element of silence "romantic." It is, rather, a prerequisite for the "right" of the male to speak for the female and as such is no doubt part of romantic plot. The declaiming advocate must resist all efforts at silencing, including *praescriptio*—the annulment of his claim, the procedural barrier to sue that would prevent his speaking. *Praescriptio*—legal formula and precedent of the *patres*—never wins in declamation, just as the *rapta* does not remain *tacita*.

27. Erikson 1963, 261.

28. Piaget 1950, 148: between eleven and fifteen the child "forms theories about everything, delighting especially in consideration of that which is not."

29. Connolly (1998) has argued for the connection between declamation's misogyny and the contrasting, positive celebration and creation of Roman virility.

30. For an account of the program of the elder Seneca's collection, see Bloomer 1997, chap. 4.

31. Scholars have long thought that these declamations derive from a note taker in Quintilian's classroom. See Winterbottom (1984, xi–xiii), who reviews this interpretation but concludes that the collection is in fact the unedited notes of the teacher for his lectures.

32. The importance of the status system for declamation, especially Roman declamation, has been exaggerated. It is true that declamations fall into questions, that division is used, and that the exercises from Quintilian's school show careful attention to division. But these divisions are fairly simple. Scholarly enthusiasm for a complex Greek theory seems to have at least two motivations: to give some status to Roman school exercises obviously so important for the history of Latin literature; to keep the analysis of these texts formal and aesthetic and difficult. Quintilian himself expresses disdain for enthusiasts of the stasis system. In the third century A.D. a teacher at Athens called status nonsense (*Rhetores graeci* 4.38, cited by Russell

1983, 41). Russell also acknowledges the pedagogical limitations of stasis theory (Russell, 72) and notes that for Ps.-Dionysios, for example, "character (*êthos*) is of central significance."

33. The teacher's instructions preserved as the *sermones* in Ps.-Quintilian include frequent directives about the treatment of persona (e.g., *Decl. Min.* 260, when to speak in the persona of the character and when to speak as an advocate; *Decl. Min.* 279.10, where the declaimer splits the husband into three: *iuvenis, maritus, impuber*). The treatment of persona can be highly self-conscious, as for example when the character of a declamation draws attention to it: in *Decl. Min.* 291 the father says he cannot keep up the persona and so will quote from what the brother said in his speech—here a persona engages in *sermocinatio*. Such notices of persona allow the speaker to engage in an attack or to employ a style on the verge of bad taste or abuse—effective but ill-mannered or potentially unsympathetic tactics excused by a sort of *dubitatio* regarding persona, e.g., *Decl. Min.* 297.11: *Haec dicerem si tecum asperius contenderem*. Similarly, as Winterbottom reports, after Håkanson (Winterbottom 1984, 429 ad 299.5), an overly declamatory *color* can be put in the mouth of a girl. Quintilian at 3.8.37 makes the connection of choice and treatment of persona with effect upon audience. Cf. 6.1.25: *ex personis quoque trahitur adfectus*.

34. Juvenal represents the schoolmasters droning on: *quis color et quod sit causae genus atque ubi summa / quaestio* (6.155–56).

35. Jerome *Ep.* 54.15.4 reports that there were commonplaces against stepmothers; cf. Quint. 2.10.5. Sen. *Controv.* 4.5, Ps.-Quint. *Decl. Mai.* 35, and Ennodius *Dictio* 15 are declamatory treatments of the same theme. See more generally Watson 1995.

36. Cic. *Cael.* 33ff. Comparison of personae is a standard technique in the *Minor Declamations*. This can involve two parties of a dispute, or, as at 306.4, what a clever, deceitful woman would have done is set against what the virtuous mother did do. *Decl. Mai.* 35 is devoted to a comparison of the stepmother and the mother. For an analysis of silence and the declamatory wife, see Polla-Mattiot 1990.

37. Of course, games have specific relations to their societies; cf. the definition given by Stone 1971, 4: "Play is recreation, then, because it continually re-creates the society in which it is carried on." Stone (10) follows Merton in stressing that dramatic play, even when fantastic, affords the child reflected views of himself in a kind of anticipatory socialization (see Merton 1957, 384–86). See also the discussion of anthropological models of play in Richlin 1992, 73–77.

38. Stewart (1979, 39) discusses ludic genres as texts that present interpretive schemes contrary to common sense, e.g., by presenting paradoxes of framing: "Ludic genres present a critique not only of conceptual classifications, but on the level of nonsense of classification itself." Declamation occurs in a play context, where roles and categories are suspended, created, and reversed. The outcome need not be radical in the sense of an inversion of social norms; but the process and learning context must be, so that the student relearns and reinterprets his own categories and roles.

39. On verbal dueling among adolescents, see Gossen 1976. For the fashioning of the male through oratorical training see Gleason 1995.

40. The severe speakers calculate the public *aestimatio* of the woman in a way reminiscent of Caesar's pretext for dismissing his wife.

41. Kaster (2001) has emphasized declamation's function of rendering familiar the violent.

Gunderson (2003) offers a psychoanalytic account of declamation's memory and reperformance of violence. Beard (1993) approached the violent, familial stories of declamation as Roman mythmaking. Berti (2007, 46 n. 1) refers to the romantic, novelistic aspect of many of the plots and also notes (47–48) the contemporary relevance of the themes of adultery (specifically, their connection to Augustus's legislation) and their connection to Roman elegy (55–56).

42. Sons flout *patria potestas* and father's wishes as best they can. For instance, in *Decl. Min.* 257, *Nuptiae inter inimicorum filios,* a son marries the daughter of his father's rich enemy in order to ransom his father. On dad's return he refuses to divorce her and is disinherited. (For references and bibliography on abdication in law and declamation see Winterbottom 1984, 327 ad 257.3.) Notably the son compares his situation to that of a slave and thus makes explicit the relations in power and law that are customarily glossed as *pietas.* Declamation and its role playing seek to restore the order of the house.

43. Kennedy (1972, 334) has pointed out "the recurring question of the relationship of children to adults" within declamation. In this he was anticipated by the sixth-century Choricius (*Decl.* 5 p. 225 F-R), who states that declamation includes disputes between parents and children. On the centrality of conflict in and for declamation, see now Berti 2007, 79, with bibliography.

44. In contrast Gleason (1995, xxiii), writing of the Second Sophistic, emphasizes that "spectatorship provided an affective education, through which the individual became attuned to a collective dramatization of status relationships."

45. Goetz 1892, 635–59, contains as an appendix four *colloquia.* The limitations of Goetz's corpus are clearly cataloged and in good measure redressed by the publication of a different *colloquium* by Dionisotti (1982), which as Dionisotti argues was probably composed in Gaul in the third century A.D.

46. Bradley (1994, 26), like Dionisotti (1982, 93), recognized the frequency and importance of commands to slaves in these texts. In exclusively formal terms, the student rehearsed thematic and athematic imperatives, presents and aorists. Specifically, the boy delivers first aorist actives, second aorist actives, present thematic active, aorist athematic actives, plural imperatives at 55, in addition to ἔστο/ω, one third-person imperative, to a slave regarding another slave at 54 (ποιησάντω a mistake [?] for ποιησάτω, although Dionisotti considers it a scribal error and reads *facia*<n>-*t* and ποιησά[ν]τω<ν>, but cf. ἐλθάτω at 62). He and/or the scribes are massively confused about the imperatives of λούω, but do know ἀνάβα (60). Significantly, the only imperatives the boy receives all have to do with reading and writing (26). In addition, the boy has a very limited use of the hortatory subjunctive: namely, ἀγῶμεν/*eamus*. To this add *lucubr*<e>*mus*, my reading for *lucubramus* (glossed ἀγριπνήσομεν). Here the Greek does not translate the Roman corruption. The limited range of imperatives learned may be explained by the fact that the *hermeneumata* as early exercises are more concerned with expressive than receptive language.

47. The thematic list is a sort of intrusion, for a separate exercise of the *hermeneumata* was *capitula nominum,* e.g., a vocabulary list on a set theme such as names of the gods. Thus the *colloquium* both reports and includes (small) versions of the *capitula nominum.*

48. Pedagogic lists could be more demanding; Dionisotti (1984, 203) cites "*idiomata generum,* lists of nouns of one gender in Latin and a different one in Greek, presumably inflicted on ancient children as part of bilingual teaching."

49. Dionisotti (1982, 122) noted of the list of magistrates: "The dignitaries apparently appear in hierarchical order."

50. *Hermeneumata* are being used in the school scenes of this exercise (Dionisotti 1982, 120).

51. Dionisotti 1982: *Quis sic facit dominus quomodo tu, intantum bibis? . . . ita hoc decet sapientem patrem familias. . . .* (103.66).

52. As Dionisotti (1982, 109) notes ad 7, dressing and undressing abound; cf. nos. 7, 13, 43, 48, 58, 72.

53. See, e.g., Bonner 1977, 135–36.

54. The preface of the *Hermeneumata Leidensia:* Goetz 1892, 30; the preface of the *Monacensia colloquia:* Goetz, 645.

55. The connection of gender roles with the process of writing has been stressed by those who combine a material and social critique of the sacred cows of education and literature— see Xavière Gauthier's response (1980) to the question "Is there such a thing as woman's writing?" Against the backdrop of the historical maleness of writing, Gauthier (among others) queries scholarly efforts to recuperate lost women's writing or voice and locates the woman writer's pursuit of women's writing in the holes of discourse, the "blank pages, gaps, borders, spaces and silence" (Gauthier, 164).

56. See Scruton 1990.

CONCLUSION

1. The advantages for slaves of a literate trade included specific legal privileges. Bradley 1984, 92: "Full freedom below thirty was possible in cases involving a blood relationship between master and slave, cases where the slave was the teacher of the owner's children, a potential wife or *procurator* for the owner, or an *alumnus*" (citing Gai. *Inst.* 1.19; 39).

2. If one limits culture to written and oral expression, perhaps the claim is tenable. Modern students of human culture would not pose so narrow a definition. In writing this claim Nietzsche would have at the least realized that the philosophical traditions would not have set speech as the end of human culture. Nietzsche also ignores the Romans; see his essay of 1873, "The History of Greek Eloquence" (1989, 213–42): "To no task did the Greeks devote such incessant labor as to eloquence. . . . Devotion to oratory is the most tenacious element of Greek culture and survives through all the curtailments of their condition. . . . Hellenic culture and power gradually concentrate on oratorical skill [*Reden-können*]." Nietzsche knew the contradictions inherent in this teleology: the loss of Hellenic power accompanies the rise of words.

3. Case studies in Latin literature can be found in Bloomer 1997.

4. Basil *Hom. Famis Sicc.* 67 C, *PG* p. 317; and *Hom.* VIII 72, *PG* 31, 309.

5. Cribiore 1996, 149.

6. Martianus Capella, *De nuptiis Philologiae et Mercurii,* ed. James Willis (Leipzig, 1983) 3.224. On the iconography of Lady Grammar, see Bagley 1990.

7. Another students' rebellion: Livy 5.27. Cf. Bonner 1977, 141; and Prudent. *Peristephanon* 9. See Lanzoni 1925; and Roberts 1993.

BIBLIOGRAPHY

Abbott, Frank F. 1909. "The Career of a Roman Student." In *Society and Politics in Ancient Rome: Essays and Sketches,* 191–214. New York.

Abbott, Norman J. S. 1980. "The Treatise *De liberis educandis* Attributed to Plutarch." PhD diss., Oxford University.

Adams, J. N. 2003. *Bilingualism and the Latin Language.* Cambridge.

Adrados, Francisco Rodríguez. 1999. *History of the Greco-Latin Fable.* Vol. 1. Leiden, Boston, and Cologne.

Agostiniani, Luciano. 1982. *Le "iscrizioni parlanti" dell'Italia antica.* Florence.

Ahlheid, Frans. 1983. *Quintilian: The Preface to Book VIII and Comparable Passages in the "Institutio oratoria."* Amsterdam.

Albini, Francesca. 1997. "Family and the Formation of Character: Aspects of Plutarch's Thought." In Judith Mossman, ed., *Plutarch and His Intellectual World: Essays on Plutarch,* 59–70. London.

Alison, P. 1993. "How Do We Identify the Use of Space in Roman Housing?" In E. M. Moorman, ed., *Functional and Spatial Analysis of Wall Painting,* 1–8. Leiden.

Amsler, Mark. 1989. *Etymology and Grammatical Discourse in Late Antiquity and the Early Middle Ages.* Amsterdam and Philadelphia.

Apple, Michael W., ed., 1982. *Cultural and Economic Reproduction in Education.* London.

Apple, Michael W., and Linda K. Christian-Smith, eds. 1991. *The Politics of the Textbook.* New York and London.

Ariès, Philip. 1962. *Centuries of Childhood: A Social History of Family Life.* Trans. Robert Baldick. New York.

Arntzenius, Otto. 1754. *Dionysii Catonis Disticha de Moribus ad Filium.* Amsterdam.

Astin, Alan E. 1967. *Scipio Aemilianus.* Oxford.

———. 1978. *Cato the Censor.* Oxford.

Atali, Carlo. 1995. "'Ars' et 'actus': Il fine dell'arte retorica secondo Quintiliano." *Rhetorica* 13.2: 161–78.

Atherton, C. A. 1988. "Hand over Fist: The Failure of Stoic Rhetoric." *CQ* 38: 392–427.

Babbitt, Frank Cole. 1927. *Plutarch Moralia.* Vol. 1. Cambridge, Mass.

Badian, E. 1972. "Ennius and His Friends." In *Entretiens Fondation Hardt* 17: 149–208. Geneva.

Bagley, Ayers. 1990. "Grammar as Teacher: A Study in the Iconics of Education." *Studies in Medieval and Renaissance Teaching* n.s. 1: 17–48.

Bagnall, Roger. 1995. *Reading Papyri, Writing Ancient History.* London.

Baker, Carolyn D., and Peter Freebody, eds. 1987. "'Constituting the Child' in Beginning School Reading Books." *British Journal of Sociology of Education* 8: 55–76.

———. 1988a. "Possible Worlds and Possible People: Interpretive Challenges in Beginning School Reading Books." *Australian Journal of Reading* 11.2: 95–104.

———. 1988b. "Talk Around Text: Constructions of Textual and Teacher Authority in Classroom Discourse." In DeCastell, Luke, and Luke 1988, 263–83.

———. 1989. *Children's First Schoolbooks: Introductions to the Culture of Literacy.* Oxford.

Barnard, Sylvia. 1990. "Cornelia and the Women of Her Family." *Latomus* 49: 383–92.

Barns, John. 1950a. "A New Gnomologium: With Some Remarks on Gnomic Anthologies (I)." *CQ* 44: 126–37.

———. 1950b. "A New Gnomologium: With Some Remarks on Gnomic Anthologies (II)." *CQ* n.s. 1: 1–19.

Barthes, Roland. 1982. "Inaugural Lecture, Collège de France." In Susan Sontag, ed., *A Barthes Reader,* 457–78. New York.

Barwick, Karl. 1964. "Zur Erklärung und Geschichte der Stasislehre der Hermagoras von Temnos." *Philologus* 108: 80–101.

Beagon, Mary. 1992. *Roman Nature: The Thought of Pliny the Elder.* Oxford.

Beard, Mary. 1986. "Cicero and Divination: The Formation of a Latin Discourse." *JRS* 76: 33–46.

———. 1993. "Looking (Harder) for Roman Myth: Dumézil, Declamation, and the Problem of Definition." In Fritz Graf, ed., *Mythos in mythenloser Gesellschaft: Das Paradigma Roms,* 44–64. Stuttgart and Leipzig.

Beard, Mary, et al. 1991. *Literacy in the Roman World.* JRA Supplement 3. Ann Arbor, Mich.

Beard, Mary, and Michael Crawford. 1985. *Rome in the Late Republic: Problems and Interpretations.* London.

Beck, Frederick. 1975. *Album of Greek Education.* Sydney.

Bedaux, Jan Baptist, and Rudi Ekkart, eds. 2000. *Pride and Joy: Children's Portraiture in the Netherlands, 1500–1700.* Amsterdam.

Beechley, Veronica, and James Donald, eds. 1985. *Subjectivity and Social Relations.* Philadelphia.

Bernays, Jacob. 1855. *Joseph Justus Scaliger.* Berlin.

Bernstein, D. 1964. "Elaborated and Restricted Codes: Their Social Origins and Some Consequences." *American Anthropologist* 66: 55–69.

Berry, Edmund G. 1958. "The *De liberis educandis* of Pseudo-Plutarch." *HSCP* 63: 387–99.

Berti, Emanuele. 2007. *Scholasticorum studia: Seneca il Vecchio e la cultura retorica e letteraria della prima età imperiale.* Pisa.

Bianca, G. G. 1963. *La pedagogia di Quintiliano*. Padua.

Birt, Theodor. 1907. *Die Buchrolle in der Kunst: Archäologisch-antiquarische Untersuchungen zum antiken Buchwesen*. Leipzig.

Bloomer, W. Martin. 1992. *Valerius Maximus and the Rhetoric of the New Nobility*. Chapel Hill, N.C., and London.

———. 1997. *Latinity and Literary Society at Rome*. Philadelphia.

———. 2001. "Declamation." In *Oxford Encyclopedia of Rhetoric*, 197–99. Oxford.

———. 2005. "Marble Latin: Encounters with the Timeless Language." In W. Martin Bloomer, ed., *The Contest of Language: Before and Beyond Nationalism*, 207–26. Notre Dame, Ind.

Boas, Marcus. 1914. "De librorum Catoniarum historia atque compositione." *Mnem.* 42: 17–46.

———. 1934. *Die Epistula Catonis*. Amsterdam.

———. 1952. *Disticha Catonis*. Amsterdam.

Bolgar, Robert R. 1969. "The Training of Elites in Greek Education." In Rupert Wilkinson, ed., *Governing Elites*, 23–49. New York.

Bömer, Franz. 1953. "Der commentarius: Zur Vorgeschichte und literarischen Form der Schriften Caesars." *Hermes* 81: 210–50.

Bonfante, Larissa. 1990. *Etruscan*. London.

Bonner, Stanley F. 1949. *Roman Declamation*. Berkeley.

———. 1977. *Education in Ancient Rome*. Berkeley.

Booth, A. D. 1976. "The Image of the Professor in Ancient Society." *EMC* 20: 1–10.

———. 1978. "The Appearance of the *Schola grammatici*." *Hermes* 106: 117–25.

———. 1979a. "Elementary and Secondary Education in the Roman Empire." *Florilegium* 1: 1–14.

———. 1979b. "The Schooling of Slaves in First-Century Rome." *TAPA* 109: 11–19.

Boskoff, Priscilla S. 1952. "Quintilian in the Late Middle Ages." *Speculum* 27: 71–78.

Bourdieu, Pierre. 1984. *Distinction: A Social Critique of the Judgement of Taste*. Trans. Richard Nice. Cambridge.

———. 1991. *Language and Symbolic Power*. Ed. and intro. John B. Thompson, trans. Gino Raymond and Matthew Adamson. Cambridge, Mass.

Bower, E. W. 1961. "Some Technical Terms in Roman Education." *Hermes* 89: 462–77.

Bowersock, Glenn. 1965. *Augustus and the Greek World*. Oxford.

———. 1969. *Greek Sophists in the Roman Empire*. Oxford.

Bradley, Keith. 1984. *Slaves and Masters in the Roman Empire: A Study in Social Control*. Brussels.

———. 1985. "Child Care at Rome: The Role of Men." *Historical Reflections* 12.3: 485–91.

———. 1986. "Wet-Nursing at Rome: A Study in Social Relations." In B. Rawson, ed., *The Family in Ancient Rome: New Perspectives*, 201–29. London.

———. 1991. *Discovering the Roman Family*. Oxford.

———. 1994a. "The Nurse and the Child at Rome: Duty, Affect, and Socialisation." *Thamyris* 1: 137–56.

———. 1994b. *Slavery and Society at Rome*. Cambridge.

Brendel, Otto. 1977. *Etruscan Art*. New York.

Brink, C. O. 1989. "Quintilian's *De causis corruptae eloquentiae* and Tacitus' *Dialogus de oratoribus*." *CQ* 39: 472–503.

Brody, Miriam. 1993. *Manly Writing: Gender, Rhetoric, and the Rise of Composition*. Carbondale and Edwardsville, Ill.

Brown, Peter. 2000. *Augustine of Hippo: A Biography*. Berkeley.

Brunner, Hellmut. 1957/1991. *Altägyptische Erziehung*. Wiesbaden.

Burke, Peter, and Roy Porter. 1987. *The Social History of Language*. Cambridge.

Butts, James R. 1986. "The 'Progymnasmata' of Theon: A New Text with Translation and Commentary." PhD diss., Claremont Graduate School.

Calboli, G. 1972. "L'oratore M. Antonio e la Rhetorica ad Herennium." *Giornale Italiano di Filologia* 24: 149–50.

Caplan, Harry. 1954. *[Cicero] Ad C. Herennium*. Cambridge, Mass., and London.

———. 1970. "The Decline of Eloquence at Rome in the First Century A.D." In A. King and H. North, eds., *Of Eloquence: Studies in Ancient and Medieval Rhetoric*, 160–95. Ithaca, N.Y.

Carson, Ann. 1990. "Putting Her in Her Place: Woman, Dirt, and Desire." In David Halperin, John Winkler, Froma Zeitlin, eds., *Before Sexuality: The Construction of Erotic Experience in the Ancient Greek World*, 135–69. Princeton, N.J.

Castorina, Emanuelle. 1952. *L'atticismo nell'evoluzione del pensiero di Cicerone*. Catania.

Cavallo, Guglielmo. 1989. "Testo, libro, lettura." In Guglielmo Cavallo, Paolo Fedeli, and Andrea Giardana, eds., *Lo spazio litterario di Roma antica*, vol. 2, *La circolazione del testo*, 307–41. Rome.

Christes, J. 1979. *Sklaven und Freigelassene als Grammatiker und Philologen in antiken Rom*. Wiesbaden.

Cicu, Luciano. 1991. "Convertere ut orator: Cicerone fra traduzione scientifica e traduzione artistica." In *Studi di filologia classica in onore di Giusto Monaco*, 849–57. Palermo.

Clark, Donald L. 1957. *Rhetoric in Greco-Roman Education*. New York.

Clarke, John Robert. 1991. *The Houses of Roman Italy, 100 B.C.–A.D. 250: Ritual, Space, and Decoration*. Berkeley.

Clarke, M. L. 1951. "The Thesis in the Roman Rhetorical Schools of the Republic." *CQ* 1: 159–66.

———. 1967. "Quintilian: A Biographical Sketch." *Greece & Rome* 14: 24–37.

———. 1968. "Cicero at School." *Greece & Rome* 15: 18–22..

———. 1971. *Higher Education in the Ancient World*. Albuquerque.

Classen, C. J. 1986. "Ciceros *orator perfectus* ein *vir bonus dicendi peritus?*" In S. Prete, ed., *Commemoratio: Studi di filologia in ricordo di Riccardo Ribuoli*, 43–55. Sassoferrato.

Clausen, Wendell. 1986. "Cicero and the New Poetry." *HSCP* 90: 159–70.

Coarelli, F. 1978. "La statue de Cornélie, mère des Gracches et la crise politique à Rome au temps de Saturninus." In *La dernier siècle de la République romaine et l'époque augustéenne*, 13–28. Strasbourg.

———. 1993. "Athenaeum." In Eva Margareta Steinby, ed., *Lexicon topographicum urbis Romae*. 6 vols. Rome.

Cohen, Edward E. 2003. "The High Cost of *Andreia* at Athens." In Rosen and Sluiter 2003, 145–65. Leiden and Boston.

Cole, Thomas. 1991a. "In Response to Nevio Zorzetti." *CJ* 86: 377–82.

———. 1991b. *The Origins of Rhetoric in Ancient Greece*. Baltimore.

Colish, Marcia. 1985. *The Stoic Tradition from Antiquity to the Early Middle Ages*. Leiden.

Collart, Paul. 1926. *Les Papyrus Bouriant*. Paris.

Colson, F. H. 1921. "Quintilian I.9 and the 'Chria' in Ancient Education." *CR* 35: 150–54.

———. 1924. *M. Fabii Quintiliani Institutionis oratoriae liber I*. Cambridge.

Connolly, Joy. 1998. "Mastering Corruption: Constructions of Identity in Roman Oratory." In Sandra Joshel and Sheila Murnaghan, eds., *Women and Slaves in Greco-Roman Culture: Differential Equations*, 130–51. New York.

———. 2003. "Like the Labors of Heracles: *Andreia* and *Paideia* in Greek Culture under Rome." In Rosen and Sluiter 2003, 286–317.

Conte, G. B. 1994. *Genres and Readers*. Trans. Glen W. Most. Baltimore.

Cook-Gumperz, Jenny, ed. 1986. *The Social Construction of Literacy*. Cambridge.

Cooper, John. 1996. *The Child in Jewish History*. Northvale, N. J., and London.

Corbeill, Anthony. 2001. "Education in the Roman Republic: Creating Traditions." In Too 2001, 261–87.

Cornell, Tim. 1991. "The Tyranny of the Evidence: A Discussion of the Possible Uses of Literacy in Etruria and Latium in the Archaic Age." In Beard et al. 1991, 7–33.

Coulter, Cornelia C. 1958. "Boccaccio's Knowledge of Quintilian." *Speculum* 33: 490–96.

Courcelle, Pierre. 1969. *Late Latin Writers and Their Greek Sources*. Trans. Harry E. Wedeck. Cambridge, Mass.

Courtney, Edward. 1993. *The Fragmentary Latin Poets*. Oxford.

———. 1999. *Archaic Latin Prose*. Atlanta.

Cousin, J. 1935/1967. *Études sur Quintilien*. 2 vols. Paris; repr., Amsterdam.

———. 1963. *Institution oratoire*, I. Paris.

Cova, P. V., et al., eds. 1990. *Aspetti della "paideia" di Quintiliano*. Milan.

Cramer, Frederick H. 1951. "Expulsion of Astrologers from Ancient Rome." *Classica et Mediaevalia* 12: 14–17.

———. 1954. *Astrology in Roman Law and Politics*. Philadelphia.

Cribiore, Rafaella. 1996. *Writing, Teachers, and Students in Graeco-Roman Egypt*. Atlanta.

———. 2001. *Gymnastics of the Mind: Greek Education in Hellenistic and Roman Egypt*. Princeton, N.J.

Cribiore, Rafaella, P. Davoli, and D. Ratzan. 2008. "A Teacher's Dipinto from Trimithis (Dakhleh Oasis)." *JRA* 21: 170–91.

Cristofani, Mauro. 1987. *Saggi di storia etrusca arcaica*. Rome.

Currie, Sarah. 1996. "The Empire of Adults: The Representation of Children on Trajan's Arch at Benevento." In Jas Elsner, ed., *Art and Text in Roman Culture*, 153–81. Cambridge.

Curtius, E. R. 1952. *European Literature and the Latin Middle Ages*. Trans. Willard R. Trask. New York.

Dale, Roger, Geoff Esland, and Madeleine MacDonald, eds. 1976. *Schooling and Capitalism: A Sociological Reader*. London and Henley.

Daly, L. W. 1950. "Roman Study Abroad." *AJP* 71: 42–58.

Dalzell, Alexander. 1955. "C. Asinius Pollio and the Early History of Recitation at Rome." *Hermathena* 86: 20–28.

D'Arms, John. 1981. *Commerce and Social Standing in Ancient Rome*. Cambridge, Mass.

Darnton, R. 1991. "History of Reading." In P. Burke, ed., *New Perspectives on Historical Writing*, 140–67. Cambridge.

Davies, J. C. 1968. "Molon's Influence on Cicero." *CQ* 18: 303–14.

Davis, A. T. 1967. *Bellum Catilinae*. Oxford.

Dawe, R. D., ed. 2000. *Philogelos*. Munich.

DeCastell, S. C., A. Luke, and C. Luke, eds. 1988. *Language, Authority, and Criticism: Readings on the School Textbook*. London and Philadelphia.

de' Fogolari, G., and Aldo L. Prosdocimi. 1987. *I veneti antichi: Lingua e cultura*. Padua.

Delaine, Janet. 1988. "Recent Research on Roman Baths." *JRA* 1: 11–32.

Della Corte, Francesco. 1946. *Enciclopedisti latini*. Genoa.

Della Corte, Matteo. 1924. *Juventus*. Arpino.

———. 1959. "Scuole e maestri in Pompei antica." *Studi Romani* 7.6: 621–34.

Delorme, Jean. 1960. *Gymnasion: Étude sur les monuments consacrés à l'éducation en Grèce*. Paris.

De Pater, W. A. 1968. "La fonction du lieu et de l'instrument dans les *Topiques*." In G. E. L. Owen, ed., *Aristotle on Dialectic: The Topics*, 165–88. Oxford.

De Robertis, Francesco. 1967. *Lavoro e lavoratori nel mondo romano*. Bari.

Diels, H. 1954. *Die Fragmente der Vorsokratiker*. Berlin.

Dilke, O. A. W. 1985. *Greek and Roman Maps*. Ithaca, N.Y.

Dingel, Joachim. 1988. *Scholastica materia: Untersuchungen zu den "Declamationes minores" und der "Institutio oratoria" Quintilians*. Berlin and New York.

Dionisotti, A. C. 1982. "From Ausonius' Schooldays? A Schoolbook and Its Relations." *JRS* 72: 83–125.

———. 1984. "Latin Grammar for Greeks and Goths." *JRS* 74: 202–8.

Dixon, Suzanne. 1992. *The Roman Family*. Baltimore and London.

Donald, James. 1985. "Beacons of the Future: Schooling, Subject, and Subjectification." In Veronica Beechley and James Donald, eds., *Subjectivity and Social Relations*, 217–18. Philadelphia.

Douglas, A. E. 1960. "Clausulae in the *Rhetorica ad Herennium* as Evidence of Its Date." *CQ* 54: 65–78.

———. 1966. *M. Tulli Ciceronis Brutus*. Oxford.

Dover, Kenneth. 1974. *Greek Popular Morality in the Time of Plato and Aristotle*. Oxford.

Dryoff, A. 1897. *Die Ethik der alten Stoa*. Berlin.

Dubuisson, M. 1989. "Non quaerere externa, domesticis esse contentos: Cicéron et le problème de la 'traduction' de grec en latin." *Ktèma: Civilisations de l'Orient, de la Grèce et de Rome antiques* 14: 201–4.

Duckworth, G. E. 1952. *The Nature of Roman Comedy: A Study in Popular Entertainment*. Princeton, N.J.

Ducos, M. 1987. "Dynasties familiales et exercice du pouvoir dans l'oeuvre de Tite-Live." *Ktema* 12: 159–67.

Dugan, John. 2001. "Preventing Ciceronianism: C. Licinius Calvus' Regimens for Sexual and Oratorical Self-Mastery." *CP* 96: 400–428.

Dunbabin, Katherine. 2003. *The Roman Banquet: Images of Conviviality*. Cambridge.

Dupont, Florence. 1997. "Recitation and the Reorganization of the Space of Public Discourse."

In Thomas Habinek and Alessandro Schiesaro, eds., *The Roman Cultural Revolution*, 44–60. Cambridge.

Dyck, Andrew R. 1997. *A Commentary on Cicero, De officiis*. Ann Arbor, Mich.

———. 2004. *A Commentary on Cicero, De legibus*. Ann Arbor, Mich.

Edmonds, J. M. 1961. *Fragments of Attic Comedy*. Leiden.

Elliot, Alison J. 1981. *Child Language*. Cambridge.

Emerson, Ralph Waldo. 1880. "Works and Days." In *Works of Ralph Waldo Emerson*, 129–50. Boston.

Erikson, E. H. 1963. *Childhood and Society*. New York.

Ernout, Alfred, and François Thomas. 1953. *Syntaxe latine*. Paris.

Eyben, Emiel. 1993. *Restless Youth in Ancient Rome*. London and New York.

Fairweather, Janet. 1981. *Seneca the Elder*. Cambridge.

Fantham, Elaine. 1978a. "Imitation and Decline: Rhetorical Theory and Practice in the First Century after Christ." *CP* 73: 102–16.

———. 1978b. "Imitation and Evolution: The Discussion of Rhetorical Imitation in Cicero *De oratore* 2.87–97 and Some Related Problems of Ciceronian Theory." *CP* 73: 1–16.

———. 1995. "The Concept of Nature and Human Nature in Quintilian's Psychology and Theory of Instruction." *Rhetorica* 13.2: 125–36.

———. 1998. "The Roman Background to Medieval Instruction: The Teaching of Quintilian." *Studies in Medieval and Renaissance Teaching* 6.2: 23–34.

Fantham, Elaine, et al., eds. 1994. *Women in the Classical World*. New York and Oxford.

Farrell, Joseph. 2001. *Latin Language and Latin Culture: From Ancient to Modern Times*. Cambridge.

Fear, A. T. 1995. "A Latin Master from Roman Spain." *Greece & Rome* 42: 57–69.

Ferrero, Leonardo. 1955. *Storia del pitagorismo nel mondo romano, dalle origini alla fine della republica*. Turin.

Finley, Moses. 1985. *The Ancient Economy*. London.

Fischel, A. Henry. 1968. "Studies in Cynicism and the Ancient Near East: The Transformation of a Chria." In J. Neusner, ed., *Religions in Antiquity: Essays in Memory of Erwin Ramsdell Goodenough*, 372–411. Leiden.

Fisher, Bonnie. 1987. "A History of the Use of Aesop's Fables as a School Text from the Classical Era through the Nineteenth Century." PhD diss., Indiana University.

Formisano, Marco. 2001. *Tecnica e scrittura: Le letterature tecnico-scientifiche nello spazio letterario tardolatino*. Rome.

Foucault, Michel. 1990. *The History of Sexuality*. Vol. 2, *The Use of Pleasure*. New York.

Fraenkel, E. 1922. *Plautinisches in Plautus*. Berlin.

France, Peter. 1995. "Quintilian and Rousseau: Oratory and Education." *Rhetorica* 13.3: 301–21.

Franits, Wayne E. 1993. *Pargons of Virtue: Women and Domesticity in Seventeenth-Century Dutch Art*. Cambridge.

Frasca, Rosella. 1996a. *Educazione e formazione a Roma*. Bari.

———. 1996b. *La multimedialità della communicazione educativa in Grecia e Roma: Scenari, percorsi*. Bari.

Fuhrmann, Manfred. 1960. *Das systematische Lehrbuch: Ein Beitrag zur Geschichte der Wissenschaften in der Antike*. Göttingen.

Gabba, Emilio. 1989. "Rome and Italy in the Second Century B.C." In *Cambridge Ancient History,* 8: 197–243. 2nd ed. Cambridge.

Gaide, Françoise. 1980. *Avianus, Fables.* Paris.

Garbarino, G. 1973. *Roma e la filosofia greca dalle origini alla fine del II sec. A.C.* Turin.

Garcia y Garcia, Laurentino. 2005. *Pupils, Teachers, and School in Pompeii: Childhood, Youth, and Culture in the Roman Era.* Trans. Anna Maria Poli. Rome.

Garnsey, Peter. 1991. "Child Rearing in Ancient Italy." In D. I. Kertzer and R. P. Saller, eds., *The Family in Italy: From Antiquity to the Present,* 48–66. New Haven, Conn.

Gathorn-Hardie, Jonathan. 1978. *The Phenomenon of the English Public School.* New York.

Gauthier, Xavière. 1980. In Elaine Marks and Isabelle de Courtivon, eds., *New French Feminisms,* 161–64. Amherst, Mass.

Gee, Emma. 2005. "The Prince and the Stars: Germanicus' Translation of Aratus." *Scholia Reviews* n.s. 14: 40.

Gehl, Paul F. 1993. *A Moral Art: Grammar, Society, and Culture in Trecento Florence.* Ithaca, N.Y., and London.

Gelzer, M. 1933. "Römische Politik bei Fabius Pictor." *Hermes* 68: 129.

———. 1936. "Die Unterdrückung der Bacchanalien bei Livius." *Hermes* 71: 275–87.

Gentili, Bruno. 1979. "Some Observations on the Theory and Practice of Translation in Archaic Roman Culture." In *Theatrical Performances in the Ancient World,* 2: 91–105. London Studies in Classical Philology. Amsterdam.

George, Michelle. 1997. "Repopulating the Roman House." In Beryl Rawson and Paul Weaver, eds., *The Roman Family in Italy: Status, Sentiment, Space,* 299–320. Oxford.

Gesche, Petra D. 2001. *Schulunterricht in Babylonien im ersten Jahrtausend v. Chr.* Münster.

Gianotti, Gian Franco. 1989. "I testi nella scuola." In Guglielmo Cavallo, Paolo Fedeli, and Andrea Giardana, eds., *Lo spazio litterario di Roma antica,* vol. 2, *La circolazione del testo,* 421–66. Rome.

Gibbs, Laura. 1999. "Beasts of Burden: The Stories and Morals of Aesop's Fables." PhD diss., University of California, Berkeley.

Gigante, Marcello. 1979. *Civiltà delle forme letterarie nell'antica Pompei.* Naples.

———. 1995. *Philodemus in Italy: The Books from Herculaneum.* Ann Arbor, Mich.

Giroux, H. A. 1983. *Ideology, Culture, and the Process of Schooling.* Philadelphia.

Giuliano, Luca. 1978. *Gioventù e istituzioni nella Roma antica.* Rome.

Gleason, Maude. 1995. *Making Men: Sophists and Self-Presentation in Ancient Rome.* Princeton, N.J.

Goetz, George. 1892. *Corpus glossariorum latinorum.* Vol. 3. Leipzig.

Goldberg, Sander. 1986. *Understanding Terence.* Princeton, N.J.

———. 1995. *Epic in Republican Rome.* New York and London.

———. 2005. *Constructing Literature in the Roman Republic.* Cambridge.

Golden, Mark. 1990. *Children and Childhood in Classical Athens.* Baltimore and London.

———. 1995. M. "Baby Talk and Child Language in Ancient Greece." In Francesco de Martino and Alan H. Sommerstein, eds., *Lo spettacolo delle voci,* 11–34. Bari.

Görler, Woldemar. 1974. *Untersuchungen zu Ciceros Philosophie.* Heidelberg.

Gossen, Gary H. 1976. "Verbal Dueling in Chamula." In Barbara Kirschenblatt-Gimlett, ed., *Speech Play: Research and Resources for Studying Linguistic Creativity,* 121–46. Philadelphia.

Graff, Harvey J. 1979. *The Literacy Myth: Literacy and Social Structure in the Nineteenth-Century City*. New York.
———. 1981. *Literacy and Social Development in the West*. Cambridge.
Grafton, Anthony. 1983. *Joseph Scaliger: A Study in the History of Classical Scholarship*. Vol. 1, *Textual Criticism and Exegesis*. Oxford.
———. 1993. *Joseph Scaliger: A Study in the History of Classical Scholarship*. Vol. 2, *Historical Chronology*. Oxford.
Granatelli, Rossella. 1995. "M. Fabio Quintiliano 'Institutio oratoria' II 1–10: Struttura e problemi interpretative." *Rhetorica* 13.2: 137–60.
Gratwick, A. S., ed. and trans. 1987. *Terence, The Brothers*. Warminster.
Green-Pedersen, Niels J. 1984. *The Tradition of the "Topica" in the Middle Ages*. Munich.
Griffith, Mark. 2001. "Public and Private in Early Greek Institutions of Education." In Too 2001, 23–84.
Grilli, Alberto. 1979. "Educazione urbana ed educazione rustica in Terenzio." In *La città antica come fatto di cultura: Atti del convegno di Como e Bellagio, 16–19 giugno 1979*, 23–34. Como.
Grillo, Antonino. 1982. *Critica del testo: Imitazione e narratologia; Ricerche sull'Ilias latina e la tradizione epica classica*. Florence.
Gruen, Erich. 1984. *The Hellenistic World and the Coming of Rome*. Berkeley.
———. 1990. *Studies in Greek Culture and Roman Policy*. Leiden.
———. 1992. *Culture and Identity in Republican Rome*. Ithaca, N.Y.
Gueraud, O., and P. Jouguet, eds. 1938. *Un livre d'écolier*. Cairo.
Gunderson, Erik. 2000. *Staging Masculinity: The Rhetoric of Performance in the Roman World*. Ann Arbor, Mich.
———. 2003. *Declamation, Paternity, and Roman Identity: Authority and the Rhetorical Self*. Cambridge.
Gwynn, Aubrey. 1926. *Roman Education from Cicero to Quintilian*. Oxford.
Haarhoff, T. J. 1958. *Schools of Gaul: A Study of Pagan and Christian Education in the Last Century of the Western Empire*. Johannesburg.
Habinek, Thomas. 1998. *The Politics of Latin Literature*. Princeton, N.J.
Hadot, Ilsetraut. 1984. *Arts libéraux et philosophie dans la pensée antique*. Paris.
Hadot, Pierre. 1995. *Philosophy as a Way of Life*. Oxford.
Hagendahl, H. 1967. *Augustine and the Latin Classics*. Göteborg.
Håkanson, L. 1982. *Quintilianus, Marcus Fabius, Declamationes XIX Maiores*. Stuttgart.
Hales, Shelley. 2003. *The Roman House and Social Identity*. Cambridge.
Hallett, Judith P. 1993. "Feminist Theory, Historical Periods, Literary Canons, and the Study of Greco-Roman Antiquity." In Rabinowitz and Richlin 1993, 44–72.
Halperin, David, John Winkler, and Froma Zeitlin, eds. 1990. *Before Sexuality: The Construction of Erotic Experience in the Ancient Greek World*. Princeton, N.J.
Hamilton, David. 1979. *Towards a Theory of Schooling*. London, New York, and Philadelphia.
Hanson, Ann Ellis. 1990. "The Medical Writers' Woman." In Halperin et al. 1990, 309–38.
Harding, Harold F. 1961. "Quintilian's Witnesses." In Raymond F. Howes, ed., *Historical Studies of Rhetoric and Rhetoricians*. 90–106. Ithaca, N.Y.
Harris, W. V. 1989. *Ancient Literacy*. Cambridge, Mass.
Hayes, Walter M. 1959. "Tiberius and the Future." *CJ* 55: 2–8.

Hazelton, Richard. 1957. "The Christianization of 'Cato': The Disticha Catonis in the Light of Late Medieval Commentaries." *Medieval Studies* 19: 157–73.

———. 1960. "Chaucer and Cato." *Speculum* 35: 357–80.

Hedrick, Charles W., Jr. 1999. "Democracy and the Athenian Epigraphical Habit." *Hesperia* 68.3: 387–439.

Hein, Guntharius. 1916. "Quaestiones Plutarches: Quo ordine Plutarchus nonnulla scripta moralia composuerit, agitur." Diss., Berlin.

Helbig, W. 1868. *Wandgemälde der vom Vesuv verschütteten Städte Campaniens.* Leipzig.

Hellegouarc'h, J. 1963. *Le vocabulaire latin des relations et des partis politiques sous la République.* Paris.

Henderson, John. 2001. *Telling Tales on Caesar: Roman Stories from Phaedrus.* Oxford.

Hesseling, D. C. 1892–93. "On Waxen Tablets with Fables of Babrius." *JHS* 13: 293–314.

Hettner, Felix. 1903. *Illustrierter Führer durch das Provincialmuseum in Trier.* Trier.

Hillscher, A. 1892. "Hominum litteratorum graecorum ante Tiberii mortem in urbe Roma commoratorum historia critica." *Jahrbuch für classische Philologie,* Suppl. 18.

Hock, Ronald F., and Edward N. O'Neill. 1986. *The Chreia in Ancient Rhetoric.* Atlanta.

Hodge, Robert, and Gunther Kress. 1993. *Language and Ideology.* London and New York.

Hohmann, Hanns. 2001. "Stasis." In Thomas O. Sloane, ed., *Encyclopedia of Rhetoric,* 741. Oxford.

Holden, H. A. 1894. *Plutarch's Life of Pericles.* New York.

Holtz, L. 1971. "Tradition et diffusion de l'oeuvre grammaticale de Pompée, commentateur de Donat." *RPh* 45: 48–83.

Holzberg, Niklas. 2001. *Die antike Fabel: Eine Einführung.* Darmstadt.

Hopkins, Keith. 1978. *Conquerors and Slaves.* Sociological Studies in Roman History 1. Cambridge.

Horna, K. 1935. "Gnome, Gnomendichtung, Gnomologium." *RE* Supplementband 6: 74–87.

Hus, Alain. 1965. *Docere et lets mots de la famille de docere: Étude de sémantique latine.* Paris.

Ingenkamp, H. G. 1971. *Plutarchs Schriften über die Heilung der Seele.* Göttingen.

Instinsky, H. U. 1971. "Zur Echtheitsfrage der Brieffragmente der Cornelia, Mutter der Gracchen." *Chiron* 1: 177–89.

Ireland, Robert. 1990. *Iulii Frontini Strategemata.* Leipzig.

Irvine, Martin. 1994. *The Making of Textual Culture: "Grammatica" and Literary Theory, 350–1100.* Cambridge.

Jaeger, Werner. 1948. *Paideia: The Ideals of Greek Culture.* Trans. G. Highet. 2 vols. Oxford.

Jahn, O. 1850. "Über römische Encyclopäden." *Berichte der Königlich Sächsischen Gesellschaft der Wissenschaften, Phil.-hist. Klasse* 2: 263 ff.

Jameson, Michael. 1990. "Private Space and the Greek City." In Oswyn Murray and Simon Price, eds., *The Greek City from Homer to Alexander,* 171–95. Oxford.

Janson, T. 1964. *Latin Prose Prefaces.* Stockholm.

Jocelyn, H. D. 1969. "The Poet Cn. Naevius, P. Cornelius Scipio, and Q. Caecilius Metellus." *Antichthon* 3: 32–47.

Johnson, R. 1966. "Quintilian's Place in European Education." In Maurice Kelley, ed., *For Service to Classical Studies: Essays in Honour of Francis Letters,* 79–101. Melbourne.

Johnson, W. A. 2000. "Toward a Sociology of Reading in Classical Antiquity." *AJP* 121: 593–627.

Johnson, W. R. 1971. *Luxuriance and Economy: Cicero and the Alien Style*. Berkeley.

Johnstone, Steve. 1994. "Virtuous Toil, Vicious Work: Xenophon on Aristocratic Style." *CP* 89: 219–40.

Joshel, Sandra. 1992. *Work, Identity, and Legal Status at Rome*. Norman, Okla., and London.

Judge, Harry G. 1982. "The English Public School: History and Society." *History of Education Quarterly* 22.4: 513–24.

Just, Marcel Adam, and Patricia A. Carpenter. 1987. *The Psychology of Reading and Language Comprehension*. Boston.

Kaster, Robert. 1988. *Guardians of Language: The Grammarian and Society in Late Antiquity*. Berkeley.

———. 1995. *De grammaticis et rhetoribus, C. Suetonius Tranquillus*. Oxford.

———. 2001. "Controlling Reason: Declamation in Rhetorical Education at Rome." In Too 2001, 317–37.

Kennedy, George. 1962. "An Estimate of Quintilian." *AJP* 83: 130–46.

———. 1969. *Quintilian*. New York.

———. 1972. *The Art of Rhetoric in the Roman World, 300 B.C.–A.D. 300*. Princeton, N.J.

———. 1991. *On Rhetoric: A Theory of Civic Discourse*. New York.

———. 2003. *Progymnasmata: Greek Textbooks of Prose Composition and Rhetoric*. Atlanta.

Kennell, Nigel M. 1995. *The Gymnasium of Virtue: Education and Culture in Ancient Sparta*. Chapel Hill, N.C., and London.

Kleijwegt, Marc. 1991. *Ancient Youth: The Ambiguity of Youth and the Absence of Adolescence in Greco-Roman Society*. Amsterdam.

Kleingünther, A. 1933. *ΠΡΩΤΟΣ ΕΥΡΕΤΗΣ: Untersuchungen zur Geschichte einer Fragestellung*. Berlin.

Konstantinovic, Isabelle. 1989. *Montaigne et Plutarch*. Geneva.

Kramer, Noah. 1958. "Education" and "Schooldays." In *History Begins at Sumer*, 35–45. London.

———. 1963. "Education: The Sumerian School." In *The Sumerians*, 229–48. Chicago.

Kress, Gunther. 1994. *Learning to Write*. London.

Krostenko, Brian. 2000. "Beyond (Dis)belief: Rhetorical Form and Religious Symbol in Cicero's *De divinatione*." *TAPA* 130: 353–91.

Krueger, Derek. 1993. "Diogenes the Cynic among the Fourth-Century Fathers." *Vigiliae Christianae* 47: 29–49.

Kubiak, David P. 1981. "The Orion Episode in Cicero's *Aratea*." *CJ* 77: 12–22.

Kühnert, Friedmar. 1960. *Allgemeinbildung und Fachbildung in der Antike*. Berlin.

Kullmann, Wolfgang, Jochen Althoff, and Markus Asper, eds. 1998. *Gattungen wissenschaftlicher Literatur in der Antike*. Tübingen.

Kurke, Leslie V. 1999. *Coins, Bodies, Games, and Gold*. Princeton, N.J.

Lamberton, Robert. 2001. *Plutarch*. New Haven, Conn., and London.

Lanzoni, F. 1925. "Le leggende di San Cassiano d'Imola." *Didaskalion* n.s. 3.2: 1–44.

Laurand, L. 1965. *Études sur le style des discours de Cicéron*. Amsterdam.

Laurence, Ray. 1996. *Roman Pompeii: Space and Society*. London.

Leeman, A. D. 1963. *Orationis ratio*. Amsterdam.

Legras, Bernard. 1998. *Éducation et culture dans le monde grec (VIIIe–Ier siècle avant J.C.)*. Paris.

Lehmann, Paul. 1959. "Die *Institutio oratoria* des Quintilianus im Mittelalter." *Erforschung der Mittelalters* 2: 1–28.

Leigh, Matthew. 2004. "Quintilian on the Emotions (*Institutio oratoria* 6 Preface and 1–2)." *JRS* 94: 122–40.

Lejeune, M. 1952. "Problèmes de philologie vénete: VII–X." *RPH* 26: 192–218.

Letta, C. 1984. "L'Italia dei mores romani nelle *Origines* di Catone." *Athenaeum* 62: 3–30 and 416–39.

Leyerle, Blake. 1997. "Appealing to Children." *JECS* 5: 243–70.

Logie, John. 2003. " 'I Have No Predecessor to Guide My Steps': Quintilian and Roman Authorship." *Rhetoric Review* 22.4: 353–73.

López, Aurora. 1998. *Modelando con palabras: La elaboración de las imágenes ejemplares de Catón y Cornelia.* Madrid.

López, Jorge Fernández. 1999. *Retórica, humanismo y filología: Quintiliano y Lorenzo Valla.* Logroño.

Loraux, Nicole. 1982. "Ponos: Sur quelques difficultés de la peine comme nom du travail." *Annali del Seminario di Studi del Mundo Classico, Archeologia e Storia Antica* 4: 171–92.

Luke, Alan. 1988. *Literacy, Textbooks, and Ideology.* London and Philadelphia.

———. 1989. "Open and Closed Texts: The Ideological/Semantic Analysis of Textbook Narratives." *Journal of Pragmatics* 13: 53–80.

MacMullen, Ramsay. 1966. *Enemies of the Roman Order: Treason, Unrest, and Alienation in the Empire.* Cambridge, Mass.

———. 1990. *Changes in the Roman Empire: Essays in the Ordinary.* Princeton, N.J.

———. 1991. "Hellenizing the Romans (2nd Century B.C.)." *Historia* 40: 419–38.

Manfredini, A. 1976. "L'editto De coercendis rhetoribus latinis del 92 a.c." *SDHI* 42: 99–138.

Mann, Jill. 1996. "Beast Epic and Fable." In F. A. C. Mantello and A. G. Rigg, eds., *Medieval Latin: An Introduction and Bibliographical Guide,* 556–61. Washington, D.C.

Marichal, R. 1992. " Les tablettes à écrire dans le monde romain." In E. Lalou, ed., *Les tablettes à écrire de l'antiquité à l'époque moderne,* 165–85. Bibliologia 12. Turnhout.

Mariotti, S. 1952. *Livio Andronico e la traduzione artistica: Saggio critico ed edizione dei frammenti dell'Odyssea.* Pubblicazioni dell'Università di Urbino. Serie di Lettere e Filosofia 1. Milan.

Marrou, H.-I. 1948/1956. *A History of Education in Antiquity.* Trans. G. Lamb. London.

———. 1958. *St. Augustin et la fin de la culture antique.* Paris.

———. 1969. "Les arts libéraux dans l'antiquité classique." In *Arts libéraux et philosophie au Moyen Age: Actes du Quatrième Congrès International de Philosophie Médiévale, 27 août– 2 sept. 1967,* 5–33. Montreal and Paris.

McEwen, Indra Kagis. 2003. *Vitruvius: Writing the Body of Architecture.* Cambridge, Mass.

McGuiness, Lucy. 1999. "Quintilian and Medieval Pedagogy: The Twelfth–Century Witness Stuttgart, Würtembergische Landesbibliothek, Theol, Octavo 68." *Bulletin du Cange: Archivum Latinitatis Medii Aevi* 57: 191–259.

McNelis, Charles. 2002. "Greek Grammarians and Roman Society during the Early Empire: Statius' Father and His Contemporaries." *CA* 21: 67–94.

Merton, Robert K. 1957. *Social Theory and Social Structure.* Glencoe, Ill.

Meurant, Alain. 2004. "Mère charnelle et mères de substitution à la naissance de Rome: Quelques aspects d'une complémentarité symbolique." In Véronique Dasen, ed., *Naissance et petite enfance dans l'antiquité*, 325–38. Fribourg.

Michel, C. 1900. *Recueil d'inscriptions grecques.* Brussels.

Mohler, S. L. 1940. "Slave Education in the Roman Empire." *TAPA* 70: 262–80.

Momigliano, Arnaldo. 1971. *Alien Wisdom: The Limits of Hellenization.* Cambridge.

Morford, Mark P. O. 1967. "Ancient and Modern in Cicero's Poetry." *CP* 62.2: 112–16.

Morgan, Teresa. 1998. *Literate Education in the Hellenistic and Roman Worlds.* Cambridge.

Mossman, Judith, 1997. "Plutarch's Dinner of the Seven Wise Men and Its Place in *Symposion* Literature." In Judith Mossman, ed., *Plutarch and His Intellectual World: Essays on Plutarch,* 119–40. London.

Mountford, James. 1964. "Music and the Romans." *Bulletin of the John Rylands Library* 47: 198–211.

Muir, James R. 1998. "The History of Educational Ideas and the Credibility of Philosophy of Education." *Educational Philosophy and Theory* 30.1: 7–25.

Murphy, James. J. 1990. "Quintilian's Influence on the Teaching of Speaking and Writing in the Middle Ages and Renaissance." In Richard Leo Enos. ed., *Oral and Written Communication: Historical Approaches,* 158–83. Newbury Park, Calif.

———, ed. 2001. *A Short History of Writing Instruction: From Ancient Greece to Modern America.* Mahwah, N.J.

Murray, P., ed. 1989. *Genius: The History of an Idea.* Oxford.

Mynors, R. A. B., ed. 1964. *Panegyrici latini.* Oxford.

Nadeau, Ray. 1959. "Classical Systems of Stases in Greek: Hermagoras to Hermogenes." *GRBS* 2: 53–71.

Narducci, Emanuele. 1989. "Le risonanze del potere." In Guglielmo Cavallo, Paolo Fedeli, and Andrea Giardana, eds., *Lo spazio litterario di Roma antica,* 2: 533–77. Rome.

Nettleship, H. 1886. "The Study of Latin Grammar among the Romans in the First Century A.D." *Journal of Philology* 15 (1886): 189–214.

Nevett, Lisa. 1997. "Perceptions of Domestic Space in Roman Italy." In Beryl Rawson and Paul Weaver, eds., *The Roman Family in Italy,* 281–98. Oxford.

———. 1999. *House and Society in the Ancient Greek World.* Cambridge.

Newton, Adam Zachary. 1995. *Narrative Ethics.* Cambridge, Mass.

Nietzsche, Friedrich. 1989. *Friedrich Nietzsche on Rhetoric and Language.* Ed. and trans. Sander L. Gilman, Carole Blair, and David J. Parent. Oxford and New York.

Nightingale, A. W. 2001. "Education in Plato's *Republic* and Aristotle's *Politics.*" In Too 2001, 133–73.

Norden, Eduard. 1918. *Antike Kunstprosa.* 3rd ed. Leipzig.

Norman, Donald A. 1982. *Learning and Memory.* San Francisco.

North, Helen. 1952. "The Use of Poetry in the Training of the Ancient Orator." *Traditio* 8: 1–33.

Ong, Walter J. 1971. "Latin Language Study as a Renaissance Puberty Rite." In *Rhetoric, Romance, and Technology: Studies in the Interaction of Expression and Culture,* 113–41. Ithaca, N.Y.

Opsomer, Jan. 1997. "Favorinus versus Epictetus on the Philosophical Heritage of Plutarch: A Debate on Epistemology." In Judith Mossman, ed., *Plutarch and His Intellectual World: Essays on Plutarch,* 17–39. London.

Orme, Nicholas. 2001. *Medieval Children.* New Haven, Conn.

Osborne, R., and S. Hornblower, eds. 1994. *Ritual, Finance, Politics: Athenian Democratic Accounts Presented to David Lewis.* Oxford.

Padley, G. A. 1985. *Grammatical Theory in Western Europe, 1500–1700.* Cambridge.

Pallotino, M. 1984. *Etruscologia.* Milan.

———. 1991. *A History of Earliest Italy.* Ann Arbor, Mich.

Palmer, R. E. A. 1990. "Studies of the Northern Campus Martius in Ancient Rome." *TAPS* 80.2: 42–45.

Pandolfini, Maristella, and Aldo L. Prosdocimi. 1990. *Alfabeteri e insegnamento della scrittura in Etruria e nell'Italia antica.* Florence.

Papageorgius, P. 1888. *Scholia in Sophoclis tragoedia vetera.* Leipzig.

Patillon, Michel. 1997. *Aelius Theon, Progymnasmata.* Paris.

Pavolini, Carlo. 1987. "Lo scavo di Piazza Celimontana: Un'indagine nel *Caput Africae*." In *L'urbs: Espace urbain et histoire,* 653–85. Collection de l'École Française de Rome 98. Rome.

Pelling, Christopher. 2002. "Childhood and Personality in Greek Biography." In *Plutarch and History,* 301–38. London.

Perry, B. E. 1952. *Aesopica.* Urbana, Ill.

Peterson, Carole, and Allyssa McCabe. 1983. *Developmental Psycholinguistics: Three Ways of Looking at a Child's Narrative.* New York and London.

Peterson, W. 1891. *Quintiliani Institutionis oratoriae liber X.* Oxford.

Petrochilos, N. 1974. *Roman Attitudes to the Greeks.* Athens.

Phillips, C. R., III. 1991. "Poetry before the Ancient City: Zorzetti and the Case of Rome." *CJ* 86: 382–89.

Piaget, Jean. 1950. *The Psychology of Intelligence.* London.

Platner, S. B., and T. Ashby. 1927. *A Topographical Dictionary of Ancient Rome.* London.

Pohlenz, M. 1955. *Die Stoa.* Göttingen.

Polla-Mattiot, Nicoletta. 1990. "Il silenzio nella τέχνη ῥητορική: Analisi della *Contr.* 2.7 di Seneca il Vecchio." In Adriano Pennacini, ed., *Retorica della communicazione nelle letterature classiche,* 233–74. Bologna.

Poncelet, R. 1957. *Cicéron traducteur de Platon.* Paris.

Possanza, Mark D. 2004. *Translating the Heavens: Aratus, Germanicus, and the Poetics of Latin Translation.* New York.

Postgate, J. P. 1919. "Seneca and Phaedrus." *CR* 33: 22–24.

Potter, David. 1994. *Prophets and Emperors.* Cambridge, Mass.

Powell, J. G. F. 1995. "Cicero's Translations from Greek." In *Cicero the Philosopher: Twelve Papers,* 273–300. Oxford.

Preisendanz, K. 1930. "Die griechischen und lateinischen Zaubertafeln." *Arch. für Papyrus Forschung* 9: 11 ff.

———. 1933. "Die griechischen und lateinischen Zaubertafeln." *Arch. für Papyrus Forschung* 11: 153 ff.

Prosdocimi, Aldo L. 1989. "Le lingue dominanti e i linguaggi locali." In Guglielmo Cavallo,

Paolo Fedeli, and Andrea Giardana, eds., *Lo spazio litterario di Roma antica,* vol. 2, *La circolazione del testo,* 20–28. Rome.

Quirke, S., and J. Spencer. 1992. *The British Museum Book of Ancient Egypt.* London.

Rabinowitz, Nancy Sorkin, and Amy Richlin, eds. 1993. *Feminist Theory and the Classics.* New York and London.

Ramage, Edwin. 1959. "The *De urbanitate* of Domitius Marsus." *CP* 54: 250–55.

Rathofer, Clemens. 1986. *Cicero's "Brutus" als literarisches Paradigma eines Auctoritas-Verhältnisses.* Frankfurt am Main.

Rawson, Beryl. 2003. *Children and Childhood in Roman Italy.* Oxford.

Rawson, Beryl, and Paul Weaver, eds. 1997. *The Roman Family in Italy: Status, Sentiment, Space.* Oxford.

Rawson, Elizabeth. 1983. *Cicero: A Portrait.* Ithaca, N.Y.

———. 1985. *Intellectual Life in the Late Roman Republic.* London.

Ray, J. D. 1986. "The Emergence of Writing in Egypt." *World Archeology* 17.3: 307–16.

Reay, Brendon. 2005. "Agriculture, Writing, and Cato's Aristocratic Self-Fashioning." *CA* 24: 331–61.

Reiff, Arno. 1959. *Interpretatio, imitatio, aemulatio: Begriff und Vorstellung der literarischen Abhängigkeit bei den Römern.* Würzburg.

Reinhardt, Tobias, and Michael Winterbottom, eds. 2006. *Quintilian, Institutio oratoria, Book 2.* Oxford.

Rémondon, Roger. 1964. "Problèmes de bilinguisme dans l'Égypte lagide (U.P.Z. I, 148)." *Chronique d'Égypte* 39: 126–46.

Reuter, Augustus. 1887. "De causis corruptae eloquentiae." Diss., Bratislava.

Reynolds, L. D., ed. 1983. *Texts and Transmissions: A Survey of the Latin Classics.* Oxford.

Reynolds, Suzanne. 1996. *Medieval Reading: Grammar, Rhetoric, and the Classical Text.* Cambridge.

Richardson, John G., ed. 1986. *Handbook of Theory and Research for the Sociology of Education.* New York.

Richardson, L., Jr. 1992. *A New Topographical Dictionary of Ancient Rome.* Baltimore and London.

Riché, Pierre. 1975. *Education and Culture in the Barbarian West, Sixth through Eighth Centuries.* Trans. John Contreni. Columbia, S.C.

Richlin, Amy. 1992. *The Garden of Priapus: Sexuality and Aggression in Roman Humor.* New York and Oxford.

———. 1993. "The Ethnographer's Dilemma and the Dream of a Lost Golden Age." In Rabinowitz and Richlin 1993, 272–303.

Risselada, Rodie. 1993. *Imperatives and Other Directive Expressions in Latin: A Study in the Pragmatics of a Dead Language.* Amsterdam.

Robb, Kevin. 1994. *Literacy and Paideia in Ancient Greece.* Oxford.

Robbins, R. H. 1998. "Methods of Teaching Grammar in the Middle Ages: *Partitiones/Schedographia.*" *Studies in Medieval and Renaissance Teaching* 6.2: 69–78.

Roberts, Michael. 1985. *Biblical Epic and Rhetorical Paraphrase in Late Antiquity.* Liverpool.

———. 1993. *Poetry and the Cult of the Martyrs: The "Liber peristephanon" of Prudentius.* Ann Arbor, Mich.

Roger, M. 1905. *L'enseignement des lettres classiques d'Ausone à Alcuin: Introduction à l'histoire des écoles carolingiennes.* Paris.

Romaine, Suzanne. 1984. *The Language of Children and Adolescents: The Acquisition of Communicative Competence.* Oxford.

Roos, Paolo. 1984. *Sentenza e proverbio nell'antichità e i 'Distichi di Catone': Il testo latino e i volgarizzamenti italiani.* Brescia.

Rosen, Ralph M., and Ineke Sluiter, eds. 2003. *Andreia: Studies in Manliness and Courage in Classical Antiquity.* Leiden and Boston.

Rosenstock, Bruce. 1992. "Fathers and Sons: Irony in the *Cratylus.*" *Arethusa* 25: 385–417.

Rouse, Richard H., and Mary A. Rouse. 1989. "Wax Tablets." *Language & Communication* 9.2–3: 175–91.

Rouselle, Aline. 1988. *Porneia: On Desire and the Body in Antiquity.* Cambridge, Mass., and Oxford.

Rowland, Robert J., Jr. 1972. "Cicero and the Greek World." *TAPA* 103: 451–61.

Russell, D. A. 1983. *Greek Declamation.* Cambridge.

Saenger, Paul. 1997. *Space between Words: The Origins of Silent Reading.* Stanford.

Saller, Richard. 1980. "Anecdotes as Historical Evidence for the Principate." *Greece & Rome* 27: 69–83.

———. 1994. *Patriarchy, Property, and Death in the Roman Family.* Cambridge.

Saller, Richard, and Brent Shaw. 1984. "Tombstones and Roman Family Relations in the Principate: Cicilians, Soldiers, and Slaves." *JRS* 74: 124–56.

Sanders, E. P. 1985. *Jesus and Judaism.* Philadelphia.

Scaffai, Marco. 1982. *Baebii Italici Ilias latina: Introduzione, edizione critica, traduzione italiano, e commento.* Bologna.

Scaliger, Joseph. 1605. *Disticha Catonis.* Paris.

Schlegel, Catherine. 2000. "Horace and His Fathers: *Satires* 1.4 and 1.6." *AJP* 121: 93–119.

Schmidt, P. L. 1975. "Die Anfänge der institutionellen Rhetorik im Rom." In Eckard Lefèvre, ed., *Monumentum Chiloniense: Studien zur augusteischen Zeit; Kieler Festrshrift für Erich Burke,* 183–216. Amsterdam.

Schmitter, Peter. 1972. "Die hellenistische Erziehung im Spiegel der Νέα Κωμῳδία und der Fabula Palliata." Diss., Rheinischen Friedrich-Wilhelms-Universität.

Schmitz, Thomas. 1997. *Bildung und Macht: Zur socialen und politischen Funktion der zweiten Sophistik in der griechischen Welt der Kaiserzeit.* Munich.

Schoeck, R. J., ed. 1966. *Roger Ascham, The Scholemaster.* Don Mills, Ontario.

Schönberger, Otto, and Eva Schönberger, eds. and trans. 2004. *Lucius Annaeus Seneca der Ältere: Sentenzen, Einteilungen, Färbungen und Redelehrern.* Würzburg.

Schussel, O. 1933. "Die Einteilung der Chrie bei Quintilian." *Hermes* 68: 245–48.

Sciarrino, Enrica. 2004. "Putting Cato the Censor's *Origines* in Its Place." *CA* 23: 323–57.

Scott, Dominic. 1995. *Recollection and Experience: Plato's Theory of Learning and Its Successors.* Cambridge.

Scruton, Roger. 1990. "Ideologically Speaking." In Christopher Ricks and Leonard Michaels, eds., *The State of the Language,* 118–19. London and Boston.

Severy, Beth. 2003. *Augustus and the Family at the Birth of the Roman Empire.* New York and London.

Sherman, W. H. 1995. *John Dee: The Politics of Reading and Writing in the English Renaissance*. Amherst, Mass.

Shorey, Paul. 1909. "*Physis, Melete, Episteme.*" *TAPA* 40: 185–201.

Sickinger, J. P. 1999. *Public Records and Archives in Classical Athens*. Chapel Hill, N.C.

Simpson, William K. 1973. "Satire of the Trades." In *The Literature of Ancient Egypt*, 329–36. New Haven, Conn., and London.

Skutsch, F. 1905. "Dicta Catonis." *RE* 5: 358–66.

Skutsch, Otto. 1985. *The Annals of Quintus Ennius*. Oxford.

Sloane, Thomas O., ed. 2001. *Encyclopedia of Rhetoric*. Oxford.

Soubiron, Jean. 1973. "L'art de la traduction." In *Cicéron, Aratea: Fragments poétiques*, 87–95. Paris.

Stadter, Philip. 1999. *A Commentary on Plutarch's "Pericles."* Chapel Hill, N.C.

Steinby, Eva Margareta, ed. 1994–2001. *Lexicon topographicum urbis Romae*. 6 vols. Rome.

Stewart, Susan. 1979. *Nonsense: Aspects of Intertextuality in Folklore and Literature*. Baltimore and London.

Stock, Brian. 1996. *Augustine the Reader: Meditation, Self-Knowledge, and the Ethics of Interpretation*. Cambridge.

Stone, Gregory P. 1971. "The Play of Little Children." In R. E. Heron and Brian Sutton-Smith, eds., *Child's Play*, 23–31. New York.

Stroh, Wilfred. 2003. "Declamatio." In Bianca-Jeanette Schröder, ed., *Studium declamatorium: Untersuchungen zu Schulübungen und Prunkreden von der Antike bus zur Neuzeit*, 5–34. Munich and Leipzig.

Stump, Eleonore, ed. and trans. 1988. *Boethius's In Ciceronis "Topica."* Ithaca, N.Y.

Sullivan, Shirley D. 2000. *Euripides' Use of Psychological Terminology*. Montreal.

Sumner, G. V. 1973. *The Orators in Cicero's "Brutus": Prosopography and Chronology*. Toronto.

Sundwall, Gavin A. 1996. "Ammianus Geographicus." *AJP* 117: 619–43.

Suolahti, Jaakko. 1963. *The Roman Censors: A Study on Social Structure*. Helsinki.

Sussman, Lewis A. 1978. *The Elder Seneca*. Leiden.

———. 1987. *The Major Declamations Ascribed to Quintilian*. Frankfurt am Main.

Swain, Simon. 1996. *Hellenism and Empire: Language, Classicism, and Power in the Greek World, A.D. 50–250*. Oxford.

Tabacco, R. 1985. "Il tiranno nelle declamazione di scuola in lingua Latina." *Memorie della Accademia delle Scienze di Torino, II*, ser. 5, 9.1–2: 1–141.

Talbert, Richard J. A. 1984. *The Senate of Imperial Rome*. Princeton, N.J.

Thomas, R. 1989. *Oral Tradition and Written Record in Classical Athens*. Cambridge.

Throop, C. Jason, and Keith M. Murphy. 2002. "Bourdieu and Phenomenology: A Critical Assessment." *Anthropological Theory* 2: 185–207.

Thulin, C. O. 1909. *Die etruskische Disciplin*. Göteburg.

Too, Yun Lee. 2000. *The Pedagogical Contract: The Economies of Teaching and Learning in the Ancient World*. Ann Arbor, Mich.

———, ed. 2001. *Education in Greek and Roman Antiquity*. Leiden.

Too, Yun Lee, and Niall Livingstone, eds. 1998. *Pedagogy and Power: Rhetorics of Classical Learning*. Cambridge.

Traina, Alfonso. 1970. *Vortit barbare: Le traduzioni poetiche da Livio Andronico a Cicerone*. Rome.

Treggiari, Susan. 1969. *Roman Freedmen during the Late Republic*. Oxford.

———. 1998. "Home and Forum: Cicero between 'Public' and 'Private.'" *TAPA* 128: 1–23.

Tucker, Nicholas. 1981. *The Child and the Book*. London.

Ullman, B. L. 1973. "Petrarch's Favorite Books." Chap. 6 in *Studies in the Italian Renaissance*, 113–33. Rome.

van Dijk, Gert-Jan. 1997. *Αἶνοι, Λόγοι, Μῦθοι: Fables in Archaic, Classical, and Hellenistic Greek Literature, with a Study of the Theory and Terminology of the Genre*. Leiden, New York, and Cologne.

van Geytenbeek, A. C. 1962. *Musonius Rufus and Greek Diatribe*. Assen.

van Leeuwen, L. 1894. "De codicillis nuper bibliotheca Ludguno-Batavae donatis." *Mnem.* 22: 223.

Vasaly, Ann. 1987. "Personality and Power: Livy's Depiction of the Appii Claudii in the First Pentad." *TAPA* 117: 203–26.

Veblen, Thorstein. 1899. *The Theory of the Leisure Class*. New York.

Vischer, R. 1965. *Das einfache Leben*. Göttingen.

Vlastos, Gregory. 1991. *Socrates, Ironist and Moral Philosopher*. Ithaca, N.Y.

von Fritz, Kurt. 1949. "Ancient Instruction in 'Grammar' according to Quintilian." *AJP* 70: 337–66.

von Gaertringen, F. Hiller, ed. 1906. *Inschriften von Priene*. Berlin.

Vössing, Konrad. 1997. *Schule und Bildung im Nordafrika der römischen Kaiserzeit*. Brussels.

Walbank, F. W. 1979. *A Historical Commentary on Polybius*. Oxford.

Wallace-Hadrill, Andrew. 1994. *Houses and Society in Pompeii and Herculaneum*. Princeton, N.J.

———. 1998. "The Social Structure of the Roman House." *Papers of the British School at Rome* 56: 43–97.

Wallace-Hadrill, Andrew, and John Rich, eds. 1991. *City and Country in the Ancient World*. London and New York.

Walsh, P. G. 1961. *Livy: His Historical Aims and Methods*. Cambridge.

Walzer, Arthur E. 2006. "Moral Philosophy and Rhetoric in the Institutes: Quintilian on Honor and Expediency." *Rhetoric Society Quarterly* 36.3: 263–80.

Waquet, Françoise. 2001. *Latin or the Empire of a Sign from the Sixteenth to the Nineteenth Centuries*. Trans. John Howe. London.

Ward, Alan. 1970. "The Early Relationships between Cicero and Pompey until 80 B.C." *Phoenix* 24.2: 119–29.

Wardle, D. 1998. *Valerius Maximus: Memorable Deeds and Sayings, Book I*. Oxford.

Wardman, Alan. 1974. *Plutarch's Lives*. Berkeley.

Watson, Patricia A. 1995. *Ancient Stepmothers: Myth, Misogyny, and Reality*. Leiden.

Webb, Ruth. 2001. "The *Progymnasmata* as Practice." In Too 2001, 289–316. Leiden.

Wells, David A. 1994. "Fatherly Advice: The Precepts of 'Gregorius,' and Gurnemanz and the School Tradition of the 'Disticha Catonis.'" *Frühmittelalterliche Studien* 28: 296–332.

Westaway, K. M. 1922. *The Educational Theory of Plutarch*. London.

Whitmarsh, Tim. 2001. *Greek Literature and the Roman Empire*. Oxford.

Wiedemann, Thomas. 1989. *Adults and Children in the Roman Empire*. New Haven, Conn.

Wightman, Edith M. 1971. *Roman Trier and the Treveri*. New York.

Wilkins, A. S. 1905. *Roman Education*. Cambridge.

Wille, G. 1967. *Musica romana: Die Bedeutung der Musik im Leben der Römer*. Amsterdam.

Williams, G. W. 1968. *Tradition and Originality in Roman Poetry*. Oxford.

Winterbottom, Michael. 1964. "Quintilian and the *vir bonus*." *JRS* 54: 90–97.

———. 1967. "Fifteenth-Century Manuscripts of Quintilian." *CQ* 17: 339–69.

———. 1974. *The Elder Seneca, Declamations*. 2 vols. Cambridge, Mass., and London.

———. 1984. *The Minor Declamations Ascribed to Quintilian*. Berlin and New York.

Wiseman, T. P. 1995. *Remus: A Roman Myth*. Cambridge.

Woodbury, L. 1978. "The Gratitude of the Locrian Maiden: Pindar, *Pyth.* 2.18–20." *TAPA* 108: 285–99.

Woodhead, A. G. 1981. *The Study of Greek Inscriptions*. 2nd ed. Oxford.

Woodside, M., St. A. 1942. "Vespasian's Patronage of Education and the Arts." *TAPA* 73: 123–29.

Wyttenbach, Daniel Albert. 1820. *Opera moralia*. Vol. 6. Leipzig.

Yegül, Fikret. 1989. *Baths and Bathing in Classical Antiquity*. New York.

Zalateo, G. 1961. "Papiri scolastici." *Aegyptus* 41: 161–235.

Zanker, Paul. 1988. *The Power of Images*. Trans. Alan Shapiro. Ann Arbor, Mich.

Ziebarth, Erich. 1913. *Aus der antiken Schule*. Bonn.

Zorzetti, Nevio. 1990. "The *Carmina Convivalia*." In Oswynn Murray, ed., *Sympotica: A Symposium on the Symposion*, 289–307. Oxford.

———. 1991. "Poetry and the Ancient City: The Case of Rome." *CJ* 86: 311–29.

INDEX

Abbott, Norman, 218n1, 220nn13,19; on *nous*, 222n40; on philosophical education, 225n66
abecedaria, Etruscan, 19, 20, 207n44
Achilles, education of, 25, 208n5
adolescence: as *aetas perfecta,* 229n30; assumption of roles in, 180; bodies during, 103; in *De liberis educandis,* 76; self-building during, 32, 120; verbal dueling in, 244n39
Adrados, Francisco Rodríguez, 234n18
Aeschines, 177
Aesop, 133; exercises using, 134
agriculture: education in, 12; Roman treatises on, 219n4. *See also* Cato the Elder, *De agri cultura*
Alexander of Aphrodisias, 241n10
alphabet, Roman, 18, 206n35
Amyot, Jacques, 219n11
animals, in fables, 123–25, 128, 136
animus: boys', 93–98, 231n45; of clients, 180; in declamation, 182; development of, 95, 97; students', 158, 197
Antiphon, tetralogies of, 177
Antonius (orator), 217n49; in *De oratore,* 48, 145, 219n8; pamphlet on oratory, 218n52
Antony, Marc: use of declamation, 178
aphorisms, in Roman education, 122
aptitude, Quintilian on, 232n56
Archias, 218n51; and Cicero, 42, 213n9, 214n24
architecture, domestic, 15, 205n23
Ariès, Philip, 218n2

Aristides, 227n11
Aristophanes, 79
Aristotle: on experience, 230n35; great-souled man of, 217n45; on rhetoric, 174; on syllogism, 174, 175; on topical invention, 174; use of *deigma,* 212n2. Works: *Sophistic Refutations,* 176; *Topica,* 174, 176
Ascham, Roger, 45
Assendelft Tablets, 237n54
Astin, Alan: on Cato, 153, 154, 155, 208n14, 209n23, 239n21
astrology, Roman use of, 40, 213n13
Athenaeum (Rome), 14
athletics, Roman opposition to, 4, 9, 31, 210n30
Atticus, literate slaves of, 15
Augustine, Saint: education of, 1, 201n3; school at Rome, 13–14; on speech, 107
Augustus: grandchildren of, 30; military training under, 15; paternalism of, 61, 62, 221n24
Ausonius, 241n4; teaching of Gratian, 172
Avianus: date of, 236n38; fables of, 127, 130; use of metonymy, 237n51; vocabulary of, 238n58

Babrius, 125; exercises using, 130, 237nn47,54; use in exercises, 127; vocabulary of, 238n58
Bacchic cult, 40
Bacon, Francis: on Plutarch, 220n11
Badian, E., 213n8
Barbaro, Francesco, 219n11
Barns, John, 155, 240n30

Elder and, 140, 142, 152, 153; Cicero in, 146–
47; copying of, 146, 150; deference in, 149;
deferral in, 165; diligence in, 148; discipline
in, 166; displacement of violence in, 165;
dissemination of, 163; economic activity in,
159; editions of, 139, 140, 150–51, 238nn1–
2,5; educational imperative of, 141–47, 149–
50; *fama* in, 147; fantasy in, 148; *figurae
etymologicae* of, 147; form of, 152, 157;
gnomology of, 158; Horace in, 164; ideal
reader of, 147–48; imaginary of, 156–60;
imperative mode of, 141–42, 146, 149, 150,
151, 159, 160–62; impulse and reaction in,
143; internalization of, 156, 161, 166; introductory epistle, 151, 156, 158, 161; legitima-
tion through, 169; male roles in, 163; manuscripts of, 151, 238n2; meditative mode
of, 165; in Middle Ages, 140, 151, 238n5;
moralizing in, 140, 150, 158, 164; paratexts
to, 157–58; paronomasia in, 147; personae
in, 181; praise and blame in, 162; progressive
learning with, 167; punishment in, 149;
reading of, 148; reception history of, 169;
Renaissance use of, 140, 150, 238n4; restraint
in, 141; roles and relationships in, 158; second person in, 161–63, 240n35; self-control
in, 141, 166, 169; self-cultivation in, 146–
47, 156, 165–66; self-preservation in, 159;
Si deus, 122, 146; situational ethics of, 160;
skills gained from, 142; students' variations
on, 157; student world of, 147–50; stylization
using, 168; texts accompanying, 151; use of
Euripides, 145, 238n10; utility of, 143; versions of, 151, 152–53; virtue in, 140, 159; in
Western education, 142; world of, 160–69.
See also Cato the Elder
distinction, creation of, 23
Domitian (emperor), and Quintilian, 88
Domitius Ahenobarbus, 41
Donald, James, 202n9, 233n1
Donatus, 152; *Ars minor,* 115
Dover, Kenneth, 225n62
dubitatio (rhetorical querying), 31

the East, wealth from, 27
educability, natural, 63
education: ancient versus modern, 114; Babylonian, 2, 201n4; discursive forms of, 114;
Egyptian, 2, 201n4; form and content in,
114; liberation of self, 193; multiple functions of, 233n1; pleasure in, 150; reform of,

113; research on, 112, 115, 126; as social
replication, 202n9; sociology of, 233n4
education, Greek: Enlightenment view of, 9;
forms of, 25–26; in New Comedy, 210n28;
philosophical thesis in, 177; poetry in, 232n53;
Spartan, 26; variety in, 202n9
education, Hellenistic, 9–10; civic, 4; curriculum
of, 10; manuals for, 55; maxims in, 140; in
Menander, 34; Plutarch's adaptation of, 193;
Roman use of, 4; Sophists' influence on, 193;
stylization in, 46; vocal training in, 38
education, Roman: advantages of, 7; aphorisms
in, 122; bilingual, 3, 24, 26, 169, 188, 191; in
biographies, 23, 24, 25; building metaphors
for, 35; *chreia* in, 8, 9, 122; as citizen training,
202n9; in comedy, 23, 31–36, 210n29; communication of status, 22; copying in, 146,
150, 197; correction in, 6, 7; cultural transfers into, 3, 9–10, 12, 24; divisions of, 4, 118,
234n13; dynamic nature of, 2; early, 22, 53,
59, 119; elite interest in, 3, 22–23, 24, 114,
178–79, 193–95; encouragement in, 150;
Enlightenment view of, 9; Etruscan influence
on, 18–21, 206n37; eugenics and, 64; versus
expertise, 61; faulty, 75; girls', 3, 13, 35, 54,
61, 125, 191, 195–96, 202n11; goals of, 5;
for governing class, 53–54, 114, 195, 199;
Greek literary authors in, 237n44; ideal, 5,
46; imagination in, 196; imitation in, 168;
imperial, 53, 54, 55, 65, 168; innovation in,
37–38; Italic culture in, 2–3, 11, 21; Latin
versus Greek, 209n17; legacy of, 8; liberal,
1–2, 58, 196; lifelong, 148; literary, 22; manliness in, 60, 61, 66, 97, 104; material evidence for, 19–20, 207nn41,44; maxims in,
140; meditative mode of, 157; memory in,
115, 116, 120–21; memory of, 23, 24–27;
moralizing in, 7–8, 84; narratives of, 5, 6,
9–10, 24; nativist versus Greek, 2–3, 9, 17,
24, 33, 35, 44–45, 52, 194; of notable men,
26, 50; origins of, 9–12, 17–21, 24, 201n5;
paraphrase in, 120, 132, 133, 216n36, 234n19;
parental supervision of, 29–31, 40; place in
educational history, 2, 3; in Plautus, 31–33,
210n29; playacting in, 198; pleasure in, 196;
progressive exercises in, 121, 126, 160, 163,
167, 169; public displays of, 24; public utility
of, 30–31; purpose of, 23; Quintilian's synthesis of, 82, 109; refounding of, 22; repetition
in, 6; restrictions on, 68; role in identity, 2;
role in legitimacy, 30, 67, 73, 81; role playing

TEXT
10/12.5 Minion Pro

DISPLAY
Minion Pro

COMPOSITOR
Integrated Composition Systems

INDEXER
Roberta Engleman

PRINTER AND BINDER
Maple-Vail Book Manufacturing Group